message category

message pattern

FinancialHistory class protocol
__class initialization__

  initialBalance: amount   Begin a financial history with amount as the amount of money on hand.

  new   Begin a financial history with 0 as the amount of money on hand.

FinancialHistory instance protocol
__transaction recording__

  receive: amount from: source   Remember that an amount of money, amount, has been received from source.

  spend: amount for: reason   Remember that an amount of money, amount, has been spent for reason.

__inquiries__

  cashOnHand   Answer the total amount of money currently on hand.

  totalReceivedFrom: source   Answer the total amount received from source, so far.

  totalSpentFor: reason   Answer the total amount spent for reason, so far.

Smalltalk–80

The Language

Adele Goldberg and David Robson

ParcPlace Systems and Xerox PARC

Addison-Wesley Publishing Company
*Reading, Massachusetts • Menlo Park, California • New York
Don Mills, Ontario • Wokingham, England • Amsterdam • Bonn
Sydney • Singapore • Tokyo • Madrid • San Juan*

This book is in the
Addison-Wesley Series in Computer Science
MICHAEL A. HARRISON
CONSULTING EDITOR

Library of Congress Cataloging in Publication Data

Goldberg, Adele.
  Smalltalk-80: the language/Adele Goldberg, Dave Robson.
    p. cm.
  Includes indexes.
  ISBN 0-201-13688-0
  1. Smalltalk-80 (Computer system)   I. Robson, David.   II. Title.
QA76.8.S635G639   1989
005.26—dc19   88-34455
                                                   CIP
Reprinted with corrections September,1989

Smalltalk-80 is a trademark of ParcPlace Systems.

6 7 8 9 10 DO 9594939291

Preface

Advances in the design and production of computer hardware have brought many more people into direct contact with computers. Similar advances in the design and production of computer software are required in order that this increased contact be as rewarding as possible. The Smalltalk-80 system is a result of a decade of research into creating computer software that is appropriate for producing highly functional and interactive contact with personal computer systems, and another five years of careful engineering and revision.

This book is a substantial revision of our original detailed account of the Smalltalk-80 system, first released in 1983. It is divided into three major parts:

Part One — an overview of the concepts and syntax of the programming language.

Part Two — an annotated and illustrated specification of the system's functionality.

Part Three — an example of the design and implementation of a moderate-size application.

The first part introduces the Smalltalk approach to information representation and manipulation. Five words—*object, message, class, instance,* and *method*—make up the vocabulary with which Smalltalk is discussed. These terms are defined and the syntax of the Smalltalk-80 programming language is introduced.

The second part of the book contains specifications of the kinds of objects already present in the Smalltalk-80 programming environment. New kinds of objects can be added by a programmer, but a wide variety of objects come with the standard system. The messages that can be sent to each kind of object are listed, commented upon, and illustrated.

The third part of the book is an example of adding new kinds of objects to the system. It describes the addition of an application to model discrete, event-driven simulations such as car washes, banks, or information systems. Some readers may find it useful to read the third part of the book immediately after reading the first part, referring to the specifications in the second part whenever the meaning of a Smalltalk-80 expression is not clear.

These three parts include corrections to errors that readers have pointed out. The original fourth part, a specification for a Smalltalk-80 virtual machine, has been eliminated. The wide availability of commercial implementations, sold or licensed by ParcPlace Systems, has created a declining need for inclusion of this part.

The Task of Book-Writing

Writing this first book about the Smalltalk-80 system was a complex task, partially due to the sociology of the system's creation, and partially due to the diverse kinds of information people require about such a system. We can divide the different reasons for the complexity of this task into four categories:

- Smalltalk is a vision.
- Smalltalk is based on a small number of concepts, but defined by unusual terminology.
- Smalltalk is a graphical, interactive programming environment.
- Smalltalk is a big system.

Smalltalk is a vision

In the early 1970's, the Xerox Palo Alto Research Center Learning Research Group began work on a vision of the ways different people might effectively and joyfully use computing power. In 1981 the name of the group was changed to the Software Concepts Group or SCG. The goal of SCG is to create a powerful information system, one in which the user can store, access and manipulate information so that the system can grow as the user's ideas grow. Both the number and kinds of system components should grow in proportion to the growth of the user's awareness of how to effectively use the system.

SCG's strategy for realizing this vision has been to concentrate on two principal areas of research: a language of description (a programming language) which serves as an interface between the models in the human mind and those in computing hardware, and a language of interaction (a user interface) which matches the human communication system to that of the computer. Smalltalk research has followed a two-to four-year cycle: create a system embodying current understanding of the software needs; implement applications that test the system's ability to support these applications; and finally, based on the resulting experience, reformulate the understanding of software needs and redesign the programming language and/or the user interface.

The Smalltalk-80 system marks the fifth time through this cycle. The research is still in progress. We hope that presenting a detailed description of the current research results will contribute to the community working towards SCG's vision. The continued unfolding of the research means that the software system described in this book is literally a "moving target" and the information in this book represents only one station on a long track. Holding the train in the station long enough to write about it made the writing task complex.

Smalltalk has few concepts

Smalltalk is based on a small number of concepts, but defined by unusual terminology. Due to the uniformity with which the object-message orientation is carried out in the system, there are very few new programming concepts to learn in order to understand Smalltalk. On the one hand, this means that the reader can be told all the concepts quickly and then explore the various ways in which these concepts are applied in the system. These concepts are presented by defining the five words mentioned earlier that make up the vocabulary of Smalltalk—object, message, class, instance, and method. These five words are defined in terms of each other, so it is almost as though the reader must know everything before knowing anything.

Smalltalk is an environment

Smalltalk is a graphical, interactive programming environment. As suggested by the personal computing vision, Smalltalk is designed so that every component in the system that is accessible to the user can be presented in a meaningful way for observation and manipulation. The user interface issues in Smalltalk revolve around the attempt to create a visual language for each object. The preferred hardware system for Smalltalk includes a high-resolution graphical display screen and a pointing device such as a graphics pen or a mouse. With these devices, the user can select information viewed on the screen and invoke messages in order to interact with that information.

One way to present the details of the Smalltalk-80 system would be to start with the user interface and to describe each facility for accessing objects. Such a presentation might begin with scenarios of the ways in which the programmer might interact with the system. Each scenario would be a snapshot of a dynamic system. In a linear, static way, the book would try to convey the dynamics of multiple access paths to a large and diverse amount of information.

These aspects of the system are an important part of what Smalltalk provides as an applications development environment. However, in order to explain how this graphical user interface really works, the reader first has to understand the programming language. Thus, this book inverts the presentation of the system by starting with the language itself. Information about the system objects that support the user interface has been separated out and, except for the kernel graphics classes, is not presented in this book. Another book on the Smalltalk-80 user interface presents a detailed treatment of the implementation of these system objects (*Smalltalk-80: The Interactive Programming Environment* by Adele Goldberg).

Smalltalk is a big system

The Smalltalk-80 system is made up of many components. It includes objects that provide the functions usually attributed to a computer operating system: automatic storage management, a file system, display handling, text and picture editing, keyboard and pointing device input, a debugger, a performance spy, processor scheduling, compilation and decompilation. There are a lot of kinds of objects to learn about.

Smalltalk is built on the model of communicating objects. Large applications are viewed in the same way as the fundamental units from which the system is built. The interaction between the most primitive objects is viewed in the same way as the highest-level interaction between the computer and the user. Objects support modularity—the functioning of any object does not depend on the internal details of other objects. The complexity of the system is reduced by this minimization of interdependencies of system components. Complexity is further reduced by grouping together similar components; this is achieved through classes in Smalltalk. Classes are the chief mechanism for extension in Smalltalk. User-defined classes become a part of the system on an equal footing with the kernel classes of the system. Subclasses support the ability to factor the system in order to avoid repetitions of the same concepts in many different places.

Managing complexity is a key contribution of the Smalltalk approach to software. The early examples of the language are very simple, taken from the kinds of programming exercises common in many programming language books. This is so examples can be short, illustrating one or two points. The value of Smalltalk may not be apparent in these examples. After all, they can be done in other languages, and probably just as well. The value of Smalltalk becomes apparent when designing and implementing large applications, or when trying to make a modification to the system itself. For example, consider a dictionary, a frequently-used data structure in the Smalltalk-80 system. It is possible to design, implement, test, and install a new representation for dictionaries without in any way disrupting the running system. This is possible as long as the message interface upon which the functioning of other system objects depends is not destroyed.

The Smalltalk-80 system supports a number of interesting design tools, notably classes and instances as units for organizing and sharing information, and subclassing as a means to inherit and to refine existing capability. Combined with the interactive way in which the program development process is carried out, the Smalltalk-80 system provides a rich environment for prototyping new applications and refining old ones.

Writing a book about such a rich system means that some things must be left out. Again, we chose to omit in this book the details of the programming interface and the way in which interactive graphical applications can be created. We focus on the language and the kernel classes of the system.

The Task of Book-Reading

This book takes for granted a certain amount of computer literacy on the part of its reader. We assume that the reader

- knows why software systems are a good idea;

- is a programmer or programming-language designer who knows at least one language well;

- is familiar with the idea of expression syntax and of evaluation of expressions by an interpreter;

- is familiar with sequencing of instructions in a computer, control structures such as iteration and recursion, and the role of data structures;

- is concerned with the need to have better control of the representation and manipulation of information in a computing system; and

- is seeking new ideas for how to create a software (application) system that supports the ability to express a software solution in a way that is closely associated with the natural expression of the solution.

The Smalltalk-80 system is based on ideas gleaned from the Simula language and from the visions of Alan Kay, who first encouraged us to try to create a uniformly object-oriented system. The current embodiment of these ideas is the result of three related activities: research carried out at the Xerox Palo Alto Research Center; cooperation with a group of stalwart participants in a project to review the research results; and the persistent efforts of a group of Xerox employees who successfully created the commercial forum for Smalltalk—ParcPlace Systems—in 1988.

In August, 1980, several hardware manufacturers were invited to review the pages of our second attempt to write a book about Smalltalk and its latest realization. Our first attempt described the Smalltalk-76 system and was abandoned in response to our desire to create a more portable system for distribution outside the Xerox research centers. Our second attempt was a book that was partially historical in nature, partially statements about a vision for personal computing, and partially functional specification for a new Smalltalk system. We thought we would entitle it *Smalltalk Dreams and Schemes* as a reflection of the dual purpose of our writing. The manufacturers who patiently reviewed our material were from Apple Computer, Digital Equipment Corporation, Hewlett-Packard, and Tektronix. These companies were chosen because they designed hardware systems. We hoped that, in reviewing the material, they would learn about our unusual software goals and would devote some time to the problem of creating hardware systems specifically for Smalltalk-like systems. We knew that hardware systems currently on the market, and even ones planned for the near future, would have insufficient power to support our goals. Instead of designing software to fit the hardware we could buy, we decided to try to get the hardware designed to fit the software we wanted. We feel that we succeeded!

The manufacturers assigned personnel from their research laboratories to the task of reading the second version of the book. This book has benefited from much discussion and hard work on the part of these reviewers. The early part of the book was completely rewritten as a result of their constructive criticism. The reviewers are responsible for our continuing to try to complete the distribution process and for our completing this book, but not for any faults in its ultimate form. Each set of reviewers implemented the system at least once in order to test our specification of the Smalltalk-80 virtual machine. The current specification reflects their careful review.

As authors of this book, we took responsibility for creating the written description of the Smalltalk-80 system. But credit for the creation of the system goes to all the members of the Software Concepts Group. To these people, we state our debt, our thanks, and our love. Dan Ingalls managed the overall systems design and development effort. Peter Deutsch on the Dorado, Glenn Krasner on the Alto, and Kim McCall on the Dolphin (also called the Xerox 1100 Scientific Information Processor), contributed expertise to the virtual machine implementations on the Xerox computers. User interface ideas, implementations, and management of the release process were carried out by James Althoff (user interface development), Robert Flegal (design of the graphics editor), Ted Kaehler (while laboring over virtual memory problems), Diana Merry (our text guru), and Steve Putz (version management). Peggy Asprey, Marc Meyer, Bill Finzer, and Laura Gould, in trying to keep their applications studies in pace with the system development, tested major changes. Copious reading of the manuscript at various stages of inception was done by Michael Rutenberg, Michael Madsen, Susanne Bodker, and Jay Trow. Editing assistance was given by Rachel Rutherford and Janet Moreland.

Chapter 18 on the Smalltalk-80 graphics kernel was revised from a paper written by Dan Ingalls for *Byte* magazine. Graphical images in Chapters 18, 19, and 20, were created by Robert Flegal (especially Figures 18.1 and 20.1), Dan Ingalls, and Adele Goldberg (especially Figures 20.2 and 20.3). Steve Putz offered valuable assistance in creating the images for Chapter 17. Images for the openings to Parts One and Two, and all images for the opening pages of Chapters 1 through 20, were created by Adele Goldberg. Images for Part Three, and all images for the opening pages of Chapters 21 through 26, were created by Robert Flegal. These images were created using the Smalltalk-80 graphics editor in combination with a low-resolution image scanner designed by Joseph Maleson.

To the participants in the review process, we also give our thanks.

With them we have set an example of cooperative scientific exchange that we hope will evolve and continue to grow. Encouragement to begin this project came from our laboratory manager, Bert Sutherland. Reviewers and implementors were: from Apple, Rick Meyers and David Casseres; from Digital Equipment Corporation, Stoney Ballard, Eric Osman, and Steve Shirron; from Hewlett-Packard, Alec Dara-Abrams, Joe Falcone, Jim Stinger, Bert Speelpenning, and Jeff Eastman; and from Tektronix, Paul McCullough, Allen Wirfs-Brock, D. Jason Penney, Larry Katz, Robert Reed, and Rick Samco. We thank their companies and administrators for their patience and willingness to depart from industry standards, at least for one brief moment—at Apple, Steve Jobs and Bruce Daniels; at Digital, Larry Samburg; at Hewlett-Packard, Paul Stoft, Jim Duley, and Ted Laliotis; and at Tektronix, Jack Grimes, and George Rhine. The folks from Tektronix prepared detailed reviews on audiotape, so we could not only see the errors of our ways, but hear them as well!

We take this opportunity to add a debt of gratitude to the faith demonstrated by the pioneers who helped Adele, Duane, Glenn, and Peter form ParcPlace Systems within Xerox in 1986: Russ Pencin, Nanette Harter, Ron Carter, David Leibs, Stephen Pope, Frank Jackson, Allan Schiffman, and Richard Steiger.

It is our hope that this book and its companion will facilitate the distribution of the Smalltalk concepts in the computer community. If it succeeds, then that success is shared by us with our colleagues at the Xerox Palo Alto Research Center.

Postscript on the Production of This Book

The original text for this book was supplied to the publisher on magnetic tape. The tape included formatting codes identifying the various types of textual entity in the manuscript. The actual format of each type of entity was supplied by the publisher. This process worked smoothly thanks in large part to the efforts and patience of Eileen Colahan of the International Computaprint Corporation and Jim DeWolf of Addison-Wesley.

Many of the graphical images that represent Smalltalk-80 screen graphics and the Part and Chapter artwork were printed on the Platemaker system developed by Gary Starkweather and the Imaging Sciences Laboratory of PARC. We would like to thank Gary, Eric Larson, and Julian Orr for making the Platemaker available to us.

Palo Alto, California

Adele Goldberg
David Robson

Contents

Smalltalk-**80**

PART ONE

Part One of this book provides an overview of the Smalltalk-80 programming language. Chapter 1 introduces the basic concepts and vocabulary of the Smalltalk-80 programming language without introducing its syntax. It describes objects, messages, classes, instances, and methods. These concepts are discussed in greater detail in the next four chapters as the relevant parts of the programming language syntax are described. Chapter 2 describes the syntax of expressions. Expressions allow objects to be referred to and messages to be described. Chapter 3 describes the basic syntax for classes and methods. Classes and methods allow new kinds of objects to be created and existing kinds to be modified. The final two chapters describe two important refinements to the role of classes in the Smalltalk-80 system. These refinements allow subclasses and metaclasses.

1

Objects and Messages

An *object* represents a component of the Smalltalk-80 software system. For example, objects represent

- numbers
- character strings
- queues
- dictionaries
- rectangles
- file directories
- text editors
- programs
- compilers
- computational processes
- financial histories
- views of information

An object consists of some private memory and a set of operations. The nature of an object's operations depends on the type of component it represents. Objects representing numbers compute arithmetic functions. Objects representing data structures store and retrieve information. Objects representing positions and areas answer inquiries about their relation to other positions and areas.

A *message* is a request for an object to carry out one of its operations. A message specifies which operation is desired, but not how that operation should be carried out. The *receiver*, the object to which the message was sent, determines how to carry out the requested operation. For example, addition is performed by sending a message to an object representing a number. The message specifies that the desired operation is addition and also specifies what number should be added to the receiver. The message does not specify how the addition will be performed. The receiver determines how to accomplish the addition. Computing is viewed as an intrinsic capability of objects that can be uniformly invoked by sending messages.

The set of messages to which an object can respond is called its *interface* with the rest of the system. The only way to interact with an object is through its interface. A crucial property of an object is that its private memory can be manipulated only by its own operations. A crucial property of messages is that they are the only way to invoke an object's operations. These properties insure that the implementation of one object cannot depend on the internal details of other objects, only on the messages to which they respond.

Messages insure the modularity of the system because they specify the type of operation desired, but not how that operation should be accomplished. For example, there are several representations of numerical values in the Smalltalk-80 system. Fractions, small integers, large integers, and floating point numbers are represented in different ways. They all understand the same message requesting the computation of their sum with another number, but each representation implies a different way to compute that sum. To interact with a number or any object, one need only know what messages it responds to, not how it is represented.

Other programming environments also use objects and messages to facilitate modular design. For example, Simula uses them for describing simulations and Hydra uses them for describing operating system facilities in a distributed system. In the Smalltalk-80 system, objects and messages are used to implement the entire programming environment. Once objects and messages are understood, the entire system becomes accessible.

An example of a commonly-used data structure in programming is a dictionary, which associates names and values. In the Smalltalk-80 system, a dictionary is represented by an object that can perform two operations: associate a name with a new value, and find the value last associated with a particular name. A programmer using a dictionary must know how to specify these two operations with messages. Dictionary objects understand messages that make requests like "associate the name *Brett* with the value *3*" and "what is the value associated with the name *Dave*?" Since everything is an object, the names, such as *Brett* or *Dave*, and the values, such as *3* or *30*, are also represented by objects. Although a curious programmer may want to know how associations are represented in a dictionary, this internal implementation information is unnecessary for successful use of a dictionary. Knowledge of a dictionary's implementation is of interest only to the programmer who works on the definition of the dictionary object itself.

An important part of designing Smalltalk-80 programs is determining which kinds of objects should be described and which message names provide a useful vocabulary of interaction among these objects. A language is designed whenever the programmer specifies the messages that can be sent to an object. Appropriate choice of objects depends, of course, on the purposes to which the object will be put and the granularity of information to be manipulated. For example, if a simulation of an amusement park is to be created for the purpose of collecting data on queues at the various rides, then it would be useful to describe objects representing the rides, workers who control the rides, the waiting lines, and the people visiting the park. If the purpose of the simulation includes monitoring the consumption of food in the park, then objects representing these consumable resources are required. If the amount of money exchanged in the park is to be monitored, then details about the cost of rides have to be represented.

In designing a Smalltalk-80 application, then, choice of objects is the first key step. There really is nothing definitive to say about the "right way" to choose objects. As in any design process, this is an acquired skill. Different choices provide different bases for extending an application or for using the objects for other purposes. The skilled Smalltalk-80 programmer is mindful that the objects created for an application might prove more useful for other applications if a semantically complete set of functions for an object is specified. For example, a dictionary whose associations can be removed as well as added is generally more useful than an add-only version.

Classes and Instances

A *class* describes the implementation of a set of objects that all represent the same kind of system component. The individual objects described by a class are called its *instances*. A class describes the form of its instances' private memories and it describes how they carry out their operations. For example, there is a system class that describes the implementation of objects representing rectangular areas. This class describes how the individual instances remember the locations of their areas and also how the instances carry out the operations that rectangular areas perform. Every object in the Smalltalk-80 system is an instance of a class. Even an object that represents a unique system component is implemented as the single instance of a class. Programming in the Smalltalk-80 system consists of creating classes, creating instances of classes, and specifying sequences of message exchanges among these objects.

The instances of a class are similar in both their public and private properties. An object's public properties are the messages that make up its interface. All instances of a class have the same message interface since they represent the same kind of component. An object's private properties are a set of *instance variables* that make up its private memory and a set of *methods* that describe how to carry out its operations. The instance variables and methods are not directly available to other objects. The instances of a class all use the same set of methods to describe their operations. For example, the instances that represent rectangles all respond to the same set of messages and they all use the same methods to determine how to respond. Each instance has its own set of instance variables, but they generally all have the same number of instance variables. For example, the instances that represent rectangles all have two instance variables.

Each class has a name that describes the type of component its instances represent. Class names will appear in a special font because they are part of the programming language. The same font will be used for all text that represents Smalltalk-80 expressions. The class whose instances represent character sequences is named String. The class whose instances represent spatial locations is named Point. The class whose instances represent rectangular areas is named Rectangle. The class whose instances represent computational processes is named Process.

Each instance variable in an object's private memory refers to one object, called its value. The values of a Rectangle's two instance variables are instances of Point that represent opposing corners of its rectangular area. The fact that Rectangles have two instance variables, or that those instance variables refer to Points is strictly internal information, unavailable outside the individual Rectangle.

Each method in a class tells how to perform the operation requested by a particular type of message. When that type of message is sent to any instance of the class, the method is executed. The methods used by all Rectangles describe how to perform their operations in terms of the two Points representing opposing corners. For example, one message asks a Rectangle for the location of its center. The corresponding method tells how to calculate the center by finding the point halfway between the opposing corners.

A class includes a method for each type of operation its instances can perform. A method may specify some changes to the object's private memory and/or some other messages to be sent. A method also specifies an object that should be returned as the value of the invoking message. An object's methods can access the object's own instance variables, but not those of any other objects. For example, the method a Rectangle uses to compute its center has access to the two Points referred to by its instance variables; however, the method cannot access the instance variables of those Points. The method specifies messages to be sent to the Points asking them to perform the required calculations.

A small subset of the methods in the Smalltalk-80 system are not expressed in the Smalltalk-80 programming language. These are called *primitive* methods. The primitive methods are built into the virtual machine and cannot be changed by the Smalltalk-80 programmer. They are invoked with messages in exactly the same way that other methods are. Primitive methods allow the underlying hardware and virtual machine structures to be accessed. For example, instances of Integer use a primitive method to respond to the message +. Other primitive methods perform disk and terminal interactions.

An Example Application

Examples are an important part of the description of a programming language and environment. Many of the examples used in this book are taken from the classes found in the standard Smalltalk-80 system. Other examples are taken from classes that might be added to the system to enhance its functionality. The first part of the book draws examples from an application that might be added to the system to maintain simple financial histories for individuals, households, clubs, or small businesses. The full application allows information about financial transactions to be entered and views of that information to be displayed. Figure 1.1 shows a view of a financial history as it might appear on a Smalltalk-80 display screen. The top two parts of the view show two views of the amount of money spent for various reasons. The next view down shows how the cash-on-hand fluctuated over time as transactions were made.

At the bottom of the picture are two areas in which the user can type in order to add new expenditures and incomes to the history. When new information is added, the three views are automatically updated. In Figure 1.2, a new expenditure for food has been added.

This application requires the addition of several classes to the system. These new classes describe the different kinds of view as well as the underlying financial history information. The class that actually records the financial information is named FinancialHistory and will be used as an example in the next four chapters. This example application will make use of several classes already in the system; it will use numbers to represent amounts of money and strings to represent the reasons for expenditures and the sources of income.

FinancialHistory is used to introduce the basic concepts of the Smalltalk-80 programming language because its functionality and implementation are easy to describe. The functionality of a class can be specified by listing the operations available through its message interface. FinancialHistory provides six operations:

1. Create a new financial history object with a certain initial amount of money available.

2. Remember that a certain amount was spent for a particular reason.

3. Remember that a certain amount was received from a particular source.

4. Find out how much money is available.

5. Find out how much has been spent for a particular reason.

6. Find out how much has been received from a particular source.

Figure 1.1   Class - Financial History

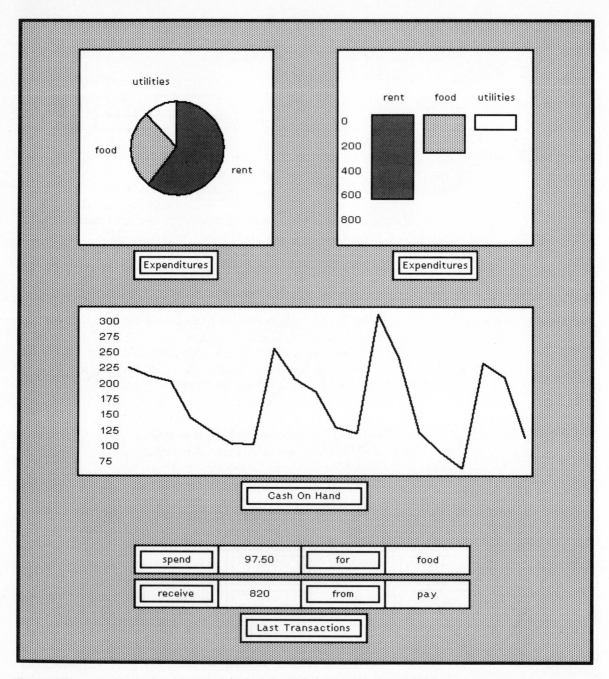

Figure 1.2

An implementation of these operations is specified in the class description shown inside the front cover of this book. The form of class descriptions will be described in Chapters 3, 4, and 5.

System Classes

The Smalltalk-80 system includes a set of classes that provides the standard functionality of a programming language and environment: arithmetic, data structures, control structures, and input/output facilities. The functionality of these classes will be specified in detail in Part Two of this book. Figure 1.3 is a diagram of the system classes presented in Part Two. Lines are drawn around groups of related classes; the groups are labeled to indicate the chapters in which the specifications of the classes can be found.

Arithmetic

The Smalltalk-80 system includes objects representing both real and rational numbers. Real numbers can be represented with an accuracy of about six digits. Integers with absolute value less than 2^{524288} can be represented exactly. Rational numbers can be represented using these integers. There are also classes for representing linear magnitudes (like dates and times) and random number generators.

Data Structures

Most of the objects in the Smalltalk-80 system function as data structures of some kind. However, while most objects also have other functionality, there is a set of classes representing more or less pure data structures. These classes represent different types of collections. The elements of some collections are unordered while the elements of others are ordered. Of the collections with unordered elements, there are bags that allow duplicate elements and sets that don't allow duplication. There are also dictionaries that associate pairs of objects. Of the collections with ordered elements, some have the order specified externally when elements are added and others determine the order based on properties of the elements themselves. The common data structures of arrays and strings are provided by classes that have associative behavior (associating indices and elements) and external ordering (corresponding to the inherent ordering of the indices).

Control Structures

The Smalltalk-80 system includes objects and messages that implement the standard control structures found in most programming languages. They provide conditional selection similar to the if-then-else statements of Algol and conditional repetition similar to its while and until state-

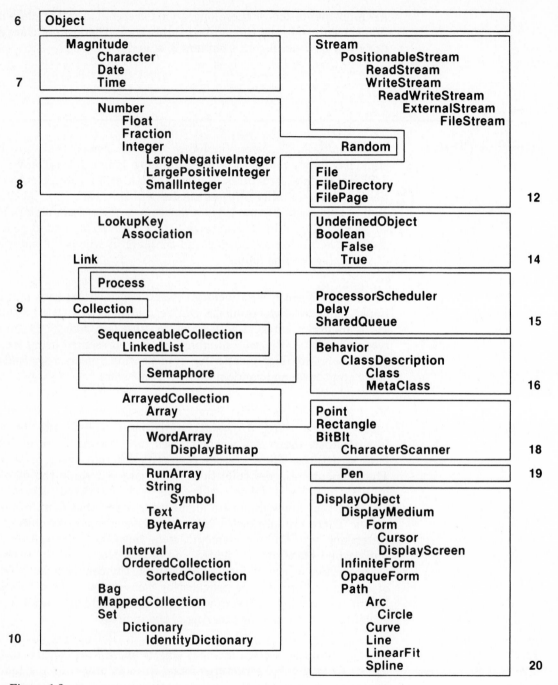

Figure 1.3

ments. Objects representing independent processes and mechanisms for scheduling and synchronous interaction are also provided. Two classes are provided to support these control structures. Booleans represent the two truth values and blocks represent sequences of actions. Booleans and blocks can also be used to create new kinds of control structures.

Programming Environment

There are several classes in the Smalltalk-80 system that assist in the programming process. There are separate classes representing the source (human-readable) form and the compiled (machine-executable) form of methods. Objects representing parsers, compilers, and decompilers translate between the two forms of method. Objects representing classes connect methods with the objects that use them (the instances of the classes).

Objects representing organizational structures for classes and methods help the programmer keep track of the system, and objects representing histories of software modification help interface with the efforts of other programmers. Even the execution state of a method is represented by an object. These objects are called *contexts* and are analogous to stack frames or activation records of other systems.

Viewing and Interacting

The Smalltalk-80 system includes classes of objects that can be used to view and edit information. Classes helpful for presenting graphical views represent points, lines, rectangles, and arcs. Since the Smalltalk-80 system is oriented toward a bitmap display, there are classes for representing and manipulating bitmap images. There are also classes for representing and manipulating the more specific use of bitmap images for character fonts, text, and cursors.

Built from these graphical objects are other objects representing rectangular windows, command menus, and content selections. There are also objects that represent the user's actions on the input devices and how these relate to the information being viewed. Classes representing specific viewing and editing mechanisms constructed from these components provide views for classes, contexts, and documents containing text and graphics. The views of classes provide the fundamental mechanism to interact with the software in the system. Smalltalk-80 views and editors are presented in a separate book.

Communication

The Smalltalk-80 system allows communication with external media. The standard external medium is a disk file system. Objects represent individual files as well as directories. If a connection to a communications network is available, it can be accessed through objects as well.

Summary of Terminology

object	A component of the Smalltalk-80 system represented by some private memory and a set of operations.
message	A request for an object to carry out one of its operations.
receiver	The object to which a message is sent.
interface	The messages to which an object can respond.
class	A description of a group of similar objects.
instance	One of the objects described by a class.
instance variable	A part of an object's private memory.
method	A description of how to perform one of an object's operations.
primitive method	An operation performed directly by the Smalltalk-80 virtual machine.
FinancialHistory	The name of a class used as an example in this book.
system classes	The set of classes that come with the Smalltalk-80 system.

2

Expression Syntax

Chapter 1 introduced the fundamental concepts of the Smalltalk-80 system. System components are represented by *objects*. Objects are *instances* of *classes*. Objects interact by sending *messages*. Messages cause *methods* to be executed. This chapter introduces an expression syntax for describing objects and messages. The next chapter introduces a syntax for describing classes and methods.

An *expression* is a sequence of characters that describes an object called the value of the expression. The syntax presented in this chapter explains which sequences of characters form legal expressions. There are four types of expression in the Smalltalk-80 programming language.

1. *Literals* describe certain constant objects, such as numbers and character strings.

2. *Variable names* describe the accessible variables. The value of a variable name is the current value of the variable with that name.

3. *Message expressions* describe messages to receivers. The value of a message expression is determined by the method the message invokes. That method is found in the class of the receiver.

4. *Block expressions* describe objects representing deferred activities. Blocks are used to implement control structures.

Expressions are found in two places, in methods and in text displayed on the screen. When a message is sent, a method from the receiver's class is selected and its expressions are evaluated. Part of the user interface allows expressions to be selected on the screen and evaluated. The details of selecting and evaluating expressions on the screen fall outside the scope of this book, since they are part of the user interface. Some examples, however, are given in Chapter 17.

Of the four types of expression listed above, only the variable names are context-dependent. An expression's location in the system determines which character sequences are legal variable names. The set of variable names available in a method's expressions depends on the class in which the method is found. For example, methods in class Rectangle and methods in class Point have access to different sets of variable names. The variables available in a class's methods will be fully described in Chapters 3, 4, and 5. The variable names available for use in expressions on the screen depend on where the expressions are displayed on the screen. All other aspects of the expression syntax are independent of the expression's location.

The syntax for expressions is summarized in the diagram that appears inside the back cover of this book. The rest of this chapter describes the four types of expression.

Literals

Five kinds of objects can be referred to by literal expressions. Since the value of a literal expression is always the same object, these expressions are also called *literal constants*. The five types of literal constant are:

1. numbers

2. individual characters

3. strings of characters

4. symbols

5. arrays of other literal constants

Numbers

Numbers are objects that represent numerical values and respond to messages that compute mathematical results. The literal representation of a number is a sequence of digits that may be preceded by a minus sign and/or followed by a decimal point and another sequence of digits. For example,

```
3
30.45
−3
0.005
−14.0
13772
```

Number literals can also be expressed in a nondecimal base by preceding the digits with a radix prefix. The radix prefix includes the value of the digit radix (always expressed in decimal) followed by the letter "r". The following examples specify numbers in octal with their corresponding decimal values.

octal	decimal
8r377	255
8r153	107
8r34.1	28.125
8r−37	−31

When the base is greater than ten, the capital letters starting with "A" are used for digits greater than nine. The following examples specify numbers in hexadecimal with their corresponding decimal values.

hexadecimal	decimal
16r106	262
16rFF	255
16rAC.DC	172.859
16r−1.C	−1.75

Number literals can also be expressed in scientific notation by following the digits of the value with an exponent suffix. The exponent suffix includes the letter "e" followed by the exponent (expressed in decimal). The number specified before the exponent suffix is multiplied by the radix raised to the power specified by the exponent.

scientific notation	decimal
1.586e5	158600.0
1.586e−3	0.001586
8r3e2	192
2r11e6	192

Characters

Characters are objects that represent the individual symbols of an alphabet. A character literal expression consists of a dollar sign followed by any character, for example,

```
$a
$M
$−
$$
$1
```

Strings

Strings are objects that represent sequences of characters. Strings respond to messages that access individual characters, replace substrings, and perform comparisons with other strings. The literal representation of a string is a sequence of characters delimited by single quotes, for example,

```
'hi'
'food'
'the Smalltalk-80 system'
```

Any character may be included in a string literal. If a single quote is to be included in a string, it must be duplicated to avoid confusion with the delimiters. For example, the string literal 'can" t'

refers to a string of the five characters $c, $a, $n, $´, and $t.

Symbols

Symbols are objects that represent strings used for names in the system. The literal representation of a symbol is a sequence of characters preceded by a pound sign, for example,

    #bill
    #M63

There are some restrictions on the characters that can be used in literal symbols. The syntax charts at the end of the book give a more accurate definition. There will never be two symbols with the same characters; each symbol is unique. This makes it possible to compare symbols efficiently.

Arrays

An array is a simple data structure object whose contents can be referenced by an integer index from one to a number that is the size of the array. Arrays respond to messages requesting access to their contents. The literal representation of an array is a sequence of other literals—numbers, characters, strings, symbols, and arrays—delimited by parentheses and preceded by a pound sign. The other literals are separated by spaces. Embedded symbols and arrays are not preceded by pound signs. An array of three numbers is described by the expression

    #(1 2 3)

An array of seven strings is described by the expression

    #('food' 'utilities' 'rent' 'household' 'transportation' 'taxes' 'recreation')

An array of two arrays and two numbers is described by the expression

    #(('one' 1) ('not' 'negative') 0 −1)

And an array of a number, a string, a character, a symbol, and another array is described by the expression

    #(9 'nine' $9 nine (0 'zero' $0 ( ) 'e' $f 'g' $h 'i'))

Variables

The memory available to an object is made up of variables. Most of these variables have names. Each variable remembers a single object and the variable's name can be used as an expression referring to that object. The objects that can be accessed from a particular place are determined by which variable names are available. For example, the contents of an object's instance variables are unavailable to other objects because the names of those variables can be used only in the methods of the object's class.

A variable name is a simple identifier, a sequence of letters and digits beginning with a letter. Some examples of variable names are:

index	bin14Total
initialIndex	HouseholdFinances
textEditor	Rectangle
bin14	IncomeReasons

There are two kinds of variables in the system, distinguished by how widely they are accessible. Private variables are accessible only to a single object. Instance variables are private. Shared variables can be accessed by more than one object. Private variable names are required to have lowercase initial letters; shared variable names are required to have uppercase initial letters. The first five example identifiers shown above refer to private variables and the last three refer to shared variables.

Another capitalization convention evident in the examples above is that identifiers formed by concatenating several words capitalize each word following the first one. This convention is not enforced by the system.

Assignments

A literal constant will always refer to the same object, but a variable name may refer to different objects at different times. The object referred to by a variable is changed when an assignment expression is evaluated. Assignments were not listed earlier as a type of expression since any expression can become an assignment by including an assignment prefix.

An assignment prefix is composed of the name of the variable whose value will be changed followed by a left arrow (←). The following example is a literal expression that has an assignment prefix. It indicates that the variable named quantity should now refer to the object representing the number 19.

quantity ← 19

The following example is a variable-name expression with an assignment prefix. It indicates that the variable named index should refer to the same object as does the variable named initialIndex.

index ← initialIndex

Other examples of assignment expressions are:

chapterName ← 'Expression Syntax'
flavors ← #('vanilla' 'chocolate' 'butter pecan' 'garlic')

More than one assignment prefix can be included, indicating that the values of several variables are changed.

index ← initialIndex ← 1

This expression indicates that both the variables named index and initialIndex should refer to the number 1. Message expressions and block expressions can also have assignment prefixes, as will be seen in the following sections.

Pseudo-variable Names	A pseudo-variable name is an identifier that refers to an object. In this way, it is similar to a variable name. A pseudo-variable name is different from a variable name in that its value cannot be changed with an assignment expression. Some of the pseudo-variables in the system are constants; they always refer to the same objects. Three important pseudo-variable names are nil, true, and false.

nil	refers to an object used as the value of a variable when no other object is appropriate. Variables that have not been otherwise initialized refer to nil.
true	refers to an object that represents logical accuracy. It is used as an affirmative response to a message making a simple yes-no inquiry.
false	refers to an object that represents logical inaccuracy. It is used as a negative response to a message making a simple yes-no inquiry.

The objects named true and false are called *Boolean* objects. They represent the answers to yes-no questions. For example, a number will respond with true or false to a message asking whether or not the number is greater than another number. Boolean objects respond to messages that compute logical functions and perform conditional control structures.

There are other pseudo-variables in the system (for example, self and super) whose values are different depending on where they are used. These will be described in the next three chapters.

Messages

Messages represent the interactions between the components of the Smalltalk-80 system. A message requests an operation on the part of the receiver. Some examples of message expressions and the interactions they represent follow.

Messages to numbers representing arithmetic operations

3 + 4	computes the sum of three and four.
index + 1	adds one to the number named index.
index > limit	inquires whether or not the number named index is greater than the number named limit.
theta sin	computes the sine of the number named theta.
quantity sqrt	computes the positive square root of the number named quantity.

Messages to linear data structures representing the addition or removal of information

list addFirst: newComponent	adds the object named newComponent as the first element of the linear data structure named list.
list removeLast	removes and returns the last element in list.

Messages to associative data structures (such as dictionaries) representing the addition or removal of information

ages at: 'Brett Jorgensen' put: 3	associates the string 'Brett Jorgensen' with the number 3 in the dictionary named ages.
addresses at: 'Peggy Jorgensen'	looks up the object associated with the string 'Peggy Jorgensen' in the dictionary named addresses.

Messages to rectangles representing graphical inquiries and calculations

frame center	answers the position of the center of the rectangle named frame.
frame containsPoint: cursorLocation	answers true if the position named cursorLocation is inside the rectangle named frame, and false otherwise.

frame intersect: clippingBox
> computes the rectangle that represents the intersection of the two rectangles named frame and clippingBox.

Messages to financial history records representing transactions and inquiries

HouseholdFinances spend: 32.50 on: 'utilities'
> informs the financial history named HouseholdFinances that $32.50 has been spent on utility bills.

HouseholdFinances totalSpentFor: 'food'
> asks HouseholdFinances how much money has been spent for food.

Selectors and Arguments

A message expression describes a receiver, *selector*, and possibly some *arguments.* The receiver and arguments are described by other expressions. The selector is specified literally.

A message's selector is a name for the type of interaction the sender desires with the receiver. For example, in the message

theta sin

the receiver is a number referred to by the variable named theta and the selector is sin. It is up to the receiver to decide how to respond to the message (in this case, how to compute the sine function of its value).

In the two message expressions

3 + 4

and

previousTotal + increment

the selectors are +. Both messages ask the receiver to calculate and return a sum. These messages each contain an object in addition to the selector (4 in the first expression and increment in the second). The additional objects in the message are arguments that specify the amount to be added.

The following two message expressions describe the same kind of operation. The receiver is an instance of FinancialHistory and will return the amount of money spent for a particular reason. The argument indicates the reason of interest. The first expression requests the amount spent for utility bills.

HouseholdFinances totalSpentOn: 'utilities'

The amount spent for food can be found by sending a message with the same selector, but with a different argument.

HouseholdFinances totalSpentOn: 'food'

The selector of a message determines which of the receiver's operations will be invoked. The arguments are other objects that are involved in the selected operation.

☐ *Unary Messages* Messages without arguments are called *unary messages*. For example, the money currently available according to HouseholdFinances is the value of the unary message expression

HouseholdFinances cashOnHand

These messages are called unary because only one object, the receiver, is involved. A unary message selector can be any simple identifier. Other examples of unary message expressions are

theta sin
quantity sqrt
nameString size

☐ *Keyword Messages* The general type of message with one or more arguments is the *keyword message*. The selector of a keyword message is composed of one or more keywords, one preceding each argument. A keyword is a simple identifier with a trailing colon. Examples of expressions describing single keyword messages are

HouseholdFinances totalSpentOn: 'utilities'
index max: limit

A message with two arguments will have a selector with two keywords. Examples of expressions describing double keyword messages are

HouseholdFinances spend: 30.45 on: 'food'
ages at: 'Brett Jorgensen' put: 3

When the selector of a multiple keyword message is referred to independently, the keywords are concatenated. The selectors of the last two message expressions are spend:on: and at:put:. There can be any number of keywords in a message, but most messages in the system have fewer than three.

□ *Binary Messages*   There is one other type of message expression that takes a single argument, the *binary message*. A binary message selector is composed of one or two nonalphanumeric characters. The only restriction is that the second character cannot be a minus sign. Binary selectors tend to be used for arithmetic messages. Examples of binary message expressions are

```
3 + 4
total − 1
total < = max
```

Returning Values

Smalltalk-80 messages provide two-way communication. The selector and arguments transmit information to the receiver about what type of response to make. The receiver transmits information back by returning an object that becomes the value of the message expression. If a message expression includes an assignment prefix, the object returned by the receiver will become the new object referred to by the variable. For example, the expression

```
sum ← 3 + 4
```

makes 7 be the new value of the variable named sum. The expression

```
x ← theta sin
```

makes the sine of theta be the new value of the variable named x. If the value of theta is 1, the new value of x becomes 0.841471. If the value of theta is 1.5, the new value of x becomes 0.997495.

The number referred to by index can be incremented by the expression

```
index ← index + 1
```

Even if no information needs to be communicated back to the sender, a receiver *always* returns a value for the message expression. Returning a value indicates that the response to the message is complete. Some messages are meant only to inform the receiver of something. Examples are the messages to record financial transactions described by the following expressions.

```
HouseholdFinances spend: 32.50 on: 'utilities'
HouseholdFinances receive: 1000 from: 'pay'
```

The receiver of these messages informs the sender only that it is finished recording the transaction. The default value returned in such cases is usually the receiver itself. So, the expression

var ← HouseholdFinances spend: 32.50 on: 'utilities'

results in var referring to the same financial history as HouseholdFinances.

Parsing

All of the message expressions shown thus far have described the receiver and arguments with literals or variable names. When the receiver or argument of a message expression is described by another message expression, the issue of how the expression is parsed arises. An example of a unary message describing the receiver of another unary message is

1.5 tan rounded

Unary messages are parsed left to right. The first message in the example is the unary selector tan sent to 1.5. The value of that message expression (a number around 14.1014) receives the unary message rounded and returns the nearest integer, 14. The number 14 is the value of the whole expression.

Binary messages are also parsed left to right. An example of a binary message describing the receiver of another binary message is

index + offset ∗ 2

The value returned by index from the message + offset is the receiver for the binary message ∗ 2.

All binary selectors have the same precedence; only the order in which they are written matters. Note that this makes mathematical expressions in the Smalltalk-80 language different from those in many other languages in which multiplication and division take precedence over addition and subtraction.

Parentheses can be used to change the order of evaluation. A message within parentheses is sent before any messages outside the parentheses. If the previous example were written as

index + (offset ∗ 2)

the multiplication would be performed before the addition.

Unary messages take precedence over binary messages. If unary messages and binary messages appear together, the unary messages will all be sent first. In the example frame width + border width * 2

the value of frame width is the receiver of the binary message whose selector is + and whose argument is the value of border width. The value of the + message is, in turn, the receiver of the binary message * 2. The expression parses as if it had been parenthesized as follows:

((frame width) + (border width)) * 2

Parentheses can be used to send binary messages before unary messages. The expression

2 * theta sin

calculates twice the sine of theta, while the expression

(2 * theta) sin

calculates the sine of twice theta.

Whenever keywords appear in an unparenthesized message, they compose a single selector. Because of this concatenation, there is no left-to-right parsing rule for keyword messages. If a keyword message is to be used as a receiver or argument of another keyword message, it must be parenthesized. The expression

frame scale: factor max: 5

describes a single two-argument keyword message whose selector is scale:max:. The expression

frame scale: (factor max: 5)

describes two single keyword messages whose selectors are scale: and max:. The value of the expression factor max: 5 is the argument for the scale: message to frame.

Binary messages take precedence over keyword messages. When unary, binary, and keyword messages appear in the same expression without parentheses, the unaries are sent first, the binaries next, and the keyword last. The example

bigFrame width: smallFrame width * 2

is evaluated as if it had been parenthesized as follows:

bigFrame width: ((smallFrame width) * 2)

In the following example, a unary message describes the receiver of a keyword message and a binary message describes the argument.

OrderedCollection new add: value * rate

To summarize the parsing rules:

1. Unary expressions parse left to right.

2. Binary expressions parse left to right.

3. Binary expressions take precedence over keyword expressions.

4. Unary expressions take precedence over binary expressions.

5. Parenthesized expressions take precedence over unary expressions.

*Formatting
Conventions*

A programmer is free to format expressions in various ways using spaces, tabs, and carriage returns. For example, multiple keyword messages are often written with each keyword-argument pair on a different line, as in

ages at: 'Brett Jorgensen'
    put: 3

or

HouseholdFinances
    spend: 30.45
    on: 'food'

The only time that a space, tab, or carriage return affects the meaning of an expression is when its absence would cause two letters or two numbers to fall next to each other.

Cascading

There is one special syntactic form called *cascading* that specifies multiple messages to the same object. Any sequence of messages can be expressed without cascading. However, cascading often reduces the need for using variables. A cascaded message expression consists of one description of the receiver followed by several messages separated by semicolons. For example,

OrderedCollection new add: 1; add: 2; add: 3

Three add: messages are sent to the result of OrderedCollection new. Without cascading, this would have required four expressions and a variable. For example, the following four expressions, separated by periods, have the same result as the cascaded expression above.

```
temp ← OrderedCollection new.
temp add: 1.
temp add: 2.
temp add: 3
```

Blocks

Blocks are objects used in many of the control structures in the Smalltalk-80 system. A block represents a deferred sequence of actions. A block expression consists of a sequence of expressions separated by periods and delimited by square brackets. For example,

```
[index ← index + 1]
```

or

```
[index ← index + 1.
 array at: index put: 0]
```

If a period follows the last expression, it is ignored, as in

```
[expenditures at: reason.]
```

When a block expression is encountered, the statements enclosed in the brackets are not executed immediately. The value of a block expression is an object that can execute these enclosed expressions at a later time, when requested to do so. For example, the expression

```
actions at: 'monthly payments'
        put: [HouseholdFinances spend: 650 on: 'rent'.
              HouseholdFinances spend: 7.25 on: 'newspaper'.
              HouseholdFinances spend: 225.50 on: 'car payment']
```

does not actually send any spend:on: messages to HouseholdFinances. It simply associates a block with the string 'monthly payments'.

The sequence of actions a block describes will take place when the block receives the unary message value. For example, the following two expressions have identical effects.

index ← index + 1

and

[index ← index + 1] value

The object referred to by the expression

actions at: 'monthly payments'

is the block containing three spend:on: messages. The execution of the
expression

(actions at: 'monthly payments') value

results in those three spend:on: messages being sent to
HouseholdFinances.

A block can also be assigned to a variable. So if the expression

incrementBlock ← [index ← index + 1]

is executed, then the expression

incrementBlock value

increments index.

The object returned after a value message is sent to a block is the
value of the last expression in the sequence. So if the expression

addBlock ← [index + 1]

is executed, then another way to increment index is to evaluate

index ← addBlock value

A block that contains no expressions returns nil when sent the message
value. The expression

[] value

has the value nil.

Control Structures

A control structure determines the order of some activities. The fundamental control structure in the Smalltalk-80 language provides that a
sequence of expressions will be evaluated sequentially. Many

nonsequential control structures can be implemented with blocks. These control structures are invoked either by sending a message to a block or by sending a message with one or more blocks as arguments. The response to one of these control structure messages determines the order of activities with the pattern of value messages it sends to the block(s).

Examining the evaluation of the following sequence of expressions gives an example of the way blocks work.

\

```
incrementBlock ← [index ← index + 1].
sumBlock ← [sum + (index * index)].
sum ← 0.
index ← 1.
sum ← sumBlock value.
incrementBlock value.
sum ← sumBlock value
```

The 15 actions taken as a result of evaluating this sequence of expressions are

1. *Assign* a block to incrementBlock.
2. *Assign* a block to sumBlock.
3. *Assign* the number 0 to sum.
4. *Assign* the number 1 to index.
5. *Send* the message value to the block sumBlock.
6. *Send* the message * 1 to the number 1.
7. *Send* the message + 1 to the number 0.
8. *Assign* the number 1 to sum.
9. *Send* the message value to the block IncrementBlock.
10. *Send* the message + 1 to the number 1.
11. *Assign* the number 2 to index.
12. *Send* the message value to the block sumBlock.
13. *Send* the message * 2 to the number 2.
14. *Send* the message + 4 to the number 1.
15. *Assign* the number 5 to sum.

An example of a control structure implemented with blocks is simple repetition, represented by a message to an integer with timesRepeat: as the selector and a block as the argument. The integer will respond by sending the block as many value messages as its own value indicates. For example, the following expression doubles the value of the variable named amount four times.

```
4 timesRepeat: [amount ← amount + amount]
```

Conditionals

Two common control structures implemented with blocks are *conditional selection* and *conditional repetition*. Conditional selection is similar to the if-then-else statements in Algol-like languages and conditional repetition is similar to the while and until statements in those languages. These conditional control structures use the two Boolean objects named true and false described in the section on pseudo-variables. Booleans are returned from messages that ask simple yes-no questions (for example, the magnitude comparison messages: $<$, $=$, $<=$, $>$, $>=$, $\sim=$).

☐ *Conditional Selection*   The conditional selection of an activity is provided by a message to a Boolean with the selector ifTrue:ifFalse: and two blocks as arguments. The only objects that understand ifTrue:ifFalse: messages are true and false. They have opposite responses: true sends value to the first argument block and ignores the second; false sends value to the second argument block and ignores the first. For example, the following expression assigns 0 or 1 to the variable parity depending on whether or not the value of the variable number is divisible by 2. The binary message \\ computes the modulus or remainder function.

```
(number \\ 2) = 0
        ifTrue: [parity ← 0]
        ifFalse: [parity ← 1]
```

The value returned from ifTrue:ifFalse: is the value of the block that was executed. The previous example could also be written

```
parity ← (number \\ 2) = 0 ifTrue: [0] ifFalse: [1]
```

In addition to ifTrue:ifFalse:, there are two single-keyword messages that specify only one conditional consequent. The selectors of these messages are ifTrue: and ifFalse:. These messages have the same effect as the ifTrue:ifFalse: message when one argument is an empty block. For example, these two expressions have the same effect.

```
index <= limit
        ifTrue: [total ← total + (list at: index)]
```

and

```
index <= limit
        ifTrue: [total ← total + (list at: index)]
        ifFalse: []
```

Since the value of an empty block is nil, the following expression would set lastElement to nil if index is greater than limit.

```
lastElement ← index > limit ifFalse: [list at: index]
```

☐ *Conditional Repetition*   The conditional repetition of an activity is provided by a message to a block with the selector whileTrue: and another block as an argument. The receiver block sends itself the message value and, if the response is true, it sends the other block value and then starts over, sending itself value again. When the receiver's response to value becomes false, it stops the repetition and returns from the whileTrue: message. For example, conditional repetition could be used to initialize all of the elements of an array named list.

```
index ← 1.
[index < = list size]
        whileTrue: [list at: index put: 0.
                       index ← index + 1]
```

Blocks also understand a message with selector whileFalse: that repeats the execution of the argument block as long as the value of the receiver is false. So, the following expressions are equivalent to the one above.

```
index ← 1.
[index > list size]
        whileFalse: [list at: index put: 0.
                        index ← index + 1]
```

The programmer is free to choose whichever message makes the intent of the repetition clearest. The value returned by both whileTrue: and whileFalse: is always nil. Two additional messages, whileTrue and whileFalse, are the equivalents to whileTrue: [] and whileFalse: [] respectively.

Block Arguments

In order to make some nonsequential control structures easy to express, blocks may take one or more arguments. Block arguments are specified by including identifiers preceded by colons at the beginning of a block. The block arguments are separated from the expressions that make up the block by a vertical bar. The following two examples describe blocks with one argument.

```
[ :array |   total ← total + array size]
```

and

```
[ :newElement |
  index ← index + 1.
  list at: index put: newElement]
```

A common use of blocks with arguments is to implement functions to be applied to all elements of a data structure. For example, many objects representing different kinds of data structures respond to the message do:, which takes a single-argument block as its argument. The object that receives a do: message evaluates the block once for each of the elements contained in the data structure. Each element is made the value of the block argument for one evaluation of the block. The following example calculates the sum of the squares of the first five primes. The result is the value of sum.

```
sum ← 0.
#(2 3 5 7 11) do: [ :prime |  sum ← sum + (prime * prime)]
```

The message collect: creates a collection of the values produced by the block when supplied with the elements of the receiver. The value of the following expression is an array of the squares of the first five primes.

```
#(2 3 5 7 11) collect: [ :prime |  prime * prime]
```

The objects that implement these control structures supply the values of the block arguments by sending the block the message value:. A block with one block argument responds to value: by setting the block argument to the argument of value: and then executing the expressions in the block. For example, evaluating the following expressions results in the variable total having the value 7.

```
sizeAdder ← [ :array |  total ← total + array size].
total ← 0.
sizeAdder value: #(a b c).
sizeAdder value: #(1 2).
sizeAdder value: #(e f)
```

Blocks can take more than one argument. All arguments are local to the block and its execution. For example

```
[ :x :y |  (x * x) + (y * y)]
```

or

```
[ :frame :clippingBox |  frame intersect: clippingBox]
```

A block must have the same number of block arguments as the number of value: keywords in the message to evaluate it. The two blocks above would be evaluated by means of a two-keyword message with selector value:value:. The two arguments of the message specify the values of the two block arguments, in order. If a block receives an evaluation message with a different number of arguments from the number of block arguments it takes, an error will be reported.

Summary of Terminology

The syntax of expressions is summarized inside the back cover of this book.

expression	A sequence of characters that describes an object.
literal	An expression describing a constant, such as a number or a string.
symbol	A string whose sequence of characters is guaranteed to be different from that of any other symbol.
array	A data structure whose elements are associated with integer indices.
variable name	An expression describing the current value of a variable.
assignment	An expression describing a change of a variable's value.
pseudo-variable name	An expression similar to a variable name. However, unlike a variable name, the value of a pseudo-variable name cannot be changed by an assignment.
receiver	The object to which a message is sent.
message selector	The name of the type of operation a message requests of its receiver.
message argument	An object that specifies additional information for an operation.
unary message	A message without arguments.
keyword	An identifier with a trailing colon.
keyword message	A message with one or more arguments whose selector is made up of one or more keywords.
binary message	A message with one argument whose selector is made up of one or two special characters.
cascading	A description of several messages to one object in a single expression.
block	A description of a deferred sequence of actions.
block argument	A parameter that must be supplied when certain blocks are evaluated.
value	A message to a block asking it to carry out the set of actions it represents.
value:	A keyword used in a message to a block that has block arguments; the corresponding message asks the block to carry out its set of actions.
ifTrue:ifFalse:	Message to a Boolean requesting conditional selection.
ifFalse:ifTrue:	Message to a Boolean requesting conditional selection.
ifTrue:	Message to a Boolean requesting conditional selection.
ifFalse:	Message to a Boolean requesting conditional selection.

whileTrue:	Message to a block requesting conditional repetition.
whileFalse:	Message to a block requesting conditional repetition.
whileTrue	Message to a block requesting conditional repetition. Equivalent to whileTrue: [].
whileFalse	Message to a block requesting conditional repetition. Equivalent to whileFalse: [].
do:	A message to a collection requesting enumeration of its elements.
collect:	A message to a collection requesting transformation of its elements.

3

Classes and Instances

Protocol Descriptions
Message Categories

Implementation Descriptions

Variable Declarations
Instance Variables
Shared Variables

Methods
Argument Names
Returning Values
The Pseudo-variable self
Temporary Variables

Primitive Methods

Summary of Terminology

Objects represent the components of the Smalltalk-80 system—the numbers, data structures, processes, disk files, process schedulers, text editors, compilers, and applications. Messages represent interactions between the components of the Smalltalk-80 system—the arithmetic, data accesses, control structures, file creations, text manipulations, compilations, and application uses. Messages make an object's functionality available to other objects, while keeping the object's implementation hidden. The previous chapter introduced an expression syntax for describing objects and messages, concentrating on how messages are used to access an object's functionality. This chapter introduces the syntax for describing methods and classes in order to show how the functionality of objects is implemented.

Every Smalltalk-80 object is an *instance* of a *class*. The instances of a class all have the same message interface; the class describes how to carry out each of the operations available through that interface. Each operation is described by a *method*. The selector of a message determines what type of operation the receiver should perform, so a class has one method for each selector in its interface. When a message is sent to an object, the method associated with that type of message in the receiver's class is executed. A class also describes what type of private memory its instances will have.

Each class has a name that describes the type of component its instances represent. A class name serves two fundamental purposes; it is a simple way for instances to identify themselves, and it provides a way to refer to the class in expressions. Since classes are components of the Smalltalk-80 system, they are represented by objects. A class's name automatically becomes the name of a globally shared variable. The value of that variable is the object representing the class. Since class names are the names of shared variables, they must be capitalized.

New objects are created by sending messages to classes. Most classes respond to the unary message new by creating a new instance of themselves. For example,

OrderedCollection new

returns a new collection that is an instance of the system class OrderedCollection. The new OrderedCollection is empty. Some classes create instances in response to other messages. For example, the class whose instances represent times in a day is Time; Time responds to the message now with an instance representing the current time. The class whose instances represent days in a year is Date; Date responds to the message today with an instance representing the current day. When a new instance is created, it automatically shares the methods of the class that received the instance creation message.

This chapter introduces two ways to present a class, one describing the functionality of the instances and the other describing the implementation of that functionality.

1. A *protocol description* lists the messages in the instances' message interface. Each message is accompanied by a comment describing the operation an instance will perform when it receives that type of message.

2. An *implementation description* shows how the functionality described in the protocol description is implemented. An implementation description gives the form of the instances' private memory and the set of methods that describe how instances perform their operations.

A third way to present classes is an interactive view called a *system browser*. The browser is part of the programming interface and is used in a running Smalltalk-80 system. Protocol descriptions and implementation descriptions are designed for noninteractive documentation like this book. The browser will be described briefly in Chapter 17.

Protocol Descriptions

A protocol description lists the messages understood by instances of a particular class. Each message is listed with a comment about its functionality. The comment describes the operation that will be performed when the message is received and what value will be returned. The comment describes *what* will happen, not *how* the operation will be performed. If the comment gives no indication of the value to be returned, then the value is assumed to be the receiver of the message.

For example, a protocol description entry for the message to a FinancialHistory with the selector spend:for: is

spend: amount for: reason   Remember that an amount of money, amount, has been spent for reason.

Messages in a protocol description are described in the form of *message patterns*. A message pattern contains a message selector and a set of argument names, one name for each argument that a message with that selector would have. For example, the message pattern

spend: amount for: reason

matches the messages described by each of the following three expressions.

```
HouseholdFinances spend: 32.50 for: 'utilities'
HouseholdFinances spend: cost+ tax for: 'food'
HouseholdFinances spend: 100 for: usualReason
```

The argument names are used in the comment to refer to the arguments. The comment in the example above indicates that the first argument represents the amount of money spent and the second argument represents what the money was spent for.

Message Categories

Messages that invoke similar operations are grouped together in *categories*. The categories have names that indicate the common functionality of the messages in the group. For example, the messages to FinancialHistory are grouped into three categories named transaction recording, inquiries, and initialization. This categorization is intended to make the protocol more readable to the user; it does not affect the operation of the class.

The complete protocol description for FinancialHistory is shown next.

FinancialHistory protocol

---

transaction recording

receive: amount from: source	Remember that an amount of money, amount, has been received from source.
spend: amount for: reason	Remember that an amount of money, amount, has been spent for reason.

inquiries

cashOnHand	Answer the total amount of money currently on hand.
totalReceivedFrom: source	Answer the total amount received from source, so far.
totalSpentFor: reason	Answer the total amount spent for reason, so far.

initialization

initialBalance: amount	Begin a financial history with amount as the amount of money on hand.

Category

A protocol description provides sufficient information for a programmer to know how to use instances of the class. From the above protocol description, we know that any instance of FinancialHistory should respond to the messages whose selectors are receive:from:, spend:for:, cashOnHand, totalReceivedFrom:, totalSpentFor:, and initialBalance:. We can guess that when we first create an instance of a FinancialHistory, the message initialBalance: should be sent to the instance in order to set values for its variables.

Implementation Descriptions

An implementation description has three parts.

1. a class name

2. a declaration of the variables available to the instances

3. the methods used by instances to respond to messages

An example of a complete implementation description for FinancialHistory is given next. The methods in an implementation description are divided into the same categories used in the protocol description. In the interactive system browser, categories are used to provide a hierarchical query path for accessing the parts of a class description. There are no special character delimiters separating the various parts of implementation descriptions. Changes in character font and emphasis indicate the different parts. In the interactive system browser, the parts are stored independently and the system browser provides a structured editor for accessing them.

class name   FinancialHistory
instance variable names   cashOnHand
                                  incomes
                                  expenditures

instance methods

transaction recording

     receive: amount from: source
        incomes at: source
            put: (self totalReceivedFrom: source) + amount.
        cashOnHand ← cashOnHand + amount
     spend: amount for: reason
        expenditures at: reason
            put: (self totalSpentFor: reason) + amount.
        cashOnHand ← cashOnHand − amount

inquiries

     cashOnHand
        ↑cashOnHand
     totalReceivedFrom: source
        (incomes includesKey: source)
          ifTrue: [↑incomes at: source]
          ifFalse: [↑0]
     totalSpentFor: reason
        (expenditures includesKey: reason)
          ifTrue: [↑expenditures at: reason]
          ifFalse: [↑0]

initialization

initialBalance: amount
    cashOnHand ← amount.
    incomes ← Dictionary new.
    expenditures ← Dictionary new

This implementation description is different from the one presented for FinancialHistory on the inside front cover of this book. The one on the inside front cover has an additional part labeled "class methods" that will be explained in Chapter 5; also, it omits the initialization method shown here.

Variable Declarations

The methods in a class have access to five different kinds of variables. These kinds of variables differ in terms of how widely they are available (their scope) and how long they persist.

There are two kinds of private variables available only to a single object.

1. *Instance variables* exist for the entire lifetime of the object.

2. *Temporary variables* are created for a specific activity and are available only for the duration of the activity.

Instance variables represent the current state of an object. Temporary variables represent the transitory state necessary to carry out some activity. Temporary variables are typically associated with a single execution of a method: they are created when a message causes the method to be executed and are discarded when the method completes by returning a value.

The three other kinds of variables can be accessed by more than one object. They are distinguished by how widely they are shared.

3. *Class variables* are shared by all the instances of a single class.

4. *Global variables* are shared by all the instances of all classes (that is, by all objects).

5. *Pool variables* are shared by the instances of a subset of the classes in the system.

The majority of shared variables in the system are either class variables or global variables. The majority of global variables refer to the classes in the system. An instance of FinancialHistory named

HouseholdFinances was used in several of the examples in the previous chapters. We used HouseholdFinances as if it were defined as a global variable name. Global variables are used to refer to objects that are not parts of other objects.

Recall that the names of shared variables (3-5) are capitalized, while the names of private variables (1-2) are not. The value of a shared variable will be independent of which instance is using the method in which its name appears. The value of instance variables and temporaries will depend on the instance using the method, that is, the instance that received a message.

Instance Variables

There are two types of instance variables, named and indexed. They differ in terms of how they are declared and how they are accessed. A class may have only named instance variables, only indexed variables, or some of each.

☐ *Named Instance Variables* An implementation description includes a set of names for the instance variables that make up the individual instances. Each instance has one variable corresponding to each instance variable name. The variable declaration in the implementation description of FinancialHistory specified three instance variable names.

instance variable names	cashOnHand
	incomes
	expenditures

An instance of FinancialHistory uses two dictionaries to store the total amounts spent and received for various reasons, and uses another variable to keep track of the cash on hand.

- expenditures refers to a dictionary that associates spending reasons with amounts spent.

- incomes refers to a dictionary that associates income sources with amounts received.

- cashOnHand refers to a number representing the amount of money available.

When expressions in the methods of the class use one of the variable names incomes, expenditures, or cashOnHand, these expressions refer to the value of the corresponding instance variable in the instance that received the message.

When a new instance is created by sending a message to a class, it has a new set of instance variables. The instance variables are initialized as specified in the method associated with the instance creation message. The default initialization method gives each instance variable a value of nil.

For example, in order for the previous example messages to HouseholdFinances to work, an expression such as the following must have been evaluated.

Class

HouseholdFinances ← FinancialHistory new initialBalance: 350

FinancialHistory new creates a new object whose three instance variables all refer to nil. The initialBalance: message to that new instance gives the three instance variables more appropriate initial values.

☐ *Indexed Instance Variables*   Instances of some classes can have instance variables that are not accessed by names. These are called *indexed instance variables.* Instead of being referred to by name, indexed instance variables are referred to by messages that include integers, called indices, as arguments. Since indexing is a form of association, the two fundamental indexing messages have the same selectors as the association messages to dictionaries—at: and at:put:. For example, instances of Array have indexed variables. If names is an instance of Array, the expression

names at: 1

returns the value of its first indexed instance variable. The expression

names at: 4 put: 'Adele'

stores the string 'Adele' as the value of the fourth indexed instance variable of names. The legal indices run from one to the number of indexed variables in the instance.

If the instances of a class have indexed instance variables, its variable declaration will include the line indexed instance variables. For example, part of the implementation description for the system class Array is

class name   Array
indexed instance variables

Each instance of a class that allows indexed instance variables may have a different number of them. All instances of FinancialHistory have three instance variables, but instances of Array may have any number of instance variables.

A class whose instances have indexed instance variables can also have named instance variables. All instances of such a class will have the same number of named instance variables, but may have different numbers of indexed variables. For example, a system class representing a collection whose elements are ordered, OrderedCollection, has indexed instance variables to hold its contents. An OrderedCollection might have more space for storing elements than is currently being used. The two named instance variables remember the indices of the first and last element of the contents.

class name	OrderedCollection
instance variable names	firstIndex
	lastIndex
indexed instance variables	

All instances of OrderedCollection will have two named variables, but one may have five indexed instance variables, another 15, another 18, and so on.

The named instance variables of an instance of FinancialHistory are private in the sense that access to the values of the variables is controlled by the instance. A class may or may not include messages giving direct access to the instance variables. Indexed instance variables are not private in this sense, since direct access to the values of the variables is available by sending messages with selectors at: and at:put:. Since these messages are the only way to access indexed instance variables, they must be provided.

Classes with indexed instance variables create new instances with the message new: instead of the usual message new. The argument of new: tells the number of indexed variables to be provided.

list ← Array new: 10

creates an Array of 10 elements, each of which is initially the special object nil. The number of indexed instance variables of an instance can be found by sending it the message size. The response to the message size

list size

is, for this example, the integer 10.

Evaluating each of the following expressions, in order,

list ← Array new: 3.
list at: 1 put: 'one'.
list at: 2 put: 'two'.
list at: 3 put: 'three'

is equivalent to the single expression

list ← #('one' 'two' 'three')

Shared Variables

Variables that are shared by more than one object come in groups called *pools*. Each class has two or more pools whose variables can be accessed by its instances. One pool is shared by all classes and contains the global variables; this pool is named Smalltalk. Each class also has a pool which is only available to its instances and contains the class variables.

Besides these two mandatory pools, a class may access some other special purpose pools shared by several classes. For example, there are several classes in the system that represent textual information; these classes need to share the ASCII character codes for characters that are not easily indicated visually, such as a carriage return, tab, or space. These numbers are included as variables in a pool named TextConstants that is shared by the classes implementing text display and text editing.

If FinancialHistory had a class variable named SalesTaxRate and shared a pool dictionary whose name is FinancialConstants, the declaration would be expressed as follows.

instance variable names	cashOnHand
	incomes
	expenditures
class variable names	SalesTaxRate
shared pools	FinancialConstants

SalesTaxRate is the name of a class variable, so it can be used in any methods in the class. FinancialConstants, on the other hand, is the name of a pool; it is the variables *in* the pool that can be used in expressions.

In order to declare a variable to be global (known to all classes and to the user's interactive system), the variable name must be inserted as a key in the dictionary Smalltalk. For example, to make AllHistories global, evaluate the expression

Smalltalk at: #AllHistories put: nil

Then use an assignment statement to set the value of AllHistories.

Methods

A method describes how an object will perform one of its operations. A method is made up of a message pattern and a sequence of expressions separated by periods. The example method shown below describes the response of a FinancialHistory to messages informing it of expenditures.

spend: amount for: reason

> exp.   { expenditures at: reason
>   put: (self totalSpentFor: reason) + amount.
>
> exp.   {cashOnHand ← cashOnHand − amount

The message pattern, **spend: amount for: reason**, indicates that this method will be used in response to all messages with selector spend:for:.

The first expression in the body of this method adds the new amount to the amount already spent for the reason indicated. The second expression is an assignment that decrements the value of cashOnHand by the new amount.

Argument Names

Message patterns were introduced earlier in this chapter. A message pattern contains a message selector and a set of argument names, one for each argument that a message with that selector would have. A message pattern matches any messages that have the same selector. A class will have only one method with a given selector in its message pattern. When a message is sent, the method with matching message pattern is selected from the class of the receiver. The expressions in the selected method are evaluated one after another. After all the expressions are evaluated, a value is returned to the sender of the message.

The argument names found in a method's message pattern are pseudo-variable names referring to the arguments of the actual message. If the method shown above were invoked by the expression

HouseholdFinances spend: 30.45 for: 'food'

the pseudo-variable name amount would refer to the number 30.45 and the pseudo-variable name reason would refer to the string 'food' during the evaluation of the expressions in the method. If the same method were invoked by the expression

HouseholdFinances spend: cost + tax for: 'food'

cost would be sent the message + tax and the value it returned would be referred to as amount in the method. If cost referred to 100 and tax to 6.5, the value of amount would be 106.5.

Since argument names are pseudo-variable names, they can be used to access values like variable names, but their values cannot be changed by assignment. In the method for spend:for:, a statement of the form

amount ← amount * taxRate

would be syntactically illegal since the value of amount cannot be reassigned.

Returning Values

The method for spend:for: does not specify what the value of the message should be. Therefore, the default value, the receiver itself, will be returned. When another value is to be specified, one or more return expressions are included in the method. Any expression can be turned into a return expression by preceding it with an uparrow (↑). The value of a variable may be returned as in

↑cashOnHand

The value of another message can be returned as in

↑expenditures at: reason

A literal object can be returned as in

↑0

Even an assignment statement can be turned into a return expression, as in

↑initialIndex ← 0

The assignment is performed first. The new value of the variable is then returned.

An example of the use of a return expression is the following implementation of totalSpentFor:.

totalSpentFor: reason
  (expenditures includesKey: reason)
    ifTrue: [↑expenditures at: reason]
    ifFalse: [↑0]

This method consists of a single conditional expression. If the expenditure reason is in expenditures, the associated value is returned; otherwise, zero is returned.

The Pseudo-variable self

Along with the pseudo-variables used to refer to the arguments of a message, all methods have access to a pseudo-variable named self that refers to the message receiver itself. For example, in the method for spend:for:, the message totalSpentFor: is sent to the receiver of the spend:for: message.

spend: amount for: reason
  expenditures at: reason
       put: (self totalSpentFor: reason) + amount.
  cashOnHand ← cashOnHand - amount

When this method is executed, the first thing that happens is that totalSpentFor: is sent to the same object (self) that received spend:for:. The result of that message is sent the message + amount, and the result of that message is used as the second argument to at:put:.

The pseudo-variable self can be used to implement recursive functions. For example, the message factorial is understood by integers in order to compute the appropriate function. The method associated with factorial is

factorial
```
self = 0 ifTrue: [↑1].
self < 0
    ifTrue: [self error: 'factorial invalid']
    ifFalse: [↑self * (self − 1) factorial]
```

The receiver is an Integer. The first expression tests to see if the receiver is 0 and, if it is, returns 1. The second expression tests the sign of the receiver because, if it is less than 0, the programmer should be notified of an error (all objects respond to the message error: with a report that an error has been encountered). If the receiver is greater than 0, then the value to be returned is

self * (self − 1) factorial

The value returned is the receiver multiplied by the factorial of one less than the receiver.

*Temporary
Variables*

The argument names and self are available only during a single execution of a method. In addition to these pseudo-variable names, a method may obtain some other variables for use during its execution. These are called *temporary variables*. Temporary variables are indicated by including a temporary variable declaration between the message pattern and the expressions of a method. A temporary declaration consists of a set of variable names between vertical bars. The method for spend:for: could be rewritten to use a temporary variable to hold the previous expenditures.

spend: amount for: reason
```
| previousExpenditures |
previousExpenditures ← self totalSpentFor: reason.
expenditures at: reason
            put: previousExpenditures + amount.
cashOnHand ← cashOnHand − amount
```

The values of temporary variables are accessible only to statements in the method and are forgotten when the method completes execution. All temporary variables initially refer to nil.

In the interactive Smalltalk-80 system, the programmer can test algorithms that make use of temporary variables. The test can be carried out by using the vertical bar notation to declare the variables for the duration of the immediate evaluation only. Suppose the expressions to be tried out include reference to the variable list. If the variable list is undeclared, an attempt to evaluate the expressions will create a syntax error message. Instead, the programmer can declare list as a temporary variable by prefixing the expressions with the declaration | list |. The expressions are separated by periods, as in the syntax of a method.

```
| list |
list ← Array new: 3.
list at: 1 put: 'one'.
list at: 2 put: 'four'.
list printString
```

The programmer interactively selects all five lines—the declaration and the expressions—and requests evaluation. The variable list is available only during the single execution of the selection.

Primitive Methods

When an object receives a message, it typically just sends other messages, so where does something *really* happen? An object may change the value of its instance variables when it receives a message, which certainly qualifies as "something happening." But this hardly seems enough. In fact, it is not enough. All behavior in the system *is* invoked by messages, however, all messages are *not* responded to by executing Smalltalk-80 methods. There are about one hundred *primitive methods* that the Smalltalk-80 virtual machine knows how to perform. Examples of messages that invoke primitives are the + message to small integers, the at: message to objects with indexed instance variables, and the new and new: messages to classes. When 3 gets the message + 4, it does not execute a Smalltalk-80 method. A primitive method returns 7 as the value of the message. The complete set of primitive methods is included in the fourth part of this book, which describes the virtual machine.

Methods that are implemented as primitive methods begin with an expression of the form

```
< primitive # >
```

where # is an integer indicating which primitive method will be followed. If the primitive fails to perform correctly, execution continues in the Smalltalk-80 method. The expression < primitive # > is followed by Smalltalk-80 expressions that handle failure situations.

Summary of Terminology

class	An object that describes the implementation of a set of similar objects.
instance	One of the objects described by a class; it has memory and responds to messages.
instance variable	A variable available to a single object for the entire lifetime of the object; instance variables can be named or indexed.
protocol description	A description of a class in terms of its instances' public message protocol.
implementation description	A description of a class in terms of its instances' private memory and the set of methods that describe how instances perform their operations.
message pattern	A message selector and a set of argument names, one for each argument that a message with this selector must have.
temporary variable	A variable created for a specific activity and available only for the duration of that activity.
class variable	A variable shared by all the instances of a single class.
global variable	A variable shared by all the instances of all classes.
pool variable	A variable shared by the instances of a set of classes.
Smalltalk	A pool shared by all classes that contains the global variables.
method	A procedure describing how to perform one of an object's operations; it is made up of a message pattern, temporary variable declaration, and a sequence of expressions. A method is executed when a message matching its message pattern is sent to an instance of the class in which the method is found
argument name	Name of a pseudo-variable available to a method only for the duration of that method's execution; the value of the argument names are the arguments of the message that invoked the method.
↑	When used in a method, indicates that the value of the next expression is to be the value of the method.
self	A pseudo-variable referring to the receiver of a message.
message category	A group of methods in a class description.
primitive method	An operation performed directly by the Smalltalk-80 virtual machine; it is not described as a sequence of Smalltalk-80 expressions.

4

Subclasses

Every object in the Smalltalk-80 system is an instance of a class. All instances of a class represent the same kind of system component. For example, each instance of Rectangle represents a rectangular area and each instance of Dictionary represents a set of associations between names and values. The fact that the instances of a class all represent the same kind of component is reflected both in the way the instances respond to messages and in the form of their instance variables.

- All instances of a class respond to the same set of messages and use the same set of methods to do so.

- All instances of a class have the same number of named instance variables and use the same names to refer to them.

- An object can have indexed instance variables only if all instances of its class can have indexed instance variables.

The class structure as described so far does not explicitly provide for any intersection in class membership. Each object is an instance of exactly one class. This structure is illustrated in Figure 4.1. In the figure, the small circles represent instances and the boxes represent classes. If a circle is within a box, then it represents an instance of the class represented by the box.

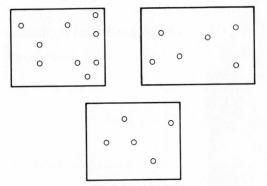

Figure 4.1

Lack of intersection in class membership is a limitation on design in an object-oriented system since it does not allow any sharing between class descriptions. We might want two objects to be substantially similar, but to differ in some particular way. For example, a floating-point number and an integer are similar in their ability to respond to arithmetic messages, but are different in the way they represent numeric values. An ordered collection and a bag are similar in that they are containers to which elements can be added and from which elements can be removed, but they are different in the precise way in which individual elements are accessed. The difference between otherwise similar objects may be externally visible, such as responding to some different messages, or it may be purely internal, such as responding to the same message by executing different methods. If class memberships are not allowed to overlap, this type of partial similarity between two objects cannot be guaranteed by the system.

The most general way to overcome this limitation is to allow arbitrary intersection of class boundaries (Figure 4.2).

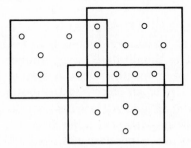

Figure 4.2

We call this approach *multiple inheritance*. Multiple inheritance allows a situation in which some objects are instances of two classes, while other objects are instances of only one class or the other. A less general relaxation of the nonintersection limitation on classes is to allow a class to include all instances of another class, but not to allow more general sharing (Figure 4.3).

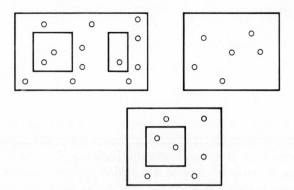

Figure 4.3

We call this approach *subclassing*. This follows the terminology of the programming language Simula, which includes a similar concept. Subclassing is strictly hierarchical; if any instances of a class are also instances of another class, then all instances of that class must also be instances of the other class.

The Smalltalk-80 system provides the subclassing form of inheritance for its classes. This chapter describes how subclasses modify their superclasses, how this affects the association of messages and methods, and how the subclass mechanism provides a framework for the classes in the system.

Subclass Descriptions

A subclass specifies that its instances will be the same as instances of another class, called its *superclass*, except for the differences that are explicitly stated. The Smalltalk-80 programmer always creates a new class as a subclass of an existing class. A system class named Object describes the similarities of *all* objects in the system, so every class will at least be a subclass of Object. A class description (protocol or implementation) specifies how its instances differ from the instances of its superclass. The instances of a superclass can not be affected by the existence of subclasses.

A subclass is in all respects a class and can therefore have subclasses itself. Each class has one superclass, although many classes may share the same superclass, so the classes form a tree structure. A class has a sequence of classes from which it inherits both variables and methods. This sequence begins with its superclass and continues with its superclass's superclass, and so on. The inheritance chain continues through the superclass relationship until Object is encountered. Object is the single root class; it is the only class without a superclass.

Recall that an implementation description has three basic parts:

1. A class name

2. A variable declaration

3. A set of methods

A subclass must provide a new class name for itself, but it inherits both the variable declaration and methods of its superclass. New variables may be declared and new methods may be added by the subclass. If instance variable names are added in the subclass variable declaration, instances of the subclass will have more instance variables than instances of the superclass. If shared variables are added, they will be accessible to the instances of the subclass, but not to instances of the superclass. All variable names added must be different from any declared in the superclass.

If a class does not have indexed instance variables, a subclass can declare that its instances will have indexed variables; these indexed variables will be in addition to any inherited named instance variables. If a class has indexed instance variables, its subclasses *must* also have indexed instance variables; a subclass can also declare new named instance variables.

If a subclass adds a method whose message pattern has the same selector as a method in the superclass, its instances will respond to messages with that selector by executing the new method. This is called *overriding* a method. If a subclass adds a method with a selector not found in the methods of the superclass, the instances of the subclass will respond to messages not understood by instances of the superclass.

To summarize, each part of an implementation description can be modified by a subclass in a different way:

1. The class name *must* be overridden.

2. Variables *may* be added.

3. Methods *may* be added or overridden.

An Example Subclass

An implementation description includes an entry, not shown in the previous chapter, that specifies its superclass. The following example is a class created as a subclass of the FinancialHistory class introduced in Chapter 3. Instances of the subclass share the function of FinancialHistory for storing information about monetary expenditures and receipts. They have the additional function of keeping track of the expenditures that are tax deductible. The subclass provides the mandatory new class name (DeductibleHistory), and adds one instance variable and four methods. One of these methods (initialBalance:) overrides a method in the superclass.

The class description for DeductibleHistory follows.

class name	DeductibleHistory
superclass	FinancialHistory
instance variable names	deductibleExpenditures
instance methods	

transaction recording

spendDeductible: amount for: reason
    self spend: amount for: reason.
    deductibleExpenditures ←
        deductibleExpenditures + amount

spend: amount for: reason deducting: deductibleAmount
    self spend: amount for: reason.
    deductibleExpenditures ←
        deductibleExpenditures + deductibleAmount

inquiries

totalDeductions
    ↑deductibleExpenditures

initialization

initialBalance: amount
    super initialBalance: amount.
    deductibleExpenditures ← 0

In order to know all the messages understood by an instance of DeductibleHistory, it is necessary to examine the protocols of DeductibleHistory, FinancialHistory, and Object. Instances of DeductibleHistory have four variables—three inherited from the superclass FinancialHistory, and one specified in the class DeductibleHistory. Class Object declares no instance variables.

Figure 4.4 indicates that DeductibleHistory is a subclass of FinancialHistory. Each box in this diagram is labeled in the upper left corner with the name of class it represents.

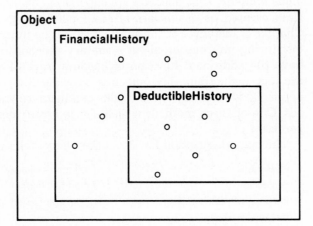

Figure 4.4

Instances of DeductibleHistory can be used to record the history of entities that pay taxes (people, households, businesses). Instances of FinancialHistory can be used to record the history of entities that do not pay taxes (charitable organizations, religious organizations). Actually, an instance of DeductibleHistory could be used in place of an instance of FinancialHistory without detection since it responds to the same messages in the same way. In addition to the messages and methods inherited from FinancialHistory, an instance of DeductibleHistory can respond to messages indicating that all or part of an expenditure is deductible. The new messages available are spendDeductible:for:, which is used if the total amount is deductible; and spend:for:deducting:, which is used if only part of the expenditure is deductible. The total tax deduction can be found by sending a DeductibleHistory the message totalDeductions.

Method Determination

When a message is sent, the methods in the receiver's class are searched for one with a matching selector. If none is found, the methods in that class's superclass are searched next. The search continues up the superclass chain until a matching method is found. Suppose we send an instance of DeductibleHistory a message with selector cashOnHand. The search for the appropriate method to execute begins in the class of the receiver, DeductibleHistory. When it is not found, the search continues by looking at DeductibleHistory's superclass, FinancialHistory. When a method with the selector cashOnHand is found there, that method is executed as the response to the message. The response to this message is to return the value of the instance variable cashOnHand. This value is found in the receiver of the message, that is, in the instance of DeductibleHistory.

The search for a matching method follows the superclass chain, terminating at class Object. If no matching method is found in any class in the superclass chain, the receiver is sent the message doesNotUnderstand:; the argument is the offending message. There is a method for the selector doesNotUnderstand: in Object that reports the error to the programmer.

Suppose we send an instance of DeductibleHistory a message with selector spend:for:. This method is found in the superclass FinancialHistory. The method, as given in Chapter 3, is

spend: amount for: reason
```
    expenditures at: reason
            put: (self totalSpentFor: reason) + amount.
    cashOnHand ← cashOnHand − amount
```

The values of the instance variables (expenditures and cashOnHand) are found in the receiver of the message, the instance of DeductibleHistory.

The pseudo-variable self is also referenced in this method; self represents the DeductibleHistory instance that was the receiver of the message.

Messages to self

When a method contains a message whose receiver is self, the search for the method for that message begins in the instance's class, regardless of which class contains the method containing self. Thus, when the expression self totalSpentFor: reason is evaluated in the method for spend:for: found in FinancialHistory, the search for the method associated with the message selector totalSpentFor: begins in the class of self, i.e., in DeductibleHistory.

Messages to self will be explained using two example classes named One and Two. Two is a subclass of One and One is a subclass of Object. Both classes include a method for the message test. Class One also includes a method for the message result1 that returns the result of the expression self test.

```
class name                    One
superclass                    Object
instance methods

    test
        ↑1
    result1
        ↑self test

class name                    Two
superclass                    One
instance methods

    test
        ↑2
```

An instance of each class will be used to demonstrate the method determination for messages to self. example1 is an instance of class One and example2 is an instance of class Two.

```
example1 ← One new.
example2 ← Two new
```

The relationship between One and Two is shown in Figure 4.5. In addition to labeling the boxes in order to indicate class names, several of the circles are also labeled in order to indicate a name referring to the corresponding instance.

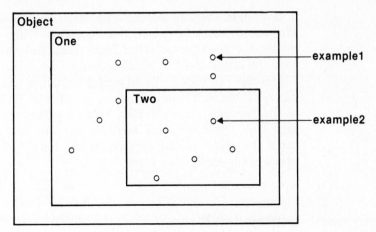

Figure 4.5

The following table shows the results of evaluating various expressions.

expression	result
example1 test	1
example1 result1	1
example2 test	2
example2 result1	2

The two result1 messages both invoke the same method, which is found in class One. They produce different results because of the message to self contained in that method. When result1 is sent to example2, the search for a matching method begins in Two. A method is not found in Two, so the search continues by looking in the superclass, One. A method for result1 is found in One, which consists of one expression, ↑self test. The pseudo-variable self refers to the receiver, example2. The search for the response to test, therefore, begins in class Two. A method for test is found in Two, which returns 2.

Messages to super

An additional pseudo-variable named super is available for use in a method's expressions. The pseudo-variable super refers to the receiver of the message, just as self does. However, when a message is sent to super, the search for a method does not begin in the receiver's class. Instead, the search begins in the superclass of the class containing the method. The use of super allows a method to access methods defined in a superclass even if the methods have been overridden in subclasses. The use of super as other than a receiver (for example, as an argument), has no different effect from using self; the use of super only affects the initial class in which messages are looked up.

Messages to super will be explained using two more example classes named Three and Four. Four is a subclass of Three, Three is a subclass of the previous example Two. Four overrides the method for the message test. Three contains methods for two new messages—result2 returns the result of the expression self result1, and result3 returns the result of the expression super test.

class name	Three
superclass	Two
instance methods	

result2
↑self result1
result3
↑super test

class name	Four
superclass	Three
instance methods	

test
↑4

Instances of One, Two, Three, and Four can all respond to the messages test and result1. The response of instances of Three and Four to messages illustrates the effect of super (Figure 4.6).

example3 ← Three new.
example4 ← Four new

An attempt to send the messages result2 or result3 to example1 or example2 is an error since instances of One or Two do not understand the messages result2 or result3.

The following table shows the results of sending various messages.

expression	result
example3 test	2
example4 result1	4
example3 result2	2
example4 result2	4
example3 result3	2
example4 result3	2

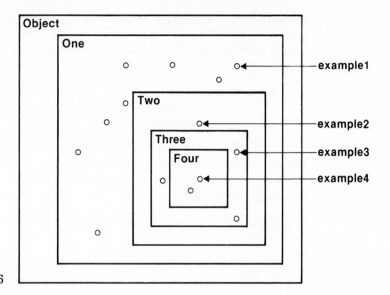

Figure 4.6

When test is sent to example3, the method in Two is used, since Three doesn't override the method. example4 responds to result1 with a 4 for the same reason that example2 responded with a 2. When result2 is sent to example3, the search for a matching method begins in Three. The method found there returns the result of the expression self result1. The search for the response to result1 also begins in class Three. A matching method is not found in Three or its superclass, Two. The method for result1 is found in One and returns the result of self test. The search for the response to test once more begins in class Three. This time, the matching method is found in Three's superclass Two.

The effect of sending messages to super will be illustrated by the responses of example3 and example4 to the message result3. When result3 is sent to example3, the search for a matching method begins in Three. The method found there returns the result of the expression super test. Since test is sent to super, the search for a matching method begins not in class Three, but in its superclass, Two. The method for test in Two returns a 2. When result3 is sent to example4, the result is still 2, even though Four overrides the message for test.

This example highlights a potential confusion: super does not mean start the search in the superclass of the receiver, which, in the last example, would have been class Three. It means start the search in the superclass of the class containing the method in which super was used, which, in the last example, was class Two. Even if Three had overridden the method for test by returning 3, the result of example4 result3 would still be 2. Sometimes, of course, the superclass of the class in which the method containing super is found is the same as the superclass of the receiver.

Another example of the use of super is in the method for initialBalance: in DeductibleHistory.

initialBalance: amount
    super initialBalance: amount.
    deductibleExpenditures ← 0

This method overrides a method in the superclass FinancialHistory. The method in DeductibleHistory consists of two expressions. The first expression passes control to the superclass in order to process the initialization of the balance.

    super initialBalance: amount

The pseudo-variable super refers to the receiver of the message, but indicates that the search for the method should skip DeductibleHistory and begin in FinancialHistory. In this way, the expressions from FinancialHistory do not have to be duplicated in DeductibleHistory. The second expression in the method does the subclass-specific initialization.

    deductibleExpenditures ← 0

If self were substituted for super in the initialBalance: method, it would result in an infinite recursion, since every time initialBalance: is sent, it will be sent again.

Abstract Superclasses

Abstract superclasses are created when two classes share a part of their descriptions and yet neither one is properly a subclass of the other. A mutual superclass is created for the two classes which contains their shared aspects. This type of superclass is called *abstract* because it was not created in order to have instances. In terms of the figures shown earlier, an abstract superclass represents the situation illustrated in Figure 4.7. Notice that the abstract class does not directly contain instances.

As an example of the use of an abstract superclass, consider two classes whose instances represent dictionaries. One class, named SmallDictionary, minimizes the space needed to store its contents; the other, named FastDictionary, stores names and values sparsely and uses a hashing technique to locate names. Both classes use two parallel lists

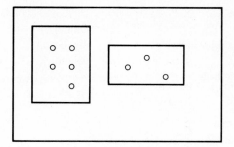

Figure 4.7

that contain names and associated values. SmallDictionary stores the names and values contiguously and uses a simple linear search to locate a name. FastDictionary stores names and values sparsely and uses a hashing technique to locate a name. Other than the difference in how names are located, these two classes are very similar: they share identical protocol and they both use parallel lists to store their contents. These similarities are represented in an abstract superclass named DualListDictionary. The relationships among these three classes is shown in Figure 4.8.

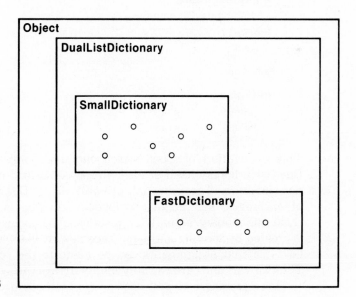

Figure 4.8

The implementation description for the abstract class, DualListDictionary is shown next.

class name	DualListDictionary
superclass	Object
instance variable names	names
	values

instance methods

accessing

at: name
> | index |
> index ← self indexOf: name.
> index = 0
>   ifTrue: [self error: 'Name not found']
>   ifFalse: [↑values at: index]

at: name put: value
> | index |
> index ← self indexOf: name.
> index = 0
>   ifTrue: [index ← self newIndexOf: name].
> ↑values at: index put: value

testing

includes: name
> ↑(self indexOf: name) ∼= 0

isEmpty
> ↑self size = 0

initialization

initialize
> names ← Array new: 0.
> values ← Array new: 0

This description of DualListDictionary uses only messages defined in DualListDictionary itself or ones already described in this or in the previous chapters. The external protocol for a DualListDictionary consists of messages at:, at:put:, includes:, isEmpty, and initialize. A new DualListDictionary (actually an instance of a subclass of DualListDictionary) is created by sending it the message new. It is then sent the message initialize so that assignments can be made to the two instance variables. The two variables are initially empty arrays (Array new: 0).

Three messages to self used in its methods are not implemented in DualListDictionary—size, indexOf:, and newIndexOf:. This is the reason that DualListDictionary is called abstract. If an instance were created, it would not be able to respond successfully to all of the necessary messages. The two subclasses, SmallDictionary and FastDictionary, must implement the three missing messages. The fact that the search always starts at the class of the instance referred to by self means that a method in a superclass can be specified in which messages are sent to self, but the corresponding methods are found in the subclass. In this way, a superclass can provide a framework for a method that is refined or actually implemented by the subclass.

SmallDictionary is a subclass of DualListDictionary that uses a minimal amount of space to represent the associations, but may take a long time to find an association. It provides methods for the three messages that were not implemented in DualListDictionary—size, indexOf:, and newIndexOf:. It does not add variables.

class name	SmallDictionary
superclass	DualListDictionary
instance methods	

accessing

size
    ↑names size

private

indexOf: name
    1 to: names size do:
       [:index | (names at: index) = name ifTrue: [↑index]].
    ↑0
newIndexOf: name
    self grow.
    names at: names size put: name.
    ↑names size
grow
    | oldNames oldValues |
    oldNames ← names.
    oldValues ← values.
    names ← Array new: names size + 1.
    values ← Array new: values size + 1.
    names replaceFrom: 1 to: oldNames size with: oldNames.
    values replaceFrom: 1 to: oldValues size with: oldValues

Since names are stored contiguously, the size of a SmallDictionary is the size of its array of names, names. The index of a particular name is determined by a linear search of the array names. If no match is found, the index is 0, signalling failure in the search. Whenever a new association is to be added to the dictionary, the method for newIndexOf: is used to find the appropriate index. It assumes that the sizes of names and values are exactly the sizes needed to store their current elements. This means no space is available for adding a new element. The message grow creates two new Arrays that are copies of the previous ones, with one more element at the end. In the method for newIndexOf:, first the sizes of names and values are increased and then the new name is stored in the new empty position (the last one). The method that called on newIndexOf: has the responsibility for storing the value.

We could evaluate the following example expressions.

expression	result
ages ← SmallDictionary new	a new, uninitialized instance
ages initialize	instance variables initialized
ages isEmpty	true
ages at: 'Brett' put: 3	3
ages at: 'Dave' put: 30	30
ages includes: 'Sam'	false
ages includes: 'Brett'	true
ages size	2
ages at: 'Dave'	30

For each of the above example expressions, we indicate in which class the message is found and in which class any messages sent to self are found.

message selector	message to self	class of method
initialize		DualListDictionary
at:put:		DualListDictionary
	indexOf:	SmallDictionary
	newIndexOf:	SmallDictionary
includes:		DualListDictionary
	indexOf:	SmallDictionary
size		SmallDictionary
at:		DualListDictionary
	indexOf:	SmallDictionary
	error:	Object

FastDictionary is another subclass of DualListDictionary. It uses a hashing technique to locate names. Hashing requires more space, but takes less time than a linear search. All objects respond to the hash message by returning a number. Numbers respond to the \\ message by returning their value in the modulus of the argument.

class name   FastDictionary
superclass   DualListDictionary
instance methods

accessing

size
```
| size |
size ← 0.
names do: [ :name | name notNil ifTrue: [size ← size + 1]].
↑size
```

initialization

initialize
```
names ← Array new: 4.
values ← Array new: 4
```

private

indexOf: name
```
| index |
index ← name hash \\ names size + 1.
[(names at: index) = name]
    whileFalse: [(names at: index) isNil
                    ifTrue: [↑0]
                    ifFalse: [index ← index \\ names size + 1]].
↑index
```

newIndexOf: name
```
| index |
names size - self size <= (names size / 4)
    ifTrue: [self grow].
index ← name hash \\ names size + 1.
[(names at: index) isNil]
    whileFalse: [index ← index \\ names size + 1].
names at: index put: name.
↑index
```

grow
```
| oldNames oldValues |
oldNames ← names.
oldValues ← values.
names ← Array new: names size * 2.
values ← Array new: values size * 2.
1 to: oldNames size do:
    [ :index |
    (oldNames at: index) isNil
        ifFalse: [self at: (oldNames at: index)
                    put: (oldValues at: index)]]
```

FastDictionary overrides DualListDictionary's implementation of initialize in order to create Arrays that already have some space allocated (Array new: 4). The size of a FastDictionary is not simply the size of one of its variables since the Arrays always have empty entries. So the size is determined by examining each element in the Array and counting the number that are not nil.

The implementation of newIndexOf: follows basically the same idea as that used for SmallDictionary except that when the size of an Array is changed (doubled in this case in the method for grow), each element is explicitly copied from the old Arrays into the new ones so that elements are rehashed. The size does not always have to be changed as is necessary in SmallDictionary. The size of a FastDictionary is changed only when the number of empty locations in names falls below a minimum. The minimum is equal to 25% of the elements.

names size − self size < = (names size / 4)

Subclass Framework Messages

As a matter of programming style, a method should not include messages to self if the messages are neither implemented by the class nor inherited from a superclass. In the description of DualListDictionary, three such messages exist—size, indexOf:, and newIndexOf:. As we shall see in subsequent chapters, the ability to respond to size is inherited from Object; the response is the number of indexed instance variables. A subclass of DualListDictionary is supposed to override this method in order to return the number of names in the dictionary.

A special message, subclassResponsibility, is specified in Object. It is to be used in the implementation of messages that cannot be properly implemented in an abstract class. That is, the implementation of size and indexOf: and newIndexOf:, by Smalltalk-80 convention, should be

self subclassResponsibility

The response to this message is to invoke the following method defined in class Object.

subclassResponsibility
    self error: ' My subclass should have overridden one of my messages. '

In this way, if a method should have been implemented in a subclass of an abstract class, the error reported is an indication to the programmer of how to fix the problem. Moreover, using this message, the programmer creates abstract classes in which all messages sent to self are implemented, and in which the implementation is an indication to the programmer of which methods must be overridden in the subclass.

By convention, if the programmer decides that a message inherited from an abstract superclass should actually *not* be implemented, the appropriate way to override the inherited method is

    self shouldNotImplement

The response to this message is to invoke the following method defined in class Object.

shouldNotImplement
    self error: ' This message is not appropriate for this object. '

There are several major subclass hierarchies in the Smalltalk-80 system that make use of the idea of creating a framework of messages whose implementations must be completed in subclasses. There are classes describing various kinds of collections (see Chapters 9 and 10). The collection classes are arranged hierarchically in order to share as much as possible among classes describing similar kinds of collections. They make use of the messages subclassResponsibility and shouldNotImplement. Another example of the use of subclasses is the hierarchy of linear measures and number classes (see Chapters 7 and 8).

Summary of Terminology		
subclass	A class that inherits variables and methods from an existing class.	
superclass	The class from which variables and methods are inherited.	
Object	The class that is the root of the tree-structured class hierarchy.	
overriding a method	Specifying a method in a subclass for the same message as a method in a superclass.	
super	A pseudo-variable that refers to the receiver of a message; differs from self in where to start the search for methods.	
abstract class	A class that specifies protocol, but is not able to fully implement it; by convention, instances are not created of this kind of class.	
subclassResponsibility	A message to report the error that a subclass should have implemented one of the superclass's messages.	
shouldNotImplement	A message to report the error that this is a message inherited from a superclass but explicitly not available to instances of the subclass.	

5

Metaclasses

Since all Smalltalk-80 system components are represented by objects and all objects are instances of a class, the classes themselves must be represented by instances of a class. A class whose instances are themselves classes is called a *metaclass*. This chapter describes the special properties of metaclasses. Examples illustrate how metaclasses are used to support instance creation and general class inquiries.

In earlier versions of the Smalltalk system, there was only one metaclass, named Class. It corresponded to the class organization depicted in Figure 5.1. As used in Chapter 4, a box denotes a class and a circle denotes an instance of the class in which it is contained. Where possible, the box is labeled with the name of the class it represents. Note that there is one circle in the box labeled Class for each box in the diagram.

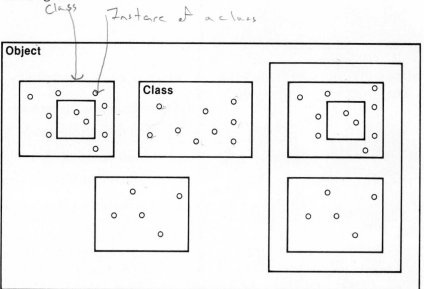

Figure 5.1

This approach had the difficulty that the message protocol of all classes was constrained to be the same since it was specified in one place. In particular, the messages used to create new instances were the same for all classes and could not take any special initialization requirements into account. With a single metaclass, all classes respond to the message new or new: by returning an instance whose instance variables all refer to nil. For most objects, nil is not a reasonable instance variable value, so new instances have to be initialized by sending another message. The programmer must ensure that every time a new or new: is sent, another message is sent to the new object so that it will be properly initialized. Examples of this kind of initialization were shown in Chapter 4 for SmallDictionary and FinancialHistory.

The Smalltalk-80 system removes the restriction that all classes have the same message protocol by making each class an instance of its own metaclass. Whenever a new class is created, a new metaclass is created for it automatically. Metaclasses are similar to other classes because they contain the methods used by their instances. Metaclasses are different from other classes because they are not themselves instances of metaclasses. Instead, they are all instances of a class called Metaclass. Also, metaclasses do not have class names. A metaclass can be accessed by sending its instance the unary message class. For example, Rectangle's metaclass can be referred to with the expression Rectangle class.

The messages of a metaclass typically support creation and initialization of instances, and initialization of class variables.

Initialization of Instances

Each class can respond to messages that request properly initialized new instances. Multiple metaclasses are needed because the initialization messages are different for different classes. For example, we have already seen that Time creates new instances in response to the message now and Date creates new instances in response to the message today.

    Time now
    Date today

These messages are meaningless to Point, the class whose instances represent two-dimensional locations. Point creates a new instance in response to a message with selector x:y: and two arguments specifying the coordinates. This message is, in turn, meaningless to Time or Date.

    Point x: 100 y: 150

Class Rectangle understands several messages that create new instances. A message with the selector origin:corner: takes Points representing the upper left and lower right corners as arguments.

    Rectangle
        origin: (Point x: 50 y: 50)
        corner: (Point x: 250 y: 300)

A message with the selector origin:extent: takes as arguments the upper left corner and a Point representing the width and height. The same rectangle could have been created by the following expression.

Rectangle
    origin: (Point x: 50 y: 50)
    extent: (Point x: 200 y: 250)

In the Smalltalk-80 system, Class is an abstract superclass for all of the metaclasses. Class describes the general nature of classes. Each metaclass adds the behavior specific to its single instance. Metaclasses may add new instance creation messages like those of Date, Time, Point, and Rectangle mentioned above, or they may redefine the fundamental new and new: messages in order to perform some default initialization.

The organization of classes and instances in the system, as described so far, is illustrated in Figure 5.2.

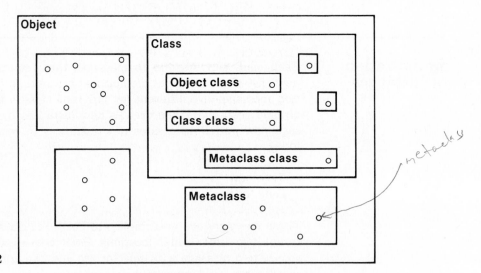

Figure 5.2

In this figure, we indicate classes Object, Metaclass, and Class, and metaclasses for each. Each circle within the box labeled Metaclass denotes a metaclass. Each box within the box labeled Class denotes a subclass of Class. There is one such box for each circle within the box labeled Metaclass. Each of these boxes contains a circle denoting its instance; these instances refer to Object or one of the subclasses of Object, but not to metaclasses.

An Example Metaclass

Since there is a one-to-one correspondence between a class and its metaclass, their descriptions are presented together. An implementation description includes a part entitled "class methods" that shows the methods added by the metaclass. The protocol for the metaclass is always found by looking at the class methods part of the implementation description of its single instance. In this way, messages sent to the class (class methods) and messages sent to instances of the class (instance methods) are listed together as part of the complete implementation description.

The following new version of the implementation description for FinancialHistory includes class methods.

class name	FinancialHistory
superclass	Object
instance variable names	cashOnHand
	incomes
	expenditures

class methods

instance creation

initialBalance: amount
↑super new setInitialBalance: amount
new
↑super new setInitialBalance: 0

instance methods

transaction recording

receive: amount from: source
incomes at: source
put: (self totalReceivedFrom: source) + amount.
cashOnHand ← cashOnHand + amount
spend: amount for: reason
expenditures at: reason
put: (self totalSpentFor: reason) + amount.
cashOnHand ← cashOnHand − amount

inquiries

cashOnHand
↑cashOnHand
totalReceivedFrom: source
(incomes includesKey: source)
ifTrue: [↑incomes at: source]
ifFalse: [↑0]
totalSpentFor: reason
(expenditures includesKey: reason)
ifTrue: [↑expenditures at: reason]
ifFalse: [↑0]

private

setInitialBalance: amount
    cashOnHand ← amount.
    incomes ← Dictionary new.
    expenditures ← Dictionary new

Three changes have been made to the implementation description.

1. One category of class methods named instance creation has been added. The category contains methods for initialBalance: and new. By convention, the category instance creation is used for class methods that return new instances.

2. The category of instance methods named initialization has been deleted. It had included a method for initialBalance:.

3. A category of instance methods named private has been added. The category contains one method for setInitialBalance:; this method contains the same expressions that were in the deleted method for initialBalance:.

This example illustrates how metaclasses create initialized instances. The instance creation methods for initialBalance: and new do not have direct access to the instance variables of the new instance (cashOnHand, incomes, and expenses). This is because the methods are not a part of the class of the new instance, but rather of the class's class. Therefore, the instance creation methods first create uninitialized instances and then send an initialization message, setInitialBalance:, to the new instance. The method for this message is found in the instance methods part of FinancialHistory's implementation description; it can assign appropriate values to the instance variables. The initialization message is not considered part of the external protocol of FinancialHistory so it is categorized as private. It is typically only sent once and only by a class method.

The old initialization message initialBalance: was deleted because the proper way to create a FinancialHistory is to use an expression such as

FinancialHistory initialBalance: 350

not

FinancialHistory new initialBalance: 350

Indeed, this second expression would now create an error since instances of FinancialHistory are no longer described as responding to initialBalance:. We could have maintained the instance method initialBalance: and implemented the class method for initialBalance: to call on it, but we try not to use the same selectors for both instance and class methods in order to improve the readability of the implementation description. However, there would be no ambiguity if the same selector were used.

Metaclass Inheritance

Like other classes, a metaclass inherits from a superclass. The simplest way to structure the inheritance of metaclasses would be to make each one a subclass of Class. This organization was shown in Figure 5.2. Class describes the general nature of classes. Each metaclass adds behavior specific to its instance. Metaclasses may add new instance creation messages or they may redefine the fundamental new and new: messages to perform some default initialization.

When metaclasses were added to the Smalltalk-80 system, one further step in class organization was taken. The metaclass subclass hierarchy was constrained to be parallel to the subclass hierarchy of the classes that are their instances. Therefore, if DeductibleHistory is a subclass of FinancialHistory, then DeductibleHistory's metaclass must be a subclass of FinancialHistory's metaclass. A metaclass typically has only one instance.

An abstract class named ClassDescription was provided to describe classes and their instances. Class and Metaclass are subclasses of ClassDescription. Since the superclass chain of all objects ends at Object and Object has no superclass, the superclass of Object's metaclass is Class. From Class, the metaclasses inherit messages that provide protocol for the creation of instances (Figure 5.3).

The superclass chain from Class leads eventually to class Object. Notice that the hierarchy of boxes with the box labeled Object class is like that of the hierarchy of boxes within the box labeled Object; this similarity illustrates the parallel hierarchies. A full description of this part of the system, including the relationship between Metaclass and its metaclass, is provided in Chapter 16.

As an example of the metaclass inheritance hierarchy, consider the implementation of initialBalance: in FinancialHistory class.

initialBalance: amount
    ↑super new setInitialBalance: amount

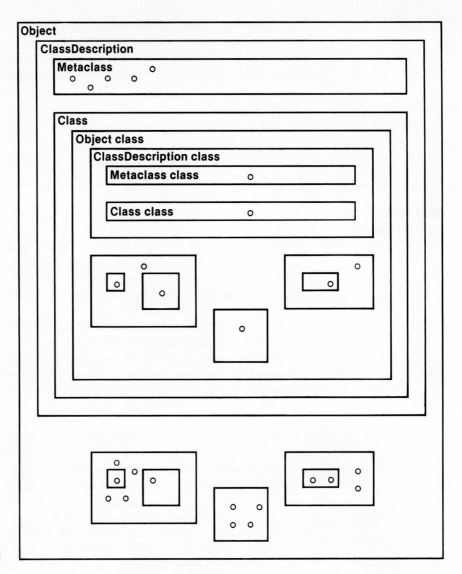

Figure 5.3

This method creates a new instance by evaluating the expression super new; it uses the method for new found in the class methods of the superclass, not the class methods found in this class. It then sends the new instance the message setInitialBalance: with the initial amount of the balance as the argument. Similarly, new is reimplemented as creating an instance using super new followed by setInitialBalance:.

new
   ↑super new setInitialBalance: 0

Figure 5.4

Where is the method for the message new sent to super actually found? The subclass hierarchy of the metaclasses parallels the hierarchy of their instances. If one class is a subclass of another, its metaclass will be a subclass of the other's metaclass, as indicated in Figure 5.3. The parallel class and metaclass hierarchies for the FinancialHistory application are shown in Figure 5.4.

If we evaluate the expression

FinancialHistory initialBalance: 350

the search for the response to initialBalance: begins in FinancialHistory class, i.e., in the class methods for FinancialHistory. A method for that selector is found there. The method consists of two messages:

1. Send super the message new.

2. Send the result of 1 the message setInitialBalance: 350.

The search for new begins in the superclass of FinancialHistory class, that is, in Object class. A method is not found there, so the search continues up the superclass chain to Class. The message selector new is found in Class, and a primitive method is executed. The result is an uninitialized instance of FinancialHistory. This instance is then sent the message setInitialBalance:. The search for the response begins in the class of the instance, i.e., in FinancialHistory (in the instance methods). A method is found there which assigns a value to each instance variable.

The evaluation of

FinancialHistory new

is carried out in a similar way. The response to new is found in FinancialHistory class (i.e., in the class methods of FinancialHistory). The remaining actions are the same as for initialBalance: with the exception of the value of the argument to setInitialBalance:. The instance creation methods must use super new in order to avoid invoking the same method recursively.

Initialization of Class Variables

The main use of messages to classes other than creation of instances is the initialization of class variables. The implementation description's variable declaration gives the names of the class variables only, not their values. When a class is created, the named class variables are created, but they all have a value of nil. The metaclass typically defines a method that initializes the class variables. By convention, the class-variable initialization method is usually associated with the unary message initialize, categorized as class initialization.

Class variables are accessible to both the class and its metaclass. The assignment of values to class variables can be done in the class methods, rather than indirectly via a private message in the instance methods (as was necessary for instance variables).

The example DeductibleHistory, this time with a class variable that needs to be initialized, is shown next. DeductibleHistory is a subclass of FinancialHistory. It declares one class variable, MinimumDeductions.

class name	DeductibleHistory
superclass	FinancialHistory
instance variable names	deductibleExpenditures
class variable names	MinimumDeductions
class methods	

instance creation

initialBalance: amount
    | newHistory |
    newHistory ← super initialBalance: amount.
    newHistory initializeDeductions.
    ↑newHistory

new
    | newHistory |
    newHistory ← super initialBalance: 0.
    newHistory initializeDeductions.
    ↑newHistory

class initialization

initialize
    MinimumDeductions ← 2300

instance methods

transaction recording

spendDeductible: amount for: reason
    self spend: amount for: reason.
    deductibleExpenditures ←
        deductibleExpenditures + amount

spend: amount for: reason deducting: deductibleAmount
    self spend: amount for: reason.
    deductibleExpenditures ←
        deductibleExpenditures + deductibleAmount

inquiries

isItemizable
    ↑deductibleExpenditures $>=$ MinimumDeductions
totalDeductions
    ↑deductibleExpenditures

private

initializeDeductions
    deductibleExpenditures ← 0

This version of DeductibleHistory adds five instance methods, one of which is isItemizable. The response to this message is true or false

PART TWO

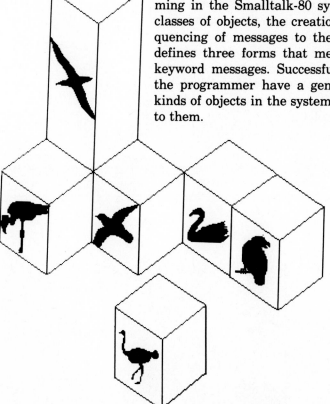

Part One provided an overview of the Smalltalk-80 language both from the semantic view of objects and message sending and from the syntactic view of the form that expressions take. The Smalltalk-80 programmer must first understand the semantics of the language: that all information is represented in the form of objects and that all processing is done by sending messages to objects. Every object is described by a class; every class, with the exception of class Object, is a subclass of another class. Programming in the Smalltalk-80 system involves the description of new classes of objects, the creation of instances of classes, and the sequencing of messages to the instances. The Smalltalk-80 syntax defines three forms that messages can take: unary, binary, and keyword messages. Successful use of the language requires that the programmer have a general knowledge of each of the basic kinds of objects in the system and of the messages that can be sent to them.

The semantics and syntax of the language are relatively simple. Yet the system is large and powerful due to the numbers of and kinds of available objects. There are eight significant categories of classes in the Smalltalk-80 system: kernel and kernel support, linear measures, numbers, collections, streams, classes, independent processes, and graphics. The protocol of these kinds of objects is reviewed in 12 chapters of Part Two. In each of these chapters, the diagram of the class hierarchy given in Chapter 1 is re-presented in order to highlight the portion of the hierarchy discussed in that chapter. Three additional chapters in Part Two provide examples of Smalltalk-80 expressions and class descriptions.

The classes in the Smalltalk-80 system are defined in a linear hierarchy. The chapters in Part Two take an encyclopedic approach to reviewing class protocol: categories of messages are defined, each message is annotated, and examples are given. In presenting the protocol of a class, however, only those messages added by the class are described. The complete message protocol is determined by examining the protocol specified in the class and in each of its superclasses. Thus it is useful to present the classes starting with a description of class Object and to proceed in a mostly depth-first manner so that inherited protocol can be understood in conjunction with the new protocol.

6

Protocol for All Objects

Testing the Functionality of an Object

Comparing Objects

Copying Objects

Accessing the Parts of an Object

Printing and Storing Objects

Error Handling

Object

Magnitude	Stream
Character	PositionableStream
Date	ReadStream
Time	WriteStream
	ReadWriteStream
Number	ExternalStream
Float	FileStream
Fraction	
Integer	Random
LargeNegativeInteger	
LargePositiveInteger	UndefinedObject
SmallInteger	Boolean
	False
	True
LookupKey	
Association	
	ProcessorScheduler
Link	Delay
	SharedQueue
Process	
	Behavior
Collection	ClassDescription
	Class
SequenceableCollection	MetaClass
LinkedList	
	Point
Semaphore	Rectangle
	BitBlt
ArrayedCollection	CharacterScanner
Array	
	Pen
WordArray	
DisplayBitmap	DisplayObject
	DisplayMedium
RunArray	Form
String	Cursor
Symbol	DisplayScreen
Text	InfiniteForm
ByteArray	OpaqueForm
	Path
Interval	Arc
OrderedCollection	Circle
SortedCollection	Curve
Bag	Line
MappedCollection	LinearFit
Set	Spline
Dictionary	
IdentityDictionary	

Everything in the system is an object. The protocol common to all objects in the system is provided in the description of class Object. This means that any and every object created in the system can respond to the messages defined by class Object. These are typically messages that support reasonable default behavior in order to provide a starting place from which to develop new kinds of objects, either by adding new messages or by modifying the response to existing messages. Examples to consider when examining Object's protocol are numeric objects such as 3 or 16.23, collections such as 'this is a string' or #(this is an array), nil or true, and class-describing objects such as Collection or SmallInteger or, indeed, Object itself.

The specification of protocol for class Object given in this chapter is incomplete. We have omitted messages pertaining to message handling, special dependency relationships, and system primitives. These are presented in Chapter 14.

Testing the Functionality of an Object

Every object is an instance of a class. An object's functionality is determined by its class. This functionality is tested in two ways: explicit naming of a class to determine whether it is the class or the superclass of the object, and naming of a message selector to determine whether the object can respond to it. These reflect two ways of thinking about the relationship among instances of different classes: in terms of the class/subclass hierarchy, or in terms of shared message protocols.

Object instance protocol

class membership

class	Answer the object which is the receiver's class.
isKindOf: aClass	Answer whether the argument, aClass, is a superclass or class of the receiver.
isMemberOf: aClass	Answer whether the receiver is a direct instance of the argument, aClass. This is the same as testing whether the response to sending the receiver the message class is the same as (==) aClass.
respondsTo: aSymbol	Answer whether the method dictionary of the receiver's class or one of its superclasses contains the argument, aSymbol, as a message selector.

Example messages and their corresponding results are

expression	*result*
3 class	SmallInteger
#(this is an array) isKindOf: Collection	true

#(this is an array) isMemberOf: Collection	false
#(this is an array) class	Array
3 respondsTo: #isKindOf:	true
#(1 2 3) isMemberOf: Array	true
Object class	Object class

Comparing Objects

Since all information in the system is represented as objects, there is a basic protocol provided for testing the identity of an object and for copying objects. The important comparisons specified in class Object are equivalence and equality testing. Equivalence (==) is the test of whether two objects are the same object. Equality (=) is the test of whether two objects represent the same component. The decision as to what it means to be "represent the same component" is made by the receiver of the message; each new kind of object that adds new instance variables typically must reimplement the = message in order to specify which of its instance variables should enter into the test of equality. For example, equality of two arrays is determined by checking the size of the arrays and then the equality of each of the elements of the arrays; equality of two numbers is determined by testing whether the two numbers represent the same value; and equality of two bank accounts might rest solely on the equality of each account identification number.

The message hash is a special part of the comparing protocol. The response to hash is an integer. Any two objects that are equal must return the same value for hash. Unequal objects may or may not return equal values for hash. Typically, this integer is used as an index to locate the object in an indexed collection (as illustrated in Chapter 3). Any time = is redefined, hash may also have to be redefined in order to preserve the property that any two objects that are equal return equal values for hash.

Object instance protocol

comparing

== anObject	Answer whether the receiver and the argument are the same object.
= anObject	Answer whether the receiver and the argument represent the same component.
~= anObject	Answer whether the receiver and the argument do not represent the same component.
~~ anObject	Answer whether the receiver and the argument are not the same object.
hash	Answer an Integer computed with respect to the representation of the receiver.
hashMappedBy: map	Answer what the receiver's hash would be if the object pointer changed according to map.

The default implementation of = is the same as that of ==.

Some specialized comparison protocol provides a concise way to test for identity with the object nil.

Object instance protocol

---

testing
  isNil   Answer whether the receiver is nil.
  notNil   Answer whether the receiver is not nil.
  isInteger   Coerces instances of Integer to answer true, otherwise false.

These messages are identical to == nil and $\sim\sim$ nil, respectively. Choice of which to use is a matter of personal style.

Some obvious examples are

expression	*result*
nil isNil	true
true notNil	true
3 isNil	false
#(a b c) = #(a b c)	true
3 = (6/2)	true
#(1 2 3) class == Array	true

Copying Objects

There are two ways to make copies of an object. The distinction is whether or not the values of the object's variables are copied. If the values are not copied, then they are shared (shallowCopy); if the values are copied, then they are not shared (deepCopy).

Object instance protocol

---

copying
  copy   Answer another instance just like the receiver.
  shallowCopy   Answer a copy of the receiver which shares the receiver's instance variables.
  deepCopy   Answer a copy of the receiver with its own copy of each instance variable.

The default implementation of copy is shallowCopy. In subclasses in which copying must result in a special combination of shared and unshared variables, the method associated with copy is usually reimplemented, rather than the method associated with shallowCopy or deepCopy.

As an example, a copy (a shallow copy) of an Array refers to the same elements as in the original Array, but the copy is a different object. Replacing an element in the copy does not change the original. Thus

expression	result
a ← #('first' 'second' 'third')	('first' 'second' 'third')
b ← a copy	('first' 'second' 'third')
a = b	true
a == b	false
(a at: 1) == (b at: 1)	true
b at: 1 put: 'newFirst'	'newFirst'
a = b	false
a ← 'hello'	'hello'
b ← a copy	'hello'
a = b	true
a == b	false

Figure 6.1 shows the relationship between shallow and deep copying. To further illustrate the distinction between shallowCopy and deepCopy, take as an example a PersonnelRecord. Suppose it is defined to include the variable insurancePlan, an instance of class Insurance. Suppose further that each instance of Insurance has a value associated with it representing the limit on medical coverage. Now suppose we have created employeeRecord as a prototypical instance of a PersonnelRecord. By "prototypical" we mean that the object has all of the initial attributes of any new instance of its class, so that instances can be created by simply copying it rather than sending a sequence of initialization messages. Suppose further that this prototypical instance is a class variable of PersonnelRecord and that the response to creating a new PersonnelRecord is to make a shallow copy of it; that is, the method associated with the message new is ↑employeeRecord copy.

Figure 6.1

As a result of evaluating the expression

joeSmithRecord ← PersonnelRecord new

joeSmithRecord refers to a copy (in particular, a shallow copy) of employeeRecord.

The prototype employeeRecord and the actual record joeSmithRecord share a reference to the same insurance plan. Company policy may change. Suppose PersonnelRecord understands the message changeInsuranceLimit: aNumber, which is implemented by having the prototypical instance of PersonnelRecord, employeeRecord, reset its insurance plan limit on medical coverage. Since this insurance plan is shared, the result of evaluating the expression

    PersonnelRecord changeInsuranceLimit: 4000

is to change the medical coverage of all employees. In the example, both the medical coverage referenced by employeeRecord and that referenced by its copy, joeSmithRecord, is changed. The message changeInsuranceLimit: is sent to the class PersonnelRecord because it is the appropriate object to broadcast a change to all of its instances.

Accessing the Parts of an Object

There are two kinds of objects in the Smalltalk-80 system, objects with named variables and objects with indexed variables. Objects with indexed variables may also have named instance variables. This distinction is explained in Chapter 3. Class Object supports six messages intended to access the indexed variables of an object. These are

Object instance protocol

accessing

at: index	Answer the value of the indexed instance variable of the receiver whose index is the argument, index. If the receiver does not have indexed variables, or if the argument is greater than the number of indexed variables, then report an error.
at: index put: anObject	Store the argument, anObject, as the value of the indexed instance variable of the receiver whose index is the argument, index. If the receiver does not have indexed variables, or if the argument is greater than the number of indexed variables, then report an error. Answer anObject.
basicAt: index	Same as at: index. The method associated with this message, however, cannot be modified in any subclass.
basicAt: index put: anObject	Same as at: index put: anObject. The method associated with this message, however, cannot be modified in any subclass.

size	Answer the receiver's number of indexed variables. This value is the same as the largest legal index.
basicSize	Same as size. The method associated with this message, however, cannot be modified in any subclass.
readFromString: aString	Create an object based on the contents of aString.
Yourself	Answer the receiver.

Notice that the accessing messages come in pairs; one message in each pair is prefixed by the word basic meaning that it is a fundamental system message whose implementation should not be modified in any subclass. The purpose of providing pairs is so that the external protocol, at:, at:put:, and size, can be overridden to handle special cases, while still maintaining a way to get at the primitive methods. (Chapter 4 includes an explanation of "primitive" methods, which are methods implemented in the virtual machine for the system.) Thus in any method in a hierarchy of class descriptions, the messages, basicAt:, basicAt:put:, and basicSize, can always be used to obtain the primitive implementations. The message basicSize can be sent to any object; if the object is not variable length, then the response is 0.

Instances of class Array are variable-length objects. Suppose letters is the Array #(a b d f j m p s). Then

expression	result
letters size	8
letters at: 3	d
letters at: 3 put: #c	c
letters	(a b c f j m p s)

Printing and Storing Objects

There are various ways to create a sequence of characters that provides a description of an object. The description might give only a clue as to the identity of an object. Or the description might provide enough information so that a similar object can be constructed. In the first case (printing), the description may or may not be in a well-formatted, visually pleasing style, such as that provided by a Lisp pretty-printing routine. In the second case (storing), the description might preserve information shared with other objects.

The message protocol of the classes in the Smalltalk-80 system support printing and storing. The implementation of these messages in class Object provides minimal capability; most subclasses override the

7

Linear Measures

Class Magnitude

Class Date

Class Time

Class Character

Object

> **Magnitude**
> **   Character**
> **   Date**
> **   Time**

      Number
          Float
          Fraction
          Integer
              LargeNegativeInteger
              LargePositiveInteger
              SmallInteger

      LookupKey
          Association

  Link

  Process

Collection

      SequenceableCollection
          LinkedList

              Semaphore

          ArrayedCollection
              Array

                  WordArray
                      DisplayBitmap

                  RunArray
                  String
                      Symbol
                  Text
                  ByteArray

          Interval
          OrderedCollection
              SortedCollection
      Bag
      MappedCollection
      Set
          Dictionary
              IdentityDictionary

Stream
          PositionableStream
              ReadStream
              WriteStream
                  ReadWriteStream
                      ExternalStream
                          FileStream

          Random

UndefinedObject
Boolean
      False
      True

ProcessorScheduler
Delay
SharedQueue

Behavior
      ClassDescription
          Class
          MetaClass

Point
Rectangle
BitBlt
      CharacterScanner

      Pen

DisplayObject
      DisplayMedium
          Form
              Cursor
              DisplayScreen
      InfiniteForm
      OpaqueForm
      Path
          Arc
              Circle
          Curve
          Line
          LinearFit
          Spline

The Smalltalk-80 system provides several classes representing objects that measure something with linear ordering. Real world examples of such measurable quantities are (1) temporal quantities such as dates and time, (2) spatial quantities such as distance, and (3) numerical quantities such as reals and rationals.

Class Magnitude

Is one number less than another number? Does one date come after another date? Does one time precede another time? Does a character come after another one in the alphabet? Is one distance the same or less than another distance?

The common protocol for answering these queries is provided in the class Magnitude. Magnitude provides the protocol for objects that have the ability to be compared along a linear dimension. Subclasses of class Magnitude include Date, Time, and Number. Classes Character (an element of a string) and LookupKey (a key in a dictionary association) are also implemented as subclasses of class Magnitude. Character is interesting as an example of immutable objects in the system and so is introduced in this chapter; LookupKey is less interesting and is deferred until needed in the chapter on collections. A class Distance is not provided in the actual Smalltalk-80 system.

Magnitude instance protocol

comparing

< aMagnitude	Answer whether the receiver is less than the argument.
< = aMagnitude	Answer whether the receiver is less than or equal to the argument.
> aMagnitude	Answer whether the receiver is greater than the argument.
> = aMagnitude	Answer whether the receiver is greater than or equal to the argument.
between: min and: max	Answer whether the receiver is greater than or equal to the argument, min, and less than or equal to the argument, max.

Although Magnitude inherits from its superclass, Object, the message = for comparing the equality of two quantifiable objects, every kind of Magnitude must redefine this message. The method associated with = in class Magnitude is

    self subclassResponsibility

If a subclass of Magnitude does not implement =, then an attempt to send the message to an instance of the subclass results in the special error message that a subclass should have implemented the message, as specified in its superclass.

An instance of a kind of Magnitude can also respond to messages that determine which of two objects that can be linearly measured is the larger or the smaller.

Magnitude instance protocol

comparing
    min: aMagnitude   Answer the receiver or the argument, whichever has the lesser magnitude.

    max: aMagnitude   Answer the receiver or the argument, whichever has the greater magnitude.

Note that protocol for the equality comparisons $==$, $\sim=$, and $\sim\sim$ is inherited from class Object. Using Integers as the example kinds of Magnitudes, we have

expression	result
3 < = 4	true
3 > 4	false
5 between: 2 and: 6	true
5 between: 2 and: 4	false
34 min: 45	34
34 max: 45	45

The programmer does not create instances of Magnitude, but only of its subclasses. This is due to the fact that Magnitude is not able to implement all of the messages it specifies, indeed, that it implements one or more of these messages by the expression self subclassResponsibility.

Class Date

Now that we have defined the general protocol of Magnitudes, it is possible to add additional protocol that supports arithmetic and inquiries about specific linear measurements. The first refinement we will examine is the subclass Date.

An instance of Date represents a specific day since the start of the Julian calendar. A day exists in a particular month and year. Class Date knows about some obvious information: (1) there are seven days in a week, each day having a symbolic name and an index 1, 2, ..., or 7; (2) there are 12 months in a year, each having a symbolic name and an index, 1, 2, ..., or 12; (3) months have 28, 29, 30, or 31 days; and (4) a particular year might be a leap year.

Protocol provided for the object, Date, supports inquiries about Dates in general as well as about a specific Date. Both Date and Time provide interesting examples of classes in the system for which special knowledge is attributed to and accessible from the class itself, rather than from its instances. This "class protocol" is specified in the metaclass of the class. Let's first look at the class protocol of Date supporting general inquiries.

Date class protocol
_____

general inquiries

    dayOfWeek: dayName   Answer the index in a week, 1, 2, .., or 7, of the day named as the argument, dayName.

    nameOfDay: dayIndex   Answer a Symbol that represents the name of the day whose index is the argument, dayIndex, where 1 is Monday, 2, is Tuesday, and so on.

    indexOfMonth: monthName   Answer the index in a year, 1, 2, .., or 12, of the month named as the argument, monthName.

    nameOfMonth: monthIndex   Answer a Symbol that represents the name of the month whose index is the argument, monthIndex, where 1 is January, 2, is February, and so on.

    daysInMonth: monthName forYear: yearInteger

                             Answer the number of days in the month whose name is monthName in the year yearInteger (the year must be known in order to account for a leap year).

    daysInYear: yearInteger   Answer the number of days in the year, yearInteger.

    leapYear: yearInteger   Answer 1 if the year yearInteger is a leap year; answer 0 otherwise.

    dateAndTimeNow   Answer an Array whose first element is the current date (an instance of class Date representing today's date) and whose second element is the current time (an instance of class Time representing the time right now).

Thus we can send the following messages.

expression	result
Date daysInYear: 1982	365
Date dayOfWeek: #Wednesday	3
Date nameOfMonth: 10	October
Date leapYear: 1972	1 (meaning it is a leap year)
Date daysInMonth: #February forYear: 1972	29
Date daysInMonth: #Feb forYear: 1971	28

Date is familar with the common abbreviations for names of months.

There are four messages that can be used to create an instance of class Date. The one commonly used in the Smalltalk-80 system, notably for marking the creation date of a file, is Date today.

Date class protocol

instance creation

today
    Answer an instance of Date representing the day the message is sent.

fromDays: dayCount
    Answer an instance of Date that is dayCount number of days before or after January 1, 1901 (depending on the sign of the argument).

newDay: day month: monthName year: yearInteger
    Answer an instance of Date that is day number of days into the month named monthName in the year yearInteger.

newDay: dayCount year: yearInteger
    Answer an instance of Date that is dayCount number of days after the beginning of the year yearInteger.

Four examples of instance creation messages are

expression	result
Date today	3 February 1982
Date fromDays: 200	20 July 1901
Date newDay: 6 month: #Feb year: 82	6 February 1982
Date newDay: 3 year: 82	3 January 1982

Messages that can be sent to an instance of Date are categorized as accessing, inquiries, arithmetic, and printing messages. Accessing and inquiries about a particular day consist of

- the day index, month index, or year
- the number of seconds, days, or months since some other date
- the total days in the date's month or year
- the days left in the date's month or year
- the first day of the date's month
- the name of the date's weekday or month
- the date of a particular weekday previous to the instance

Simple arithmetic is supported in the protocol of class Date.

arithmetic

addDays: dayCount	Answer a Date that is dayCount number of days after the receiver.
subtractDays: dayCount	Answer a Date that is dayCount number of days before the receiver.
subtractDate: aDate	Answer an Integer that represents the number of days between the receiver and the argument, aDate.

Such arithmetic is useful, for example, in order to compute due dates for books in a library or fines for late books. Suppose dueDate is an instance of Date denoting the day a book was supposed to be returned to the library. Then

    Date today subtractDate: dueDate

computes the number of days for which the borrower should be fined. If a book is being borrowed today and it can be kept out for two weeks, then

    Date today addDays: 14

is the due date for the book. If the librarian wants to quit work 16 days before Christmas day, then the date of the last day at work is

    (Date newDay: 25 month: #December year: 1982) subtractDays: 16

An algorithm to determine the fine a borrower must pay might first compare today's date with the due date and then, if the due date has past, determine the fine as a 10-cent multiple of the number of days overdue.

    Date today < dueDate
        ifTrue: [fine ← 0]
        ifFalse: [fine ← 0.10 * (Date today subtractDate: dueDate)]

Class Time

An instance of class Time represents a particular second in a day. Days start at midnight. Time is a subclass of Magnitude. Like class Date, Time can respond to general inquiry messages that are specified in the class protocol.

Time class protocol

general inquiries

millisecondClockValue	Answer the number of milliseconds since the millisecond clock was last reset or rolled over to 0.
millisecondsToRun: timedBlock	Answer the number of milliseconds timedBlock takes to return its value.
timeWords	Answer the seconds (in Greenwich Mean Time) since Jan. 1, 1901. The answer is a four-element ByteArray (ByteArray is described in Chapter 10).
totalSeconds	Answer the total seconds from Jan. 1, 1901, corrected for time zone and daylight savings time.
dateAndTimeNow	Answer an Array whose first element is the current date (an instance of class Date that represents today's date) and whose second element is the current time (an instance of class Time that represents the time right now). The result of sending this message to Time is identical to the result of sending it to Date.

The only non-obvious inquiry is millisecondsToRun: timedBlock. An example is

    Time millisecondsToRun: [Date today]

where the result is the number of milliseconds it took the system to compute today's date. Because there is some overhead in responding to this message, and because the resolution of the clock affects the result, the careful programmer should determine the machine-dependent uncertainties associated with selecting reasonable arguments to this message.

A new instance of Time can be created by sending Time the message now; the corresponding method reads the current time from a system clock. Alternatively, an instance of Time can be created by sending the message fromSeconds: secondCount, where secondCount is the number of seconds since midnight.

Time class protocol

instance creation

now	Answer an instance of Time representing the second the message is sent.
fromSeconds: secondCount	Answer an instance of Time that is secondCount number of seconds since midnight.

Accessing protocol for instances of class Time provide information as to the number of hours (hours), minutes (minutes) and seconds (seconds) that the instance represents.

Arithmetic is also supported.

Time instance protocol

arithmetic

    addTime: timeAmount   Answer an instance of Time that is the argument, timeAmount, after the receiver.

    subtractTime: timeAmount   Answer an instance of Time that is the argument, timeAmount, before the receiver.

In the messages given above, the arguments (timeAmount) may be either Dates or Times. For this to be possible, the system must be able to convert a Date and a Time to a common unit of measurement; it converts them to seconds. In the case of Time, the conversion is to the number of seconds since midnight; in the case of Date, the conversion is to the number of seconds between a time on January 1, 1901, and the same time in the receiver's day. To support these methods, instances of each class respond to the conversion message asSeconds.

Time instance protocol

converting

    asSeconds   Answer the number of seconds since midnight that the receiver represents.

Date instance protocol

converting

    asSeconds   Answer the number of seconds between a time on January 1, 1901, and the same time in the receiver's day.

Arithmetic for Time can be used in ways analogous to that for Date. Suppose the amount of time a person spends working on a particular project is to be logged so that a customer can be charged an hourly fee. Suppose the person started work at startTime and worked continuously during the day until right now; the phone rings and the customer wants to know today's charges. At that moment, the bill at $5.00 an hour is

(Time now subtractTime: startTime) hours * 5

ignoring any additional minutes or seconds. If a charge for any fraction of an hour over 30 minutes is to be charged as a full hour then an additional $5.00 is added if

(Time now subtractTime: startTime) minutes > 30

Who is more productive, the worker who finished the job with time logged at timeA or the worker with time timeB? The answer is the first worker if timeA < timeB. Comparing protocol is inherited from the superclasses Magnitude and Object.

Suppose times are computed across days, for example, in computing the time of a car in a four-day rally. If the first day of the rally started at startTime on day startDate, then the time for a car arriving at the finish line right now is computed as follows.

Let the start time be 6:00 a.m.

startTime ← Time fromSeconds: (60*60*6).

on February 2, 1982

startDate ← Date newDay: 2 month: #Feb year: 82.

The time that has passed up to the start of the current day is

todayStart ← (((Time fromSeconds: 0) addTime: Date today)
        subtractTime: startDate)
            subtractTime: startTime

That is, add all the seconds since Jan. 1, 1901, up to the start of today and then subtract all the seconds since Jan. 1, 1901, up to the start of the start date. This is equivalent to adding the number of seconds in the number of elapsed days, but then the programmer would have to do all the conversions.

(Date today subtractDate: startDate) * 24*60*60)

By adding the current time, we have the elapsed rally time for the car.

todayStart addTime: Time now

Class Character

Class Character is the third subclass of class Magnitude we shall examine. It is a kind of Magnitude because instances of class Character form an ordered sequence about which we can make inquiries such as whether one character precedes (<) or succeeds (>) another character alphabetically. There are 256 instances of class Character in the system. Each one is associated with a code in an extended ASCII character set.

Characters can be expressed literally by preceding the alphabetic character by a dollar sign ($); thus, $A is the Character representing the capital letter "A". Protocol for creating instances of class Character consists of

Character class protocol

instance creation

value: anInteger
    Answer an instance of Character whose value is the argument, anInteger. The value is associated with an element of the ASCII character set. For example, Character value: 65 is a capital "A".

digitValue: anInteger
    Answer an instance of Character whose digit value is the argument, anInteger. For example, answer $9 if the argument is 9; answer $0 for 0; answer $A for 10, and $Z for 35. This method is useful in parsing numbers into strings. Typically, only Characters up to $F are useful (for base 16 numbers).

Class protocol, that is, the set of messages to the object Character, provides a vocabulary for accessing characters that are not easy to distinguish when printed: backspace, cr, esc, newPage (that is, form feed), space, and tab.

Messages to instances of Character support accessing the ASCII value and the digit value of the instance and testing the type of character. The only state of a Character is its value which can never change. Objects that can not change their internal state are called *immutable objects*. This means that, once created, they are not destroyed and then recreated when they are needed again. Rather, the 256 instances of Character are created at the time the system is initialized and remain in the system. Whenever a new Character whose code is between 0 and 255 is requested, a reference is provided to an already existing Character. In this way the 256 Characters are unique. Besides Characters, the Smalltalk-80 system includes SmallIntegers and Symbols as immutable objects.

Character instance protocol

accessing

asciiValue
    Answer the number corresponding to the ASCII encoding for the receiver.

digitValue
    Answer the number corresponding to the numerical radix represented by the receiver (see the instance creation message digitValue: for the correspondences).

testing

isAlphaNumeric
    Answer true if the receiver is a letter or a digit.

isDigit
    Answer whether the receiver is a digit.

isLetter
    Answer whether the receiver is a letter.

isLowercase
    Answer whether the receiver is a lowercase letter.

isUppercase
    Answer whether the receiver is an uppercase letter.

isSeparator   Answer whether the receiver is one of the separator characters in the expression syntax: space, cr, tab, line feed, or form feed.

isVowel   Answer whether the receiver is one of the vowels: a, e, i, o, or u, in upper or lowercase.

Instance protocol also provides conversion of a character into upper- or lowercase (asLowercase and asUppercase) and into a symbol (asSymbol).

A simple alphabetic comparison demonstrates the use of comparing protocol for instances of Character. Suppose we wish to know if one string of characters precedes another string in the telephone book. Strings respond to the message at: to retrieve the element whose index is the argument; elements of Strings are Characters. Thus 'abc' at: 2 is $b. In the following we assume we are specifying a method in class String whose message selector is min:. The method returns a String, either the receiver of the message min: or its argument, whichever is collated first alphabetically.

min: aString
```
    1 to: self size do:
        [ :index |
        (index > aString size) ifTrue: [↑aString].
        (self at: index) > (aString at: index) ifTrue: [↑aString].
        (self at: index) < (aString at: index) ifTrue: [↑self]].
    ↑self
```

The algorithm consists of two statements. The first is an iteration over each element of the receiver. The iteration stops when either (1) the argument, aString, no longer has a character with which to compare the next character in the receiver (i.e., index > aString size); (2) the next character in self comes after the next character in aString (i.e., (self at: index) > (aString at: index)); or (3) the next character in self comes before the next character in aString. As an example of (1), take the comparison of 'abcd' and 'abc' which terminates when index = 4; the answer is that 'abc' is first alphabetically. For (2), suppose we compare 'abde' with 'abce'. When index = 3, $d > $c is true; the answer is 'abce'. For (3), compare 'az' with 'by' which terminates when index = 1; the answer is 'az'. In the case that the receiver has fewer characters than the argument, even when the receiver is the initial substring of the argument, the first statement will complete and the second statement is evaluated; the result is the receiver. An example is the comparison of 'abc' and 'abcd'.

Note that arithmetic on characters is not supported. For example, the following expression is incorrect.

a ← $A + 1

The error occurs because a Character does not understand the message +.

8

Numerical Classes

Protocol of the Number Classes

Classes Float **and** Fraction

Integer Classes

Class Random: **A Random Number Generator**

Object

Magnitude
    Character
    Date
    Time

Number
    Float
    Fraction
    Integer
        LargeNegativeInteger
        LargePositiveInteger
        SmallInteger

LookupKey
    Association

Link

Process

Collection

SequenceableCollection
    LinkedList

        Semaphore

    ArrayedCollection
    Array

        WordArray
            DisplayBitmap

        RunArray
        String
            Symbol
        Text
        ByteArray

    Interval
    OrderedCollection
        SortedCollection
Bag
MappedCollection
Set
    Dictionary
        IdentityDictionary

Stream
    PositionableStream
        ReadStream
        WriteStream
            ReadWriteStream
                ExternalStream
                    FileStream

Random

UndefinedObject
Boolean
    False
    True

ProcessorScheduler
Delay
SharedQueue

Behavior
    ClassDescription
        Class
        MetaClass

Point
Rectangle
BitBlt
    CharacterScanner

    Pen

DisplayObject
    DisplayMedium
        Form
            Cursor
            DisplayScreen
    InfiniteForm
    OpaqueForm
    Path
        Arc
            Circle
        Curve
        Line
        LinearFit
        Spline

One of the major goals of the Smalltalk programming system is to apply a single metaphor for information processing as uniformly as possible. The Smalltalk metaphor, as described in earlier chapters, is one of objects that communicate by sending messages. This metaphor is very similar to the one used in Simula for implementing simulation systems. One of the greatest challenges to the application of the Smalltalk metaphor to all aspects of a programming system has been in the area of arithmetic. Simula used the object/message metaphor only for the higher level interactions in the simulations it implemented. For arithmetic, as well as most algorithmic control structures, Simula relied on the embedded Algol programming language with its built-in number representations, operations, and syntax. The contention that even the addition of two integers should be interpreted as message-sending met with a certain amount of resistance in the early days of Smalltalk. Experience has demonstrated that the benefits of this extreme uniformity in the programming language outweigh any inconvenience in its implementation. Over several versions of Smalltalk, implementation techniques have been developed to reduce the message-sending overhead for the most common arithmetic operations so that there is now almost no cost for the benefits of uniformity.

Objects that represent numerical values are used in most systems done in Smalltalk (as with most other programming languages). Numbers are naturally used to perform mathematical computations; they are also used in algorithms as indices, counters, and encodings of states or conditions (often called flags). Integral numbers are also used as collections of binary digits (bits) that perform boolean masking operations with each other.

Each different kind of numerical value is represented by a class. The number classes have been implemented so that all numbers behave as if they were of the most general type. The actual class of a particular number object is determined by how much of the full generality is needed to represent its value. Therefore the external protocol of all number objects is inherited from the class Number. Number has three subclasses: Float, Fraction, and Integer. Integer has three subclasses: SmallInteger, LargePositiveInteger, and LargeNegativeInteger. Integral numbers provide further protocol to support treating the number as a sequence of bits. This protocol is specified in the class Integer. Numbers in the system are instances of Float, Fraction, SmallInteger, LargePositiveInteger, or LargeNegativeInteger. Classes Number and Integer specify shared protocol, but they do not specify particular representations for numeric values. Therefore no instances of Number or Integer are created.

Unlike other objects that may change their internal state, the only state of a number is its value, which should never change. The object 3, for example, should never change its state to 4, or disastrous effects could occur.

Protocol of the Number Classes

Number defines the protocol of all numeric objects. Its messages support standard arithmetic operations and comparisons. Most of these must be implemented by subclasses of Number since they depend on the actual representation of values.

The protocol of arithmetic messages consists of the usual binary operators such as +, −, * and /, and several unary and keyword messages for computing the absolute value of a number, the negation of a number, or the integer quotient or remainder of a number. The category for arithmetic messages is as follows.

Number instance protocol

arithmetic

+ aNumber	Answer the sum of the receiver and the argument, aNumber.
− aNumber	Answer the difference between the receiver and the argument, aNumber.
* aNumber	Answer the result of multiplying the receiver by the argument, aNumber.
/ aNumber	Answer the result of dividing the receiver by the argument, aNumber. Note that since as much precision as possible is retained, if the division is not exact, the result will be an instance of Fraction.
// aNumber	Answer the integer quotient defined by division with truncation toward negative infinity.
\\ aNumber	Answer the integer remainder defined by division with truncation toward negative infinity. This is the modulo operation.
abs	Answer a Number that is the absolute value (positive magnitude) of the receiver.
negated	Answer a Number that is the negation of the receiver.
quo: aNumber	Answer the integer quotient defined by division with truncation toward zero.
rem: aNumber	Answer the integer remainder defined by division with truncation toward zero.
reciprocal	Answer 1 divided by the receiver. Report an error to the user if the receiver is 0.

Some examples follow.

expression	result
1 + 10	11
5.6 − 3	2.6
5 − 2.6	2.4
(−4) abs	4
6 / 2	3

7 / 2	(7/2), a Fraction with numerator 7 and denominator 2
7 reciprocal	(1/7), a Fraction with numerator 1 and denominator 7

Arithmetic messages that return integral quotients and remainders from a division operation follow two conventions. One convention truncates the resulting number toward zero, the other toward negative infinity. These are the same for positive results since zero and negative infinity are in the same direction. For negative results, the two conventions round in different directions. The protocol for Number provides for both conventions.

The following table shows the relationships among the selectors.

result	truncate toward negative infinity	truncate toward zero
quotient	//	quo:
remainder	\\	rem:

Examples include:

expression	result
6 quo: 2	3
7 quo: 2	3
(7 quo: 2) + 1	4
7 quo: 2 + 1	2
7 rem: 2	1
7 // 2	3
7 \\ 2	1
7 \\ 2 +1	2
−7 quo: 2	−3
−7 rem: 2	−1
−7 // 2	−4
−7 \\ 2	1

The result of quo:, rem:, or // is always to return a value whose sign is positive if the receiver and argument have the same sign, and negative if their signs are different. \\ always produces a positive result.

Additional mathematical functions are

Number instance protocol

mathematical functions

exp	Answer a floating point number that is the exponential of the receiver.
ln	Answer the natural log of the receiver.
log: aNumber	Answer the log base aNumber of the receiver.
floorLog: radix	Answer the floor of the log base radix of the receiver, where the floor is the integer nearest the receiver toward negative infinity.
raisedTo: aNumber	Answer the receiver raised to the power of the argument, aNumber.
raisedToInteger: anInteger	Answer the receiver raised to the power of the argument, anInteger, where the argument must be a kind of Integer.
sqrt	Answer a floating point number that is the positive square root of the receiver.
squared	Answer the receiver multiplied by itself.

Some examples are

expression	result
2.718284 ln	1.0
6 exp	403.429
2 exp	7.38906
7.38906 ln	1.99998 (that is, 2)
2 log: 2	1.0
2 floorLog: 2	1
6 log: 2	2.58496
6 floorLog: 2	2
6 raisedTo: 1.2	8.58579
6 raisedToInteger: 2	36
64 sqrt	8.0
8 squared	64

Properties of numbers that deal with whether a number is even or odd and negative or positive can be tested with the following messages.

Number instance protocol

testing

even	Answer whether the receiver is an even number.
odd	Answer whether the receiver is an odd number.
negative	Answer whether the receiver is less than 0.
positive	Answer whether the receiver is greater than or equal to 0.
strictlyPositive	Answer whether the receiver is greater than 0.
sign	Answer 1 if the receiver is greater than 0, answer -1 if less than 0, else answer 0.

Properties of numbers that deal with truncation and round off are supplied by the following protocol.

Number instance protocol
___

truncation and round off

ceiling	Answer the integer nearest the receiver toward positive infinity.
floor	Answer the integer nearest the receiver toward negative infinity.
truncated	Answer the integer nearest the receiver toward zero.
truncateTo: aNumber	Answer the next multiple of the argument, aNumber, that is nearest the receiver toward zero.
rounded	Answer the integer nearest the receiver.
roundTo: aNumber	Answer the multiple of the argument, aNumber, that is nearest the receiver.

Whenever a Number must be converted to an Integer, the message truncated can be used. So we have

expression	*result*
16.32 ceiling	17
16.32 floor	16
−16.32 floor	−17
−16.32 truncated	−16
16.32 truncated	16
16.32 truncateTo: 5	15
16.32 truncateTo: 5.1	15.3
16.32 rounded	16
16.32 roundTo: 6	18
16.32 roundTo: 6.3	18.9

The protocol provided in class Number includes various messages for converting a number into another kind of object or a different unit of representation. Numbers can represent various unit measurements such as degrees and radians. The following two messages perform conversions.

Number instance protocol
___

converting

degreesToRadians	The receiver is assumed to represent degrees. Answer the conversion to radians.
radiansToDegrees	The receiver is assumed to represent radians. Answer the conversion to degrees.

So that

    30 degreesToRadians = 0.523599
    90 degreesToRadians = 1.5708

Trigonometric and logarithmic functions are included in the protocol for mathematical functions. The receiver for the trigonometric functions cos, sin, and tan is an angle measured in radians; the result of the functions arcCos, arcSin and arcTan is the angle measured in radians.

In the following examples, 30 degrees is given as 0.523599 radians; 90 degrees is 1.5708 radians.

expression	result
0.523599 sin	0.5
0.523599 cos	0.866025
0.523599 tan	0.57735
1.5708 sin	1.0
0.57735 arcTan	0.523551
1.0 arcSin	1.5708

When a kind of Integer is asked to add itself to another kind of Integer, the result returned will naturally also be a kind of Integer. The same is true for the sum of two Floats; the class of the result will be the same as the class of the operands. If the two operands are SmallIntegers and the absolute value of their sum is too large to be represented as a SmallInteger, the result will be a LargePositiveInteger or a LargeNegativeInteger. The determination of the appropriate class of result when the operands are of different classes is somewhat more complicated. Two design criteria are that there be as little loss of information as possible and that commutative operations produce the same result regardless of which operand is the receiver of the message and which is the argument. So for example, 3.1 * 4 will return the same result as 4 * 3.1.

The appropriate representation for the result of operations on numbers of different classes is determined by a numerical measure of generality assigned to each class. Classes said to have more generality will have a larger number for this generality measure. Each class must be able to convert its instances into equal-valued instances of more general classes. The measure of generality is used to decide which of the operands should be converted. In this way, the arithmetic operations obey the law of commutativity with no loss of numerical information. When the differences between two classes of numbers are only a matter of precision (where "precision" is a measure of the information provided in a number), the more precise class is assigned a higher degree of generality. We have arbitrarily assigned approximate numbers a higher generality in cases where precision was not the issue (so, Float is more general than Fraction).

The generality hierarchy for the kinds of numbers in the Smalltalk-80 system, with most general listed first, is

Float
Fraction
LargePositiveInteger, LargeNegativeInteger
SmallInteger

The messages in the Number protocol designed to support the necessary coercions are categorized as "coercing" messages.

Number instance protocol
_____

coercing

coerce: aNumber

Answer a number representing the argument, aNumber, that is the same kind of Number as the receiver. This method must be defined by all subclasses of Number.

generality

Answer the number representing the ordering of the receiver in the generality hierarchy.

retry: aSymbol coercing: aNumber

An arithmetic operation denoted by the symbol, aSymbol, could not be performed with the receiver and the argument, aNumber, as the operands because of the difference in representation. Coerce either the receiver or the argument, depending on which has the lower generality, and then try the arithmetic operation again. If the symbol is the equals sign, answer false if the argument is not a Number. If the generalities are the same, then retry:coercing: should not have been sent, so report an error to the user.

Thus if we try to evaluate 32.45 * 4, the multiplication of a Float by a SmallInteger will result in evaluating the expression

32.45 retry: #* coercing: 4

and the argument 4 will be coerced to 4.0 (Float has higher generality than SmallInteger). Then the multiplication will be carried out successfully.

Defining a hierarchy of the numbers in terms of a numerical measure of generality works for the kinds of numbers provided in the basic Smalltalk-80 system because the generality is transitive for these kinds of numbers. However, it does not provide a technique that can be used for all kinds of numbers.

Intervals (described in detail in Chapter 10) can be created by sending one of two messages to a number. For each element of such an interval, a block can be evaluated with the element as the block value.

Number instance protocol

intervals

to: stop	Answer an Interval from the receiver up to the argument, stop, with each next element computed by incrementing the previous one by 1.
to: stop by: step	Answer an Interval from the receiver up to the argument, stop, with each next element computed by incrementing the previous one by step.
to: stop do: aBlock	Create an Interval from the receiver up to the argument, stop, incrementing by 1. Evaluate the argument, aBlock, for each element of the Interval.
to: stop by: step do: aBlock	Create an Interval from the receiver up to the argument, stop, incrementing by step. Evaluate the argument, aBlock, for each element of the Interval.

Thus if we evaluate

```
a ← 0.
10 to: 100 by: 10 do: [ :each | a ← a + each]
```

the final value of a will be 550.

If a is the array #('one' 'two' 'three' 'four' 'five'), then each element of the array can be accessed by indices that are in the interval from 1 to the size of the array. The following expression changes each element so that only the initial characters are kept.

```
1 to: a size do: [ :index | a at: index put: ((a at: index) at: 1)]
```

The resulting array is #('o' 't' 't' 'f' 'f'). Note that, like an array, elements of a string can be accessed using the messages at: and at:put:. Messages to objects like strings and arrays are detailed in Chapters 9 and 10.

Classes Float and Fraction

The classes Float and Fraction provide two representations of non-integral values. Floats are representations of real numbers that may be approximate; they represent about 6 digits of accuracy with a range between plus or minus 10 raised to the power plus or minus 32. Some examples are

```
8.0
13.3
```

0.3
2.5e6
1.27e−30
−12.987654e12

Fractions are representations of rational numbers that will always be exact. All arithmetic operations on a Fraction answer a reduced fractional result.

Instances of Float can be created by literal notation in methods (for example, 3.14159) or as the result of an arithmetic operation, one argument of which is another Float.

Instances of Fraction can be created as a result of an arithmetic operation if one of the operands is a Fraction and the other is not a Float. (If it were a Float, the result would be a Float since the generality number of Float is higher than that of Fraction). Instances of Fraction can also be created when the mathematical division operation (/) is performed on two Integers and the result is not integral. In addition, class protocol for Fraction supports sending a message of the form numerator: numInteger denominator: denInteger in order to create an instance.

Float responds to the message pi to return the corresponding constant. It adds truncation and round off protocol to return the fraction and integer parts of the receiver (fractionPart and integerPart), and it adds converting protocol to convert the receiver to a Fraction (asFraction). Similarly class Fraction adds converting protocol to convert the receiver to a Float (asFloat).

Integer Classes

Class Integer adds protocol particular to integral numbers. It has three subclasses. One is class SmallInteger, which provides a space-economical representation for a substantial range of integral values that occur frequently in counting and indexing. The representation limits the range to a little less than the magnitudes representable by a single machine word. Large integers, which are represented by instances of LargePositiveInteger or LargeNegativeInteger depending on the sign of the integer, do not have a limit to their magnitude. The cost in providing the generality of large integers is longer computation time. Thus if the result of an arithmetic operation on a large integer is representable as a small integer, it will in fact be a small integer.

In addition to the messages inherited from the class Number, class Integer adds converting protocol (asCharacter, asFloat and asFraction), further printing (printOn: aStream base: b, printStringRadix: baseInteger), and enumerating protocol. Thus 8 printStringRadix: 2 is 2r1000.

For enumerating, it is possible to evaluate a block repetitively an integral number of times using the message timesRepeat: aBlock. Take as an example

a ← 1.
10 timesRepeat: [a ← a + a]

where the block has no arguments. The resulting value of a is 2^{10}, or 1024.

Class Integer provides factorization and divisibility protocol not specified for numbers in general.

Integer instance protocol

factorization and divisibility	
factorial	Answer the factorial of the receiver. The receiver must not be less than 0.
gcd: anInteger	Answer the greatest common divisor of the receiver and the argument, anInteger.
lcm: anInteger	Answer the least common multiple of the receiver and the argument, anInteger.

Examples are

expression	*result*
3 factorial	6
55 gcd: 30	5
6 lcm: 10	30

In addition to the numerical properties of integers, some algorithms make use of the fact that integers can be interpreted as a sequence of bits. Thus protocol for bit manipulation is specified in Integer.

Integer instance protocol

bit manipulation	
allMask: anInteger	Treat the argument anInteger as a bit mask. Answer whether *all* of the bits that are 1 in anInteger are 1 in the receiver.
anyMask: anInteger	Treat the argument anInteger as a bit mask. Answer whether *any* of the bits that are 1 in anInteger are 1 in the receiver.
noMask: anInteger	Treat the argument anInteger as a bit mask. Answer whether *none* of the bits that are 1 in anInteger are 1 in the receiver.
bitAnd: anInteger	Answer an Integer whose bits are the logical *and* of the receiver's bits and those of the argument anInteger.
bitOr: anInteger	Answer an Integer whose bits are the logical *or* of the receiver's bits and those of the argument anInteger.

bitXor: anInteger	Answer an Integer whose bits are the logical *xor* of the receiver's bits and those of the argument anInteger.
bitAt: index	Answer the bit (0 or 1) at position index of the receiver.
bitInvert	Answer an Integer whose bits are the complement of the receiver.
highBit	Answer the index of the high order bit of the binary representation of the receiver.
bitShift: anInteger	Answer an Integer whose value (in two's-complement representation) is the receiver's value (in two's-complement representation) shifted left by the number of bits indicated by the argument, anInteger. Negative arguments shift right. Zeros are shifted in from the right in left shifts. The sign bit is extended in right shifts.

Some examples follow. Note that the default radix for printing an Integer is 10.

expression	result
2r111000111000111	29127
2r101010101010101	21845
2r101000101000101	20805
2r000111000111000	3640
29127 allMask: 20805	true
29127 allMask: 21845	false
29127 anyMask: 21845	true
29127 noMask: 3640	true
29127 bitAnd: 3640	0
29127 bitOr: 3640	32767
32767 radix: 2	2r111111111111111
29127 bitOr: 21845	30167
30167 printStringRadix: 2	2r111010111010111
3640 bitShift: 1	7280

Class Random: A Random Number Generator

Many applications require random choices of numbers. Random numbers are useful, for example, in statistical applications and data encryption algorithms. Class Random is a random number generator that is included in the standard Smalltalk-80 system. It provides a simple way of obtaining a sequence of random numbers that will be uniformly distributed over the interval between, but not including, 0.0 and 1.0.

An instance of class Random maintains a seed from which the next random number is generated. The seed is initialized in a pseudo-random way. An instance of Random is sent the message next whenever a new random number is desired.

A random number generator can be created with the expression

rand ← Random new

The expression

rand next

can then be evaluated whenever a new random number is needed. The response is a number (Float) between 0.0 and 1.0.

The implementation of next is based on Lehmer's linear congruential method as presented in Knuth, Volume 1 [D. E. Knuth, *The Art of Computer Programming: Fundamental Algorithms,* Volume 1, Reading, Mass: Addison Wesley, 1968].

next
```
| temp |
"Lehmer's linear congruential method with modulus m = 2 raisedTo: 16,
a = 27181 odd, and 5 = a \\ 8, c = 13849 odd, and c / m approxi-
mately 0.21132"
[seed ← 13849 + (27181 * seed) bitAnd: 8r177777.
temp ← seed / 65536.0.
temp = 0] whileTrue.
↑temp
```

It is also possible to send an instance of class Random the messages next: anInteger, to obtain an OrderedCollection of anInteger number of random numbers, and nextMatchFor: aNumber, to determine whether the next random number is equal to aNumber.

Suppose we want to select one of 10 integers, 1, ..., 10, using the random number generator rand. The expression to be evaluated is

(rand next * 10) truncated + 1

That is,

expression	result
rand next	a random number between 0 and 1
rand next * 10	a random number between 0 and 10
(rand next * 10) truncated	an integer $> = 0$ and $< = 9$
(rand next * 10) truncated + 1	an integer $> = 1$ and $< = 10$

9

Protocol for All Collection Classes

Object

Magnitude
    Character
    Date
    Time

    Number
        Float
        Fraction
        Integer
            LargeNegativeInteger
            LargePositiveInteger
            SmallInteger

    LookupKey
        Association

Link

Process

Collection

SequenceableCollection
    LinkedList

        Semaphore

    ArrayedCollection
        Array

        WordArray
            DisplayBitmap

        RunArray
        String
            Symbol
        Text
        ByteArray

    Interval
    OrderedCollection
        SortedCollection
Bag
MappedCollection
Set
    Dictionary
        IdentityDictionary

Stream
    PositionableStream
        ReadStream
        WriteStream
            ReadWriteStream
                ExternalStream
                    FileStream

    Random

UndefinedObject
Boolean
    False
    True

ProcessorScheduler
Delay
SharedQueue

Behavior
    ClassDescription
        Class
        MetaClass

Point
Rectangle
BitBlt
    CharacterScanner

    Pen

DisplayObject
    DisplayMedium
        Form
            Cursor
            DisplayScreen
    InfiniteForm
    OpaqueForm
    Path
        Arc
            Circle
        Curve
        Line
        LinearFit
        Spline

A collection represents a group of objects. These objects are called the *elements* of the collection. For example, an Array is a collection. The Array

#('word' 3 5 $G (1 2 3))

is a collection of five elements. The first one is a String, the second and third are SmallIntegers, the fourth element is a Character, and the fifth is itself an Array. The first element, the String, is also a collection; in this case, it is a collection of four Characters.

Collections provide basic data structures for programming in the Smalltalk-80 system. Elements of some of the collections are unordered and elements of other collections are ordered. Of the collections with unordered elements, Bags allow duplicate elements and Sets do not allow duplication. There are also Dictionaries that associate pairs of objects. Of the collections with ordered elements, some have the order specified externally when the elements are added (OrderedCollections, Arrays, Strings) and others determine the order based on the elements themselves (SortedCollections). For example, the common data structures of arrays and strings are provided by classes that associate integer indices and elements and that have external ordering corresponding to the ordering of the indices.

This chapter introduces the protocol shared by all collections. Each message described in this chapter is understood by any kind of collection, unless that collection specifically disallows it. Descriptions of each kind of collection are provided in the next chapter.

Collections support four categories of messages for accessing elements:

- messages for adding new elements

- messages for removing elements

- messages for testing occurrences of elements

- messages for enumerating elements

A single element or several elements can be added or removed from a collection. It is possible to test whether a collection is empty or whether it includes a particular element. It is also possible to determine the number of times a particular element occurs in the collection. Enumeration allows one to access the elements without removing them from the collection.

Adding, Removing, and Testing Elements

The basic protocol for collections is specified by the superclass of all collection classes, named Collection. Class Collection is a subclass of class Object. The protocol for adding, removing, and testing elements follows.

Collection instance protocol

adding

add: newObject	Include the argument, newObject, as one of the receiver's elements. Answer newObject.
addAll: aCollection	Include all the elements of the argument, aCollection, as the receiver's elements. Answer aCollection.

removing

remove: oldObject	Remove the argument, oldObject, from the receiver's elements. Answer oldObject unless no element is equal to oldObject, in which case, report that an error occurred.
remove: oldObject ifAbsent: anExceptionBlock	Remove the argument, oldObject, from the receiver's elements. If several of the elements are equal to oldObject, only one is removed. If no element is equal to oldObject, answer the result of evaluating anExceptionBlock. Otherwise, answer oldObject.
removeAll: aCollection	Remove each element of the argument, aCollection, from the receiver. If successful for each, answer aCollection. Otherwise report that an error occurred.

testing

includes: anObject	Answer whether the argument, anObject, is equal to one of the receiver's elements.
isEmpty	Answer whether the receiver contains any elements.
occurrencesOf: anObject	Answer how many of the receiver's elements are equal to the argument, anObject.

In order to demonstrate the use of these messages, we introduce the collection lotteryA

(272 572 852 156)

and the collection lotteryB

(572 621 274)

We will assume that these two collections, representing numbers drawn in a lottery, are instances of Bag, a subclass of Collection. Collection itself is abstract in the sense that it describes protocol for all collections. Collection does not provide sufficient representation for storing elements and so it is not possible to provide implementations in Collection of all of its messages. Because of this incompleteness in the definition of Collection, it is not useful to create instances of Collection. Bag is concrete in the sense that it provides a representation for storing elements and implementations of the messages not implementable in its superclass.

All collections respond to size in order to answer the number of their elements. So we can determine that

lotteryA size

is 4 and

lotteryB size

is 3. Then, evaluating the messages in order, we have

expression	result	lotteryA *if it changed*
lotteryA isEmpty	false	
lotteryA includes: 572	true	
lotteryA add: 596	596	Bag (272 572 852 156 596)
lotteryA addAll: lotteryB	Bag (572 621 274)	Bag (272 274 852 156 596 572 572 621)
lotteryA occurrencesOf: 572	2	
lotteryA remove: 572	572	Bag (272 274 852 156 596 572 621)
lotteryA size	7	
lotteryA removeAll: lotteryB	Bag (572 621 274)	Bag (272 852 596 156)
lotteryA size	4	

Note that the add: and remove: messages answer the argument rather than the collection itself so that computed arguments can be accessed. The message remove: deletes only one occurrence of the argument, not all occurrences.

Blocks were introduced in Chapter 2. The message remove: oldObject ifAbsent: anExceptionBlock makes use of a block in order to specify the behavior of the collection if an error should occur. The argument anExceptionBlock is evaluated if the object referred to by oldObject is not an element of the collection. This block can contain code to deal with the error or simply to ignore it. For example, the expression

lotteryA remove: 121 ifAbsent: []

does nothing when it is determined that 121 is not an element of lotteryA.

The default behavior of the message remove: is to report the error by sending the collection the message error: 'object is not in the collection'. (Recall that the message error: is specified in the protocol for all objects and is therefore understood by any collection.)

Enumerating Elements

Included in the instance protocol of collections are several enumeration messages that support the ability to list the elements of a collection and to supply each element in the evaluation of a block. The basic enumeration message is do: aBlock. It takes a one-argument block as its argument and evaluates the block once for each of the elements of the collection. As an example, suppose letters is a collection of Characters and we want to know how many of the Characters are a or A.

```
count ← 0.
letters do: [ :each | each asLowercase == $a
                ifTrue: [count ← count + 1]]
```

That is, increment the counter, count, by 1 for each element that is an upper- or lowercase a. The desired result is the final value of count. We can use the equivalence test (==) rather than equality since objects representing Characters are unique.

Six enhancements of the basic enumeration messages are specified in the protocol for all collections. The description of these enumeration messages indicates that "a new collection like the receiver" is created for gathering the resulting information. This phrase means that the new collection is an instance of the same class as that of the receiver. For example, if the receiver of the message select: is a Set or an Array, then the response is a new Set or Array, respectively. In the Smalltalk-80 system, the only exception is in the implementation of class Interval, which returns a new Array, not a new Interval, from these enumeration messages. The reason for this exception is that the elements of an Interval are created when the Interval is first created; it is not possible to store elements into an existing Interval.

Collection instance protocol

enumerating

do: aBlock	Evaluate the argument, aBlock, for each of the receiver's elements.
select: aBlock	Evaluate the argument, aBlock, for each of the receiver's elements. Collect into a new collection like that of the receiver, only those elements for which aBlock evaluates to true. Answer the new collection.

reject: aBlock	Evaluate the argument, aBlock, for each of the receiver's elements. Collect into a new collection like that of the receiver only those elements for which aBlock evaluates to false. Answer the new collection.
collect: aBlock	Evaluate the argument, aBlock, for each of the receiver's elements. Answer a new collection like that of the receiver containing the values returned by the block on each evaluation.
detect: aBlock	Evaluate the argument, aBlock, for each of the receiver's elements. Answer the first element for which aBlock evaluates to true. If none evaluates to true, report an error.
detect: aBlock ifNone: exceptionBlock	Evaluate the argument, aBlock, for each of the receiver's elements. Answer the first element for which aBlock evaluates to true. If none evaluates to true, evaluate the argument, exceptionBlock. exceptionBlock must be a block requiring no arguments.
inject: thisValue into: binaryBlock	Evaluate the argument, binaryBlock, once for each element in the receiver. The block has two arguments: the second is an element from the receiver; the first is the value of the previous evaluation of the block, starting with the argument, thisValue. Answer the final value of the block.

Each enumeration message provides a concise way to express a sequence of messages for testing or gathering information about the elements of a collection.

Selecting and Rejecting

We could have determined the number of occurrences of the character a or A using the message select:.

(letters select: [:each | each asLowercase = = $a]) size

That is, create a collection containing only those elements of letters that are a or A, and then answer the size of the resulting collection.

We could also have determined the number of occurrences of the character a or A using the message reject:.

(letters reject: [:each | each asLowercase ~~ $a]) size

That is, create a collection by eliminating those elements of letters that are not a or A, and then answer the size of the resulting collection.

The choice between select: and reject: should be based on the best expression of the test. If the selection test is best expressed in terms of acceptance, then select: is easier to use if the selection test is best expressed in terms of rejection, then reject: is easier to use. In this example, select: would be preferred.

As another example, assume employees is a collection of workers, each of whom responds to the message salary with his or her gross earnings. To make a collection of all employees whose salary is at least $10,000, use

employees select: [:each | each salary > = 10000]

or

employees reject: [:each | each salary < 10000]

The resulting collections are the same. The choice of which message to use, select: or reject:, depends on the way the programmer wishes to express the criterion "at least $10,000."

Collecting

Suppose we wish to create a new collection in which each element is the salary of each worker in the collection employees.

employees collect: [:each | each salary]

The resulting collection is the same size as employees. Each of the elements of the new collection is the salary of the corresponding element of employees.

Detecting

Suppose we wish to find one worker in the collection of employees whose salary is greater than $20,000. The expression

employees detect: [:each | each salary > 20000]

will answer with that worker, if one exists. If none exists, then employees will be sent the message error: ′ object is not in the collection′ . Just as in the specification of the removing messages, the programmer has the option to specify the exception behavior for an unsuccessful detect:. The next expression answers one worker whose salary exceeds $20,000, or, if none exists, answers nil.

employees detect: [:each | each salary > 20000] ifNone: [nil]

Injecting

In the message inject:into:, the first argument is the initial value that takes part in determining the result; the second argument is a two-argument block. The first block argument names the variable that refers to the result; the second block argument refers to each element of the collection. An example using this message sums the salaries of the workers in the collection employees.

employees
        inject: 0
        into: [:subTotal :nextWorker | subTotal + nextWorker salary]

where the initial value of 0 increases by the value of the salary for each worker in the collection, employees. The result is the final value of sub-Total.

By using the message inject:into:, the programmer can locally specify temporary variable names and can avoid separate initialization of the object into which the result is accumulated. For example, in an earlier expression that counted the number of occurrences of the Characters a and A in the collection letters, we used a counter, count.

```
count ← 0.
letters do: [ :each | each asLowercase = = $a
                    ifTrue: [count ← count + 1]]
```

An alternative approach is to use the message inject:into:. In the example expression, the result is accumulated in count. count starts at 0. If the next character (nextElement) is a or A, then add 1 to count; otherwise add 0.

```
letters inject: 0
        into: [ :count :nextElement |
              count + (nextElement asLowerCase = = $a
                            ifTrue: [1]
                            ifFalse: [0])]
```

Instance Creation

In the beginning of this chapter, examples were given in which new collections were expressed as literals. These collections were Arrays and Strings. For example, an expression for creating an array is

```
#('first' 'second' 'third')
```

where each element is a String expressed literally.

The messages new and new: can be used to create instances of particular kinds of collections. In addition, the class protocol for all collections supports messages for creating instances with one, two, three, or four elements. These messages provide a shorthand notation for creating kinds of collections that are not expressible as literals.

Collection class protocol

instance creation

with: anObject   Answer an instance of the collection containing anObject.

with: firstObject with: secondObject
> Answer an instance of the collection containing firstObject and secondObject as elements.

with: firstObject with: secondObject with: thirdObject
> Answer an instance of the collection containing firstObject, secondObject, and thirdObject as elements.

with: firstObject with: secondObject with: thirdObject with: fourthObject
> Answer an instance of the collection, containing firstObject, secondObject, thirdObject, and fourthObject as the elements.

For example, Set is a subclass of Collection. To create a new Set with three elements that are the Characters s, e, and t, evaluate the expression

Set with: $s with: $e with: $t

Note that the rationale for providing these four instance creation messages, no more and no fewer, is that this number satisfies the uses to which collections are put in the system itself.

Conversion Among Collection Classes

A complete description and understanding of the permissible conversions between kinds of collections depends on a presentation of all the subclasses of Collection. Here we simply note that five messages are specified in the converting protocol for all collections in order to convert the receiver to a Bag, a Set, an OrderedCollection, and a SortedCollection. These messages are specified in class Collection because it is possible to convert any collection into any of these kinds of collections. The ordering of elements from any collection whose elements are unordered, when converted to a collection whose elements are ordered, is arbitrary.

Collection instance protocol

converting
    asBag
> Answer a Bag whose elements are those of the receiver.

    asSet
> Answer a Set whose elements are those of the receiver (any duplications are therefore eliminated).

    asOrderedCollection
> Answer an OrderedCollection whose elements are those of the receiver (ordering is possibly arbitrary).

asSortedCollection	Answer a SortedCollection whose elements are those of the receiver, sorted so that each element is less than or equal to ($<=$) its successors.
asSortedCollection: aBlock	Answer a SortedCollection whose elements are those of the receiver, sorted according to the argument aBlock.

Thus if lotteryA is a Bag containing elements

272 572 852 156 596 272 572

then

lotteryA asSet

is a Set containing elements

852 596 156 572 272

and

lotteryA asSortedCollection

is a SortedCollection containing elements ordered (the first element is listed as the leftmost one)

156 272 272 572 572 596 852

10

Hierarchy of the Collection Classes

Object

Magnitude
    Character
    Date
    Time

    Number
      Float
      Fraction
      Integer
        LargeNegativeInteger
        LargePositiveInteger
        SmallInteger

LookupKey
    Association

Link

    Process

Collection

    SequenceableCollection
    LinkedList

    Semaphore

    ArrayedCollection
    Array

    WordArray
      DisplayBitmap

    RunArray
    String
      Symbol
    Text
    ByteArray

    Interval
    OrderedCollection
      SortedCollection
Bag
MappedCollection
Set
    Dictionary
      IdentityDictionary

Stream
    PositionableStream
      ReadStream
      WriteStream
        ReadWriteStream
          ExternalStream
            FileStream

    Random

UndefinedObject
Boolean
    False
    True

ProcessorScheduler
Delay
SharedQueue

Behavior
    ClassDescription
      Class
      MetaClass

Point
Rectangle
BitBlt
    CharacterScanner

    Pen

DisplayObject
    DisplayMedium
      Form
        Cursor
        DisplayScreen
    InfiniteForm
    OpaqueForm
    Path
      Arc
        Circle
      Curve
      Line
      LinearFit
      Spline

Figure 10.1 provides a road map for distinguishing among the various collection classes in the system. Following the choices in the figure is a useful way to determine which kind of collection to use in an implementation.

One distinction among the classes is whether or not a collection has a well-defined order associated with its elements. Another distinction is that elements of some collections can be accessed through externally-known names or *keys*. The type of key defines another way of distinguishing among kinds of collections. Some are integer indices, implicitly assigned according to the order of the elements; others are explicitly assigned objects that serve as lookup keys.

One unordered collection with external keys is a Dictionary. Its keys are typically instances of String or LookupKey; the comparison for matching keys is equality (=). Dictionary has a subclass, IdentityDictionary, whose external keys are typically Symbols. Its comparison for matching keys is equivalence (==). Elements of a Bag or a Set are unordered and not accessible through externally-known keys. Duplicates are allowed in a Bag, but not allowed in a Set.

All ordered collections are kinds of SequenceableCollections. Elements of all SequenceableCollections are accessible through keys that are integer indices. Four subclasses of SequenceableCollection support different ways in which to create the ordering of elements. An additional distinction among the SequenceableCollection classes is whether the elements can be any object or whether they are restricted to be instances of a particular kind of object.

The order of elements is determined externally for OrderedCollections, LinkedLists, and ArrayedCollections. For OrderedCollection and LinkedList, the programmer's sequence for adding and removing elements defines the ordering of the elements. An element of an OrderedCollection can be any object, while that of a LinkedList must be a kind of Link. The different ArrayedCollections in the system include Array, String, and ByteArray. The elements of an Array or a RunArray can be any kind of object, elements of a String or of a Text must be Characters, and those of a ByteArray must be SmallIntegers between 0 and 255.

The order of elements is determined internally for Intervals and SortedCollections. For an Interval, the ordering is an arithmetic progression that is specified at the time the instance is created. For a SortedCollection, the ordering is specified by a sorting criterion determined by evaluating a block known to the collection. Elements of an Interval must be Numbers; elements of a SortedCollection can be any kind of object.

In addition to the collection classes already mentioned, MappedCollection is a Collection that represents an indirect access path to a collection whose elements are accessible via external keys. The

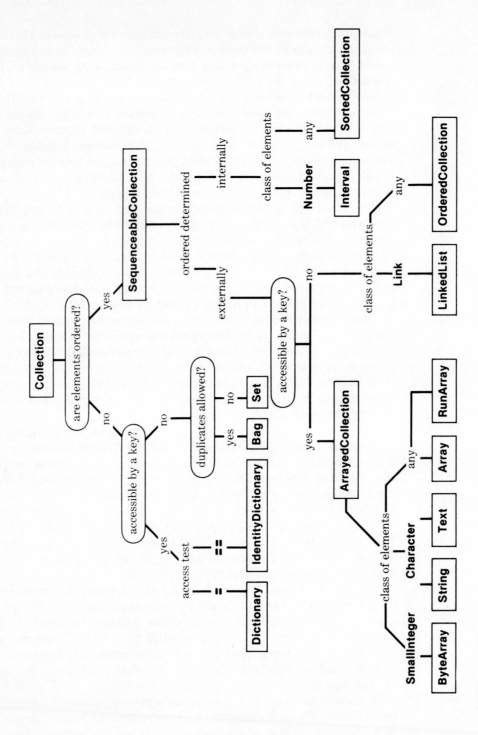

Figure 10.1

mapping from one set of external keys to the collection is determined at the time the MappedCollection is created.

The remainder of this chapter explores each of the collection subclasses, describing any additions to the message protocols and providing simple examples.

Class Bag

A Bag is the simplest kind of collection. It represents collections whose elements are unordered and have no external keys. It is a subclass of Collection. Since its instances do not have external keys, they cannot respond to the messages at: and at:put:. The message size answers the total number of elements in the collection.

A Bag is nothing more than a group of elements that behaves according to the protocol of all collections. The general description of collections does not restrict the number of occurrences of an element in an individual collection. Class Bag emphasizes this generality by specifying an additional message for adding elements.

Bag instance protocol
___

adding
    add: newObject withOccurrences: anInteger
                         Include the argument, newObject, as an element of the receiver, anInteger number of times. Answer the argument, newObject.

Consider the example class Product which represents a grocery item and its price. A new Product may be created using the message of: name at: price, and the price of an instance is accessible by sending it the message price. Filling one's grocery bag may be expressed by

```
sack ← Bag new.
sack add: (Product of: #steak at: 5.80).
sack add: (Product of: #potatoes at: 0.50) withOccurrences: 6.
sack add: (Product of: #carrots at: 0.10) withOccurrences: 4.
sack add: (Product of: #milk at: 2.20)
```

Then the grocery bill is determined by the expression

```
amount ← 0.
sack do: [ :eachProduct | amount ← amount + eachProduct price]
```

or

```
                    sack inject: 0
                        into: [ :amount :eachProduct | amount + eachProduct price]
```

to be $11.40. Note that the messages add:, do:, and inject:into: to a Bag are inherited from its superclass, Collection.

A Bag is unordered, so that, although enumeration messages are supported, the programmer cannot depend on the order in which elements are enumerated.

Class Set

Class Set represents collections whose elements are unordered and have no external keys. Its instances cannot respond to the messages at: and at:put:. A Set is like a Bag except that its elements cannot be duplicated. The adding messages add the element only if it is not already in the collection. Class Set is a subclass of class Collection.

Classes Dictionary and IdentityDictionary

Class Dictionary represents a set of associations between keys and values. The elements of a Dictionary are instances of class Association, a simple data structure for storing and retrieving the members of the key-value pair.

An alternative way of thinking about a Dictionary is that it is a collection whose elements are unordered but have explicitly assigned keys or names. From this perspective, the elements of a Dictionary are arbitrary objects (values) with external keys. These alternative ways of thinking about a Dictionary are reflected in the message protocol of the class. Messages inherited from class Collection—includes:, do:, and other enumeration messages—are applied to the *values* of the Dictionary. That is, these messages refer to the values of each association in the Dictionary, rather than to the keys or to the associations themselves.

Messages inherited from class Object—at: and at:put:—are applied to the keys of the Dictionary. The at: and at:put: paradigm is extended for the associations and the values by adding messages associationAt: and keyAtValue:. In order to provide additional control when looking up elements in a Dictionary, the message at:ifAbsent: is provided; using it, the programmer can specify the action to take if the element whose key is the first argument is not found. The inherited message at: reports an error if the key is not found.

Dictionary instance protocol

accessing

at: key ifAbsent: aBlock	Answer the value named by the argument, key. If key is not found, answer the result of evaluating aBlock.
associationAt: key	Answer the association named by the argument, key. If key is not found, report an error.
associationAt: key ifAbsent: aBlock	
	Answer the association named by the argument, key. If key is not found, answer the result of evaluating aBlock.
keyAtValue: value	Answer the name for the argument, value. If there is no such value, answer nil. Since values are not necessarily unique, answer the name for the first one encountered in the search.
keyAtValue: value ifAbsent: exceptionBlock	
	Answer the key for the argument, value. If there is no such value, answer the result of evaluating exceptionBlock.
keys	Answer a Set containing the receiver's keys.
values	Answer a Bag containing the receiver's values (includes any duplications).

As an example of the use of a Dictionary, suppose opposites is a Dictionary of word Symbols and their opposites.

```
opposites ← Dictionary new.
opposites at: #hot put: #cold.
opposites at: #push put: #pull.
opposites at: #stop put: #go.
opposites at: #come put: #go
```

Alternatively, an element can be added using the message add: by creating an Association as the argument.

```
opposites add: (Association key: #front value: #back).
opposites add: (Association key: #top value: #bottom)
```

The Dictionary, opposites, now consists of

key	value
hot	cold
push	pull
stop	go
come	go
front	back
top	bottom

We can use the testing protocol inherited from class Collection to test the values in the Dictionary. Notice that includes: tests the inclusion of a value, not a key.

expression	result
opposites size	6
opposites includes: #cold	true
opposites includes: #hot	false
opposites occurrencesOf: #go	2
opposites at: #stop put: #start	start

The fourth example indicates that, although a key can appear only once in a Dictionary, a value can be associated with any number of keys. The last example re-associates the key #stop with a new value, #start. Additional messages are provided in class Dictionary for testing associations and keys.

Dictionary instance protocol

dictionary testing
    includesAssociation: anAssociation

> Answer whether the receiver has an element (association between a key and a value) that is equal to the argument, anAssociation.

    includesKey: key

> Answer whether the receiver has a key equal to the argument, key.

Then we can try

expression	result

opposites
  includesAssociation:
    (Association
      key: #come
      value: #go)
	true

opposites includesKey: #hot	true

Similarly, the removing protocol specified in class Collection is extended to provide access by reference to associations and keys, as well as to values. However, the message remove: itself is not appropriate for a Dictionary; in removing an element, mention of the key is required.

Dictionary instance protocol
___

dictionary removing

    removeAssociation: anAssociation

	Remove the key and value association, anAssociation, from the receiver. Answer anAssociation.
removeKey: key	Remove key (and its associated value) from the receiver. If key is not in the receiver, report an error. Otherwise, answer the value associated with key.
removeKey: key ifAbsent: aBlock	Remove key (and its associated value) from the receiver. If key is not in the receiver, answer the result of evaluating aBlock. Otherwise, answer the value named by key.

For example

---

expression	result

opposites
  removeAssociation:
    (Association
      key: #top
      value: #bottom)
	The association whose key is #top and value is #bottom. opposites has one less element.

opposites removeKey: #hot	The association whose key is #hot and whose value is #cold. This association is removed from opposites.

opposites
  removeKey: #cold
  ifAbsent: [opposites
      at: #cold
      put: #hot]
	hot

As a result of the last example, the association of #cold with #hot is now an element of opposites.

The message do: evaluates its argument, a block, for each of the Dictionary's values. The collection enumerating protocol, inherited from class Collection, is again extended in order to provide messages for enumerating over the associations and the keys. Messages supporting uses of reject: and inject:into: are not provided.

Dictionary instance protocol

dictionary enumerating

associationsDo: aBlock	Evaluate aBlock for each of the receiver's key/value associations.
keysDo: aBlock	Evaluate aBlock for each of the receiver's keys.

We thus have three possible ways of enumerating over a Dictionary. Suppose newWords is a Set of vocabulary words that a child has not yet learned. Any word in opposites is now part of the child's repertoire and can be removed from newWords. Evaluating the following two expressions removes these words (the first removes the values, the second the keys).

```
opposites do: [ :word | newWords remove: word ifAbsent: []].
opposites keysDo: [ :word | newWords remove: word ifAbsent: []]
```

Note that if a word from opposites is not in newWords, then nothing (no error report) happens. Alternatively, one expression, enumerating the Associations, can be used.

```
opposites associationsDo:
        [ :each |
          newWords remove: each key ifAbsent: [].
          newWords remove: each value ifAbsent: []]
```

The accessing messages keys and values can be used to obtain collections of the words in the opposites dictionary. Assuming the evaluation of all previous example expressions, then

```
opposites keys
```

returns the Set whose elements are

```
push come front stop cold
```

and

```
opposites values
```

returns the Bag whose elements are

```
pull go back start hot
```

Class Sequenceable-Collection

Class SequenceableCollection represents collections whose elements are ordered and are externally named by integer indices. SequenceableCollection is a subclass of Collection and provides the protocol for accessing, copying, and enumerating elements of a collection when it is known that there is an ordering associated with the elements. Since the elements are ordered, there is a well-defined first and last element of the collection. It is possible to ask the index of a particular element (indexOf:) and the index of the beginning of a sequence of elements within the collection (indexOfSubCollection:startingAt:). All collections inherit messages from class Object for accessing indexed variables. As described in Chapter 6, these are at:, at:put:, and size. In addition, SequenceableCollections support putting an object at all positions named by the elements of a Collection (atAll:put:), and putting an object at all positions in the sequence (atAllPut:). Sequences of elements within the collection can be replaced by the elements of another collection (replaceFrom:to:with: and replaceFrom:to:with:startingAt:).

SequenceableCollection instance protocol

accessing

atAll: aCollection put: anObject   Associate each element of the argument, aCollection (an Integer or other external key), with the second argument, anObject.

atAllPut: anObject   Put the argument, anObject, as every one of the receiver's elements.

first   Answer the first element of the receiver. Report an error if the receiver contains no elements.

last   Answer the last element of the receiver. Report an error if the receiver contains no elements.

indexOf: anElement   Answer the first index of the argument, anElement, within the receiver. If the receiver does not contain anElement, answer 0.

indexOf: anElement ifAbsent: exceptionBlock   Answer the first index of the argument, anElement, within the receiver. If the receiver does not contain anElement, answer the result of evaluating the argument, exceptionBlock.

indexOfSubCollection: aSubCollection startingAt: anIndex   If the elements of the argument, aSubCollection, appear, in order, in the receiver, then answer the index of the first element of the first such occurrence. If no such match is found, answer 0.

indexOfSubCollection: aSubCollection startingAt: anIndex
ifAbsent: exceptionBlock   Answer the index of the receiver's first element, such that that element equals the first

element of the argument, aSubCollection, and the next elements equal the rest of the elements of aSubCollection. Begin the search of the receiver at the element whose index is the argument, anIndex. If no such match is found, answer the result of evaluating the argument, exceptionBlock.

replaceFrom: start to: stop with: replacementCollection

Associate each index between start and stop with the elements of the argument, replacementCollection. Answer the receiver. The number of elements in replacementCollection must equal stop-start+1.

replaceFrom: start to: stop with: replacementCollection startingAt: repStart

Associate each index between start and stop with the elements of the argument, replacementCollection, starting at the element of replacementCollection whose index is repStart. Answer the receiver. No range checks are performed, except if the receiver is the same as replacementCollection but repStart is not 1, then an error reporting that indices are out of range will occur.

Examples of using these accessing messages, using instances of String, are

expression	result
' aaaaaaaaaa ' size	10
' aaaaaaaaaa ' atAll: (2 to: 10 by: 2) put: $b	' abababababab '
' aaaaaaaaaa ' atAllPut: $b	' bbbbbbbbbb '
' This string ' first	$T
' This string ' last	$g
' ABCDEFGHIJKLMNOP ' indexOf: $F	6
' ABCDEFGHIJKLMNOP ' indexOf: $M ifAbsent: [0]	13
' ABCDEFGHIJKLMNOP ' indexOf: $Z ifAbsent: [0]	0
' The cow jumped ' indexOfSubCollection: ' cow ' startingAt: 1	5
' The cow jumped ' replaceFrom: 5 to: 7 with: ' dog '	' The dog jumped '
' The cow jumped ' replaceFrom: 5 to: 7 with: ' the spoon ran ' startingAt: 5	' The spo jumped '

Any of these examples could be similarly carried out with an instance of any subclass of SequenceableCollection, for example, with an Array. For the Array, #(The brown jug), replacement of brown by black is carried out by evaluating the expression

#(The brown jug) replaceFrom: 2 to: 2 with: #(black)

Notice that the last argument must be an Array as well. And notice that the replacement messages do not change the size of the original collection (the receiver), although they do alter the collection. It may be preferrable to preserve the original by creating a copy. The copying protocol of SequenceableCollections supports copying a sequence of elements in the collection, copying the entire collection with part of it replaced, copying the entire collection with an element deleted, or copying the entire collection with one or more elements concatenated.

SequenceableCollection instance protocol

---

copying

, aSequenceableCollection	This is the concatenation operation. Answer a copy of the receiver with each element of the argument, aSequenceableCollection, added, in order.
copyFrom: start to: stop	Answer a copy of a subset of the receiver, starting from element at index start until element at index stop.
copyReplaceAll: oldSubCollection with: newSubCollection	
	Answer a copy of the receiver in which all occurrences of oldSubCollection have been replaced by newSubCollection.
copyReplaceFrom: start to: stop with: replacementCollection	
	Answer a copy of the receiver satisfying the following conditions: If stop is less than start, then this is an insertion; stop should be exactly start-1. start = 1 means insert before the first character. start = size + 1 means append after last character. Otherwise, this is a replacement; start and stop have to be within the receiver's bounds.
copyWith: newElement	Answer a copy of the receiver that is 1 bigger than the receiver and has newElement as the last element.
copyWithout: oldElement	Answer a copy of the receiver in which all occurrences of oldElement have been left out.

Using the replace and copy messages, a simple text editor can be devised. The Smalltalk-80 system includes class String as well as class Text, the latter providing support for associating the characters in the String with font or emphasis changes in order to mix character fonts, bold, italic, and underline. The message protocol for Text is that of a SequenceableCollection with additional protocol for setting the emphasis codes. For illustration purposes, we use an instance of class String, but remind the reader of the analogous application of editing messages for an instance of class Text. Assume that line is initially an empty string

line ← String new: 0

Then

expression	result

line ← line copyReplaceFrom: 1
      to: 0
      with: 'this is the first line tril'
	'this is the first line tril'

line ← line copyReplaceAll: 'tril' with: 'trial'	'this is the first line trial'

line ← line copyReplaceFrom:
      (line size + 1)
      to: (line size)
      with: 'and so on'
	'this is the first line trialand so on'

line indexOfSubCollection: 'trial' startingAt: 1	24

line ← line copyReplaceFrom: 29
      to: 28
      with: ' '
	'this is the first line trial and so on'

The last two messages of the copying protocol given above are useful in obtaining copies of an Array with or without an element. For example

expression	result
#(one two three) copyWith: #four	(one two three four)
#(one two three) copyWithout: #two	(one three)

Because the elements of a SequenceableCollection are ordered, enumeration is in order, starting with the first element and taking each successive element until the last. Reverse enumeration is also possible, using the message reverseDo: aBlock. Enumeration of two SequenceableCollections can be done together so that pairs of elements, one from each collection, can be used in evaluating a block.

SequenceableCollection instance protocol

enumerating
    findFirst: aBlock   Evaluate aBlock with each of the receiver's elements as the argument. Answer the index of the first element for which the argument, aBlock evaluates to true.

findLast: aBlock	Evaluate aBlock with each of the receiver's elements as the argument. Answer the index of the last element for which the argument, aBlock evaluates to true.
reverseDo: aBlock	Evaluate aBlock with each of the receiver's elements as the argument, starting with the last element and taking each in sequence up to the first. For SequenceableCollections, this is the reverse of the enumeration for do:. aBlock is a one-argument block.
with: aSequenceableCollection do: aBlock	
	Evaluate aBlock with each of the receiver's elements along with the corresponding element from aSequenceableCollection. aSequenceableCollection must be the same size as the receiver, and aBlock must be a two-argument block.

The following expressions create the Dictionary, opposites, which was introduced in an earlier example.

```
opposites ← Dictionary new.
#(come cold front hot push stop)
        with: #(go hot back cold pull start)
        do: [ :key :value | opposites at: key put: value]
```

The Dictionary now has six associations as its elements.

Any SequenceableCollection can be converted to an Array or a MappedCollection. The messages are asArray and mappedBy: aSequenceableCollection.

Subclasses of Sequenceable-Collection

Subclasses of SequenceableCollection are OrderedCollection, LinkedList, and Interval. ArrayedCollection is a subclass representing a collection of elements with a fixed range of integers as external keys. Subclasses of ArrayedCollection are, for example, Array and String.

Class OrderedCollection

OrderedCollections are ordered by the sequence in which objects are added and removed from them. The elements are accessible by external keys that are indices. The accessing, adding, and removing protocols are augmented to refer to the first and last elements, and to elements preceding or succeeding other elements.

OrderedCollections can act as *stacks* or *queues*. A stack is a sequential list for which all additions and deletions are made at one end of the list (called either the "rear" or the "front") of the list. It is often called a *last-in first-out* queue.

usual vocabulary	OrderedCollection *message*
push newObject	addLast: newObject
pop	removeLast
top	last
empty	isEmpty

A queue is a sequential list for which all additions are made at one end of the list (the "rear"), but all deletions are made from the other end (the "front"). It is often called a *first-in first-out* queue.

usual vocabulary	OrderedCollection *message*
add newObject	addLast: newObject
delete	removeFirst
front	first
empty	isEmpty

The message add: to an OrderedCollection means "add the element as the last member of the collection" and remove: means "remove the argument as an element." The message protocol for OrderedCollections, in addition to that inherited from classes Collection and SequenceableCollection, follows.

OrderedCollection instance protocol

accessing

    after: oldObject   Answer the element after oldObject in the receiver. If the receiver does not contain oldObject or if the receiver contains no elements after oldObject, report an error.

    before: oldObject   Answer the element before oldObject in the receiver. If the receiver does not contain oldObject or if the receiver contains no elements before oldObject, report an error.

adding

    add: newObject after: oldObject   Add the argument, newObject, as an element of the receiver. Put it in the sequence just succeeding oldObject. Answer newObject. If oldObject is not found, then report an error.

add: newObject before: oldObject	Add the argument, newObject, as an element of the receiver. Put it in the sequence just preceding oldObject. Answer newObject. If oldObject is not found, then report an error.
addAllFirst: anOrderedCollection	Add each element of the argument, anOrderedCollection, at the beginning of the receiver. Answer anOrderedCollection.
addAllLast: anOrderedCollection	Add each element of the argument, anOrderedCollection, to the end of the receiver. Answer anOrderedCollection.
addFirst: newObject	Add the argument, newObject, to the beginning of the receiver. Answer newObject.
addLast: newObject	Add the argument, newObject, to the end of the receiver. Answer newObject.

removing

removeFirst	Remove the first element of the receiver and answer it. If the receiver is empty, report an error.
removeLast	Remove the last element of the receiver and answer it. If the receiver is empty, report an error.

Class
SortedCollection

Class SortedCollection is a subclass of OrderedCollection. The elements in a SortedCollection are ordered by a function of two elements. The function is represented by a two-argument block called the sort block. It is possible to add an element only with the message add:; messages such as addLast: that allow the programmer to specify the order of inserting are disallowed for SortedCollections.

An instance of class SortedCollection can be created by sending SortedCollection the message sortBlock:. The argument to this message is a block with two-arguments, for example,

SortedCollection sortBlock: [:a :b | a < = b]

This particular block is the default sorting function when an instance is created simply by sending SortedCollection the message new. Thus examples of the four ways to create a SortedCollection are

SortedCollection new
SortedCollection sortBlock: [:a :b | a > b]
anyCollection asSortedCollection
anyCollection asSortedCollection: [:a :b | a > b]

It is possible to determine the block and to reset the block using two additional accessing messages to instances of SortedCollection. When the block is changed, the elements of the collection are, of course, re-sorted. Notice that the same message is sent to the class itself (sortBlock:) to create an instance with a particular sorting criterion, and to an instance to change its sorting criterion.

SortedCollection class protocol

---

instance creation
    sortBlock: aBlock   Answer an instance of SortedCollection such that its elements will be sorted according to the criterion specified in the argument, aBlock.

SortedCollection instance protocol

---

accessing
    sortBlock   Answer the block that is the criterion for sorting elements of the receiver.
    sortBlock: aBlock   Make the argument, aBlock, be the criterion for ordering elements of the receiver.

Suppose we wish to maintain an alphabetical list of the names of children in a classroom.

children ← SortedCollection new

The initial sorting criterion is the default block [:a :b | a <= b]. The elements of the collection can be Strings or Symbols because, as we shall show presently, these kinds of objects respond to the comparison messages <, >, <=, and >=.

expression	result
children add: #Joe	Joe
children add: #Bill	Bill
children add: #Alice	Alice
children	SortedCollection (Alice Bill Joe)
children add: #Sam	Sam

children
  sortBlock: [:a :b | a > b]
	SortedCollection
	  (Sam Joe Bill Alice)

children add: #Henrietta	Henrietta

children	SortedCollection
	  (Sam Joe Henrietta
	  Bill Alice)

The sixth message in the example reversed the order in which elements are stored in the collection, children.

Class LinkedList

LinkedList is another subclass of SequenceableCollection whose elements are explicitly ordered by the sequence in which objects are added and removed from them. Like OrderedCollection, the elements of a LinkedList can be referred to by external keys that are indices. Unlike OrderedCollection, where the elements may be any object, the elements of a LinkedList are homogeneous; each must be an instance of class Link or of a subclass of Link.

A Link is a record of a reference to another Link. Its message protocol consists of three messages. The same message (nextLink:) is used to create an instance of Link with a particular reference, and to change the reference of an instance.

Link class protocol

---

instance creation
    nextLink: aLink   Create an instance of Link that references the argument, aLink.

Link instance protocol

---

accessing
    nextLink   Answer the receiver's reference.
    nextLink: aLink   Set the receiver's reference to be the argument, aLink.

Since class Link does not provide a way to record a reference to the actual element of the collection, it is treated as an abstract class. That is, instances of it are not created. Rather, subclasses are defined that provide the mechanisms for storing one or more elements, and instances of the subclasses are created.

Since LinkedList is a subclass of SequenceableCollection, its instances can respond to the accessing, adding, removing, and enumerating messages defined for all collections. Additional protocol for LinkedList consists of

---

LinkedList instance protocol

---

adding
    addFirst: aLink   Add aLink to the beginning of the receiver's list. Answer aLink.
    addLast: aLink   Add aLink to the end of the receiver's list. Answer aLink.

removing
    removeFirst   Remove the receiver's first element and answer it. If the receiver is empty, report an error.
    removeLast   Remove the receiver's last element and answer it. If the receiver is empty, report an error.

An example of a subclass of Link in the Smalltalk-80 system is class Process. Class Semaphore is a subclass of LinkedList. These two classes are discussed in Chapter 15, which is about multiple independent processes in the system.

The following is an example of the use of LinkedList. Link does not provide instance information other than a reference to another Link. So, as an example, assume that there is a subclass of Link named Entry. Entry adds the ability to store one object. The instance creation message for an Entry is for: anObject, and its accessing message is element.

class name	Entry
superclass	Link
instance variable names	element
class methods	

instance creation

    for: anObject
        ↑self new setElement: anObject

instance methods

accessing
    element
        ↑element
printing
    printOn: aStream
        aStream nextPutAll: ′Entry for: ′, element printString
private
    setElement: anObject
        element ← anObject

The classes LinkedList and Entry can then be used as follows.

expression	result
list ← LinkedList new	LinkedList ()
list add: (Entry for: 2)	Entry for: 2
list add: (Entry for: 4)	Entry for: 4
list addLast: (Entry for: 5)	Entry for: 5
list addFirst: (Entry for: 1)	Entry for: 1
list	LinkedList (Entry for: 1 Entry for: 2 Entry for: 4 Entry for: 5)
list isEmpty	false
list size	4

list inject: 0
  into: [:value :each |
    (each element)
      + value]
	12

list last	Entry for: 5
list first	Entry for: 1
list removeFirst	Entry for: 1
list removeLast	Entry for: 5
list first = = list last	true

Class Interval

Another kind of SequenceableCollection is a collection of numbers representing a mathematical progression. For example, the collection might consist of all the integers in the interval from 1 to 100; or it might consist of all even integers in the interval from 1 to 100. Or the collection might consist of a series of numbers where each additional number in the series is computed from the previous one by multiplying it by 2. The series might start with 1 and end with the last number that is less than or equal to 100. This would be the sequence 1, 2, 4, 8, 16, 32, 64.

A mathematical progression is characterized by a first number, a limit (maximum or minimum) for the last computed number, and a method for computing each succeeding number. The limit could be positive or negative infinity. An arithmetic progression is one in which the computation method is simply the addition of an increment. For example, it could be a series of numbers where each additional number in the series is computed from the previous one by adding a negative 20. The series might start with 100 and end with the last number that is greater than or equal to 1. This would be the sequence 100, 80, 60, 40, 20.

In the Smalltalk-80 system, the class of collections called Intervals consists of finite arithmetic progressions. In addition to those messages inherited from its superclasses SequenceableCollection and Collection, class Interval supports messages for initialization and for accessing those values that characterize the instance. New elements cannot be added or removed from an Interval.

The class protocol of Interval consists of the following messages for creating instances.

Interval class protocol

instance creation

from: startInteger to: stopInteger   Answer an instance of class Interval, starting with the number startInteger, ending with the number stopInteger, and using the increment 1 to compute each successive element.

from: startInteger to: stopInteger by: stepInteger

> Answer an instance of Interval, starting with the number startInteger, ending with the number stopInteger, and using the increment stepInteger to compute each successive element.

All messages appropriate to SequenceableCollections can be sent to an Interval. In addition, the instance protocol of Interval provides a message for accessing the increment of the arithmetic progression (increment).

Class Number supports two messages that provide a shorthand for expressing new Intervals—to: stop and to: stop by: step. Thus to create an Interval of all integers from 1 to 10, evaluate either

Interval from: 1 to: 10

or

1 to: 10

To create an Interval starting with 100 and ending with 1, adding a negative 20 each time, evaluate either

Interval from: 100 to: 1 by: −20

or

100 to: 1 by: −20

This is the sequence 100, 80, 60, 40, 20. The Interval need not consist of Integers—to create an Interval between 10 and 40, incrementing by 0.2, evaluate either

Interval from: 10 to: 40 by: 0.2

or

10 to: 40 by: 0.2

This is the sequence 10, 10.2, 10.4, 10.6, 10.8, 11.0, ... and so on.

Note that we could provide the more general case of a progression by replacing the numeric value of step by a block. When a new element is to be computed, it would be done by sending the current value as the argument of the message value: to the block. The computations of size and do: would have to take this method of computation into account.

The message do: to an Interval provides the function of the usual for-loop in a programming language. The Algol statement

for i := 10 **step** 6 **until** 100 **do**
      begin
      <statements>
      end

is represented by

(10 to: 100 by: 6) do: [:i | statements]

Numbers respond to the message to:by:do: as though the expression had been written as given in the example. So that iteration can be written without parentheses as

10 to: 100 by: 6 do: [:i | statements]

To increment by 1 every sixth numeric element of an OrderedCollection, numbers, evaluate

6 to: numbers size
  by: 6
  do: [:index | numbers at: index put: (numbers at: index) + 1]

The Interval created is 6, 12, 18, ..., up to the index of the last element of numbers. If the size of the collection is less than 6 (the supposedly first index), nothing happens. Otherwise elements at position 6, 12, 18, and so on, until the last possible position, are replaced.

Class ArrayedCollection

As stated earlier, class ArrayedCollection is a subclass of SequenceableCollection. It represents a collection of elements with a fixed range of integers as external keys. ArrayedCollection has five subclasses in the Smalltalk-80 system—Array, String, Text, RunArray, and ByteArray.

An Array is a collection whose elements are any objects. It provides the concrete representation for storing a collection of elements that have integers as external keys. Several examples of the use of Arrays have already been given in this chapter.

A String is a collection whose elements are Characters. Many examples of the use of Strings have been given in this and in previous chapters. Class String provides additional protocol for initializing and comparing its instances.

Text represents a String that has font and emphasis changes. It is used in storing information needed for creating textual documents in the Smalltalk-80 system. An instance of Text has two instance variables, the String and an instance of RunArray in which an encoding of the font and emphasis changes is stored.

Class RunArray provides a space-efficient storage of data that tends to be constant over long runs of the possible indices. It stores repeated elements singly and then associates with each single element a number that denotes the consecutive occurrences of the element. For example, suppose the Text representing the String 'He is a good boy.' is to be displayed with the word "boy" in bold, and further suppose that the code for the font is 1 and for its boldface version is 2. Then the RunArray for the Text that is associated with 'He is a good boy.' (a String of 17 Characters) consists of 1 associated with 13, 2 associated with 3, and 1 associated with 1. That is, the first 13 Characters are in font 1, the next three in font 2, and the last in font 1.

A ByteArray represents an ArrayedCollection whose elements are integers between 0 and 255. The implementation of a ByteArray stores two bytes to a 16-bit word; the class supports additional protocol for word and double-word access. ByteArrays are used in the Smalltalk-80 system for storing time in milliseconds.

Class String

As stated earlier, the class protocol for String adds messages for creating a copy of another String (fromString: aString) or for creating a String from the Characters in a Stream (readFrom: aStream). The main significance of this second message is that pairs of embedded quotes are read and stored as one element, the quote character. In addition, class String adds comparing protocol like that specified in class Magnitude. We introduced some of these messages earlier in the description of class SortedCollection.

String instance protocol

comparing

< aString	Answer whether the receiver collates before the argument, aString. The collation sequence is ASCII with case differences ignored.
< = aString	Answer whether the receiver collates before the argument, aString, or is the same as aString. The collation sequence is ASCII with case differences ignored.
> aString	Answer whether the receiver collates after the argument, aString. The collation sequence is ASCII with case differences ignored.

> = aString	Answer whether the receiver collates after the argument, aString, or is the same as aString. The collation sequence is ASCII with case differences ignored.
match: aString	Treat the receiver as a pattern that can contain characters # and *. Answer whether the argument, aString, matches the pattern in the receiver. Matching ignores upper/lower case differences. Where the receiver contains the character #, aString may contain any single character. Where the receiver contains *, aString may contain any sequence of characters, including no characters.
sameAs: aString	Answer whether the receiver collates precisely with the argument, aString. The collation sequence is ASCII with case differences ignored.

We have not as yet given examples of using the last two messages.

expression	result
' first string ' sameAs: ' first string '	true
' First String ' sameAs: ' first string '	true
' First String ' = ' first string '	false
' #irst string ' match: ' first string '	true
' * string ' match: ' any string '	true
' *.st ' match: ' filename.st '	true
' first string ' match: ' first * '	false

Strings can be converted to all lowercase characters or all uppercase characters. They can also be converted to instances of class Symbol.

String instance protocol

converting

asLowercase	Answer a String made up from the receiver whose characters are all lowercase.
asUppercase	Answer a String made up from the receiver whose characters are all uppercase.
asSymbol	Answer the unique Symbol whose characters are the characters of the receiver.

Therefore we have

expression	result
' first string ' asUppercase	' FIRST STRING '
' First String ' asLowercase	' first string '
' First ' asSymbol	First

Class Symbol

Symbols are arrays of Characters that are guaranteed to be unique. Thus

'a string' asSymbol == 'a string' asSymbol

answers true. Class Symbol provides two instance creation messages in its class protocol for this purpose.

Symbol class protocol	
instance creation	
intern: aString	Answer a unique Symbol whose characters are those of aString.
internCharacter: aCharacter	Answer a unique Symbol of one character, the argument, aCharacter.

In addition, Symbols can be expressed literally using the character # as a prefix to an identifier, a binary selector, a keyword, or a concatenation of keywords. For example, #dave is a Symbol of four Characters. Symbols print without this prefix notation.

Class MappedCollection

Class MappedCollection is a subclass of Collection. It represents an access mechanism for referencing a subcollection of a collection whose elements are named. This mapping can determine a reordering or filtering of the elements of the collection. The basic idea is that a MappedCollection refers to a *domain* and a *map*. The domain is a Collection that is to be accessed indirectly through the external keys stored in the map. The map is a Collection that associates a set of external keys with another set of external keys. This second set of keys must be external keys that can be used to access the elements of the domain. The domain and the map, therefore, must be instances of Dictionary or of a subclass of SequenceableCollection.

Take, for example, the Dictionary of word Symbols, opposites, introduced earlier.

key	*value*
come	go
cold	hot
front	back
hot	cold
push	pull
stop	start

Suppose we create another Dictionary of synonym Symbols for some of the keys of the entries in opposites and refer to it by the variable name alternates.

key	value
cease	stop
enter	come
scalding	hot
shove	push

Then we can provide a MappedCollection by evaluating the expression

words ← MappedCollection collection: opposites map: alternates

Through words, we can access the elements of opposites. For example, the value of the expression words at: #cease is start (i.e., the value of the key cease in alternatives is stop; the value of the key stop in opposites is start). We can determine which part of opposites is referenced by words by sending words the message contents.

words contents

The result is a Bag containing the symbols start go cold pull.

The message at:put: is an indirect way to change the domain collection. For example

expression	result
words at: #scalding	cold
words at: #cease	start
words at: #cease put: #continue	continue
opposites at: #stop	continue

Summary of Conversions Among Collections

In the sections describing the various kinds of collections, we have indicated which collections can be converted to which other collections. In summary, any collection can be converted to a Bag, a Set, an OrderedCollection, or a SortedCollection. All collections except Bags and Sets can be converted to an Array or a MappedCollection. Strings and Symbols can be converted into one another; but no collection can be converted into an Interval or a LinkedList.

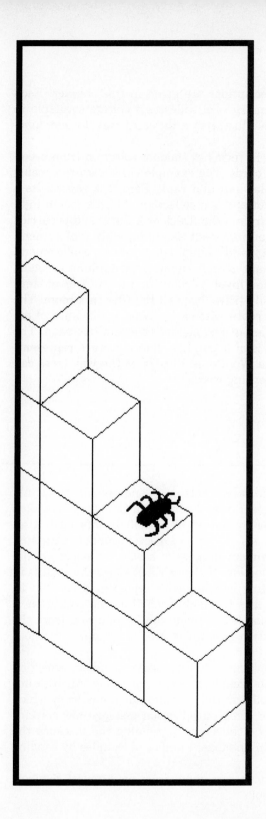

11

Three Examples That Use Collections

Three examples of class descriptions are given in this chapter. Each example makes use of the numeric and collections objects available in the Smalltalk-80 system; each illustrates a different way to add functionality to the system.

Card games can be created in terms of random selection from a collection representing a deck of cards. The example class Card represents a playing card with a particular suit and rank. CardDeck represents a collection of such Cards; a CardHand is a collection of Cards for an individual player. Selecting cards from a CardDeck or a CardHand is carried out using example classes that represent sampling with replacement, SampleSpaceWithReplacement, and sampling without replacement, SampleSpaceWithoutReplacement. A well-known programming problem, the drunken cockroach problem, involves counting the number of steps it takes a cockroach to randomly travel over all the tiles in a room. The solution given in this chapter represents each tile as an instance of example class Tile and the bug as an instance of DrunkenCockroach. The third example in this chapter is of a tree-like data structure represented by classes Tree and Node; a WordNode illustrates the way trees can be used to store strings representing words.

Random Selection and Playing Cards	The Smalltalk-80 class Random, which acts as a generator for randomly selected numbers between 0 and 1, was described in Chapter 8. Random provides the basis for sampling from a set of possible events; such a set is known as a *sample space*. A simple form of discrete random sampling can be obtained in which a random number is used to to select an element from a sequenceable collection. If the selected element remains in the collection, then the sampling is done "with replacement"—that is, every element of the collection is available each time the collection is sampled. Alternatively, the sampled element can be removed from the collection each time the collection is sampled; this is sampling "without replacement."

Class SampleSpaceWithReplacement represents random selection with replacement from a sequenceable collection of items. An instance of the class is created by specifying the collection of items from which random sampling will be done. This initialization message has selector data:. We then sample from the collection by sending the instance the message next. Or we can obtain anInteger number of samples by sending the message next: anInteger.

For example, suppose we wish to sample from an Array of Symbols representing the names of people.

> people ← SampleSpaceWithReplacement
>   data: #(sally sam sue sarah steve)

Each time we wish to select a name from the Array, we evaluate the expression

> people next

The response is one of the Symbols, sally, sam, sue, sarah, or steve. By evaluating the expression

> people next: 5

an OrderedCollection of five samples is selected. Instances of SampleSpaceWithReplacement respond to messages isEmpty and size to test whether any elements exist in the sample space and how many elements exist. Thus the response to

> people isEmpty

is false; and the response to

> people size

is 5.

An implementation of class SampleSpaceWithReplacement is given next. Comments, delimited by double quotes, are given in each method to indicate its purpose.

class name	SampleSpaceWithReplacement
superclass	Object
instance variable names	data
	rand

class methods

instance creation

data: aSequenceableCollection
> "Create an instance of SampleSpaceWithReplacement such that the argument, aSequenceableCollection, is the sample space."
> ↑self new setData: aSequenceableCollection

instance methods

accessing

next
> "The next element selected is chosen at random from the data collection. The index into the data collection is determined by obtaining a

Three Examples That Use Collections

random number between 0 and 1, and normalizing it to be within the range of the size of the data collection."
self isEmpty
   ifTrue: [self error: 'no values exist in the sample space'].
↑data at: (rand next * data size) truncated + 1

next: anInteger

"Answer an OrderedCollection containing anInteger number of selections from the data collection."
| aCollection |
aCollection ← OrderedCollection new: anInteger.
anInteger timesRepeat: [aCollection addLast: self next].
↑aCollection

testing

isEmpty

"Answer whether any items remain to be sampled."
↑self size = 0

size

"Answer the number of items remaining to be sampled."
↑data size

private

setData: aSequenceableCollection

"The argument, aSequenceableCollection, is the sample space. Create a random number generator for sampling from the space."
data ← aSequenceableCollection.
rand ← Random new

The class description declares that each instance has two variables whose names are data and rand. The initialization message, data:, sends the new instance the message setData: in which data is bound to a SequenceableCollection (the value of the argument of the initialization message) and rand is bound to a new instance of class Random.

SampleSpaceWithReplacement is not a subclass of Collection because it implements only a small subset of the messages to which Collections can respond. In response to the messages next and size to a SampleSpaceWithReplacement, the messages at: and size are sent to the instance variable data. This means that any collection that can respond to at: and size can serve as the data from which elements are sampled. All SequenceableCollections respond to these two messages. So. for example, in addition to an Array as illustrated earlier, the data can be an Interval. Suppose we wish to simulate the throw of a die. Then the elements of the sample space are the positive integers 1 through 6.

die ← SampleSpaceWithReplacement data: (1 to: 6)

A throw of the die is obtained by evaluating

die next

The response from this message is one of the Integers, 1, 2, 3, 4, 5, or 6.

We could select a card from a deck of cards in a similar way if the collection associated with the instance of SampleSpaceWithReplacement consists of elements representing playing cards. In order to play card games, however, we have to be able to deal a card out to a player and remove it from the deck. So, we have to use random selection without replacement.

To implement random selection without replacement, we define the response to the message next as removing the selected element. Since all SequenceableCollections do not respond to the message remove:, (for example, Interval does not) we either must check the argument of the initialization message or we must convert the argument to an acceptable kind of collection. Since all OrderedCollections respond to the two messages, and since all collections can be converted to an OrderedCollection, we can use the conversion approach. The method associated with setData: sends its argument the message asOrderedCollection in order to accomplish the goal.

Class SampleSpaceWithoutReplacement is defined to be a subclass of SampleSpaceWithReplacement. The methods associated with the messages next and setData: are overridden; the remaining messages are inherited without modification.

class name	SampleSpaceWithoutReplacement
superclass	SampleSpaceWithReplacement
instance methods	

accessing

next
    ↑data remove: super next

private

setData: aCollection
    data ← aCollection asOrderedCollection.
    rand ← Random new

Notice that the method for next depends on the method implemented in the superclass (super next). The superclass's method checks to make certain that the sample space is not empty and then randomly selects an element. After determining the selected element, the subclass's method removes the element from data. The result of the remove: message is the argument, so that the result of the message next to a SampleSpaceWithoutReplacement is the selected element.

Now let's implement a simple card game. Suppose the sample space data for the card game are instances of a class Card where each Card knows its suit and rank. An instance of Card is created by sending it the message suit:rank:, specifying the suit (heart, club, spade, or diamond) and its rank (1, 2, ..., 13) as the two arguments. A Card responds to the messages suit and rank with the appropriate information.

class name	Card
superclass	Object
instance variable names	suit
	rank

class methods

instance creation

suit: aSymbol rank: anInteger
    "Create an instance of Card whose suit is the argument, aSymbol, and whose rank is the argument, anInteger."
    ↑self new setSuit: aSymbol rank: anInteger

instance methods

accessing

suit
    "Answer the receiver's suit."
    ↑suit
rank
    "Answer the receiver's rank."
    ↑rank

private

setSuit: aSymbol rank: anInteger
    suit ← aSymbol.
    rank ← anInteger

A deck of cards, cardDeck, is created by the following expressions.

```
cardDeck ← OrderedCollection new: 52.
#(heart club spade diamond) do:
    [ :eachSuit |
        1 to: 13 do: [ :n | cardDeck add: (Card suit: eachSuit rank: n)]]
```

The first expression creates an OrderedCollection for 52 elements. The second expression is an enumeration of the ranks 1 through 13 for each of the four suits: heart, club, spade, and diamond. Each element of the OrderedCollection is set to be a Card with a different suit and rank.

The ability to sample from this deck of cards is obtained by creating an instance of SampleSpaceWithoutReplacement with the card deck as the collection from which samples will be taken

cards ← SampleSpaceWithoutReplacement data: cardDeck

To deal a card, evaluate the expression

cards next

The response to this message is an instance of class Card.

Another way to provide a deck of playing cards is illustrated in the description of example class CardDeck. The basic idea is to store a linear list of cards; next means supply the first card in the list. A card can be returned to the deck by placing it at the end or by inserting it at some random position. The linear list is made random by *shuffling*—that is, randomly ordering the cards.

In the implementation of class CardDeck provided next, we store an initial version of the deck of cards as a class variable. It is created using the expressions given earlier. A copy of this variable is made as an instance variable whenever a new instance is created; it is shuffled before cards are dealt out. Each subsequent shuffle of the deck uses the current state of the instance variable, not of the class variable. Of course, the shuffling process, since it is based on the use of an instance of SampleSpaceWithoutReplacement, is quite uniform. A simulation of real shuffling involves first splitting the deck approximately in half and then interleaving the two halves. The interleaving involves selecting chunks from one half and then the other half. Indeed, such a simulation may be more random than an actual person's shuffling; a person's shuffling ability might be observable and predictable.

Messages to a CardDeck, such as return:, next, and shuffle, are useful in creating card games.

class name	CardDeck
superclass	Object
instance variable names	cards
class variable names	InitialCardDeck
class methods	

class initialization

initialize
```
"Create a deck of 52 playing cards."
InitialCardDeck ← OrderedCollection new: 52.
#(heart club spade diamond) do:
    [ :aSuit |
        1 to: 13
        do: [ :n | InitialCardDeck add: (Card suit: aSuit rank: n)]]
```

instance creation

new
> "Create an instance of CardDeck with an initial deck of 52 playing cards."
> ↑super new cards: InitialCardDeck copy

instance methods

accessing

next
> "Deal (give out) the next card."
> ↑cards removeFirst

return: aCard
> "Put the argument, aCard, at the bottom of the deck."
> cards addLast: aCard

shuffle
> | sample tempDeck |
> sample ← SampleSpaceWithoutReplacement data: cards.
> tempDeck ← OrderedCollection new: cards size.
> cards size timesRepeat: [tempDeck addLast: sample next].
> self cards: tempDeck

testing

isEmpty
> "Answer whether any more cards remain in the deck."
> ↑cards isEmpty

private

cards: aCollection
> cards ← aCollection

The class CardDeck must be initialized by evaluating the expression

CardDeck initialize

In the implementation of CardDeck, cards is the instance variable and is therefore the deck of cards used in playing a game. To play a game, an instance of CardDeck is created

CardDeck new

and then each card is dealt by sending this new instance the message next. When a card is put back in the deck, the CardDeck is sent the message return:. Shuffling always shuffles whichever cards are currently in the deck. If a full CardDeck is to be reused after a round of play, any cards taken from the deck must be returned.

Note the implementation of the message shuffle. A sample space without replacement, sample, is created for a copy of the current deck of cards. A new OrderedCollection, tempDeck, is created for storing randomly selected cards from this sample space. Sampling is done from sample for each possible card; each selected card is added to the tempDeck. Once all the available cards have been shuffled into it, tempDeck is stored as the current game deck.

Suppose we create a simple card game in which there are four players and a dealer. The dealer deals out cards to each of the players. If at least one of the players has between 18 and 21 points, the game ends with the "prize" divided among each of these players. Points are counted by adding up the ranks of the cards. A player with more than 21 points is not dealt new cards.

Each player is represented by an instance of class CardHand that represents a card hand. A CardHand knows the cards it is dealt and can determine its total point count (in response to the message points).

class name	CardHand
superclass	Object
instance variable names	cards
class methods	

instance creation

new
    ↑super new setCards

instance methods

accessing

take: aCard
    "The argument, aCard, is added to the receiver."
    cards add: aCard

returnAllCardsTo: cardDeck
    "Place all of the receiver's cards into the deck of cards referred to by the argument, cardDeck, and remove these cards from the receiver's hand."
    cards do: [:eachCard | cardDeck return: eachCard].
    self setCards

inquiries

points
"Answer the sum of the ranks of the receiver's cards."
↑cards inject: 0 into: [:value :nextCard | value + nextCard rank]

private

setCards
cards ← OrderedCollection new

We create a Set of four players. Each player is represented by an instance of CardHand. The dealer's cards are the gameCards. The dealer (that is, the programmer) starts by shuffling the deck; there is no winner yet. There may be more than one winner; winners will be listed in the Set, winners.

```
players ← Set new.
4 timesRepeat: [players add: CardHand new].
gameCards ← CardDeck new.
gameCards shuffle
```

As long as there is no winner, each player with less than 21 points is given another card from the gameCards. Before dealing a card to each eligible player, the dealer looks to see if there are any winners by testing the points for each player.

```
[ winners ← players select: [ :each | each points between: 18 and: 21].
  winners isEmpty and: [gameCards isEmpty not]]
      whileTrue:
        [players do:
          [ :each |
            each points < 21 ifTrue: [each take: gameCards next]]
```

The condition for continuing to play is a block with two expressions. The first expression determines the winners, if any. The second expression tests to see if there are any winners yet (winners isEmpty) and, if not, if there are any more cards to deal out (gameCards isEmpty not). If there are no winners and more cards, the game continues. The game consists of an enumeration of each player; each player takes another card (each take: gameCards next) only if the number of card points is less than 21 (each points < 21).

To play again, all cards have to be returned to the game deck, which is then shuffled.

```
players do: [ :each | each returnAllCardsTo: gameCards].
gameCards shuffle
```

The players and dealer are ready to play again.

The Drunken Cockroach Problem

We can use some of the collection classes to solve a well-known programming problem. The problem is to measure how long it takes a drunken cockroach to touch each tile of a floor of square tiles which is N tiles wide and M tiles long. To slightly idealize the problem: in a given "step" the cockroach is equally likely to try to move to any of nine tiles, namely the tile the roach is on before the step and the tiles immediately surrounding it. The cockroach's success in moving to some of these tiles will be limited, of course, if the cockroach is next to a wall of the room. The problem is restated as counting the number of steps it takes the cockroach to land on *all* of the tiles at least once.

One straightforward algorithm to use to solve this problem starts with an empty Set and a counter set to 0. After each step, we add to the Set the tile that the cockroach lands on and increment a counter of the number of steps. Since no duplication is allowed in a Set, we would be done when the number of elements in the Set reaches N*M. The solution would be the value of the counter.

While this solves the simplest version of the problem, we might also like to know some additional information, such as how many times each tile was visited. To record this information, we can use an instance of class Bag. The size of the Bag is the total number of steps the cockroach took; the size of the Bag when it is converted to a Set is the total number of distinct tiles touched by the cockroach. When this number reaches N*M, the problem is solved. The number of occurrences of each tile in the Bag is the same as the number of times the roach visited each tile.

Each tile on the floor can be labeled with respect to its row and its column. The objects representing tiles in the solution we offer are instances of class Tile. A commented implementation of class Tile follows.

class name	Tile
superclass	Object
instance variable names	location
	floorArea

instance methods

accessing

location
    "Answer the location of the receiver on the floor."
    ↑location

location: aPoint
    "Set the receiver's location on the floor to be the argument, aPoint."
    location ← aPoint

floorArea: aRectangle

"Set the floor area to be the rectangular area represented by the argument, aRectangle."
floorArea ← aRectangle

moving

neighborAt: deltaPoint

"Create and answer a new Tile that is at the location of the receiver changed by the x and y amounts represented by the argument, deltaPoint. Keep the location of the newTile within the boundries of the floor area."
| newTile |
newTile ← Tile new floorArea: floorArea.
newTile location: ((location + deltaPoint max: floorArea origin)
                              min: floorArea corner).
↑newTile

comparing

= aTile

"Answer whether the receiver is equal to the argument, aTile."
↑(aTile isKindOf: Tile) and: [location = aTile location]

hash

↑location hash

A Tile refers to its row and column locations, each of which must be at least 1 and no larger than the width or length of the floor. Therefore, in addition to remembering its location, a Tile must remember the maximum floor space in which it can be placed. A Tile can be sent the message neighborAt: aPoint in order to determine a Tile at one of the locations next to it. This new Tile must be at a location within the boundaries of the floor.

The way we will simulate the cockroach's walk is to select a direction in terms of changes in the x-y coordinates of the cockroach's location. Given the location of the cockroach (tile x,y), there are 9 tiles to which the insect can move unless the tile is along one of the edges. We will store the possible changes of x and y in an OrderedCollection that is the data for random selection. The OrderedCollection will contain Points as elements; the Points are direction vectors representing all the possible combinations of moves. We create this collection by the expressions

Directions ← OrderedCollection new: 9.
(−1 to: 1) do: [:x | (−1 to: 1) do: [:y | Directions add: x@y]]

Directions, then, is a collection with elements

−1@−1, −1@0, −1@1, 0@−1, 0@0, 0@1, 1@−1, 1@0, 1@1

As part of the drunken walk simulation, we will generate a random number for selecting an element from this OrderedCollection of possible moves. As an alternative to using a random number generator directly, we could use the previous example's SampleSpaceWithReplacement with Directions as the sample space.

Suppose the cockroach starts on the Tile that is at location 1@1. Each time the cockroach is supposed to take a step, we obtain an element from the collection, Directions. This element is then the argument of the message neighborAt: to the Tile. In the following, assume Rand is an instance of class Random.

>   tile neighborAt:
>   (Directions at: ((Rand next * Directions size) truncated + 1)).

The resulting new tile location is the place where the cockroach landed.

Each tile position has to be remembered in order to be able to report on whether every location has been touched and how many steps were required. By storing each tile in a Bag, a tally is kept of the number of times the cockroach landed in each location. So at each step, a new tile is created that is a copy of the previous tile. This new tile is changed according to the randomly selected direction and is added to the Bag. When the number of unique elements of the Bag equals the total number of tiles, the cockroach is done.

Only two messages are needed in class DrunkenCockroach. One is a command to have the cockroach take a walk around a specific floor area until every tile on the floor has been touched. This is the message walkWithin:startingAt:. The second is an inquiry as to the number of steps the cockroach has taken so far; this is the message numberOfSteps. We can also inquire about the number of times the roach stepped on a particular tile by sending the DrunkenCockroach the message timesSteppedOn:. The collection of direction vectors (as described earlier) is created as a class variable of DrunkenCockroach; the random number generator Rand is also a class variable of DrunkenCockroach.

class name	DrunkenCockroach
superclass	Object
instance variable names	currentTile
	tilesVisited
class variable names	Directions
	Rand
class methods	

class initialization

initialize

> "Create the collection of direction vectors and the random number generator."

Three Examples That Use Collections

```
Directions ← OrderedCollection new: 9.
(−1 to: 1) do: [ :x | (−1 to: 1) do: [ :y | Directions add: x@y]].
Rand ← Random new
```

instance creation

new

```
↑super new setVariables
```

instance methods

simulation

walkWithin: aRectangle startingAt: aPoint

```
| numberTiles |
tilesVisited ← Bag new.
currentTile location: aPoint.
currentTile floorArea: aRectangle.
numberTiles ← (aRectangle width + 1) * (aRectangle height + 1).
tilesVisited add: currentTile.
[tilesVisited asSet size < numberTiles] whileTrue:
    [currentTile ← currentTile neighborAt:
        (Directions at: (Rand next * Directions size) truncated + 1).
    tilesVisited add: currentTile]
```

data

numberOfSteps

```
↑tilesVisited size
```

timesSteppedOn: aTile

```
↑tilesVisited occurrencesOf: aTile
```

private

setVariables

```
currentTile ← Tile new.
tilesVisited ← Bag new
```

We can now send the following messages in order to experiment with a drunken cockroach. Initialize the class and create an instance.

```
DrunkenCockroach initialize.
cockroach ← DrunkenCockroach new
```

Obtain the results of 10 experiments with a 5 by 5 room.

```
results ← OrderedCollection new: 10.
10 timesRepeat:
        [cockroach walkWithin: (1@1 corner: 5@5) startingAt: (1@1).
        results add: cockroach numberOfSteps]
```

The average of the 10 results is the average number of steps it took the drunken cockroach to solve the problem.

```
(results inject: 0 into: [ :sum :exp | sum + exp]) / 10
```

Note that in the implementation of the DrunkenCockroach message walkWithin:startingAt:, the termination condition is whether the Bag, when converted to a Set, has N*M elements. A faster way to make this test would be to add the message uniqueElements to the class Bag so that the conversion to a Set is not done each time through the iteration.

(For those readers wishing to try this change, the method to be added to class Bag is

uniqueElements
    ↑contents size

Then the message walkWithin:startingAt: can be changed so that the termination condition is tilesVisited uniqueElements < numberTiles.)

Traversing Binary Trees

A *tree* is an important nonlinear data structure that is useful in computer algorithms. A tree structure means that there is a branching relationship between elements. There is one element designated as the root of the tree. If there is only one element, then it is the root. If there are more elements, then they are partitioned into disjoint (sub)trees. A *binary tree* is either the root only, the root with one binary (sub)tree, or the root together with two binary (sub)trees. A complete description of the genealogy of tree structures is provided by Knuth in Volume 1 of the *Art of Computer Programming*. Here we assume the reader is familiar with the idea so that we can demonstrate how to specify the data structure as a Smalltalk-80 class.

We will define a class Tree in a way that corresponds to the definition of LinkedList. Elements of a Tree will be Nodes that are like the Links of LinkedLists, able to make connections to other elements. The Tree will reference the root node only.

A node is simple to represent as a Smalltalk-80 object with two instance variables, one refers to the *left* node and another to the *right* node. We choose to treat the order of the nodes to support *in-order traversal*. That is, in enumerating the nodes, visit the left subnode first, the root second, and the right subnode third. If a node has no subnodes, then it is called a *leaf*. We define the *size* of the node to be 1 plus the size of its subnodes, if any. Thus a leaf is a node of size 1, and a node with two leaves as subnodes has size 3. The size of a tree is the size of its root node. This definition of *size* corresponds to the general notion of size for collections.

Messages to a Node give access to the left node, the right node, and the last or end node. It is also possible to remove a subnode (remove:ifAbsent:) and the root (rest).

class name	Node
superclass	Object
instance variable names	leftNode
	rightNode

class methods

instance creation

left: lNode right: rNode
    "Create an instance of a Node with the arguments lNode and rNode as the left and right subnodes, respectively."
    | newNode |
    newNode ← self new.
    newNode left: lNode.
    newNode right: rNode.
    ↑newNode

instance methods

testing

isLeaf
    "Answer whether the receiver is a leaf, that is, whether it is a node without any subnodes."
    ↑leftNode isNil & rightNode isNil

accessing

left
    ↑leftNode

left: aNode
    leftNode ← aNode

right
    ↑rightNode

right: aNode
    rightNode ← aNode

size
↑1 + (leftNode isNil
            ifTrue: [0]
            ifFalse: [leftNode size])
      + (rightNode isNil
            ifTrue: [0]
            ifFalse: [rightNode size])

end
| aNode |
aNode ← self.
[aNode right isNil] whileFalse: [aNode ← aNode right].
↑aNode

removing

remove: subnode ifAbsent: exceptionBlock
"Assumes the root, self, is not the one to remove."
self isLeaf ifTrue: [↑exceptionBlock value].
leftNode = subnode
    ifTrue: [leftNode ← leftNode rest. ↑subnode].
rightNode = subnode
    ifTrue: [rightNode ← rightNode rest. ↑subnode].
leftNode isNil
    ifTrue: [↑rightNode remove: subnode ifAbsent: exceptionBlock].
↑leftNode
    remove: subnode
    ifAbsent:
        [rightNode isNil
            ifTrue: [exceptionBlock value]
            ifFalse:
                [rightNode remove: subnode
                            ifAbsent: exceptionBlock]]

rest
leftNode isNil
    ifTrue: [↑rightNode]
    ifFalse: [leftNode end right: rightNode.
            ↑leftNode]

enumerating

do: aBlock
leftNode isNil ifFalse: [leftNode do: aBlock].
aBlock value: self.
rightNode isNil ifFalse: [rightNode do: aBlock]

If Node is a leaf, it is denoted by

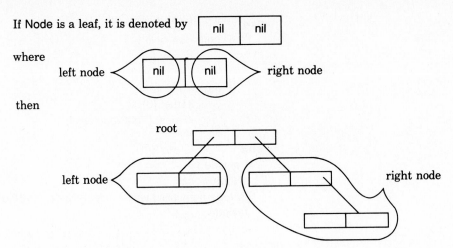

where

left node

right node

then

root

left node

right node

Enumeration uses in-order traversal, first applying the left subnode as the value of the block, then the root, and third the right subnode. The block must be defined for a block argument that is a Node.

Next we provide a Tree as a kind of SequenceableCollection whose elements are Nodes. A Tree has one instance variable which we name root; root is either nil or it is an instance of Node. As a subclass of SequenceableCollection, class Tree implements messages add: anElement, remove: anElement ifAbsent: exceptionBlock, and do: aBlock. Basically, the methods associated with each of these messages checks to see whether the tree is empty (root isNil) and, if not, passes the appropriate message to root. The check on "empty" is inherited from Collection. The intention is that the programmer who uses a tree structure accesses the elements of that structure only via an instance of class Tree.

class name	Tree
superclass	SequenceableCollection
instance variable names	root
instance methods	

testing

isEmpty
↑root isNil

accessing

first
| save |
self emptyCheck.
save ← root.

    [save left isNil] whileFalse: [save ← save left].
    ↑save

last
    self emptyCheck.
    ↑root end

size
    self isEmpty
      ifTrue: [↑0]
      ifFalse: [↑root size]

adding

add: aNode
    ↑self addLast: aNode

addFirst: aNode
    "If the collection is empty, then the argument, aNode, is the new root;
    otherwise, it is the left node of the current first node."
    self isEmpty
      ifTrue: [↑root ← aNode]
      ifFalse: [self first left: aNode].
    ↑aNode

addLast: aNode
    "If the collection is empty, then the argument, aNode, is the new root;
    otherwise it is the last element of the current root."
    self isEmpty
      ifTrue: [root ← aNode]
      ifFalse: [self last right: aNode].
    ↑aNode

removing

remove: aNode ifAbsent: exceptionBlock
    "First check the root. If not found, move down the tree checking each
    node."
    self isEmpty ifTrue: [↑exceptionBlock value].
    root = aNode
      ifTrue: [root ← root rest. ↑aNode]
      ifFalse: [↑root remove: aNode ifAbsent: exceptionBlock]

removeFirst
    self emptyCheck.
    ↑self remove: self first ifAbsent: []

removeLast
    self emptyCheck.
    ↑self remove: self last ifAbsent: []

enumerating

do: aBlock
    self isEmpty ifFalse: [root do: aBlock]

Note that the removing messages do not remove the subtree beginning with the node to be removed, only the node itself.

A Binary Word Tree

The definition of a Node, like that of a Link, is all structure without content. We have left the content of each Node to be specified by a subclass. Suppose we wish to use a kind of Node to store words represented as Strings. We call this class WordNode. An instance of WordNode is created by sending WordNode the message for:, if no subnodes are specified, or for:left:right: if the two subnodes are specified. So a WordNode illustrated as

is created by evaluating the expression

    WordNode for: ′cat′

A WordNode that looks like

is created by evaluating the expression

    WordNode for: ′cat′
            left: (WordNode for: ′dog′)
            right: (WordNode for: ′goat′)

An implementation for the class WordNode follows. Notice that equality (=) is redefined to mean that the words in the Nodes are the same; this means that the inherited removing messages will remove a subnode if its word is the same as the word of the argument.

class name	WordNode
superclass	Node
instance variable names	word
class methods	

instance creation

    for: aString
      ↑self new word: aString

for: aString left: lNode right: rNode
　| newNode |
　newNode ← super left: lNode right: rNode.
　newNode word: aString.
　↑newNode

instance methods

accessing

word
　↑word
word: aString
　word ← aString

comparing

= aWordNode
　↑(aWordNode isKindOf: WordNode) and: [word = aWordNode word]
hash
　↑word hash

A sequence of expressions follows to illustrate the use of WordNode. Note that no effort is made in the definition of WordNode to support inserting elements so that each word collates alphabetically when the tree is traversed. An interested reader might add an insert: aWordNode message to WordNode that maintains the alphabetic sort.

tree ← Tree new.

tree add: (WordNode for: ′cat′)

tree addFirst: (WordNode for: ′frog′)

tree addLast: (WordNode for: ′horse′ left: (WordNode for: ′monkey′) right: nil)

tree addFirst: (WordNode for: 'ape')

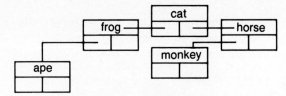

tree remove: (WordNode for: 'horse')

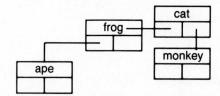

tree remove: (WordNode for: 'frog')

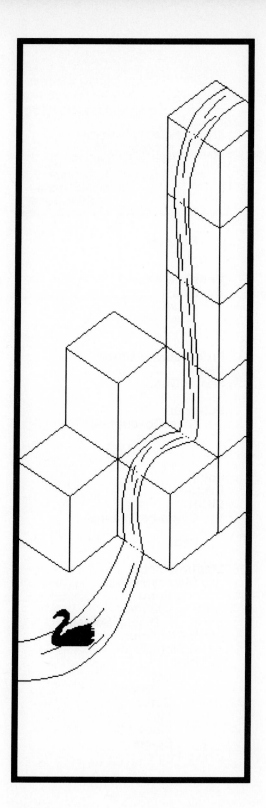

12

Protocol for Streams

```
Object

    Magnitude
        Character
        Date
        Time

        Number
            Float
            Fraction
            Integer
                LargeNegativeInteger
                LargePositiveInteger
                SmallInteger


        LookupKey
            Association

    Link

        Process

    Collection

        SequenceableCollection
            LinkedList

                Semaphore

            ArrayedCollection
                Array

                WordArray
                    DisplayBitmap

                RunArray
                String
                    Symbol
                Text
                ByteArray

            Interval
            OrderedCollection
                SortedCollection
        Bag
        MappedCollection
        Set
            Dictionary
                IdentityDictionary
```

```
Stream
        PositionableStream
            ReadStream
            WriteStream
                ReadWriteStream
                ExternalStream
                    FileStream
```

```
        Random


    UndefinedObject
    Boolean
        False
        True


    ProcessorScheduler
    Delay
    SharedQueue

    Behavior
        ClassDescription
            Class
                MetaClass

    Point
    Rectangle
    BitBlt
        CharacterScanner

        Pen

    DisplayObject
        DisplayMedium
            Form
                Cursor
                DisplayScreen
        InfiniteForm
        OpaqueForm
        Path
            Arc
                Circle
            Curve
            Line
            LinearFit
            Spline
```

The collection classes provide the basic data structure for storing objects together as nonlinear and linear groups. The protocol for these classes makes it possible directly to access (store and retrieve) individual elements. It also, through the enumeration messages, supports noninterruptible accessing of all of the elements, in order. However, it does not support intermingling the two kinds of accessing operations—enumerating and storing. Nor does the collection protocol support accessing individual elements, one at a time, unless an external position reference is separately maintained.

Unless an easily computed external name for each element exists, interruptible enumeration of individual elements can not be carried out efficiently. It is possible, for example, sequentially to read elements of an OrderedCollection using a combination of first and after:, as long as the elements of the collection are unique. An alternative approach involves the collection itself remembering, in some way, which element was last accessed. We call this the "position reference" in the discussion that follows. The possibility of shared access to a sequence of elements, however, means that it is necessary to maintain a separate, external memory of the last element accessed.

Class Stream represents the ability to maintain a position reference into a collection of objects. We use the phrase *streaming over a collection* to mean accessing the elements of a collection in such a way that it is possible to enumerate or store each element, one at a time, possibly intermingling these operations. By creating several Streams over the same collection, it is possible to maintain multiple position references into the same collection.

There are a number of ways to maintain a position reference for streaming over a collection. A common one is to use an integer as an index. This approach can be used for any collection whose elements are externally named by an integer. All SequenceableCollections fall into this category. As we shall describe later, such a Stream is represented in the Smalltalk-80 system by the class PositionableStream. A second way to maintain a position reference is to use a *seed* for a generator of objects. An example of this kind of Stream in the Smalltalk-80 system is class Random which was already presented in Chapter 8. And a third way is to maintain a non-numerical position reference, such as a reference to a node in a sequence; this approach is illustrated in this chapter by an example class that supports streaming over a linked list or a tree structure.

Class Stream

Class Stream, a subclass of class Object, is a superclass that specifies the accessing protocol for streaming over collections. Included in this protocol are messages for reading (retrieving) and writing (storing) into the collection, although not all the subclasses of class Stream can support both kinds of accessing operations. The basic reading message is next; its response is the next element in the collection that is referenced by the Stream. Given the ability to access the next element, more general reading messages can be supported. These are next: anInteger, which responds with a collection of anInteger number of elements; nextMatchFor: anObject, which reads the next element and answers whether it is equal to the argument, anObject; and contents, which answers a collection of all of the elements.

Stream instance protocol

accessing—reading

next	Answer the next object accessible by the receiver.
next: anInteger	Answer the next anInteger number of objects accessible by the receiver. Generally, the answer will be a collection of the same class as the one accessed by the receiver.
nextMatchFor: anObject	Access the next object and answer whether it is equal to the argument, anObject.
contents	Answer all of the objects in the collection accessed by the receiver. Generally, the answer will be a collection of the same class as the one accessed by the receiver.

The basic writing message is nextPut: anObject; this means to store the argument, anObject, as the next element accessible by the receiver. If both read and write messages are possible, a next message following a nextPut: anElement does not read the element just stored, but rather the one after it in the collection. Writing messages also include nextPutAll: aCollection, which stores all of the elements in the argument into the collection accessed by the receiver, and next: anInteger put: anObject, which stores the argument, anObject, as the next anInteger number of elements.

Stream instance protocol

accessing—writing

nextPut: anObject	Store the argument, anObject, as the next element accessible by the receiver. Answer anObject.
nextPutAll: aCollection	Store the elements in the argument, aCollection, as the next elements accessible by the receiver. Answer aCollection.
next: anInteger put: anObject	Store the argument, anObject, as the next anInteger number of elements accessible by the receiver. Answer anObject.

The reading and writing messages each determine if a next element can be read or written and, if not, an error is reported. The programmer might therefore wish to determine whether accessing is still feasible; this is accomplished by sending the Stream the message atEnd.

Stream instance protocol
---

testing
    atEnd
        Answer whether the receiver cannot access any more objects.

Noninterrupted reading of elements that are applied as arguments to a block can be done by sending the message do: aBlock, similar to the enumerating message supported by the collection classes.

Stream instance protocol
---

enumerating
    do: aBlock
        Evaluate the argument, aBlock, for each of the remaining elements that can be accessed by the receiver.

The implementation of this enumeration message depends on sending the messages atEnd and next to the message receiver. We show this method as an example of the use of these messages.

do: aBlock
    [self atEnd] whileFalse: [aBlock value: self next]

Each kind of Stream must specify its instance creation messages. In general, a Stream can not be created simply by sending the message new because the Stream must be informed of which collection it accesses and what is its initial position reference.

As a simple example, let's assume that the collection accessed by a Stream is an Array and that the Stream is called accessor. The contents of the Array are the Symbols

Bob Dave Earl Frank Harold Jim Kim Mike Peter Rick Sam Tom

and the position reference is such that Bob is the next accessible element. Then

expression	result
accessor next	Bob
accessor next	Dave
accessor nextMatchFor: #Bob	false

accessor		
accessor nextMatchFor: #Frank	true	
accessor next	Harold	
accessor nextPut: #James	James	
accessor contents	(Bob Dave Earl Frank Harold James Kim Mike Peter Rick Sam Tom)	
accessor nextPutAll: #(Karl Larry Paul)	(Karl Larry Paul)	
accessor contents	(Bob Dave Earl Frank Harold James Karl Larry Paul Rick Sam Tom)	
accessor next: 2 put: #John	John	
accessor contents	(Bob Dave Earl Frank Harold James Karl Larry Paul John John Tom)	
accessor next	Tom	
accessor atEnd	true	

Positionable Streams

Please note that in versions of the Smalltalk-80 system that implement external streaming, a newer hierarchy to distinguish between ExternalStreams and InternalStreams may exist. In the introduction to this chapter we indicated three possible approaches that a Stream might use in order to maintain a position reference. The first one we will present uses an integer index which is incremented each time the Stream is accessed. The Stream accesses only those kinds of collections whose elements have integers as external keys; these include all of the subclasses of SequenceableCollection.

Class PositionableStream is a subclass of class Stream. It provides additional protocol appropriate to Streams that can reposition their position references, but, it is an abstract class because it does not provide an implementation of the inherited messages next and nextPut: anObject. The implementation of these messages is left to the subclasses of PositionableStream—ReadStream, WriteStream, and ReadWriteStream.

A PositionableStream is created by sending the class one of two instance creation messages, on: aCollection or on: aCollection from: firstIndex to: lastIndex. The argument, aCollection, is the collection the Stream accesses; in the second case, a copy of a subcollection of aCollection is accessed, i.e., the one delimited by the two arguments firstIndex and lastIndex.

PositionableStream class protocol

___

instance creation
> on: aCollection
>> Answer an instance of a kind of PositionableStream that streams over the argument, aCollection.

> on: aCollection from: firstIndex to: lastIndex
>> Answer an instance of a kind of PositionableStream that streams over a copy of a subcollection of the argument, aCollection, from firstIndex to lastIndex.

PositionableStream supports additional protocol for accessing and testing the contents of the collection. Accessing handles positioning up to, through, and skipping over an element of the stream. The following are some examples of the protocol.

PositionableStream instance protocol

___

testing
> isEmpty
>> Answer true if the collection the receiver accesses has no elements; otherwise, answer false.

accessing
> peek
>> Answer the next element in the collection (as in the message next), but do not change the position reference. Answer nil if the receiver is at the end.

> peekFor: anObject
>> Determine the response to the message peek. If it is the same as the argument, anObject, then increment the position reference and answer true. Otherwise answer false and do not change the position reference.

> upTo: anObject
>> Answer a collection of elements starting with the next element accessed by the receiver, and up to, not inclusive of, the next element that is equal to anObject. If anObject is not in the collection, answer the entire rest of the collection.

Since a PositionableStream is known to store an explicit position reference, protocol for accessing that reference is supported. In particular, the reference can be reset to access the beginning, the end, or any other position of the collection.

PositionableStream instance protocol

___

positioning
> position
>> Answer the receiver's current position reference for accessing the collection.

> position: anInteger
>> Set the receiver's current position reference for accessing the collection to be the argument, anInteger. If the argument is not within

	the bounds of the receiver's collection, report an error.
reset	Set the receiver's position reference to the beginning of the collection.
setToEnd	Set the receiver's position reference to the end of the collection.
skip: anInteger	Set the receiver's position reference to be the current position plus the argument, anInteger, possibly adjusting the result so as to remain within the bounds of the collection.
skipThrough: anObject	Set the receiver's position reference to be past the next occurrence of the argument, anObject, in the collection. Answer whether such an occurrence existed.

Class ReadStream

Class ReadStream is a concrete subclass of PositionableStream that represents an accessor that can only read elements from its collection. We can create an example similar to the previous one to demonstrate the use of the additional protocol provided in class PositionableStream and inherited by all ReadStreams. None of the nextPut:, next:put:, nor nextPutAll: messages can be successfully sent to a ReadStream.

accessor ←
      ReadStream on: #(Bob Dave Earl Frank Harold Jim Kim Mike
                 Peter Rick Sam Tom)

expression	*result*
accessor next	Bob
accessor nextMatchFor: #Dave	true
accessor peek	Earl
accessor next	Earl
accessor peekFor: #Frank	true
accessor next	Harold
accessor upTo: #Rick	(Jim Kim Mike Peter)
accessor position	10
accessor skip: 1	the accessor itself
accessor next	Tom
accessor atEnd	true
accessor reset	the accessor itself
accessor skipThrough: #Frank	the accessor itself
accessor next	Harold

Class WriteStream

Class WriteStream is a subclass of PositionableStream representing accessors for writing elements into a collection. None of the next, next:, nor do: messages can be successfully sent to a WriteStream.

WriteStreams are used throughout the Smalltalk-80 system as a part of the methods for printing or storing a string description of any object. Each object in the system can respond to the messages printOn: aStream and storeOn: aStream. The methods associated with these messages consist of a sequence of messages to the argument, which is a kind of Stream that allows writing elements into the collection it accesses. These messages are nextPut:, where the argument is a Character, and nextPutAll:, where the argument is a String or a Symbol. An example will illustrate this idea.

Class Object printing protocol, as described in Chapter 6, includes the message printString. An implementation of this message is

printString
```
    | aStream |
    aStream ← WriteStream on: (String new: 16).
    self printOn: aStream.
    ↑aStream contents
```

If a collection is sent the message printString, then the answer is a String that is a description of the instance. The method creates a WriteStream that the collection can store into, sends the message printOn: to the collection, and then responds with the contents of the resulting WriteStream. The message storeString to any object is similarly implemented in class Object, the difference being that the second expression consists of the message storeOn: aStream rather than printOn: aStream.

The general way in which collections print a description of themselves is to print their class name followed by a left parenthesis, followed by a description of each element separated by spaces, and terminated by a right parenthesis. So if a Set has four elements—the Symbols one, two, three, and four—then it prints on a Stream as

    Set (one two three four)

An OrderedCollection with the same elements prints on a Stream as

    OrderedCollection (one two three four)

and so on.

Recall that the definition of printOn: and storeOn: given in Chapter 6 is that any suitable description can be provided for printOn:, but the description created by storeOn: must be a well-formed expression that, when evaluated, re-constructs the object it purports to describe.

Here is a possible implementation in class Collection for printOn:.

printOn: aStream
    aStream nextPutAll: self class name.
    aStream space.
    aStream nextPut: $(.
    self do:
        [:element |
            element printOn: aStream.
            aStream space].
    aStream nextPut: $)

Notice that the message **space** is sent to the WriteStream (aStream). It, and a number of other messages are provided in class WriteStream to support concise expressions for storing delimiters into such Streams. They are

WriteStream instance protocol
_____

character writing

cr	Store the return character as the next element of the receiver.
crtab	Store the return character and a single tab character as the next two elements of the receiver.
crtab: anInteger	Store the return character as the next element of the receiver, followed by anInteger number of tab characters.
space	Store the space character as the next element of the receiver.
tab	Store the tab character as the next element of the receiver.

Thus to construct the String

```
' name          city

bob             New York
joe             Chicago
bill            Rochester
'
```

from two corresponding Arrays,

    names ← # (bob joe bill)
    cities ← # ('New York' 'Chicago' 'Rochester')

evaluate the expressions

```
aStream ← WriteStream on: (String new: 16).
aStream nextPutAll: ' name ' .
aStream tab.
aStream nextPutAll: ' city ' .
aStream cr; cr.
names with: cities do:
        [ :name :city |
          aStream nextPutAll: name.
          aStream tab.
          aStream nextPutAll: city.
          aStream cr]
```

then the desired result is obtained by evaluating aStream contents.

Suppose a collection already exists and we wish to append further information into it by using Stream protocol. Class WriteStream supports instance creation protocol that accepts a collection and sets the position reference for writing to the end.

WriteStream class protocol

---

instance creation
  with: aCollection
                                    Answer an instance of WriteStream accessing
                                    the argument, aCollection, but positioned to
                                    store the next element at the end of it.
  with: aCollection from: firstIndex to: lastIndex
                                    Answer an instance of WriteStream accessing
                                    the subcollection of the argument, aCollection,
                                    from locaton firstIndex to lastIndex, but posi-
                                    tioned to store the next element at the end of
                                    the subcollection.

Thus if a String referred to as header already existed, containing

'name   city

    ,

then the previous example String would be constructed by

```
aStream ← WriteStream with: header.
names with: cities do:
        [ :name :city |
          aStream nextPutAll: name.
          aStream tab.
          aStream nextPutAll: city.
          aStream cr].
aStream contents
```

Class ReadWriteStream

Class ReadWriteStream is a subclass of WriteStream that represents an accessor that can both read and write elements into its collection. It supports all the protocol of both ReadStream and WriteStream, as given above. As in all system classes, check the actual classes using the browser to determine additional capability.

Streams of Generated Elements

Of the three ways to create a position reference for streaming over a collection, the second way cited in the introduction to this chapter was to specify a *seed* by which the next elements of the collection can be generated. This kind of Stream only permits reading the elements, not writing. The reference, however, can be repositioned by resetting the seed.

Class Random, introduced in Chapter 8, is a subclass of Stream that determines its elements based on an algorithm employing a number as a seed. Random provides a concrete implementation for next and atEnd. Because the size of the collection is infinite, it never ends; moreover, Random can not respond to the message contents. It can respond to the message do:, but the method will never end without the programmer's purposeful intervention.

The following is an implementation of class Random; the reader is referred to Chapters 11 and 21 for examples making use of instances of the class. The implementations for do: and nextMatchFor: anObject are inherited from class Stream.

class name	Random
superclass	Stream
instance variable names	seed
class methods	

instance creation

   new
      ↑self basicNew setSeed

instance methods

testing

   atEnd
      ↑false

accessing

   next
      | temp |
      "Lehmer's linear congruential method with modulus m = 2 raisedTo:

16, a = 27181 odd, and 5 = a \\ 8, c = 13849 odd, and c/m approximately 0.21132″
[seed ← 13849 + (27181 * seed) bitAnd: 8r177777.
 temp ← seed / 65536.0.
 temp = 0] whileTrue.
↑temp

private

setSeed
    "For pseudo-random seed, get a time from the system clock. It is a
    large positive integer; just use the lower 16 bits."
    seed ← Time millisecondClockValue bitAnd: 8r177777

Another possible example of a stream of generated elements are the
probability distributions that are presented in Chapter 21. The superclass ProbabilityDistribution is implemented as a subclass of Stream. The
message next: anInteger is inherited from Stream. Each kind of
ProbabilityDistribution determines whether it is "read-only" and, if so,
implements nextPut: as self shouldNotImplement. Class SampleSpace,
another example in Chapter 21, maintains a collection of data items
and implements nextPut: anObject as adding to the collection.

Streams for Collections Without External Keys

The third way to maintain a position reference for streaming over a collection cited in the introduction to this chapter was to maintain a non-
numerical reference. This would be useful in cases where the elements
of the collection cannot be accessed by external keys or where such access is not the most efficient means to retrieve an element.

Streaming over instances of class LinkedList provides an example in
which the elements can be accessed by indexes as the external keys, but
each such access requires a search down the chain of linked elements.
It is more efficient to maintain a reference to a particular element in
the collection (a kind of Link) and then to access the next element by requesting the current elements nextLink. Both reading and writing into
the LinkedList can be supported by such a Stream.

Suppose we create a subclass of Stream that we call LinkedListStream.
Each instance maintains a reference to a LinkedList and a position reference to an element in the collection. Since both reading and writing
are supported, the messages next, nextPut:, atEnd, and contents must be
implemented. (Note that these four messages are defined in class
Stream as self subclassResponsibility.) A new instance of
LinkedListStream is created by sending it the message on: aLinkedList.

class name	LinkedListStream
superclass	Stream
instance variable names	collection
	currentNode

class methods

instance creation

on: aLinkedList
 ↑self basicNew setOn: aLinkedList

instance methods

testing

atEnd
 ↑currentNode isNil

accessing

next
 | saveCurrentNode |
 saveCurrentNode ← currentNode.
 self atEnd
 ifFalse: [currentNode ← currentNode nextLink].
 ↑saveCurrentNode

nextPut: aLink
 | index previousLink |
 self atEnd ifTrue: [↑collection addLast: aLink].
 index ← collection indexOf: currentNode.
 index = 1
 ifTrue: [collection addFirst: aLink]
 ifFalse: [previousLink ← collection at: index - 1.
 previousLink nextLink: aLink].
 aLink nextLink: currentNode nextLink.
 currentNode ← aLink nextLink.
 ↑aLink

contents
 ↑collection

private

setOn: aLinkedList
 collection ← aLinkedList.
 currentNode ← aLinkedList first

Now suppose in order to demonstrate the use of this new kind of Stream we make up a LinkedList of nodes that are instances of class WordLink; class WordLink is a subclass of Link that stores a String or a Symbol.

class name	WordLink
superclass	Link
instance variable names	word
class methods	

instance creation

for: aString
⇑self new word: aString

instance methods

accessing

word
⇑word
word: aString
word ← aString

comparing

= aWordLink
⇑word = aWordLink word

printing

printOn: aStream
aStream nextPutAll: ' a WordLink for'.
aStream nextPutAll: word

From the above we can see that an instance of WordLink for the word #one is created by

WordLink for: #one

Its print string is

' a WordLink for one'

We can then create a LinkedList of WordLinks and then a LinkedListStream that accesses this LinkedList.

```
list ← LinkedList new.
list add: (WordLink for: #one).
list add: (WordLink for: #two).
list add: (WordLink for: #three).
list add: (WordLink for: #four).
list add: (WordLink for: #five).
accessor ← LinkedListStream on: list
```

Then an example sequence of messages to accessor is

expression	result
accessor next	a WordLink for one
accessor next	a WordLink for two
accessor nextMatchFor: (WordLink for: #three)	true
accessor nextPut: (WordLink for: #insert)	a WordLink for insert
accessor contents	LinkedList (a WordLink for one a WordLink for two a WordLink for three a WordLink for insert a WordLink for five)
accessor next	a WordLink for five
accessor atEnd	true

Similarly, traversing the nodes of a tree structure, such as that of class Tree given in Chapter 11, can be done by a kind of Stream that maintains a reference to a current node and then accesses the next element by accessing the current node's left tree, root, or right tree. This kind of Stream is slightly more complicated to implement than that for a LinkedList because it is necessary to retain knowledge of whether the left or right tree has been traversed and back references to the *father* of the current node. The order of traversal of the tree structure can be implemented in the Stream, ignoring the method by which subtrees were added to the structure. Thus, although we used in-order traversal in the implementations of class Tree and class Node, we can stream over a Tree with postorder traversal by implementing the messages next and nextPut: appropriately.

External Streams and File Streams

The Streams we have examined so far make the assumption that the elements of the collection can be any objects, independent of representation. For communicating with input/output devices, such as a disk, however, this assumption is not valid. In these cases, the elements are stored as binary, byte-sized elements that may prefer to be accessed as numbers, strings, words (two bytes), or bytes. Thus we have a need to support a mixture of nonhomogeneous accessing messages for reading and writing these different-sized "chunks" of information.

Class ExternalStream is a subclass of class ReadWriteStream. Its purpose is to add the nonhomogeneous accessing protocol. This includes protocol for positioning as well as accessing.

ExternalStream instance protocol

nonhomogeneous accessing

nextNumber: n	Answer the next n bytes of the collection accessed by the receiver as a positive SmallInteger or LargePositiveInteger.
nextNumber: n put: v	Store the argument, v, which is a positive SmallInteger or LargePositiveInteger, as the next n bytes of the collection accessed by the receiver. If necessary, pad with zeros.
nextString	Answer a String made up of the next elements of the collection accessed by the receiver.
nextStringPut: aString	Store the argument, aString, in the collection accessed by the receiver.
nextWord	Answer the next two bytes from the collecton accessed by the receiver as an Integer.
nextWordPut: anInteger	Store the argument, anInteger, as the next two bytes of the collection accessed by the receiver.

nonhomogeneous positioning

padTo: bsize	Skip to the next boundary of bsize characters, and answer how many characters were skipped.
padTo: bsize put: aCharacter	Skip—writing the argument, aCharacter, into the collection accessed by the receiver in order to pad the collection—to the next boundary of bsize characters and answer how many characters were written (padded).
padToNextWord	Make the position reference even (on word boundary), answering the padding character, if any.
padToNextWordPut: aCharacter	Make the position reference even (on word boundary), writing the padding character, aCharacter, if necessary.
skipWords: nWords	Position after nWords number of words.
wordPosition	Answer the current position in words.
wordPosition: wp	Set the current position in words to be the argument, wp.

Class FileStream is a subclass of ExternalStream. All accesses to external files are done using an instance of FileStream. A FileStream acts as though it were accessing a large sequence of bytes or characters; the elements of the sequence are assumed to be Integers or Characters. The protocol for a FileStream is essentially that of class ExternalStream and its superclasses. In addition, protocol is provided to set and to test the status of the sequence the FileStream is streaming over.

Classes ExternalStream and FileStream are provided in the Smalltalk-80 system as the framework in which a file system can be created. Additional protocol in class FileStream assumes that a file system is based on a framework consisting of a directory or dictionary of files, where a file is a sequence of file pages. A file is uniquely identified both by an alphanumeric name and a serial number. User programs typically do not access a file or its pages directly; rather they access it as a sequence of characters or bytes through a FileStream. Thus the programmer can create a FileStream as an accessor to a file using an expression of the form

```
FileStream fileNamed: 'name.smalltalk'
```

The FileStream can then be sent sequences of reading and writing messages as specified in the protocol of this chapter.

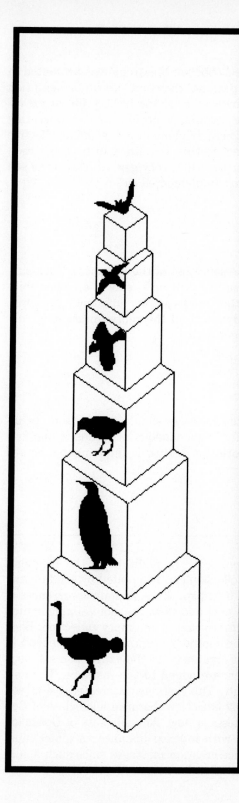

13

Implementation of the Basic Collection Protocol

Class Collection

Subclasses of Collection
Class Bag
Class Set
Class Dictionary
SequenceableCollections
Subclasses of SequenceableCollection
Class MappedCollection

The protocol for the classes in the Collection hierarchy was presented in Chapters 9 and 10. This chapter presents the complete implementation of class Collection and the implementation of the basic protocol for instance creation, accessing, testing, adding, removing, and enumerating for each subclass of Collection. These implementations make effective use of a framework in class Collection that is refined in its subclasses. Messages in Collection are implemented in a very general way or as self subclassResponsibility. Messages are implemented as

> self subclassResponsibility

if the method depends on the representation of the instances. Each subclass must override such messages to fulfill any "subclass responsibilities." Subclasses may override other messages, for efficiency purposes, with a new method that takes advantage of the representation. A subclass may implement some messages with

> self shouldNotImplement

which results in a report that the message should not be sent to instances of the class. For example, SequenceableCollections cannot respond to remove:ifAbsent:; therefore the method is implemented as self shouldNotImplement.

Class Collection

☐ Collection *instance creation protocol* In addition to the messages new and new:, an instance of a Collection can be created by sending any one of four messages made up of one, two, three, or four occurrences of the keyword with:. The messages new and new: are not reimplemented in Collection; they produce an instance that is an empty collection. Each of the other four instance creation methods is specified in Collection in a similar way. First an instance is created (with the expression self new) and then the arguments, in order, are added to the instance. The new instance is returned as the result. The instance is created using self new, rather than super new or self basicNew, because a subclass of Collection might reimplement the message new. Any subclass of Collection that represents fixed-size objects with indexed instance variables must reimplement the following instance creation messages since such a subclass cannot provide an implementation for new.

class name	Collection
superclass	Object
class methods	

instance creation

with: anObject
> | newCollection |
> newCollection ← self new.
> newCollection add: anObject.
> ↑newCollection

with: firstObject with: secondObject
> | newCollection |
> newCollection ← self new.
> newCollection add: firstObject.
> newCollection add: secondObject.
> ↑newCollection

with: firstObject with: secondObject with: thirdObject
> | newCollection |
> newCollection ← self new.
> newCollection add: firstObject.
> newCollection add: secondObject.
> newCollection add: thirdObject.
> ↑newCollection

with: firstObject with: secondObject with: thirdObject
with: fourthObject
> | newCollection |
> newCollection ← self new.
> newCollection add: firstObject.
> newCollection add: secondObject.
> newCollection add: thirdObject.
> newCollection add: fourthObject.
> ↑newCollection

The implementation of each of the instance creation messages depends on the ability of the newly-created instance to respond to the message add:. Class Collection cannot provide implementations of the following messages because they depend on the representation used by a subclass:

> add: anObject
> remove: anObject ifAbsent: aBlock
> do: aBlock

All other messages in the basic collection protocol are implemented in terms of these three messages. Each subclass must implement the three basic messages; each can then reimplement any others in order to improve its performance.

☐ Collection *adding protocol* The protocol for adding elements to a collection is implemented in class Collection as follows.

adding

add: anObject
   self subclassResponsibility
addAll: aCollection
   aCollection do: [:each | self add: each].
   ↑aCollection

Notice that the implementation of addAll: depends on both do: and add:. The order of adding elements from the argument, aCollection, depends on both the order in which the collection enumerates its elements (do:) and the manner in which the elements are included into this collection (add:).

☐ Collection *removing protocol* The messages remove: and removeAll: are implemented in terms of the basic message remove:ifAbsent:, which must be provided in a subclass. These methods report an error if the element to be removed is not in the collection. The method remove:ifAbsent: can be used to specify different exception behavior.

removing

remove: anObject ifAbsent: exceptionBlock
   self subclassResponsibility

remove: anObject
   self remove: anObject ifAbsent: [self errorNotFound]

removeAll: aCollection
   aCollection do: [:each | self remove: each].
   ↑aCollection

private

errorNotFound
   self error: ′Object is not in the collection′

As usual, the category private refers to messages introduced to support the implementations of other messages; it is not to be used by other objects. Most error messages that are used more than once will be specified as private messages in order to create the literal message string once only.

☐ Collection *testing protocol* All the messages in the protocol for testing the status of a collection can be implemented in Collection.

testing

isEmpty
    ↑self size = 0

includes: anObject
    self do: [:each | anObject = each ifTrue: [↑true]].
    ↑false

occurrencesOf: anObject
    | tally |
    tally ← 0.
    self do: [:each | anObject = each ifTrue: [tally ← tally + 1]].
    ↑tally

The implementations of includes: and occurrencesOf: depend on the subclass's implementation of the basic enumerating message do:. The block argument of do: in the method for includes: terminates as soon as an element equal to the argument is found. If no such element is found, the last expression (↑false) is evaluated. The response to isEmpty and includes: are Boolean objects, true or false. The message size is inherited from class Object, but is reimplemented in Collection because size, as defined in Object, is only nonzero for variable-length objects.

accessing

size
    | tally |
    tally ← 0.
    self do: [:each | tally ← tally + 1].
    ↑tally

This is a low-performance approach to computing the size of a collection which, as we shall see, is reimplemented in most of the subclasses.

☐ Collection *enumerating protocol* An implementation of all of the messages that enumerate the elements of collections, except do:, can be provided in class Collection.

enumerating

do: aBlock
    self subclassResponsibility

collect: aBlock
    | newCollection |
    newCollection ← self species new.
    self do: [:each | newCollection add: (aBlock value: each)].
    ↑newCollection

detect: aBlock
    ↑self detect: aBlock ifNone: [self errorNotFound]

detect: aBlock ifNone: exceptionBlock
    self do: [:each | (aBlock value: each) ifTrue: [↑each]].
    ↑exceptionBlock value

inject: thisValue into: binaryBlock
    | nextValue |
    nextValue ← thisValue.
    self do: [:each | nextValue ← binaryBlock value: nextValue value: each].
    ↑nextValue

reject: aBlock
    ↑self select: [:element | (aBlock value: element) = = false]

select: aBlock
    | newCollection |
    newCollection ← self species new.
    self do: [:each | (aBlock value: each) ifTrue: [newCollection add: each]].
    ↑newCollection

In the methods associated with collect: and select:, the message species is sent to self. This message was not shown in Chapter 9 because it is not part of the external protocol of collections. It is categorized as private to indicate the intention for internal use only. The message is implemented in class Object as returning the class of the receiver.

    private

species
    ↑self class

Thus the expression

    self species new

means "create a new instance of the same class as that of the receiver."

For some collections, it may not be appropriate to create a "similar" instance in this way; a new collection that is like it may not be an instance of its class. Such a collection will override the message species. In particular, an Interval responds that its species is Array (because it is not possible to modify an Interval); the species of a MappedCollection is the species of the collection it maps (since the MappedCollection is simply acting as an accessor for that collection).

If a collection cannot create an instance by simply sending the class the message new, it must reimplement messages collect: and select:. Since reject: is implemented in terms of select:, it need not be reimplemented.

The method for inject:into: evaluates the block argument once for each element in the receiver. The block is also provided with its own value from each previous evaluation; the initial value is provided as the argument of inject:. The final value of the block is returned as the value of the inject:into: message.

The reason for the introduction of two messages, detect: and detect:ifNone:, is similar to the reason for the two removing messages, remove: and remove:ifAbsent:. The general case (detect:) reports an error if no element meeting the detection criterion is found; the programmer can avoid this error report by specifying an alternative exception (detect:ifNone:).

☐ Collection *converting protocol*   The protocol for converting from any collection into a Bag, Set, OrderedCollection, or SortedCollection is implemented in a straightforward way—create a new instance of the target collection, then add to it each element of the receiver. In most cases, the new instance is the same size as the original collection. In the case of OrderedCollections, elements are added at the end of the sequence (addLast:), regardless of the order of enumerating from the source.

converting

asBag
   | aBag |
   aBag ← Bag new.
   self do: [:each | aBag add: each].
   ↑aBag

asOrderedCollection
   | anOrderedCollection |
   anOrderedCollection ← OrderedCollection new: self size.
   self do: [:each | anOrderedCollection addLast: each].
   ↑anOrderedCollection

asSet
   | aSet |
   aSet ← Set new: self size.
   self do: [:each | aSet add: each].
   ↑aSet

asSortedCollection
   | aSortedCollection |
   aSortedCollection ← SortedCollection new: self size.
   aSortedCollection addAll: self.
   ↑aSortedCollection

asSortedCollection: aBlock
   | aSortedCollection |
   aSortedCollection ← SortedCollection new: self size.
   aSortedCollection sortBlock: aBlock.
   aSortedCollection addAll: self.
   ↑aSortedCollection

☐ Collection *printing protocol*   The implementations of the printOn: and storeOn: messages in Object are overridden in Collection. Collections print in the form

className (element element element)

Collections store themselves as an expression from which an equal collection can be constructed. This takes the form of

((className new))

or

((className new) add: element; yourself)

or

((className new) add: element; add: element; yourself)

with the appropriate number of cascaded messages for adding each element, depending on whether the collection has no, one, or more elements. The message yourself returns the receiver of the message. It is used in cascaded messages to guarantee that the result of the cascaded message is the receiver. All objects respond to the message yourself; it is defined in class Object.

The general methods for printing and storing are

printing

printOn: aStream
```
    | tooMany |
    tooMany ← aStream position + self maxPrint.
    aStream nextPutAll: self class name, '('.
    self do:
       [ :element |
        aStream position > tooMany
          ifTrue: [aStream nextPutAll: '...etc...)'. ↑self].
        element printOn: aStream.
        aStream space].
    aStream nextPut: $)
```
storeOn: aStream
```
    | noneYet |
    aStream nextPutAll: '(('.
    aStream nextPutAll: self class name.
    aStream nextPutAll: 'new)'.
    noneYet ← true.
    self do:
       [ :each |
        noneYet
          ifTrue: [noneYet ← false]
```

```
            ifFalse: [aStream nextPut: $;].
        aStream nextPutAll: 'add:'.
        aStream store: each].
    noneYet ifFalse: [aStream nextPutAll: '; yourself'].
    aStream nextPut: $)
```

private

maxPrint
↑5000

These methods make use of instances of a kind of Stream that acts as an accessor for a String. The method printOn: sets a threshold for the length of the String to be created; a long collection may print as

className (element element ...etc...)

The threshold is determined as the response to the message maxPrint which is set at 5000 characters. Subclasses can override the private message maxPrint in order to modify the threshold.

Note that this technique of using a method rather than a variable is a way of providing a parameter in a method. A variable cannot be used as the parameter because the variable, to be accessible to all instances, would have to be a class variable. Subclasses cannot specify a class variable whose name is the same as a class variable in one of its superclasses; thus if a subclass wants to change the value of the variable, it will do so for instances of its superclass as well. This is not the desired effect.

The printing format is modified in several subclasses. Array does not print its class name; Intervals print using the shorthand notation of the messages to: and to:by: to a Number. A Symbol prints its characters (without the # prefix of the literal form of a Symbol); a String prints its characters delimited by single quotes.

The storeOn: message is reimplemented in ArrayedCollection and several of its subclasses because instances are created using new: anInteger rather than simply new. Arrays, Strings, and Symbols store in their literal forms. Arrays do if possible. Intervals use the shorthand notation of messages to: and to:by:. MappedCollections store using the converting message mappedBy: that is sent to the collection that is indirectly accessed.

Subclasses of Collection

For each subclass of Collection, we show the methods that implement the three required messages (add:, remove:ifAbsent:, and do:) and the messages in the adding, removing, testing, and enumerating protocols that are reimplemented. New collection protocol for a particular sub-class as specified in Chapter 9 will generally not be presented in this chapter.

Class Bag

Bag represents an unordered collection in which an element can appear more than once. Since the elements of Bags are unordered, the messages at: and at:put: are reimplemented to report an error.

Instances of Bag have an instance of Dictionary as a single instance variable named contents. Each unique element of a Bag is the key of an Association in contents; the value of an Association is an Integer representing the number of times the element appears in the Bag. Removing an element decrements the tally; when the tally falls below 1, the Association is removed from contents. Bag implements new, size, includes:, and occurrencesOf:. A new instance must initialize its instance variable to be a Dictionary. The reimplementation of size is made efficient by summing all the values of elements of contents. The arguments of the testing messages are used as keys of contents. In implementing includes:, the responsibility for checking is passed to contents. In order to answer the query occurrencesOf: anObject, the method checks that anObject is included as a key in contents and then looks up the value (the tally) associated with it.

class name	Bag
superclass	Collection
instance variable names	contents
class methods	

instance creation

new
    ↑super new setDictionary

instance methods

accessing

at: index
    self errorNotKeyed
at: index put: anObject
    self errorNotKeyed
size
    | tally |
    tally ← 0.
    contents do: [:each | tally ← tally + each].
    ↑tally

testing

includes: anObject
    ↑contents includesKey: anObject

occurrencesOf: anObject
    (self includes: anObject)
        ifTrue: [↑contents at: anObject]
        ifFalse: [↑0]

private

setDictionary
    contents ← Dictionary new

(in Collection)

private

errorNotKeyed
    self error:
        self class name, ' s do not respond to keyed accessing messages '

To add an element is to add it once, but Bags can add multiple times. The implementation of add: calls on add:withOccurrences:. Removing an element checks the number of occurrences, decrementing the tally or removing the element as a key in contents if the tally is less than 1.

adding

add: newObject
    ↑self add: newObject withOccurrences: 1

add: newObject withOccurrences: anInteger
    contents at: newObject
        put: anInteger + (self occurrencesOf: newObject).
    ↑newObject

removing

remove: oldObject ifAbsent: exceptionBlock
    | count |
    count ← self occurrencesOf: oldObject.
    count = 0 ifTrue: [↑exceptionBlock value].
    count = 1
      ifTrue: [contents removeKey: oldObject]
      ifFalse: [contents at: oldObject put: count − 1]].
    ↑oldObject

Enumerating the elements of a Bag means selecting each element of the Dictionary and evaluating a block with the key of that element (i.e., the actual Bag element is the key of the Dictionary). This has to be done multiple times, once for each occurrence of the element, as indicated by the value associated with the key.

enumerating

do: aBlock
    contents associationsDo:
        [:assoc | assoc value timesRepeat: [aBlock value: assoc key]]

Class Set

The elements of Sets are unordered like those of Bags, so the messages at: and at:put: produce an error report. A Set may not contain an element more than once, therefore, every insertion of an element must, in theory, check the entire collection. To avoid searching all elements, a Set determines where in its indexed instance variables to start a search for a particular element by using a hashing technique.

Each Set has an instance variable named tally. Maintaining this tally of the number of elements avoids the inefficiencies involved in determining the size of the Set by counting every non-nil element. Thus new, new:, and size are reimplemented; the first two in order to initialize the variable tally and the last simply to respond with the value of tally.

class name	Set
superclass	Collection
instance variable names	tally
class methods	

instance creation

new
    ↑self new: 2
new: anInteger
    ↑(super new: anInteger) setTally

instance methods

accessing

at: index
    self errorNotKeyed
at: index put: anObject
    self errorNotKeyed
size
    ↑tally

private

setTally
    tally ← 0

In the method for new:, super is used in order to avoid recursion. A private message of Set, findElementOrNil:, hashes the argument to produce the index at which to begin the probe of the Set. The probe proceeds until the argument, anObject, is found, or until nil is encountered. The response is the index of the last position checked. Then the testing messages are implemented as

testing

includes: anObject
↑(self basicAt: (self findElementOrNil: anObject)) ~~ nil

occurrencesOf: anObject
(self includes: anObject)
   ifTrue: [↑1]
   ifFalse: [↑0]

The number of occurrences of any element in the Set is never more than 1. The three basic messages must make use of basicAt: and basicAt:put: because Sets report an error if at: or at:put: is used.

adding

add: newObject
| index |
newObject isNil ifTrue: [↑newObject].
index ← self findElementOrNil: newObject.
(self basicAt: index) isNil
   ifTrue: [self basicAt: index put: newObject. tally ← tally + 1].
↑newObject

removing

remove: oldObject ifAbsent: aBlock
| index |
index ← self find: oldObject ifAbsent: [↑aBlock value].
self basicAt: index put: nil.
tally ← tally − 1.
self fixCollisionsFrom: index.
↑oldObject

enumerating

do: aBlock
tally = 0 ifTrue: [↑self].
1 to: self basicSize do:
  [:index |
   (self basicAt: index) == nil
     ifFalse: [aBlock value: (self basicAt: index)]]

The private message find:ifAbsent: calls on findElementOrNil:; if the element, oldObject, is not found, the argument aBlock is evaluated. In order to guarantee that the hashing/probing technique works properly, remaining elements might need to be compacted whenever one is removed (fixCollisionsFrom:). These methods are good examples of when the accessing messages basicAt:, basicAt:put:, and basicSize must be used.

Class Dictionary

A Dictionary is a collection of Associations. Class Dictionary uses a hashing technique to locate its elements which is like that of its superclass, Set, but hashes on the keys in the Associations instead of on the Associations themselves. Most of the accessing messages for Dictionary are reimplemented to treat the values of the Associations as the elements, not the Associations themselves.

Dictionary implements at: and at:put:, but redefines the argument associated with the keyword at: to be any key in the Dictionary (not necessarily an Integer index). The argument of includes: is the value of one of the Associations in the Dictionary, not one of the Associations themselves. The message do: enumerates the values, not the Associations. The argument to remove: is also a value, but this is an inappropriate way to delete from a Dictionary because elements are referenced with keys. Either removeAssociation: or removeKey: should be used. Thus the messages remove: and remove:ifAbsent: should not be implemented for Dictionary.

Much of the work in the accessing protocol is done in private messages, either those inherited from Set or similar ones for finding a key (findKeyOrNil:).

class name	Dictionary
superclass	Set
instance methods	

accessing

at: key
  ↑self at: key ifAbsent: [self errorKeyNotFound]
at: key put: anObject
  | index element |
  index ← self findKeyOrNil: key.
  element ← self basicAt: index.
  element isNil
    ifTrue:
      [self basicAt: index put: (Association key: key value: anObject).
      tally ← tally + 1]
      "element is an Association. The key already exists, change its
        value."
    ifFalse:
      [element value: anObject].
  ↑anObject
at: key ifAbsent: aBlock
  | index |
  index ← self findKey: key ifAbsent: [↑aBlock value].
  ↑(self basicAt: index) value

testing

includes: anObject
"Revert to the method used in Collection."
self do: [:each | anObject = each ifTrue: [↑true]].
↑false

adding

add: anAssociation
| index element |
index ← self findKeyOrNil: anAssociation key.
element ← self basicAt: index.
element isNil
    ifTrue: [self basicAt: index put: anAssociation.
            tally ← tally + 1]
    ifFalse: [element value: anAssociation value].
↑anAssociation

removing

remove: anObject ifAbsent: aBlock
self shouldNotImplement

enumerating

do: aBlock
self associationsDo: [:assoc | aBlock value: assoc value]

private

errorKeyNotFound
self error: 'key not found'

Notice the similarity between at:put: and add:. The difference is in the action taken if the element is not found—in the case of at:put:, a new Association is created and stored in the Dictionary; in the case of add:, the argument, anAssociation, is stored so that any shared reference to the Association is preserved.

The message collect: is reimplemented in order to avoid the problems of collecting possibly identical values into a Set which would result in throwing away duplications. The message select: is reimplemented in order to select Associations by applying their values as the arguments to the block.

enumerating

collect: aBlock
| newCollection |
newCollection ← Bag new.
self do: [:each | newCollection add: (aBlock value: each)].
↑newCollection

select: aBlock
    | newCollection |
    newCollection ← self species new.
    self associationsDo:
        [:each |
          (aBlock value: each value) ifTrue: [newCollection add: each]].
    ↑newCollection

IdentityDictionary overrides at:, at:put:, and add: in order to implement checking for identical keys instead of equal keys. An IdentityDictionary is implemented as two parallel ordered collections of keys and values, rather than as a single collection of Associations. Thus do: must also be reimplemented. The implementation is not shown.

Sequenceable-Collections

SequenceableCollection is the superclass for all collections whose elements are ordered. Of the messages we are examining, remove:ifAbsent: is specified as being inappropriate for SequenceableCollections in general, since the order of elements might have been externally specified and it is assumed that they should be removed in order. Because SequenceableCollections are ordered, elements are accessed using at:; the implementation is provided in class Object. The message do: is implemented by accessing each element at index 1 through the size of the collection. SequenceableCollections are created using the message new:. Therefore, collect: and select: must be reimplemented to create the new collection using new: rather than new. The methods for collect: and select: shown next use a WriteStream in order to access the new collection, and the message at: in order to access elements of the original collection.

class name	SequenceableCollection
superclass	Collection
instance methods	

accessing

size
    self subclassResponsibility

removing

remove: oldObject ifAbsent: anExceptionBlock
    self shouldNotImplement

enumerating

do: aBlock
    | index length |
    index ← 0.
    length ← self size.

```
    [(index ← index + 1) < = length]
       whileTrue: [aBlock value: (self at: index)]
collect: aBlock
    | aStream index length |
    aStream ← WriteStream on: (self species new: self size).
    index ← 0.
    length ← self size.
    [(index ← index + 1) < = length]
       whileTrue: [aStream nextPut: (aBlock value: (self at: index))].
    ↑aStream contents
select: aBlock
    | aStream index length |
    aStream ← WriteStream on: (self species new: self size).
    index ← 0.
    length ← self size.
    [(index ← index + 1) < = length]
       whileTrue:
          [(aBlock value: (self at: index))
              ifTrue: [aStream nextPut: (self at: index)]].
    ↑aStream contents
```

Notice that size is declared as a subclass responsibility in SequenceableCollection. The method inherited from the superclass Collection uses do: to enumerate and thereby count each element. But the method for do: as specified in SequenceableCollection determines the limit for indexing by requesting the size of the collection. Therefore, size must be reimplemented in order not to be stated in terms of do:.

Subclasses of Sequenceable-Collection

☐ *Class* LinkedList   Elements of LinkedList are instances of Link or of one of its subclasses. Each LinkedList has two instance variables, a reference to the first and to the last elements. Adding an element is assumed to be interpreted as adding to the end (addLast:); the method for addLast: is to make the element the next link of the current last link. Removing an element means that the element's preceding link must reference the element's succeeding link (or nil). If the element to be removed is the first one, then its succeeding link becomes the first one.

class name	LinkedList
superclass	SequenceableCollection
instance variable names	firstLink
	lastLink

instance methods

accessing

```
at: index
    | count element size |
    count ← 1.
```

```
            element ← self first.
            size ← self size.
            [count > size] whileFalse:
                [count = index
                    ifTrue: [↑element]
                    ifFalse: [count ← count + 1.
                            element ← element nextLink]].
            ↑self errorSubscriptBounds: index
    at: index put: element
            self error: 'Do not store into a LinkedList using at:put:'
```

adding

```
    add: aLink
            ↑self addLast: aLink
    addLast: aLink
            self isEmpty
                ifTrue: [firstLink ← aLink]
                ifFalse: [lastLink nextLink: aLink].
            lastLink ← aLink.
            ↑aLink
```

removing

```
    remove: aLink ifAbsent: aBlock
            | tempLink |
            aLink == firstLink
                ifTrue:
                    [firstLink ← aLink nextLink.
                     aLink == lastLink ifTrue: [lastLink ←nil]]
                ifFalse:
                    [tempLink ← firstLink.
                     [tempLink isNil ifTrue: [↑aBlock value].
                      tempLink nextLink == aLink]
                            whileFalse: [tempLink ← tempLink nextLink].
                     tempLink nextLink: aLink nextLink.
                     aLink == lastLink ifTrue: [lastLink ← tempLink]].
            aLink nextLink: nil.
            ↑aLink
```

enumerating

```
    do: aBlock
            | aLink |
            aLink ← firstLink.
            [aLink isNil] whileFalse:
                [aBlock value: aLink.
                 aLink ← aLink nextLink]
```

A nil link signals the end of the LinkedList. Thus the enumerating message do: is implemented as a simple loop that continues until a nil is encountered in the collection.

□ *Class* Interval   Intervals are SequenceableCollections whose elements are computed. Therefore, messages for adding and removing cannot be supported. Since elements are not explicitly stored, all accessing (at:, size, and do:) requires a computation. Each method checks to see if the last element computed is to be incremented (positive step) or decremented (negative step) in order to determine whether the limit (stop) has been reached.

class name	Interval
superclass	SequenceableCollection
instance variable names	start
	stop
	step

class methods

instance creation

from: startInteger to: stopInteger
    ↑self new
        setFrom: startInteger
        to: stopInteger
        by: 1
from: startInteger to: stopInteger by: stepInteger
    ↑self new
        setFrom: startInteger
        to: stopInteger
        by: stepInteger

instance methods

accessing

size
    step < 0
        ifTrue: [start < stop
                ifTrue: [↑0]
                ifFalse: [↑stop − start // step + 1]]
        ifFalse: [stop < start
                ifTrue: [↑0]
                ifFalse: [↑stop − start // step + 1]]
at: index
    (index >= 1 and: [index <= self size])
        ifTrue: [↑start + (step * (index − 1))]
        ifFalse: [self errorSubscriptBounds: index]

at: index put: anObject
self error: 'you cannot store into an Interval'

adding

add: newObject
self error: 'elements cannot be added to an Interval'

removing

remove: newObject
self error: 'elements cannot be removed from an Interval'

enumerating

do: aBlock
```
| aValue |
aValue ← start.
step < 0
   ifTrue: [[stop <= aValue]
                 whileTrue: [aBlock value: aValue.
                                  aValue ← aValue + step]]
   ifFalse: [[stop >= aValue]
                  whileTrue: [aBlock value: aValue.
                                   aValue ← aValue + step]]
```

collect: aBlock
```
| nextValue i result |
result ← self species new: self size.
nextValue ← start.
i ← 1.
step < 0
   ifTrue: [[stop <= nextValue]
                 whileTrue:
                         [result at: i put: (aBlock value: nextValue).
                          nextValue ← nextValue + step.
                          i ← i + 1]]
   ifFalse: [[stop >= nextValue]
                  whileTrue:
                          [result at: i put: (aBlock value: nextValue).
                           nextValue ← nextValue + step.
                           i ← i + 1]].
↑result
```

private

setFrom: startInteger to: stopInteger by: stepInteger
```
start ← startInteger.
stop ← stopInteger.
step ← stepInteger
```

☐ ArrayedCollections—Array, ByteArray, String, Text, *and* Symbol
ArrayedCollection is a subclass of SequenceableCollection; each
ArrayedCollection is a variable-length object. All instance creation
methods are reimplemented to use new:, not new. ArrayedCollections are
fixed-length so add: is disallowed; in its superclass, remove: was already
disallowed and do: was implemented. Only size, therefore, is
implemented in ArrayedCollection—it is a system primitive that reports
the number of indexed instance variables.

Of the subclasses of ArrayedCollection, Array, and ByteArray do not
reimplement any of the messages we are examining in this chapter.
Accessing messages for String—at:, at:put:, and size—are system primitives; in Text, all accessing messages are passed as messages to the instance variable string (which is an instance of String). Symbol disallows
at:put: and returns String as its species.

☐ OrderedCollections *and* SortedCollections   OrderedCollection stores
an ordered, contiguous sequence of elements. Since OrderedCollections
are expandable, some efficiency is gained by allocating extra space for
the sequence. Two instance variables, firstIndex and lastIndex, point to
the first and the last actual elements in the sequence.

The index into OrderedCollection is converted to be within the range
of firstIndex to lastIndex for accessing messages (at: and at:put:) and the
size is simply one more than the difference between the two indices.
Adding an element is interpreted to be adding to the end; if there is no
room at the end, the collection is copied with additional space allocated
(makeRoomAtLast is the private message that does this work). The actual location for storing an element is the computed index position after
lastIndex. If an element is removed, then the remaining elements must
be moved up so that elements remain contiguous (removeIndex:).

class name	OrderedCollection
superclass	SequenceableCollection
instance variable names	firstIndex
	lastIndex

class methods

instance creation

new
　　↑self new: 10
new: anInteger
　　↑(super new: anInteger) setIndices

instance methods

accessing

size
　　↑lastIndex − firstIndex + 1

Implementation of the Basic Collection Protocol

at: anInteger
  (anInteger < 1 or: [anInteger + firstIndex − 1 > lastIndex])
    ifTrue: [self errorNoSuchElement]
    ifFalse: [↑super at: anInteger + firstIndex − 1]
at: anInteger put: anObject
  | index |
  index ← anInteger truncated.
  (index < 1 or: [index + firstIndex − 1 > lastIndex])
    ifTrue: [self errorNoSuchElement]
    ifFalse: [↑super at: index + firstIndex − 1 put: anObject]

adding

add: newObject
  ↑ self addLast: newObject
addLast: newObject
  lastIndex = self basicSize ifTrue: [self makeRoomAtLast].
  lastIndex ← lastIndex + 1.
  self basicAt: lastIndex put: newObject.
  ↑newObject

removing

remove: oldObject ifAbsent: absentBlock
  | index |
  index ← firstIndex.
  [index < = lastIndex]
    whileTrue:
      [oldObject = (self basicAt: index)
          ifTrue: [self removeIndex: index.
                  ↑oldObject]
          ifFalse: [index ← index + 1]].
  ↑absentBlock value

private

setIndices
  firstIndex ← self basicSize // 2 max: 1.
  lastIndex ← firstIndex − 1 max: 0
errorNoSuchElement
  self error:
    ' attempt to index non-existent element in an ordered collection '

The enumerating messages do:, collect:, and select: are each
reimplemented—do: in order to provide better performance than the
method provided in SequenceableCollection.

enumerating

do: aBlock
| index |
index ← firstIndex.
[index < = lastIndex]
   whileTrue:
     [aBlock value: (self basicAt: index).
     index ← index + 1]

collect: aBlock
| newCollection |
newCollection ← self species new.
self do: [:each | newCollection add: (aBlock value: each)].
↑newCollection

select: aBlock
| newCollection |
newCollection ← self copyEmpty.
self do: [:each | (aBlock value: each) ifTrue: [newCollection add: each]].
↑newCollection

In the method for select:, the new collection is created by sending the original collection the message copyEmpty. This message creates a new collection with enough space allocated to hold all the elements of the original, although all the elements might not be stored. In this way, time taken in expanding the new collection is avoided.

SortedCollection is a subclass of OrderedCollection. The message at:put: reports an error, requesting the programmer to use add:; add: inserts the new element according to the value of the instance variable sortBlock. The determination of the position for insertion is done as a "bubble sort." collect: is also reimplemented to create an OrderedCollection rather than a SortedCollection for collecting the values of the block. The code is not shown; a bubble sort looks the same in the Smalltalk-80 language as it would in most programming languages.

Class
MappedCollection

Instances of MappedCollection have two instance variables—domain and map. The value of domain is either a Dictionary or a SequenceableCollection; its elements are accessed indirectly through map. The message add: is disallowed. Both at: and at:put: are reimplemented in MappedCollection in order to support the indirect access from map to the elements of domain. The size of a MappedCollection is the size of its map.

class name	MappedCollection
superclass	Collection
instance variable names	domain
	map

class methods

instance creation

collection: domainCollection map: mapCollection
↑super new setCollection: domainCollection map: mapCollection
new
self error: 'use collection:map: to create a MappedCollection'

instance methods

accessing

at: anIndex
↑domain at: (map at: anIndex)
at: anIndex put: anObject
↑domain at: (map at: anIndex) put: anObject
size
↑map size

adding

add: newObject
self shouldNotImplement

enumerating

do: aBlock
map do:
   [:mapValue | aBlock value: (domain at: mapValue)]
collect: aBlock
| aStream |
aStream ← WriteStream on: (self species new: self size).
self do: [:domainValue |
          aStream nextPut: (aBlock value: domainValue)].
↑aStream contents
select: aBlock
| aStream |
aStream ← WriteStream on: (self species new: self size).
self do:
   [:domainValue |
     (aBlock value: domainValue)
          ifTrue: [aStream nextPut: domainValue]].
↑aStream contents

private

setCollection: domainCollection map: mapCollection
domain ← domainCollection.
map ← mapCollection
species
↑domain species

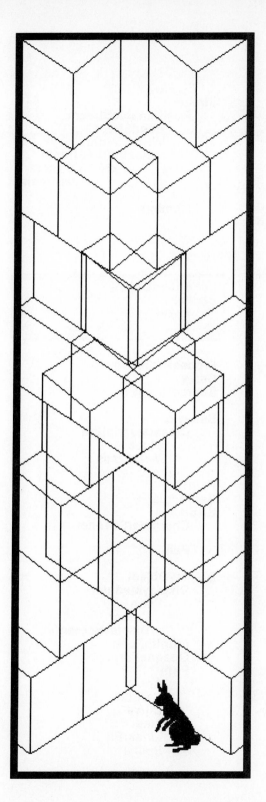

14

Kernel Support Classes

Class UndefinedObject

Classes Boolean, True, **and** False

Additional Protocol for Class Object
Dependence Relationships Among Objects
Message Handling
System Primitive Messages

Object

Magnitude
    Character
    Date
    Time

    Number
        Float
        Fraction
        Integer
            LargeNegativeInteger
            LargePositiveInteger
            SmallInteger

    LookupKey
        Association

Link

    Process

Collection

    SequenceableCollection
        LinkedList

        Semaphore

    ArrayedCollection
        Array

        WordArray
            DisplayBitmap

        RunArray
        String
            Symbol
        Text
        ByteArray

    Interval
    OrderedCollection
        SortedCollection
Bag
MappedCollection
Set
    Dictionary
        IdentityDictionary

Stream
    PositionableStream
        ReadStream
        WriteStream
            ReadWriteStream
                ExternalStream
                    FileStream

    Random

UndefinedObject
Boolean
    False
    True

ProcessorScheduler
Delay
SharedQueue

Behavior
    ClassDescription
        Class
        MetaClass

Point
Rectangle
BitBlt
    CharacterScanner

    Pen

DisplayObject
    DisplayMedium
        Form
            Cursor
            DisplayScreen
    InfiniteForm
    OpaqueForm
    Path
        Arc
            Circle
        Curve
        Line
        LinearFit
        Spline

Class
UndefinedObject

The object nil represents a value for uninitialized variables. It also represents meaningless results. It is the only instance of class UndefinedObject.

The purpose of including class UndefinedObject in the system is to handle error messages. The typical error in evaluating Smalltalk-80 expressions is that some object is sent a message it does not understand. Often this occurs because a variable is not properly initialized—in many cases, the variable name that should refer to some other object refers to nil instead. The error message is of the form

className does not understand messageSelector

where className mentions the class of the receiver and messageSelector is the selector of the erroneously-sent message.

Note, if nil were an instance of Object, then a message sent to it in error would state

Object does not understand messageSelector

which is less explicit than stating that an undefined object does not understand the message. At the price of a class description, it was possible to improve on the error message.

Tests to see if an object is nil are handled in class Object, but reimplemented in UndefinedObject. In class Object, messages isNil and notNil are implemented as

    isNil
      ↑false
    notNil
      ↑true

In class UndefinedObject, messages isNil and notNil are implemented as

    isNil
      ↑true
    notNil
      ↑false

so that no conditional test in Object is required.

Classes Boolean,
True, **and** False

Protocol for logical values is provided by the class Boolean; logical values are represented by subclasses of Boolean—True and False. The subclasses add no new protocol; they reimplement many messages to have better performance than the methods in the superclass. The idea is similar to that in testing for nil in Object and UndefinedObject; true knows that it represents logical truth and false knows that it represents logical falsehood. We show the implementation of some of the controlling protocol to illustrate this idea.

The logical operations are

Boolean instance protocol
_____

logical operations

& aBoolean	Evaluating conjunction. Answer true if both the receiver and the argument are true.
| aBoolean	Evaluating disjunction. Answer true if either the receiver or the argument is true.
not	Negation. Answer true if the receiver is false, answer false if the receiver is true.
eqv: aBoolean	Answer true if the receiver is equivalent to the argument, aBoolean.
xor: aBoolean	Exclusive OR. Answer true if the receiver is not equivalent to aBoolean.

These conjunction and disjunction operations are "evaluating"—this means that the argument is evaluated regardless of the value of the receiver. This is in contrast to and: and or: in which the receiver determines whether to evaluate the argument.

Boolean instance protocol
_____

controlling

and: alternativeBlock	Nonevaluating conjunction. If the receiver is true, answer the value of the argument; otherwise, answer false without evaluating the argument.
or: alternativeBlock	Nonevaluating disjunction. If the receiver is false, answer the value of the argument; otherwise, answer true without evaluating the argument.
ifTrue: trueAlternativeBlock ifFalse: falseAlternativeBlock	Conditional statement. If the receiver is true, answer the result of evaluating trueAlternativeBlock; otherwise answer the result of evaluating falseAlternativeBlock.
ifFalse: falseAlternativeBlock ifTrue: trueAlternativeBlock	Conditional statement. If the receiver is true, answer the result of evaluating trueAlternativeBlock; otherwise answer the result of evaluating falseAlternativeBlock.
ifTrue: trueAlternativeBlock	Conditional statement. If the receiver is true, answer the result of evaluating trueAlternativeBlock; otherwise answer nil.
ifFalse: falseAlternativeBlock	Conditional statement. If the receiver is false, answer the result of evaluating falseAlternativeBlock; otherwise answer nil.

The arguments to and: and or: must be blocks in order to defer evaluation. Conditional statements are provided as messages ifTrue:ifFalse:, ifFalse:ifTrue:, ifTrue:, and ifFalse:, as already specified and exemplified throughout the previous chapters. The messages are implemented in the subclasses of class Boolean so that the appropriate argument block is evaluated.

In class True, the methods are

> **ifTrue: trueAlternativeBlock ifFalse: falseAlternativeBlock**
> ↑trueAlternativeBlock value
>
> **ifFalse: falseAlternativeBlock ifTrue: trueAlternativeBlock**
> ↑trueAlternativeBlock value
>
> **ifTrue: trueAlternativeBlock**
> ↑trueAlternativeBlock value
>
> **ifFalse: falseAlternativeBlock**
> ↑nil

In class False, the methods are

> **ifTrue: trueAlternativeBlock ifFalse: falseAlternativeBlock**
> ↑falseAlternativeBlock value
>
> **ifFalse: falseAlternativeBlock ifTrue: trueAlternativeBlock**
> ↑falseAlternativeBlock value
>
> **ifTrue: trueAlternativeBlock**
> ↑nil
>
> **ifFalse: falseAlternativeBlock**
> ↑falseAlternativeBlock value

If x is 3, then

$$x > 0 \text{ ifTrue: } [x \leftarrow x - 1] \text{ ifFalse: } [x \leftarrow x + 1]$$

is interpreted as $x > 0$ evaluates to true, the sole instance of class True; the method for ifTrue:ifFalse: is found in class True, so the block $[x \leftarrow x - 1]$ is evaluated without further testing.

In this way, the message lookup mechanism provides an effective implementation of conditional control with no additional primitive operations or circular definitions.

Additional Protocol for Class Object

Protocol for class Object, shared by all objects, was introduced in Chapter 6. Several categories of messages were not included in that early discussion. Most of these are part of Object's protocol to provide system support for message handling, dependence relationships, primitive message handling, and system primitives.

*Dependence
Relationships
Among Objects*

Information in the Smalltalk-80 system is represented by objects. The variables of objects themselves refer to objects; in this sense, objects are explicitly related or dependent on one another. Classes are related to their superclasses and metaclasses; these classes share external and internal descriptions and are thereby dependent on one another. These forms of dependency are central to the semantics of the Smalltalk-80 language. They coordinate descriptive information among objects.

An additional kind of dependency is supported in class Object. Its purpose is to *coordinate* activities among different objects. Specifically, its purpose is to be able to link one object, say A, to one or more other objects, say B, so B can be informed if A changes in any way. Upon being informed when A changes and the nature of the change, B can decide to take some action such as updating its own status. The concept of *change* and *update*, therefore, are integral to the support of this third kind of object dependence relationship.

The protocol in class Object is

Object instance protocol

---

dependents access

addDependent: anObject	Add the argument, anObject, as one of the receiver's dependents.
removeDependent: anObject	Remove the argument, anObject, as one of the receiver's dependents.
dependents	Answer an OrderedCollection of the objects that are dependent on the receiver, that is, the objects that should be notified if the receiver changes.

and then justify left initialize-release

release	Remove references to objects that may refer back to the receiver. This message is reimplemented by any subclass that creates references to dependents; the expression super release is included in any such reimplementation.

updating

changed	The receiver changed in some general way; inform all the dependents by sending each dependent an update: message.
changed: aParameter	The receiver changed; the change is denoted by the argument, aParameter. Usually the argument is a Symbol that is part of the dependent's change protocol; the default behavior is to use the receiver itself as the argument. Inform all of the dependents.
update: aParameter	An object on whom the receiver is dependent has changed. The receiver updates its status accordingly (the default behavior is to do nothing).
broadcast: aSymbol	Send the argument, aSymbol, as a unary message to all of the receiver's dependents.

broadcast: aSymbol with: anObject

> Send the argument, aSymbol, as a keyword message with argument, anObject, to all of the receiver's dependents.

changeRequest

> Receiver wants to change; check with all dependents that it is okay.

change RequestFrom: requestor

> Receiver wants to change; check with all dependents except requestor.

Take, as an example, the objects that model traffic lights. A typical traffic light at a street corner is an object with three lights, each a different color. Only one of these lights can be ON at a given moment. In this sense, the ON-OFF status of each of the three lights is dependent on the status of the other two. There are a number of ways to create this relationship. Suppose we create the class Light as follows.

class name	Light
superclass	Object
instance variable names	status
class methods	

instance creation

setOn
    ↑self new setOn
setOff
    ↑self new setOff

instance methods

status

turnOn
    self isOff
        ifTrue: [status ← true. self changed]
turnOff
    self isOn
        ifTrue: [status ← false]

testing

isOn
    ↑status
isOff
    ↑status not

change and update

update: aLight
    aLight == self ifFalse: [self turnOff]

private

setOn
    status ← true
setOff
    status ← false

The model is very simple. A Light is either on or off, so a status flag is kept as an instance variable; it is true if the Light is on, false if the Light is off. Whenever a Light is turned on (turnOn), it sends itself the changed message. Any other status change is not broadcast to the dependents on the assumption that a Light is turned off in reaction to turning on another Light. The default response to changed is to send all dependents the message update: self (i.e., the object that changed is the argument to the update: message). Then update: is implemented in Light to mean turn off. If the parameter is the receiver, then, of course, the update: is ignored.

The class TrafficLight is defined to set up any number of coordinated lights. The instance creation message with: takes as its argument the number of Lights to be created. Each Light is dependent on all other Lights. When the TrafficLight is demolished, the dependencies among its Lights are disconnected (the message inherited from class Object for disconnecting dependents is release; it is implemented in TrafficLight in order to broadcast the message to all Lights).

class name	TrafficLight
superclass	Object
instance variable names	lights
class methods	

instance creation

with: numberOfLights
    ↑self new lights: numberOfLights

instance methods

operate

turnOn: lightNumber
    (lights at: lightNumber) turnOn

initialize-release

release
    super release.
    lights do: [:eachLight | eachLight release].
    lights ← nil

private

lights: numberOfLights

```
lights ← Array new: (numberOfLights max: 1).
lights at: 1 put: Light setOn.
2 to: numberOfLights do:
    [ :index | lights at: index put: Light setOff].
lights do:
    [ :eachLight |
      lights do:
        [ :dependentLight |
          eachLight ~~ dependentLight
            ifTrue: [eachLight addDependent: dependentLight]]]
```

The private initialization method is lights: numberOfLights. Each light is created turned off except for the first light. Then each light is connected to all the other lights (using the message addDependent:). The simulated TrafficLight operates by some round robin, perhaps timed, sequencing through each light, turning it on. A simple example shown below creates the TrafficLight with the first light on, and then turns on each of the other lights, one at a time. A simulation of a traffic corner might include different models for controlling the lights.

```
trafficLight ← TrafficLight with: 3.
trafficLight turnOn: 2.
trafficLight turnOn: 3
```

The message turnOn: to a TrafficLight sends the message turnOn to the designated Light. If the Light is currently off, then it is set on and the message changed sent. The message changed sends update: to each dependent Light; if a dependent light is on, it is turned off.

A particularly important use of this dependency protocol is to support having multiple graphical images of an object. Each image is dependent on the object in the sense that, if the object changes, the image must be informed so that it can decide whether the change affects the displayed information. The user interface to the Smalltalk-80 system makes liberal use of this support for broadcasting notices that an object has changed; this is used to coordinate the contents of a sequence of menus of possible actions that the user can take with respect to the contents of information displayed on the screen. Menus themselves can be created by linking possible actions together, in a way similar to the way we linked together the traffic lights.

Message Handling

All processing in the Smalltalk-80 system is carried out by sending messages to objects. For reasons of efficiency, instances of class Message are only created when an error occurs and the message state must be stored in an accessible structure. Most messages in the system, therefore, do not take the form of directly creating an instance of Message and transmitting it to an object.

In some circumstances, it is useful to compute the message selector of a message transmission. For example, suppose that a list of possible message selectors is kept by an object and, based on a computation, one of these selectors is chosen. Suppose it is assigned as a value of a variable selector. Now we wish to transmit the message to some object, say, to receiver. We can not simply write the expression as

receiver selector

because this means—send the object referred to by receiver the unary message selector. We could, however, write

receiver perform: selector

The result is to transmit the value of the argument, selector, as the message to receiver. Protocol to support this ability to send a computed message to an object is provided in class Object. This protocol includes methods for transmitting computed keyword as well as unary messages.

Object instance protocol

---

message handling

perform: aSymbol
    Send the receiver the unary message indicated by the argument, aSymbol. The argument is the selector of the message. Report an error if the number of arguments expected by the selector is not zero.

perform: aSymbol with: anObject
    Send the receiver the keyword message indicated by the arguments. The first argument, aSymbol, is the selector of the message. The other argument, anObject, is the argument of the message to be sent. Report an error if the number of arguments expected by the selector is not one.

perform: aSymbol with: firstObject with: secondObject
    Send the receiver the keyword message indicated by the arguments. The first argument, aSymbol, is the selector of the message. The other arguments, firstObject and secondObject, are the arguments of the message to be sent. Report an error if the number of arguments expected by the selector is not two.

perform: aSymbol with: firstObject with: secondObject with: thirdObject
    Send the receiver the keyword message indicated by the arguments. The first argument, aSymbol, is the selector of the message. The other arguments, firstObject, secondObject, and thirdObject, are the arguments of the message to be sent. Report an error if the number of arguments expected by the selector is not three.

perform: selector withArguments: anArray
    Send the receiver the keyword message indicated by the arguments. The argument, selector, is the selector of the message. The

arguments of the message are the elements of anArray. Report an error if the number of arguments expected by the selector is not the same as the size of anArray.

One way in which this protocol can be used is as a decoder of user commands. Suppose for example that we want to model a very simple calculator in which operands precede operators. A possible implementation represents the calculator as having (1) the current result, which is also the first operand, and (2) a possibly undefined second operand. Each operator is a message selector understood by the result. Sending the message clear, once, resets the operand; sending the message clear when the operand is reset will reset the result.

class name	Calculator
superclass	Object
instance variable names	result
	operand

class methods

instance creation

new
    ↑super new initialize

instance methods

accessing

result
    ↑result

calculating

apply: operator
    (result respondsTo: operator)
        ifFalse: [self error: ' operation not understood'].
    operand isNil
        ifTrue: [result ← result perform: operator]
        ifFalse: [result ← result perform: operator with: operand]
clear
    operand isNil
        ifTrue: [result ← 0]
        ifFalse: [operand ← nil]
operand: aNumber
    operand ← aNumber

private

initialize
    result ← 0

An example illustrates the use of the class Calculator.

hp ← Calculator new

Create hp as a Calculator. The instance variables are initialized with result 0 and operand nil.

hp operand: 3

Imagine the user has pressed the key labeled 3 and set the operand.

hp apply: # +

The user selects addition. The method for apply determines that the operator is understood and that the operand is not nil; therefore, the result is set by the expression

result perform: operator with: operand

which is equivalent to

0 + 3

The method sets result to 3; operand remains 3 so that

hp apply: # +

again adds 3, so the result is now 6.

hp operand: 1.
hp apply: # −.
hp clear.
hp apply: #squared

The result was 6, subtract 1, and compute the square; result is now 25.

System Primitive
Messages

There are a number of messages specified in class Object whose purpose is to support the needs of the overall system implementation. They are categorized as system primitives. These are messages that provide direct access to the state of an instance and, to some extent, violate the principle that each object has sovereign control over storing values into its variables. However, this access is needed by the language interpreter. It is useful in providing class description/development utilities for the programming environment. Examples of these messages are instVarAt: anInteger and instVarAt: anInteger put: anObject which retrieve and store the values of named instance variables, respectively.

Object instance protocol

system primitives

become: otherObject	Swap the instance pointers of the receiver and the argument, otherObject. All variables in the entire system that pointed to the receiver will now point to the argument and vice versa. Report an error if either object is a SmallInteger.
instVarAt: index	Answer a named variable in the receiver. The numbering of the variables corresponds to the order in which the named instance variables were defined.
instVarAt: index put: value	Store the argument, value, into a named variable in the receiver. The number of variables corresponds to the order in which the named instance variables were defined. Answer value.
nextInstance	Answer the next instance after the receiver in the enumeration of all instances of this class. Answer nil if all instances have been enumerated.
asOop	Answer an Integer that is unique to the receiver.

Probably the most unusual and effective of the system primitive messages is the message become: otherObject. The response to this message is to swap the instance pointer of the receiver with that of the argument, otherObject. An example of the use of this message is found in the implementation of the message grow in several of the collection classes. The message grow is sent when the number of elements that can be stored in a (fixed-length) collection have to be increased without copying the collection; copying is undesirable because all shared references to the collection must be preserved. Thus a new collection is created, its elements stored, and then the original collection transforms into (becomes) the new one. All pointers to the original collection are replaced by pointers to the new one.

The following is the method for grow as specified in class SequenceableCollection.

grow
    | newCollection |
    newCollection ← self species new: self size + self growSize
    newCollection replaceFrom: 1 to: self size with: self.
    ↑self become: newCollection
growSize
    ↑ 10

Subclasses can redefine the response to the message growSize in order to specify alternative numbers of elements by which to expand.

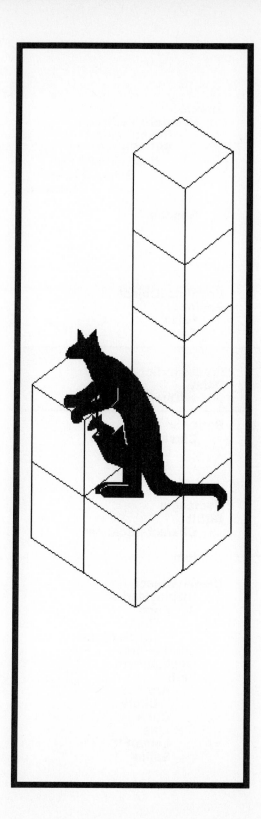

15

Multiple Independent Processes

Processes
Scheduling
Priorities

Semaphores
Mutual Exclusion
Resource Sharing
Hardware Interrupts

Class SharedQueue

Class Delay

Object

    Magnitude
        Character
        Date
        Time

        Number
            Float
            Fraction
            Integer
                LargeNegativeInteger
                LargePositiveInteger
                SmallInteger

        LookupKey
            Association

    Link

    Process

    Collection

        SequenceableCollection
            LinkedList

        Semaphore

        ArrayedCollection
            Array

                WordArray
                    DisplayBitmap

                RunArray
                String
                    Symbol
                Text
                ByteArray

            Interval
            OrderedCollection
                SortedCollection
            Bag
            MappedCollection
            Set
                Dictionary
                    IdentityDictionary

    Stream
        PositionableStream
            ReadStream
            WriteStream
                ReadWriteStream
                    ExternalStream
                        FileStream

        Random

    UndefinedObject
    Boolean
        False
        True

    ProcessorScheduler
    Delay
    SharedQueue

    Behavior
        ClassDescription
            Class
            MetaClass

    Point
    Rectangle
    BitBlt
        CharacterScanner

        Pen

    DisplayObject
        DisplayMedium
            Form
                Cursor
                DisplayScreen
        InfiniteForm
        OpaqueForm
        Path
            Arc
                Circle
            Curve
            Line
            LinearFit
            Spline

The Smalltalk-80 system provides support for multiple independent processes with three classes named Process, ProcessorScheduler, and Semaphore. A Process represents a sequence of actions that can be carried out independently of the actions represented by other Processes. A ProcessorScheduler schedules the use of the Smalltalk-80 virtual machine that actually carries out the actions represented by the Processes in the system. There may be many Processes whose actions are ready to be carried out and ProcessorScheduler determines which of these the virtual machine will carry out at any particular time. A Semaphore allows otherwise independent processes to synchronize their actions with each other. Semaphores provide a simple form of synchronous communication that can be used to create more complicated synchronized interactions. Semaphores also provide synchronous communication with asynchronous hardware devices such as the user input devices and realtime clock.

Semaphores are often not the most useful synchronization mechanism. Instances of SharedQueue and Delay use Semaphores to satisfy the two most common needs for synchronization. A SharedQueue provides safe transfer of objects between independent processes and a Delay allows a process to be synchronized with the real time clock.

Processes

A *process* is a sequence of actions described by expressions and performed by the Smalltalk-80 virtual machine. Several of the processes in the system monitor asynchronous hardware devices. For example, there are processes monitoring the keyboard, the pointing device, and the realtime clock. There is also a process monitoring the available memory in the system. The most important process to the user is the one that performs the actions directly specified by the user, for example, editing text, graphics, or class definitions. This user interface process must communicate with the processes monitoring the keyboard and pointing device to find out what the user is doing. Processes might be added that update a clock or a view of a user-defined object.

A new process can be created by sending the unary message fork to a block. For example, the following expression creates a new process to display three clocks named EasternTime, MountainTime, and PacificTime on the screen.

```
[EasternTime display.
 MountainTime display.
 PacificTime display] fork
```

The actions that make up the new process are described by the block's expressions. The message fork has the same effect on these expressions as does the message value, but it differs in the way the result of the message is returned. When a block receives value, it waits to return until all of its expressions have been executed. For example, the following expression does not produce a value until all three clocks have been completely displayed.

```
[EasternTime display.
 MountainTime display.
 PacificTime display] value
```

The value returned from sending a block value is the value of the last expression in the block. When a block receives fork, it returns immediately, usually before its expressions have been executed. This allows the expressions following the fork message to be executed independently of the expressions in the block. For example, the following two expressions would result in the contents of the collection nameList being sorted independently of the three clocks being displayed.

```
[EasternTime display.
 MountainTime display.
 PacificTime display] fork.
alphabeticalList ← nameList sort
```

The entire collection may be sorted before any of the clocks are displayed or all of the clocks may be displayed before the collection begins sorting. The occurrence of either one of these extreme cases or an intermediate case in which some sorting and some clock display are interspersed is determined by the way that display and sort are written. The two processes, the one that sends the messages fork and sort, and the one that sends display, are executed independently. Since a block's expressions may not have been evaluated when it returns from fork, the value of fork must be independent of the value of the block's expressions. A block returns itself as the value of fork.

Each process in the system is represented by an instance of class Process. A block's response to fork is to create a new instance of Process and schedule the processor to execute the expressions it contains. Blocks also respond to the message newProcess by creating and returning a new instance of Process, but the virtual machine is not scheduled to execute its expressions. This is useful because, unlike fork, it provides a reference to the Process itself. A Process created by newProcess is called *suspended* since its expressions are not being executed. For example, the following expression creates two new Processes but does not result in either display or sort being sent.

clockDisplayProcess ← [EasternTime display] newProcess.
sortingProcess ← [alphabeticalList ← nameList sort] newProcess

The actions represented by one of these suspended Processes can actually be carried out by sending the Process the message resume. The following two expressions would result in display being sent to EasternTime and sort being sent to nameList.

clockDisplayProcess resume.
sortingProcess resume

Since display and sort would be sent from different Processes, their execution may be interleaved. Another example of the use of resume is the implementation of fork in BlockContext.

fork
> self newProcess resume

A complementary message, suspend, returns a Process to the suspended state in which the processor is no longer executing its expressions. The message terminate prevents a Process from ever running again, whether it was suspended or not.

Process instance protocol

---

changing process state
    resume   Allow the receiver to be advanced.
    suspend   Stop the advancement of the receiver in such a way that it can resume its progress later (by sending it the message resume).
    terminate   Stop the advancement of the receiver forever.

Blocks also understand a message with selector newProcessWith: that creates and returns a new Process supplying values for block arguments. The argument of newProcessWith: is an Array whose elements are used as the values of the block arguments. The size of the Array should be equal to the number of block arguments the receiver takes. For example,

displayProcess ← [:clock | clock display]
                newProcessWith: (Array with: MountainTime)

The protocol of BlockContext (or BlockClosure in newer systems) that allows new Processes to be created is shown on the following page.

BlockContext instance protocol

scheduling

fork	Create and schedule a new Process for the execution of the expressions the receiver contains.
newProcess	Answer a new suspended Process for the execution of the expressions the receiver contains. The new Process is not scheduled.
newProcessWith: argumentArray	Answer a new suspended Process for the execution of the expressions the receiver contains supplying the elements of argumentArray as the values of the receiver's block arguments.

Scheduling

The Smalltalk-80 virtual machine has only one processor capable of carrying out the sequence of actions a Process represents. So when a Process receives the message resume, its actions may not be carried out immediately. The Process whose actions are currently being carried out is called *active*. Whenever the active Process receives the message suspend or terminate, a new active Process is chosen from those that have received resume. The single instance of class ProcessorScheduler keeps track of all of the Processes that have received resume. This instance of ProcessorScheduler has the global name Processor. The active Process can be found by sending Processor the message activeProcess. For example, the active Process can be terminated by the expression

    Processor activeProcess terminate

This will be the last expression executed in that Process. Any expressions following it in a method would never be executed. Processor will also terminate the active Process in response to the message terminateActive.

    Processor terminateActive

Priorities

Ordinarily, Processes are scheduled for the use of the processor on a simple first-come first-served basis. Whenever the active Process receives suspend or terminate, the Process that has been waiting the longest will become the new active Process. In order to provide more control of when a Process will run, Processor uses a very simple priority mechanism. There are a fixed number of priority levels numbered by ascending integers. A Process with a higher priority will gain the use of the processor before a Process with a lower priority, independent of the order of their requests. When a Process is created (with either fork or newProcess), it will receive the same priority as the Process that created it. The priority of a Process can be changed by sending it the message priority: with the priority as an argument. Or the priority of a Process can be specified when it is forked by using the message forkAt: with the priority as an argument. For example, consider the following expressions executed in a Process at priority 4.

```
wordProcess ← [['now'  displayAt: 50@100] forkAt: 6.
               ['is'  displayAt: 100@100] forkAt: 5.
                'the'  displayAt: 150@100]
                            newProcess.
wordProcess priority: 7.
'time'  displayAt: 200@100.
wordProcess resume.
'for'  displayAt: 250@100
```

The sequence of displays on the screen would be as follows.

			time	
		the	time	
now		the	time	
now	is	the	time	
now	is	the	time	for

Priorities are manipulated with a message to Processes and a message to BlockContexts.

Process instance protocol

---

accessing

    priority: anInteger   Set the receiver's priority to be anInteger.

BlockContext instance protocol

---

scheduling

    forkAt: priority   Create a new process for the execution of the expressions the receiver contains. Schedule the new process at the priority level priority.

The methods in the Smalltalk-80 system do not actually specify priorities with literal integers. The appropriate priority to use is always obtained by sending a message to Processor. The messages used to obtain priorities are shown in the protocol for class ProcessorScheduler.

One other message to Processor allows other Processes with the same priority as the active Process to gain access to the processor. The ProcessorScheduler responds to the message yield by suspending the active Process and placing it on the end of the list of Processes waiting at its priority. The first Process on the list then becomes the active Process. If there are no other Processes at the same priority, yield has no effect.

ProcessorScheduler instance protocol

---

accessing
    activePriority   Answer the priority of the currently running process.

    activeProcess   Answer the currently running process.

process state change
    terminateActive   Terminate the currently running process.

    yield   Give other processes at the priority of the currently running process a chance to run.

priority names
    highIOPriority   Answer the priority at which the most time critical input/output processes should run.

    lowIOPriority   Answer the priority at which most input/output processes should run.

    systemBackgroundPriority   Answer the priority at which system background processes should run.

    timingPriority   Answer the priority at which the system processes keeping track of real time should run.

    userBackgroundPriority   Answer the priority at which background processes created by the user should run.

    userInterruptPriority   Answer the priority at which processes created by the user and desiring immediate service should run.

    userSchedulingPriority   Answer the priority at which the user interface processes should run.

The messages to ProcessorScheduler requesting priorities were listed in alphabetical order above since this is the standard for protocol descriptions. The same messages are listed below from highest priority to lowest priority along with some examples of Processes that might have that priority.

    timingPriority   The Process monitoring the real time clock (see description of class Wakeup later in this chapter).

    highIOPriority   The Process monitoring the local network communication device.

    lowIOPriority   The Process monitoring the user input devices and the Process distributing packets from the local network.

    userInterruptPriority   Any Process forked by the user interface that should be executed immediately.

    userSchedulingPriority   The Process performing actions specified through the user interface (editing, viewing, programming, and debugging).

userBackgroundPriority	Any Process forked by the user interface that should be executed only when nothing else is happening.
systemBackgroundPriority	A system Process that should be executed when nothing else is happening.

Semaphores

The sequence of actions represented by a Process is carried out asynchronously with the actions represented by other Processes. The function of one Process is independent of the function of another. This is appropriate for Processes that never need to interact. For example, the two Processes shown below that display clocks and sort a collection probably do not need to interact with each other at all.

```
[EasternTime display.
 MountainTime display.
 PacificTime display ] fork.
alphabeticalList ← nameList sort
```

However, some Processes that are substantially independent must interact occasionally. The actions of these loosely dependent Processes must be synchronized while they interact. Instances of Semaphore provide a simple form of synchronized communication between otherwise independent Processes. A Semaphore provides for the synchronized communication of a simple (∼1 bit of information) signal from one process to another. A Semaphore provides a nonbusy wait for a Process that attempts to consume a signal that has not been produced yet. Semaphores are the only safe mechanism provided for interaction between Processes. Any other mechanisms for interaction should use Semaphores to insure their synchronization.

Communication with a Semaphore is initiated in one Process by sending it the message signal. On the other end of the communication, another Process waits to receive the simple communication by sending wait to the same Semaphore. It does not matter in which order the two messages are sent, the Process waiting for a signal will not proceed until one is sent. A Semaphore will only return from as many wait messages as it has received signal messages. If a signal and two waits are sent to a Semaphore, it will not return from one of the wait messages. When a Semaphore receives a wait message for which no corresponding signal was sent, it suspends the process from which the wait was sent.

Semaphore instance protocol

communication

signal	Send a signal through the receiver. If one or more Processes have been suspended trying to receive a signal, allow the one that has been waiting the longest to proceed. If no Process is waiting, remember the excess signal.
wait	The active Process must receive a signal through the receiver before proceeding. If no signal has been sent, the active Process will be suspended until one is sent.

The processes that have been suspended will be resumed in the same order in which they were suspended. A Process's priority is only taken into account by Processor when scheduling it for the use of the processor. Each Process waiting for a Semaphore will be resumed on a first-come first-served basis, independent of its priority. A Semaphore allows a Process to wait for a signal that has not been sent without using processor capacity. The Semaphore does not return from wait until signal has been sent. One of the main advantages of creating an independent process for a particular activity is that, if the process requires something that is not available, other processes can proceed while the first process waits for it to become available. Examples of things that a process may require and that may or may not be available are hardware devices, user events (keystrokes or pointing device movements), and shared data structures. A specific time of day can also be thought of as something that might be required for a process to proceed.

Mutual Exclusion

Semaphores can be used to ensure mutually exclusive use of certain facilities by separate Processes. For example, a Semaphore might be used to provide a data structure that can be safely accessed by separate Processes. The following definition of a simple first-in first-out data structure does not have any provision for mutual exclusion.

class name	SimpleQueue
superclass	Object
instance variable names	contentsArray
	readPosition
	writePosition

class methods

instance creation

new
    ↑self new: 10

new: size
    ↑super new init: size

instance methods

accessing

next
```
| value |
readPosition = writePosition
    ifTrue: [self error: 'empty queue']
    ifFalse: [value ← contentsArray at: readPosition.
             contentsArray at: readPosition put: nil.
             readPosition ← readPosition + 1.
             ↑value]
```

nextPut: value
```
writePosition > contentsArray size
    ifTrue: [self makeRoomForWrite].
contentsArray at: writePosition put: value.
writePosition ← writePosition + 1.
↑value
```

size
```
↑writePosition - readPosition
```

testing

isEmpty
```
↑writePosition = readPosition
```

private

init: size
```
contentsArray ← Array new: size.
readPosition ← 1.
writePosition ← 1
```

makeRoomForWrite
```
| contentsSize |
readPosition = 1
    ifTrue: [contentsArray grow]
    ifFalse:
        [contentsSize ← writePosition − readPosition.
        1 to: contentsSize do:
            [ :index |
             contentsArray
                 at: index
                 put: (contentsArray at: index + readPosition − 1)].
        readPosition ← 1.
        writePosition ← contentsSize + 1]
```

A SimpleQueue remembers its contents in an Array named contentsArray and maintains two indices into the contentsArray named readPosition and writePosition. New contents are added at writePosition and removed at readPosition. The private message makeRoomForWrite is sent when there is no room at the end of contentsArray for remembering a new object. If contentsArray is completely full, its size is increased. Otherwise, the contents are moved to the first of contentsArray.

The problem with sending to a SimpleQueue from different Processes is that more than one Process at a time may be executing the method for next or nextPut:. Suppose a SimpleQueue were sent the message next from one Process, and had just executed the expression

value ← contentsArray at: readPosition

when a higher priority Process woke up and sent another next message to the same SimpleQueue. Since readPosition has not been incremented, the second execution of the expresson above will bind the same object to value. The higher priority Process will remove the reference to the object from contentsArray, increment the readPosition and return the object it removed. When the lower priority Process gets control back, readPosition has been incremented so it removes the reference to the next object from contentsArray. This object should have been the value of one of the next messages, but it is discarded and both next messages return the same object.

To ensure mutual exclusion, each Process must wait for the same Semaphore before using a resource and then signal the Semaphore when it is finished. The following subclass of SimpleQueue provides mutual exclusion so that its instances can be used from separate Processes.

class name	SimpleSharedQueue
superclass	SimpleQueue
instance variable names	accessProtect
instance methods	

accessing

next
```
| value |
accessProtect wait.
value ← super next.
accessProtect signal.
↑value
```

nextPut: value
```
accessProtect wait.
super nextPut: value.
accessProtect signal.
↑value
```

private

init: size
    super init: size.
    accessProtect ← Semaphore new.
    accessProtect signal

Since mutual exclusion is a common use of Semaphores, they include a message for it. The selector of this message is critical:. The implementation of critical: is as follows.

critical: aBlock
    | value |
    self wait.
    value ← aBlock value.
    self signal.
    ↑value

A Semaphore used for mutual exclusion must start out with one excess signal so the first Process may enter the critical section. Class Semaphore provides a special initialization message, forMutualExclusion, that signals the new instance once.

Semaphore instance protocol

mutual exclusion
    critical: aBlock   Execute aBlock when no other critical blocks
                                        are executing.

Semaphore class protocol

instance creation
    forMutualExclusion   Answer a new Semaphore with one excess sig-
                                        nal.

The implementation of SimpleSharedQueue could be changed to read as follows.

class name	SimpleSharedQueue
superclass	SimpleQueue
instance variable names	accessProtect
instance methods	

accessing

next
    | value |
    accessProtect critical: [value ← super next].
    ↑value

nextPut: value
    accessProtect critical: [super nextPut: value].
    ↑value

private

init: size
super init: size.
accessProtect ← Semaphore forMutualExclusion

Resource Sharing

In order for two Processes to share a resource, mutually exclusive access to it is not enough. The Processes must also be able to communicate about the availability of the resource. SimpleSharedQueue will not get confused by simultaneous accesses, but if an attempt is made to remove an object from an empty SimpleSharedQueue, an error occurs. In an environment with asynchronous Processes, it is inconvenient to guarantee that attempts to remove objects (by sending next) will be made only after they have been added (by sending nextPut:). Therefore, Semaphores are also used to signal the availability of shared resources. A Semaphore representing a resource is signalled after each unit of the resource is made available and waited for before consuming each unit. Therefore, if an attempt is made to consume a resource before it has been produced, the consumer simply waits.

Class SafeSharedQueue is an example of how Semaphores can be used to communicate about the availability of resources. SafeSharedQueue is similar to SimpleSharedQueue, but it uses another Semaphore named valueAvailable to represent the availability of the contents of the queue. SafeSharedQueue is not in the Smalltalk-80 system, it is described here only as an example. SharedQueue is the class that is actually used to communicate between processes in the system. SharedQueue provides functionality similar to SafeSharedQueue's. The protocol specification for SharedQueue will be given later in this chapter.

class name	SafeSharedQueue
superclass	SimpleQueue
instance variable names	accessProtect
	valueAvailable

instance methods

accessing

next
| value |
valueAvailable wait.
accessProtect critical: [value ← super next].
↑value
nextPut: value
accessProtect critical: [super nextPut: value].
valueAvailable signal.
↑value

private

init: size
    super init: size.
    accessProtect ← Semaphore forMutualExclusion.
    valueAvailable ← Semaphore new

Hardware
Interrupts

Instances of Semaphore are also used to communicate between hardware devices and Processes. In this capacity, they take the place of interrupts as a means of communicating about the changes of state that hardware devices go through. The Smalltalk-80 virtual machine is specified to signal Semaphores on three conditions.

- user event: a key has been pressed on the keyboard, a button has been pressed on the pointing device, or the pointing device has moved.

- timeout: a specific value of the millisecond clock has been reached.

- low space: available object memory has fallen below certain limits.

These three Semaphores correspond to three Processes monitoring user events, the millisecond clock and memory utilization. Each monitoring Process sends wait to the appropriate Semaphore suspending itself until something of interest happens. Whenever the Semaphore is signalled, the Process will resume. The virtual machine is notified about these three types of monitoring by primitive methods. For example, the timeout signal can be requested by a primitive method associated with the message signal:atTime: to Processor.

Class Wakeup is an example of how one of these Semaphores can be used. Wakeup provides an alarm clock service to Processes by monitoring the millisecond clock. Wakeup is not in the Smalltalk-80 system; it is described here only as an example. Delay is the class that actually monitors the millisecond clock in the Smalltalk-80 system. Delay provides functionality similar to Wakeup's. The protocol specification for Delay will be given later in this chapter.

Wakeup provides a message that suspends the sending Process for a specified number of milliseconds. The following expression suspends its Process for three quarters of a second.

Wakeup after: 750

When Wakeup receives an after: message, it allocates a new instance which remembers the value of the clock at which the wakeup should occur. The new instance contains a Semaphore on which the active Process will be suspended until the wakeup time is reached. Wakeup keeps all of its instances in a list sorted by their wakeup times. A Process monitors the virtual machine's millisecond clock for the earliest of these wakeup times and allows the appropriate suspended Process to proceed. This Process is created in the class method for initializeTimingProcess. The Semaphore used to monitor the clock is referred to by a class variable named TimingSemaphore. The virtual machine is informed that the clock should be monitored with the following message found in the instance method for nextWakeup.

Processor signal: TimingSemaphore atTime: resumptionTime

The list of instances waiting for resumption is referred to by a class variable named PendingWakeups. There is another Semaphore named AccessProtect that provides mutually exclusive access to PendingWakeups.

class name	Wakeup
superclass	Object
instance variable names	alarmTime
	alarmSemaphore
class variable names	PendingWakeups
	AccessProtect
	TimingSemaphore

class methods

alarm clock service

after: millisecondCount
    (self new sleepDuration: millisecondCount) waitForWakeup

class initialization

initialize
    TimingSemaphore ← Semaphore new.
    AccessProtect ← Semaphore forMutualExclusion.
    PendingWakeups ← SortedCollection new.
    self initializeTimingProcess
initializeTimingProcess
    [[true]
        whileTrue:
            [TimingSemaphore wait.
             AccessProtect wait.
             PendingWakeups removeFirst wakeup.
             PendingWakeups isEmpty
                ifFalse: [PendingWakeups first nextWakeup].
             AccessProtect signal]]
                    forkAt: Processor timingPriority

instance methods

process delay

waitForWakeup
AccessProtect wait.
PendingWakeups add: self.
PendingWakeups first == self
    ifTrue: [self nextWakeup].
AccessProtect signal.
alarmSemaphore wait

comparison

< otherWakeup
↑alarmTime < otherWakeup wakeupTIme

accessing

wakeupTime
↑alarmTime

private

nextWakeup
Processor signal: TimingSemaphore atTime: resumptionTime
sleepDuration: millisecondCount
alarmTime ← Time millisecondClockValue + millisecondCount.
alarmSemaphore ← Semaphore new
wakeup
alarmSemaphore signal

Class
SharedQueue

Class SharedQueue is the system class whose instances provide safe communication of objects between Processes. Both its protocol and its implementation are similar to the SafeSharedQueue example shown earlier in this chapter.

SharedQueue instance protocol

accessing

next	Answer with the first object added to the receiver that has not yet been removed. If the receiver is empty, suspend the active Process until an object is added to it.
nextPut: value	Add value to the contents of the receiver. If a Process has been suspended waiting for an object, allow it to proceed.

Class Delay

A Delay allows a Process to be suspended for a specified amount of time. A Delay is created by specifying how long it will suspend the active Process.

halfMinuteDelay ← Delay forSeconds: 30.
shortDelay ← Delay forMilliseconds: 50

Simply creating a Delay has no effect on the progress of the active Process. It is in response to the message wait that a Delay suspends the active Process. The following expressions would both suspend the active Process for 30 seconds.

halfMinuteDelay wait.
(Delay forSeconds: 30) wait

Delay class protocol

---

instance creation
    forMilliseconds: millisecondCount   Answer with a new instance that will suspend the active Process for millisecondCount milliseconds when sent the message wait.

    forSeconds: secondCount   Answer with a new instance that will suspend the active Process for secondCount seconds when sent the message wait.

    untilMilliseconds: millisecondCount
         Answer with a new instance that will suspend the active Process until the millisecond clock reaches the value millisecondCount.

    general inquiries
        millisecondClockValue   Answer with the current value of the millisecond clock.

Delay instance protocol

---

accessing
    resumptionTime   Answer with the value of the millisecond clock at which the delayed Process will be resumed.

process delay
    wait   Suspend the active Process until the millisecond clock reaches the appropriate value.

A trivial clock can be implemented with the following expression.

[[true] whileTrue:
        [Time now printString displayAt: 100@100.
        (Delay forSeconds: 1) wait]] fork

The current time would be displayed on the screen once a second.

16

Protocol for Classes

Class Behavior

Class ClassDescription

Class Metaclass

Class Class

Object

Magnitude
    Character
    Date
    Time

    Number
        Float
        Fraction
        Integer
            LargeNegativeInteger
            LargePositiveInteger
            SmallInteger

    LookupKey
        Association

Link

    Process

Collection

    SequenceableCollection
    LinkedList

        Semaphore

    ArrayedCollection
    Array

        WordArray
            DisplayBitmap

        RunArray
        String
            Symbol
        Text
        ByteArray

    Interval
    OrderedCollection
        SortedCollection
    Bag
    MappedCollection
    Set
        Dictionary
            IdentityDictionary

Stream
    PositionableStream
        ReadStream
        WriteStream
            ReadWriteStream
                ExternalStream
                    FileStream

    Random

UndefinedObject
Boolean
    False
    True

ProcessorScheduler
Delay
SharedQueue

Behavior
    ClassDescription
        Class
        MetaClass

Point
Rectangle
BitBlt
    CharacterScanner

    Pen

DisplayObject
    DisplayMedium
        Form
            Cursor
            DisplayScreen
    InfiniteForm
    OpaqueForm
    Path
        Arc
            Circle
        Curve
        Line
        LinearFit
        Spline

We have now introduced the protocol for most of the classes that describe the basic components of the Smalltalk-80 system. One notable exception is the protocol for the classes themselves. Four classes—Behavior, ClassDescription, Metaclass, and Class—interact to provide the facilities needed to describe new classes. Creating a new class involves compiling methods and specifying names for instance variables, class variables, pool variables, and the class itself.

Chapters 3, 4, and 5 introduced the basic concepts represented by these classes. To summarize from that discussion, the Smalltalk-80 programmer specifies a new class by creating a subclass of another class. For example, class Collection is a subclass of Object; class Array is a subclass of ArrayedCollection (whose superclass chain terminates with Object).

1. Every class is ultimately a subclass of class Object, except for Object itself, which has no superclass. In particular, Class is a subclass of ClassDescription, which is a subclass of Behavior which is a subclass of Object.

There are two kinds of objects in the system, ones that can create instances of themselves (classes) and ones that can not.

2. Every object is an instance of a class.

Each class is itself an instance of a class. We call the class of a class, its metaclass.

3. Every class is an instance of a metaclass.

Metaclasses are not referenced by class names as are other classes. Instead, they are referred to by a message expression sending the unary message class to the instance of the metaclass. For example, the metaclass of Collection is referred to as Collection class; the metaclass of Class is referred to as Class class.

In the Smalltalk-80 system, a metaclass is created automatically whenever a new class is created. A metaclass has only one instance. The messages categorized as "class methods" in the class descriptions are found in the metaclass of the class. This follows from the way in which methods are found; when a message is sent to an object, the search for the corresponding method begins in the class of the object. When a message is sent to Dictionary, for example, the search begins in the metaclass of Dictionary. If the method is not found in the metaclass, then the search proceeds to the superclass of the metaclass. In this case, the superclass is Set class, the metaclass for Dictionary's superclass. If necessary, the search follows the superclass chain to Object class.

In the diagrams in this chapter, all arrows with solid lines denote a subclass relationship; arrows with dashed lines an instance relationship. A ---> B means A is an instance of B. Solid gray lines indicate the class hierarchy; solid black lines indicate the metaclass hierarchy.

Figure 16.1

Since the superclass chain of all objects ends at Object as shown in Figure 16.1, and Object has no superclass, the superclass of Object's metaclass is not determined by the rule of maintaining a parallel hierarchy. It is at this point that Class is found. The superclass of Object class is Class.

4. All metaclasses are (ultimately) subclasses of Class (Figure 16.2).

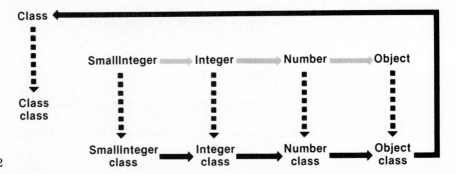

Figure 16.2

Since metaclasses are objects, they too must be instances of a class. Every metaclass is an instance of Metaclass. Metaclass itself is an instance of a metaclass. This is a point of circularity in the system—the metaclass of Metaclass must be an instance of Metaclass.

5. Every metaclass is an instance of Metaclass (Figure 16.3).

Figure 16.4 shows the relationships among Class, ClassDescription, Behavior, and Object, and their respective metaclasses. The class hierarchy follows a chain to Object, and the metaclass hierarchy follows a chain through Object class to Class and on to Object. While the methods of

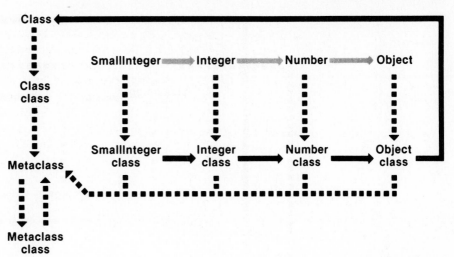

Figure 16.3

Object support the behavior common to all objects, the methods of Class and Metaclass support the behavior common to all classes.

6. The methods of Class and its superclasses support the behavior common to those objects that are classes.

7. The methods of instances of Metaclass add the behavior specific to particular classes.

The correspondence between the class and metaclass hierarchies is shown in Figure 16.5, in which the part of the number hierarchy and the behavior hierarchy of the last two figures are combined.

Figure 16.4

Figure 16.5

Class Behavior

Class Behavior defines the minimum state necessary for objects that have instances. In particular, Behavior defines the state used by the Smalltalk-80 interpreter. It provides the basic interface to the compiler. The state described by Behavior includes a class hierarchy link, a method dictionary, and a description of instances in terms of the number and the representation of their variables.

The message protocol for class Behavior will be described in four categories—*creating, accessing, testing,* and *enumerating.* These categories and their subcategories, as outlined below, provide a model for thinking about the functionality of classes in the Smalltalk-80 system.

Outline of Protocol for All Classes

creating
- creating a method dictionary
- creating instances
- creating a class hierarchy

accessing
- accessing the contents of the method dictionary
- accessing instances and variables: instance, class, and pool
- accessing the class hierarchy

testing
- testing the contents of the method dictionary
- testing the form of the instances
- testing the class hierarchy

enumerating
- enumerating subclasses and instances

☐ Behavior's *Creating Protocol* The methods in a class description are stored in a dictionary we refer to as the *method dictionary*. It is also sometimes called a message dictionary. The keys in this dictionary are message selectors; the values are the compiled form of methods (instances of CompiledMethod). The protocol for creating the method dictionary supports compiling methods as well as adding the association between a selector and a compiled method. It also supports accessing both the compiled and noncompiled (source) versions of the method.

Behavior instance protocol

creating method dictionary

methodDictionary: aDictionary	Store the argument, aDictionary, as the method dictionary of the receiver.
addSelector: selector withMethod: compiledMethod	
	Add the message selector, selector, with the corresponding compiled method, compiledMethod, to the receiver's method dictionary.
removeSelector: selector	Remove the argument, selector (which is a Symbol representing a message selector), from the receiver's method dictionary. If the selector is not in the method dictionary, report an error.
compile: code	The argument, code, is either a String or an object that converts to a String or it is a PositionableStream accessing an object that is or converts to a String. Compile code as the source code in the context of the receiver's variables. Report an error if the code can not be compiled.

compile: code notifying: requestor	Compile the argument, code, and enter the result in the receiver's method dictionary. If an error occurs, send an appropriate message to the argument, requestor.
recompile: selector	Compile the method associated with the message selector, selector.
decompile: selector	Find the compiled code associated with the argument, selector, and decompile it. Answer the resulting source code as a String. If the selector is not in the method dictionary, report an error.
compileAll	Compile all the methods in the receiver's method dictionary.
compileAllSubclasses	Compile all the methods in the receiver's subclasses' method dictionaries.

Instances of classes are created by sending the message new or new:. These two messages can be overridden in the method dictionary of a metaclass in order to supply special initialization behavior. The purpose of any special initialization is to guarantee that an instance is created with variables that are themselves appropriate instances. We have demonstrated this idea in many previous chapters. Look, for example, at the definition of class Random in Chapter 12; the method dictionary of Random class (the class methods) contains an implementation for new in which a new instance is sent the message setSeed; this initialization guarantees that the random number generation algorithm refers to a variable that is an appropriate kind of number.

Suppose a class overrides the method for new and then one of its subclasses wishes to do the same in order to avoid the behavior created by its superclass's change. The method for the first class might be

new
    ↑super new setVariables

where the message setVariables is provided in the protocol for instances of the class. By sending the message new to the pseudo-variable super, the method for creating an instance as specified in class Behavior is evaluated; the result, the new instance, is then sent the message setVariables. In the subclass, it is not possible to utilize the message super new because this will invoke the method of the first class—precisely the method to be avoided. In order to obtain the basic method in Behavior for creating an instance, the subclass must use the expression self basicNew. The message basicNew is the primitive instance creation message that should not be reimplemented in any subclass. In Behavior, new and basicNew are identical. A similar pair for creating variable-length objects, new: and basicNew:, are also provided in the protocol of class Behavior. (Note, this technique of dual messages is also used in class Object for accessing messages such as at: and at:put:.)

Behavior instance protocol

instance creation

new	Answer an instance of the receiver with no indexed variables. Send the receiver the message new: 0 if the receiver is indexable.
basicNew	Same as new, except this method should not be overridden in a subclass.
new: anInteger	Answer an instance of the receiver with anInteger number of indexed variables. Report an error if the receiver is not indexable.
basicNew: anInteger	Same as basicNew, except this method should not be overridden in a subclass.

The protocol for creating classes includes messages for placing the class within the hierarchy of classes in the system. Since this hierarchy is linear, there is only a need to set the superclass and to add or remove subclasses.

Behavior instance protocol

creating a class hierarchy

superclass: aClass	Set the superclass of the receiver to be the argument, aClass.
addSubclass: aClass	Make the argument, aClass, be a subclass of the receiver.
removeSubclass: aClass	Remove the argument, aClass, from the subclasses of the receiver.

Although the creating protocol for Behavior makes it possible to write expressions for creating a new class description, the usual approach is to take advantage of the graphical environment in which the Smalltalk-80 language is embedded, and to provide an interface in which the user fills out graphically-presented forms to specify information about the various parts of a class.

☐ Behavior's *Accessing Protocol*   The messages that access the contents of a method dictionary distinguish among the selectors in the class's locally specified method dictionary, and those in the method dictionaries of the class and each of its superclasses.

Behavior instance protocol

accessing the method dictionary

selectors	Answer a Set of all the message selectors specified in the receiver's local method dictionary.
allSelectors	Answer a Set of all the message selectors that instances of the receiver can understand. This consists of all message selectors in the receiver's method dictionary and in the dictionaries of each of the receiver's superclasses.

compiledMethodAt: selector	Answer the compiled method associated with the argument, selector, a message selector in the receiver's local method dictionary. Report an error if the selector can not be found.
sourceCodeAt: selector	Answer a String that is the source code associated with the argument, selector, a message selector in the receiver's local method dictionary. Report an error if the selector can not be found.
sourceMethodAt: selector	Answer a Text for the source code associated with the argument, selector, a message selector in the receiver's local method dictionary. This Text provides boldface emphasis for the message pattern part of the method. Report an error if the selector can not be found.

An instance can have named instance variables, indexed instance variables, class variables, and dictionaries of pool variables. Again, the distinction between locally specified variables and variables inherited from superclasses is made in the accessing protocol.

Behavior instance protocol

accessing instances and variables

allInstances	Answer a Set of all direct instances of the receiver.
someInstance	Answer an existing instance of the receiver.
instanceCount	Answer the number of instances of the receiver that currently exist.
instVarNames	Answer an Array of the instance variable names specified in the receiver.
subclassInstVarNames	Answer a Set of the instance variable names specified in the receiver's subclasses.
allInstVarNames	Answer an Array of the names of the receiver's instance variables, those specified in the receiver and in all of its superclasses. The Array ordering is the order in which the variables are stored and accessed by the Smalltalk-80 interpreter.
classVarNames	Answer a Set of the class variable names specified locally in the receiver.
allClassVarNames	Answer a Set of the names of the receiver's and the receiver's superclasses' class variables.
sharedPools	Answer a Set of the names of the pools (dictionaries) that are specified locally in the receiver.
allSharedPools	Answer a Set of the names of the pools (dictionaries) that are specified in the receiver and each of its superclasses.

Thus, for example,

expression	result
OrderedCollection instVarNames	('firstIndex' 'lastIndex')
OrderedCollection subclassInstVarNames	Set ('sortBlock')
SortedCollection allInstVarNames	('firstIndex' 'lastIndex' 'sortBlock')
String classVarNames	Set (StringBlter)
String allClassVarNames	Set (StringBlter DependentsFields ErrorRecursion)
Text sharedPools	a Set containing one element, TextConstants, a Dictionary

The accessing protocol includes messages for obtaining collections of the superclasses and subclasses of a class. These messages distinguish between a class's immediate superclass and subclasses, and all classes in the class's superclass chain.

Behavior instance protocol

accessing class hierarchy

subclasses	Answer a Set containing the receiver's immediate subclasses.
allSubclasses	Answer a Set of the receiver's subclasses and the receiver's descendent's subclasses.
withAllSubclasses	Answer a Set of the receiver, the receiver's subclasses and the receiver's descendent's subclasses.
superclass	Answer the receiver's immediate superclass.
allSuperclasses	Answer an OrderedCollection of the receiver's superclass and the receiver's ancestor's superclasses. The first element is the receiver's immediate superclass, followed by its superclass, and so on; the last element is always Object.

Thus, for example

expression	result
String superclass	ArrayedCollection
ArrayedCollection subclasses	Set (Array ByteArray RunArray Bitmap String Text)

ArrayedCollection
  allSubclasses
	Set (Array ByteArray
	  RunArray Bitmap
	  String Text
	  DisplayBitmap Symbol
	  CompiledMethod)

ArrayedCollection
  withAllSubclasses
	Set
	  (ArrayedCollection
	  Array ByteArray
	  RunArray Bitmap
	  String Text
	  DisplayBitmap Symbol
	  CompiledMethod)

ArrayedCollection
  allSuperclasses
	OrderedCollection
	  (SequenceableCollection
	  Collection Object)

ArrayedCollection
  class allSuperclasses
	OrderedCollection
	  (SequenceableCollection
	  class Collection class
	  Object class Class
	  ClassDescription
	  Behavior Object)

☐ Behavior's *Testing Protocol*   Testing protocol provides the messages needed to find out information about the structure of a class and the form of its instances. The structure of a class consists of its relationship to other classes, its ability to respond to messages, the class in which a message is specified, and so on.

The contents of a method dictionary can be tested to find out which class, if any, implements a particular message selector, whether a class can respond to a message, and which methods reference particular variables or literals. These messages are all useful in creating a programming environment in which the programmer can explore the structure and functionality of objects in the system.

Behavior instance protocol

testing the method dictionary hasMethods	Answer whether the receiver has any methods in its (local) method dictionary.
includesSelector: selector	Answer whether the message whose selector is the argument, selector, is in the local method dictionary of the receiver's class.
canUnderstand: selector	Answer whether the receiver can respond to the message whose selector is the argument.

The selector can be in the method dictionary of the receiver's class or any of its superclasses.

whichClassIncludesSelector: selector

Answer the first class on the receiver's superclass chain where the argument, selector, can be found as a message selector. Answer nil if no class includes the selector.

whichSelectorsAccess: instVarName

Answer a Set of selectors from the receiver's local method dictionary whose methods access the argument, instVarName, as a named instance variable.

whichSelectorsReferTo: anObject Answer a Set of selectors whose methods access the argument, anObject.

scopeHas: name ifTrue: aBlock Determine whether the variable name, name, is within the scope of the receiver, i.e., it is specified as a variable in the receiver or in one of its superclasses. If so, evalaute the argument, aBlock.

Thus, for example

expression	*result*

OrderedCollection
    includesSelector:
        #addFirst:
	true

SortedCollection includesSelector: #size	false
SortedCollection canUnderstand: #size	true

SortedCollection
    whichClassIncludesSelector:
        #size
	OrderedCollection

OrderedCollection
    whichSelectorsAccess:
        #firstIndex
	Set
	  (makeRoomAtFirst
	  before: size
	  makeRoomAtLast
	  insert:before:
	  remove:ifAbsent:
	  addFirst: first
	  removeFirst find:
	  removeAllSuchThat:
	  at: at:put: reverseDo:
	  do: setIndices:)

The last example expression is useful in determining which methods must be changed if an instance variable is renamed or deleted. In addition to the messages intended for external access, the Set includes all messages implemented in support of the implementation of the external messages.

The testing protocol includes messages to a class that test how its variables are stored, whether the number of variables is fixed-length or variable-length, and the number of named instance variables.

Behavior instance protocol
---

testing the form of the instances

isPointers	Answer whether the variables of instances of the receiver are stored as pointers (words).
isBits	Answer whether the variables of instances of the receiver are stored as bits (i.e., not pointers).
isBytes	Answer whether the variables of instances of the receiver are stored as bytes (8-bit integers).
isWords	Answer whether the variables of instances of the receiver are stored as words.
isFixed	Answer true if instances of the receiver do not have indexed instance variables; answer false otherwise.
isVariable	Answer true if instances of the receiver do have indexed instance variables; answer false otherwise.
instSize	Answer the number of named instance variables of the receiver.

So we have

expression	result
LinkedList isFixed	true
String isBytes	true
Integer isBits	false
Float isWords	true
OrderedCollection isFixed	false
OrderedCollection instSize	2

oc ← OrderedCollection
    with: $a
    with: $b
    with: $c
	OrderedCollection
	    ($a $b $c)

oc size	3

The last four example lines show that instances of OrderedCollection are variable-length; the instance oc has three elements. In addition, instances of OrderedCollection have two named instance variables.

There are four kinds of classes in the system. Classes that have indexed instance variables are called *variable-length* and classes that do not are called *fixed-length*. The variables of all fixed-length classes are stored as pointers (word-sized references). The variables of variable-length classes can contain pointers, bytes, or words. Since a pointer is a word-sized reference, an object that contains pointers will answer true when asked whether it contains words, but the inverse is not always the case. Initialization messages specified in Class and itemized in a later section support creation of each kind of class.

Behavior instance protocol
_____

testing the class hierarchy
    inheritsFrom: aClass   Answer whether the argument, aClass, is on the receiver's superclass chain.

    kindOfSubclass   Answer a String that is the keyword that describes the receiver as a class: either a regular (fixed length) subclass, a variableSubclass, a variableByteSubclass, or a variableWordSubclass.

Thus

expression	result
String inheritsFrom: Collection	true
String kindOfSubclass	' variableByteSubclass: '
Array kindOfSubclass	' variableSubclass: '
Float kindOfSubclass	' variableWordSubclass: '
Integer kindOfSubclass	' subclass: '

□ Behavior's *Enumerating Protocol* Messages specified in class Behavior also support listing out particular sets of objects associated with a class and applying each as the argument of a block. This enumeration of objects is similar to that provided in the collection classes, and consists of enumerating over all subclasses, superclasses, instances, and instances of subclasses. In addition, two messages support selecting those subclasses or superclasses for which a block evaluates to true.

Behavior instance protocol
_____

enumerating
    allSubclassesDo: aBlock   Evaluate the argument, aBlock, for each of the receiver's subclasses.

    allSuperclassesDo: aBlock   Evaluate the argument, aBlock, for each of the receiver's superclasses.

    allInstancesDo: aBlock   Evaluate the argument, aBlock, for each of the current instances of the receiver.

allSubinstancesDo: aBlock	Evaluate the argument, aBlock, for each of the current instances of the receiver's subclasses.
selectSubclasses: aBlock	Evaluate the argument, aBlock, for each of the receiver's subclasses. Collect into a Set only those subclasses for which aBlock evaluates to true. Answer the resulting Set.
selectSuperclasses: aBlock	Evaluate the argument, aBlock, with each of the receiver's superclasses. Collect into a Set only those superclasses for which aBlock evaluates to true. Answer the resulting Set.

As an example, in order to understand the behavior of an instance of the collection classes, it might be useful to know which subclasses of Collection implement the adding message addFirst:. With this information, the programmer can track down which method is actually evaluated when the message addFirst: is sent to a collection. The following expression collects each such class into a Set named subs.

```
subs ← Set new.
Collection allSubclassesDo:
        [ :class |
        (class includesSelector: #addFirst:)
            ifTrue: [subs add: class]]
```

The same information is accessible from

```
Collection selectSubclasses:
                [ :class | class includesSelector: #addFirst:]
```

Both create a Set of the three subclasses LinkedList, OrderedCollection, and RunArray.

The following expression returns a collection of the superclasses of SmallInteger that implement the message =.

```
SmallInteger selectSuperclasses:
                [ :class | class includesSelector: #=]
```

The response is

```
Set (Integer Magnitude Object )
```

Several subclasses of Collection implement the message first. Suppose we wish to see a list of the code for each implementation. The following expressions print the code on the file whose name is 'classMethods.first'.

```
| aStream |
aStream ← FileStream fileNamed: 'classMethods.first'.
Collection allSubclassesDo:
        [ :class |
          (class includesSelector: #first)
            ifTrue:
                [class name printOn: aStream.
                 aStream cr.
                 (class sourceCodeAt: #first) printOn: aStream.
                 aStream cr; cr]].
aStream close
```

The resulting contents of the file is

```
SequenceableCollection
'first
    self emptyCheck.
    ↑self at: 1'
OrderedCollection
'first
    self emptyCheck.
    ↑self basicAt: firstIndex'
Interval
'first
    ↑start'
LinkedList
'first
    self emptyCheck.
    ↑firstLink'
```

The protocol described in the next sections is not generally used by programmers, but may be of interest to system developers. The messages described are typically accessed in the programming environment by selecting items from a menu presented in a graphically-oriented interface.

Although most of the facilities of a class are specified in the protocol of Behavior, a number of the messages can not be implemented because Behavior does not provide a complete representation for a class. In particular, Behavior does not provide a representation for instance variable names and class variable names, nor for a class name and a comment about the class.

Representations for a class name, class comment, and instance variable names are provided in ClassDescription, a subclass of Behavior. ClassDescription has two subclasses, Class and Metaclass. Class describes the representation for class variable names and pool variables. A metaclass shares the class and pool variables of its sole instance. Class adds additional protocol for adding and removing class variables and pool variables, and for creating the various kinds of subclasses. Metaclass adds an initialization message for creating a subclass of itself, that is, a message for creating a metaclass for a new class.

Class
ClassDescription

ClassDescription represents class naming, class commenting, and naming instance variables. This is reflected in additional protocol for accessing the name and comment, and for adding and removing instance variables.

ClassDescription instance protocol	
accessing class description	
name	Answer a String that is the name of the receiver.
comment	Answer a String that is the comment for the receiver.
comment: aString	Set the receiver's comment to be the argument, aString.
addInstVarName: aString	Add the argument, aString, as one of the receiver's instance variables.
removeInstVarName: aString	Remove the argument, aString, as one of the receiver's instance variables. Report an error if aString is not found.

ClassDescription was provided as a common superclass for Class and Metaclass in order to provide further structuring to the description of a class. This helps support a general program development environment. Specifically, ClassDescription adds structure for organizing the selector/method pairs of the method dictionary. This organization is a simple categorization scheme by which the subsets of the dictionary are grouped and named, precisely the way we have been grouping and naming messages throughout the chapters of this book. ClassDescription also provides the mechanisms for storing a full class description on an external stream (a file), and the mechanisms by which any changes to the class description are logged.

The classes themselves are also grouped into system category classifications. The organization of the chapters of this part of the book parallels that of the system class categories, for example, magnitudes, numbers, collections, kernel objects, kernel classes, and kernel support. Protocol for message and class categorization includes the following messages.

organization of messages and classes

category	Answer the system organization category for the receiver.
category: aString	Categorize the receiver under the system category, aString, removing the receiver from any previous category.
removeCategory: aString	Remove each of the messages categorized under the name aString and then remove the category itself.
whichCategoryIncludesSelector: selector	
	Answer the category of the argument, selector, in the organization of the receiver's method dictionary, or answer nil if the selector can not be found.

Given a categorization of the messages, ClassDescription is able to support a set of messages for copying messages from one method dictionary to another, retaining or changing the category name. Messages to support copying consists of

copy: selector from: aClass
copy: selector from: aClass classified: categoryName
copyAll: arrayOfSelectors from: class
copyAll: arrayOfSelectors from: class classified: categoryName
copyAllCategoriesFrom: aClass
copyCategory: categoryName from: aClass
copyCategory: categoryName
     from: aClass
     classified: newCategoryName

The categorization scheme has an impact on protocol for compiling since a compiled method must be placed in a particular category. Two messages are provided: compile: code classified: categoryName and compile: code classified: categoryName notifying: requestor.

We also note, for the next example, that ClassDescription supports special printing protocol so that arguments to the compiling messages can be computed. These are

printing

classVariablesString	Answer a String that contains the names of each class variable in the receiver's variable declaration.
instanceVariablesString	Answer a String that contains the names of each instance variable in the receiver's variable declaration.

sharedPoolsString

Answer a String that contains the names of each pool dictionary in the receiver's variable declaration.

Take as an example the creation of a class named AuditTrail. This class should be just like LinkedList, except that removing elements should not be supported. Therefore, the class can be created by copying the accessing, testing, adding, and enumerating protocol of LinkedList. We assume that the elements of an AuditTrail are instances of a subclass of Link that supports storing the audit information. First, let's create the class. We assume that we do not know internal information about LinkedList so that the superclass name and variables must be accessed by sending messages to LinkedList.

```
LinkedList superclass
        subclass: #AuditTrail
        instanceVariableNames: LinkedList instanceVariablesString
        classVariableNames: LinkedList classVariablesString
        poolDictionaries: LinkedList sharedPoolsString
        category: 'Record Keeping'.
```

AuditTrail is created as a subclass of whichever class is the superclass for LinkedList (LinkedList superclass). Now we copy the categories we are interested in from class LinkedList.

```
AuditTrail copyCategory: #accessing from: LinkedList.
AuditTrail copyCategory: #testing from: LinkedList.
AuditTrail copyCategory: #adding from: LinkedList.
AuditTrail copyCategory: #enumerating from: LinkedList.
AuditTrail copyCategory: #private from: LinkedList.
```

AuditTrail declared two instance variable names, firstLink and lastLink, and copied messages first, last, size, isEmpty, add:, addFirst:, and addLast:. We also copied all the messages in the category private on the assumption that at least one of them is needed in the implementation of the external messages.

Some messages in ClassDescription that support storing the class description on an external stream are

ClassDescription instance protocol

filing

fileOutOn: aFileStream

Store a description of the receiver on the file accessed by the argument, aFileStream.

fileOutCategory: categoryName

Create a file whose name is the name of the receiver concatenated by an extension, '.st'. Store on it a description of the messages categorized as categoryName.

fileOutChangedMessages: setOfChanges on: aFileStream

> The argument, setOfChanges, is a collection of class/message pairs that were changed. Store a description of each of these pairs on the file accessed by the argument, aFileStream.

We can write a description of class AuditTrail on the file 'AuditTrail.st' by evaluating the expression

AuditTrail fileOutOn: (FileStream fileNamed: 'AuditTrail.st')

Class Metaclass
The primary role of a metaclass in the Smalltalk-80 system is to provide protocol for initializing class variables and for creating initialized instances of the metaclass's sole instance. Thus the key messages added by Metaclass are themselves initialization messages—one is sent to Metaclass itself in order to create a subclass of it, and one is sent to an instance of Metaclass in order to create its sole instance.

Metaclass class protocol

---

instance creation
    subclassOf: superMeta

> Answer an instance of Metaclass that is a subclass of the metaclass, superMeta.

Metaclass instance protocol

---

class hierarchy
name: newName
    inEnvironment: aSystemDictionary
    subclassOf: superClass
    instanceVariableNames: stringOfInstVarNames
    variable: variableBoolean
    words: wordBoolean
    pointers: pointerBoolean
    classVariableNames: stringOfClassVarNames
    poolDictionaries: stringOfPoolNames
    category: categoryName
    comment: commentString
    changed: changed

> Each of these arguments, of course, is needed in order to create a fully initialized class.

The Smalltalk-80 programming environment provides a simplified way, using graphical interface techniques, in which the user specifies the information to create new classes.

Class Class

Instances of Class describe the representation and behavior of objects. Class adds more comprehensive programming support facilities to the basic ones provided in Behavior and more descriptive facilities to the ones provided in ClassDescription. In particular, Class adds the representation for class variable names and shared (pool) variables.

Class instance protocol

accessing instances and variables

addClassVarName: aString	Add the argument, aString, as a class variable of the receiver. The first character of aString must be capitalized; aString can not already be a class variable name.
removeClassVarName: aString	Remove the receiver's class variable whose name is the argument, aString. Report an error if it is not a class variable or if it is still being used in a method of the class.
addSharedPool: aDictionary	Add the argument, aDictionary, as a pool of shared variables. Report an error if the dictionary is already a shared pool in the receiver.
removeSharedPool: aDictionary	Remove the argument, aDictionary, as one of the receiver's pool dictionaries. Report an error if the dictionary is not one of the receiver's pools.
classPool	Answer the dictionary of class variables of the receiver.
initialize	Initialize class variables.

Additional accessing messages store a description of the class on a file, where the file has the same name as that of the class (fileOut), and remove the class from the system (removeFromSystem).

A variety of messages for creating one of the four kinds of subclasses in the system are specified in the method dictionary of Class. In addition, Class provides a message for renaming a class (rename: aString); this message is provided in Class rather than in ClassDescription because it is not an appropriate message to send to a metaclass.

Class instance protocol

instance creation

subclass: classNameString
    instanceVariableNames: stringInstVarNames
    classVariableNames: stringOfClassVarNames
    poolDictionaries: stringOfPoolNames
    category: categoryNameString

Create a new class that is a fixed-length (regular) subclass of the receiver. Each of the arguments provides the information needed to initialize the new class and categorize it.

Three other messages, like the one above except that the first keyword is variableSubclass:, variableByteSubclass:, or variableWordSubclass, support the creation of the other kinds of classes. Note also that the system requires that a subclass of a variable-length class be a variable-length class. When possible, the system makes the appropriate conversion; otherwise, an error is reported to the programmer.

Suppose that every time we created a new subclass, we wanted to install messages for storing and retrieving the instance variables of that class. For example, if we create a class Record with instance variable names name and address, we wish to provide messages name and address, to respond with the values of these variables, and name: argument and address: argument, to set the values of these variables to the value of the message argument. One way to accomplish this is to add the following method to the instance protocol of class Class, subclass creation.

```
accessingSubclass: className
    instanceVariableNames: instVarString
    classVariableNames: classVarString
    poolDictionaries: stringOfPoolNames
    category: categoryName
| newClass |
newClass ← self subclass: className
            instanceVariableNames: instVarString
            classVariableNames: classVarString
            poolDictionaries: stringOfPoolNames
            category: categoryName.
newClass instVarNames do:
    [ :aName |
     newClass compile: (aName , '
    ↑', aName) classified: #accessing.
     newClass compile: (aName , ': argument
    ', aName, ' ← argument.
    ↑argument') classified: #accessing].
↑newClass
```

The method creates the class as usual, then, for each instance variable name, compiles two methods. The first is of the form

```
name
    ↑name
```

and the second is of the form

```
name: argument
    name ← argument.
    ↑argument
```

So, if we create the class Record, we can do so by sending Object the following message.

```
Object accessingSubclass: #Record
        instanceVariableNames: 'name address'
        classVariableNames: ''
        poolDictionaries: ''
        category: 'Example'.
```

The message is found in the method dictionary of Class, and creates the following four messages in the category accessing of class Record.

accessing

name
  ↑name
name: argument
  name ← argument.
  ↑argument
address
  ↑address
address: argument
  address ← argument.
  ↑argument

17

The Programming Interface

This chapter shows how a programmer adds new classes to the system and then tests and debugs their behavior using the Smalltalk-80 programming environment. The chapter presents a scenario of how a programmer might add class FinancialHistory to the system. FinancialHistory was used in the first part of this book as an example class. Its protocol and implementation descriptions can be found inside the front cover of this book. This example scenario is not intended as an exhaustive survey of the Smalltalk-80 programming interface. It is intended as an overview that provides motivation for the kinds of graphics support described in subsequent chapters.

A user and the Smalltalk-80 programming environment interact through a *bitmap display screen*, a *keyboard*, and a *pointing device*. The display is used to present graphical and textual views of information to the user. The keyboard is used to present textual information to the system. The pointing device is used to select information on the display screen. Smalltalk-80 uses an indirect pointing device called a *mouse*. A *cursor* on the screen shows the location currently being pointed to by the mouse. The cursor is moved by moving the mouse over a flat surface. The mouse has three buttons, which are used to make different kinds of selection.

Views

The display screen contains one or more rectangular areas called *views*. The views are displayed on a gray background and may overlap. Each view has a title shown at its upper left corner. Figure 17.1 shows the Smalltalk screen with two overlapping views on it. Their titles are Workspace and System Browser. These two views contain only text; other views might contain pictures or both text and pictures.

The view toward the top of the figure is a *workspace*. It contains text that can be edited or evaluated. The view towards the bottom of the figure is a *system browser*. It allows the class descriptions in the system to be viewed and edited. The arrow in the lower right part of the browser is the cursor. It shows the current location of the mouse. At the lower right corner of each figure in this chapter will be a small rectangle containing three ovals arranged side by side. These ovals represent the three mouse buttons. When one of the buttons is pressed, the corresponding oval will be filled in. The buttons will be referred to as the *left*, *middle*, and *right* buttons, even though they may not be arranged side by side on some mice.

A variety of information is typically visible on the Smalltalk-80 display screen. In order to take some action, the user indicates what part of the visible information should be affected. The general activity of directing attention to a particular piece of information is called *selec-*

Figure 17.1

tion. The system gives visual feedback to indicate the current selection. The most common feedback mechanism is to complement a rectangular area of the screen, changing black to white and white to black. To begin using the system, one of the views is selected. The selected view is indicated by complementing only its title. The selected view will be completely displayed, obscuring the overlapping parts of any other views. In Figure 17.1, the browser is the selected view.

A different view can be selected by moving the cursor into part of its rectangular frame that hasn't been overlapped by other views, and then pressing the left button on the mouse. In Figure 17.2, the workspace has been selected. Note that the left mouse button is pressed. The workspace now obscures the overlapped part of the browser.

Text Selections

The Smalltalk-80 text editor provides the ability to select text and to perform editing operations on that selected text. For example, to replace the sequence of characters the standard with my special in the workspace, the old characters are selected and then the new characters are typed.

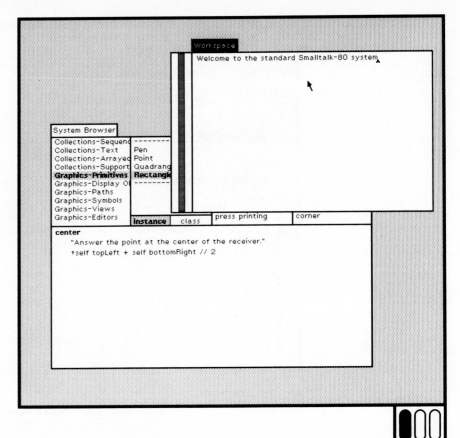

Figure 17.2

Characters are selected using the left mouse button. The cursor is positioned at one end of the selection and the mouse button is pressed (Figure 17.3).

The text selection is now empty—it contains no characters. The position of an empty selection is shown with a carat (an inverted "v"). The

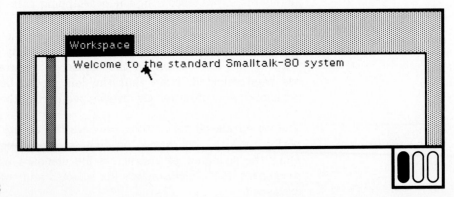

Figure 17.3

carat is partially obscured by the cursor in Figure 17.3. While the mouse button remains pressed, the cursor is moved to the other end of the characters to be selected. The selected characters are shown in a complemented rectangle (Figure 17.4).

When the button is released, the selection is complete (Figure 17.5). When characters are typed on the keyboard, they replace the selected characters. After typing the new characters, the selection is empty and positioned at the end of the new characters (Figure 17.6).

Figure 17.4

Figure 17.5

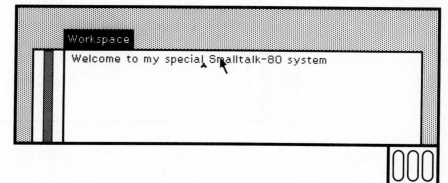

Figure 17.6

Menu Selections

Another kind of selection used in the user interface is called *menu selection*. The middle and right mouse buttons are used to select commands from one of two menus. When one of these buttons is pressed, a menu appears at the location of the cursor. The menu obtained by pressing the middle button contains commands relevant to the contents of the selected view. When the view contains editable text, as does the workspace, these commands relate to text manipulation. The menu obtained by pressing the right button contains commands relevant to the selected view itself. The middle-button menu may be different in different views, but the right-button menu is always the same.

Characters can be deleted from a piece of text by selecting the characters and then invoking the *cut* command from the middle-button menu. In the next picture, the characters special have been selected and the middle button has been pressed. The menu of commands relevant to the contents of the view has appeared. While the button is held down, the cursor is moved to select the *cut* command in the menu (Figure 17.7). When the button is released, the selected command is carried out. In this example, the selected text is removed (Figure 17.8).

Figure 17.7

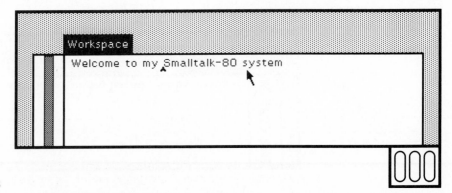

Figure 17.8

A text selection can be treated as a Smalltalk-80 expression and evaluated. There are two commands in the middle-button menu to carry out such an operation, doIt and printIt. Selecting doIt simply evaluates the selected expression and discards the resulting value. Selecting printIt evaluates the selected expression and prints its value after the expression. For example, after typing and selecting the expression Time now, printIt will print out the resulting new instance of Time (Figure 17.9). The printed result becomes the current text selection (Figure 17.10).

Figure 17.9

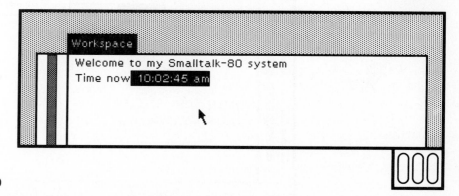

Figure 17.10

If the cursor is moved outside the menu before the button is released, no command is carried out.

Browsers

A browser is a view of the classes in the Smalltalk-80 system. Existing classes are examined and changed using a browser. New classes are added to the system using a browser. A browser consists of five rectangular subviews. Along the top are four subviews showing lists. Each list may or may not have one of its items selected. The selected item in each list is complemented. The contents of the list cannot be edited through the view, they can only be selected. Below the four list subviews is a subview showing some text. That subview is similar to the workspace, allowing the text to be edited. The selections in the four lists determine what text is visible in the lower subview. When a selection has been made in all four lists, the lower subview shows a Smalltalk-80 method. The method is found in a class determined by the selections in the two lists on the left. The method within that class is determined by the selections in the two lists on the right. The browser in Figure 17.11 is showing the method used by Rectangles to respond to the message center.

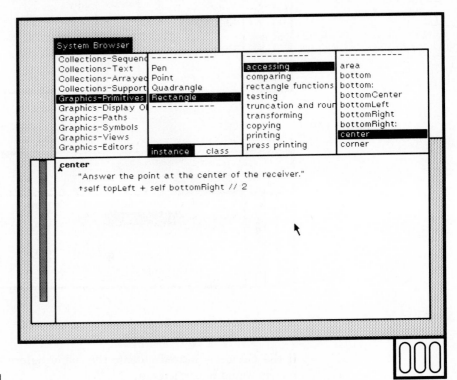

Figure 17.11

The classes in the system are organized into categories. The leftmost list in the browser shows the categories of classes in the system. When a category is selected, the classes in that category are shown in the next list to the right. In the example, the category Graphics-Primitives is selected. That category has four classes in it. When one of these classes is selected, its message categories are shown in the next list to its right.

Since Rectangle is selected, the categories in its instance protocol are displayed. At the bottom of the second list, two rectangular areas are labeled instance and class. One of these will be selected at all times. If class is selected, then the next list to the right shows the categories of class messages; if instance is selected, the list shows the categories of instance messages. When a message category is selected, the selectors of messages in that category are shown in the rightmost list. When one of these message selectors is selected, the corresponding method is displayed in the subview at the bottom of the browser. The method displayed can be edited and the old version can be replaced by the edited version, if desired.

List Selections

A selection is made in a list by placing the cursor over an item and then pressing and releasing the left mouse button. In Figure 17.12, another item is selected in the browser's rightmost list. Therefore, another method is presented in the lower text subview.

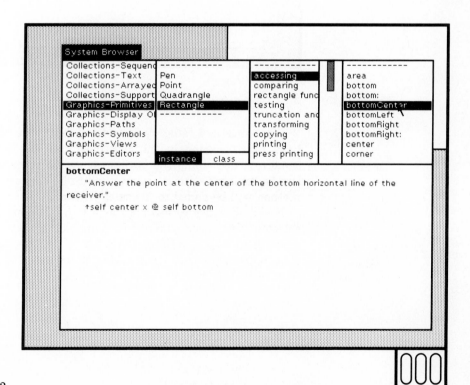

Figure 17.12

If the left button is pressed and released while the cursor is over the item already selected, that item is deselected (Figure 17.13).

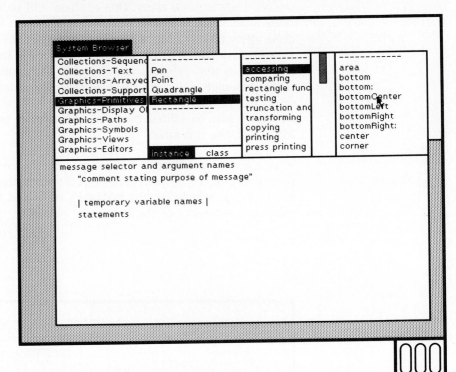

Figure 17.13

When a message category is selected, but none of its message selectors have been selected in the rightmost list, the lower subview contains some text describing the various syntactic parts of a method. This text can be replaced with a new method to be added to the system. The new method will be added to the selected category.

If a class category has been selected, but none of its classes has been selected, the lower subview contains some text describing the various parts of a class definition. This text is in the form of a message to a class (Object, in this case) asking it to create a new subclass of itself (Figure 17.14).

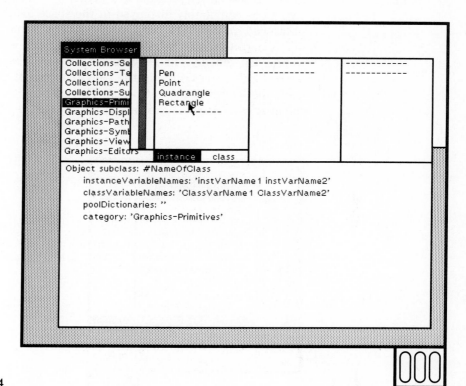

Figure 17.14

Scrolling

A view may not be large enough to show all of the information it might. For example, many of the lists viewed by the browser are too long to be completely displayed in the space available. The view can be positioned on different parts of the list by using a *scroll bar*. A scroll bar is a rectangular area that appears to the left of the subview containing the cursor. The gray box in the scroll bar indicates which part of the total list is visible in the view. The height of the scroll bar represents the length of the entire list. The part of the scroll bar occupied by the gray box indicates the part of the list that is visible.

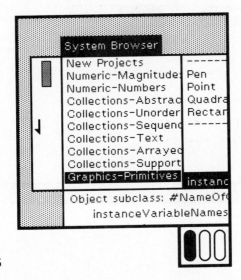

Figure 17.15

By moving the mouse into the scroll bar, another part of the list can be shown. This is called *scrolling*. When the cursor is in the right half of the scroll bar, it takes the shape of an upward pointing arrow. If the left mouse button is pressed, the items in the list appears to move up in the subview and new items become visible at the bottom. When the cursor is in the left half of the scroll bar, its shape is a downward pointing arrow; pressing the left button makes an earlier part of the list visible. For example, the browser's leftmost list can be scrolled to show categories earlier in the list (Figure 17.15).

Views containing text can also be scrolled if the view is too small to show all the text.

Class Definitions

A new class can be added to the system by selecting a class category and editing the text describing the parts of a class definition. The FinancialHistory example will be added to the category named New Projects.

While text is being changed in the lower subview, it may not accurately represent a class definition or a method. The accept command in the middle-button menu is used to indicate that the editing has been completed and the class definition or method should be added to the system (Figures 17.16 and 17.17).

Figure 17.16

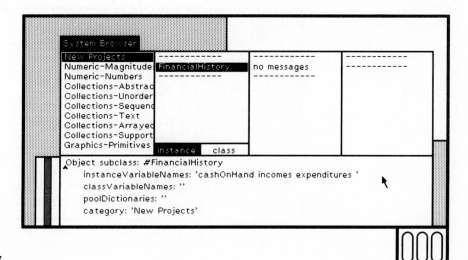

Figure 17.17

The menu that appears when the middle button is pressed is different in each of the browser's subviews. In the subview showing the classes in a category, the menu includes an item called **definition**. This command causes the class definition of an existing class to be displayed (Figures 17.18 and 17.19).

This class definition can then be modified with the standard text editing operations. After changing the text, **accept** must be selected again in the middle-button menu. For example, an instance variable could be added to all Rectangles by adding its name to the appropriate place in the class definition.

Figure 17.18

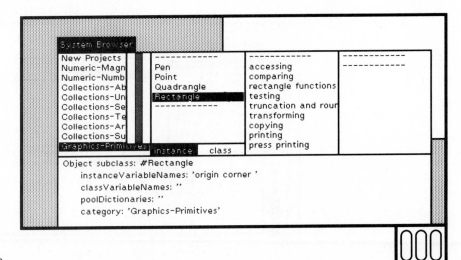

Figure 17.19

Another item in the middle-button menu for the class list is categories. When it is selected, the message categorization is shown in the bottom subview (Figures 17.20 and 17.21).

Figure 17.20

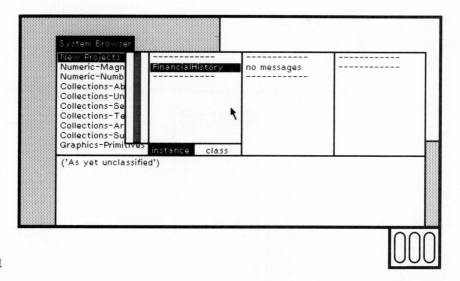

Figure 17.21

The new class has a single, empty message category called As yet unclassified.

The categorization can be changed by editing the text and selecting accept (Figures 17.22 and 17.23). Notice the change in the third subview from the left of Figure 17.23. There are now three categories, transaction recording, inquiries, and private.

Figure 17.22

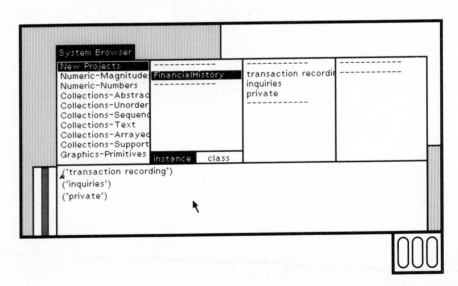

Figure 17.23

After a new class has been added to the system, methods can be added by selecting categories and editing method templates (Figures 17.24 and 17.25).

Notice the change in the rightmost subview of Figure 17.25. The selector of the new method is added to the (previously empty) list and becomes the current selection.

Figure 17.24

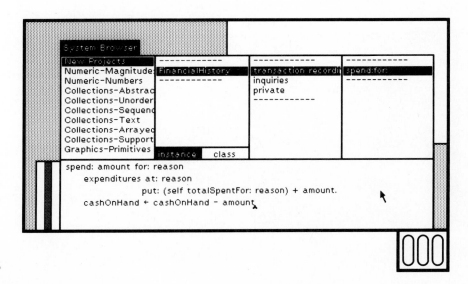

Figure 17.25

Testing

After the methods shown in Chapter 5 have been added to FinancialHistory, instances can be created and tested by sending them messages. First, a new global variable will be added to the system by sending the message at:put: to the dictionary of global variables whose name is Smalltalk. The first argument of at:put: is the name of the global variable and the second is the initial value. This global variable will be used to refer to the instance being tested (Figure 17.26).

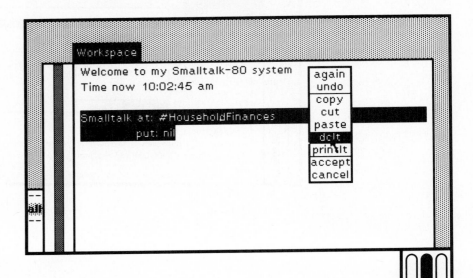

Figure 17.26

Messages are sent to HouseholdFinances by typing expressions in the workspace and evaluating them by invoking the commands doIt or printIt (Figure 17.27). Several expressions can be selected and evaluated at one time. The expressions are separated by periods (Figure 17.28).

Figure 17.27

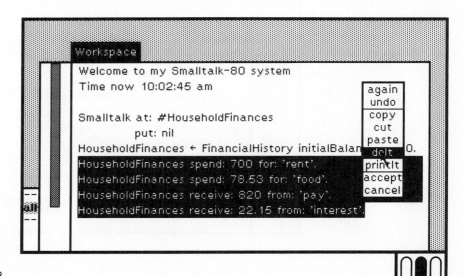

Figure 17.28

Selecting printIt instead of doIt displays the result following the expression (Figures 17.29 and 17.30).

Figure 17.29

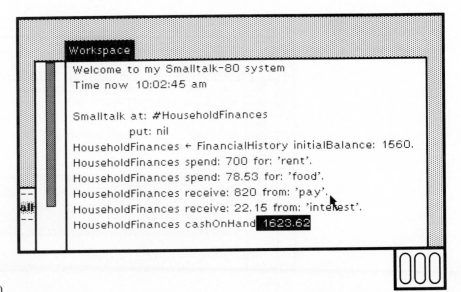

Figure 17.30

An inspector is a view of an object's instance variables. An inspector is created by sending inspect to the object whose instance variables are to be viewed (Figure 17.31).

After inspect has been sent, the user is prompted for a rectangular area in which to display the inspector. The shape of the cursor is changed to indicate that the upper left corner of the rectangular area should be specified (Figure 17.32).

Figure 17.31

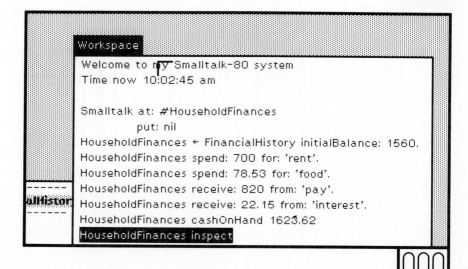

Figure 17.32

The cursor is moved to the desired location and the left mouse button is pressed and held down. The shape of the cursor is changed again to indicate that the lower right corner of the rectangular area should now be specified. As long as the left mouse button remains pressed, the prospective new rectangular frame is displayed (Figure 17.33).

When the button is released, the inspector is displayed in the selected area (Figure 17.34).

The title of the inspector is the name of the inspected object's class.

Figure 17.33

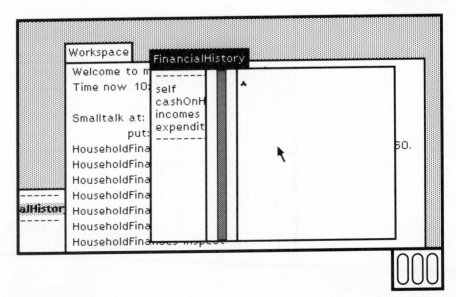

Figure 17.34

An inspector has two subviews. The left subview shows a list containing self and the names of the object's instance variables. When one of the elements of the list is selected, the corresponding value is printed in the subview to the right (Figures 17.35 and 17.36). The text that appears in the righthand subview is obtained as a result of sending printString to the selected object. Selecting the element self at the top of the list, prints the object being inspected (Figure 17.37).

Figure 17.35

Figure 17.36

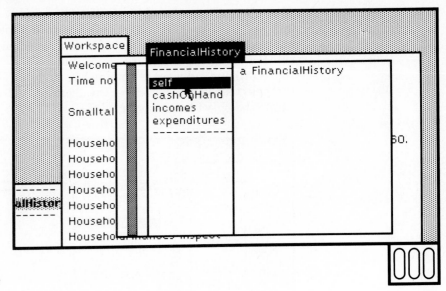

Figure 17.37

Error Reporting

When an error is encountered, the process in which the error occurred is suspended and a view of that process is created. Suspended processes can be viewed in two ways, with *notifiers* and with *debuggers*. A notifier provides a simple description of the process at the time of the error. A debugger provides a more detailed view and also the ability to change the state of the suspended process before resuming it.

As an example of error reporting, we will follow the addition and debugging of several new methods in FinancialHistory. The following methods contain several errors which will be "discovered" in the testing process. The intention of these new methods is to allow a FinancialHistory to give a summary report of its state.

```
report
    | reportStream |
    reportStream ← WriteStream on: (String new: 10).
    reportStream cr.
    reportStream nextPutAll: 'Expenses'.
    reportStream cr.
    self expenseReasons do:
        [ :reason | reportStream tab.
                reportStream nextPutAll: reason.
                reportStream tab.
                reportStream nextPutAll: (self totalSpentFor: reason).
                reportStream cr].
```

```
            reportStream nextPutAll: 'Incomes'.
            reportStream cr.
            self incomeSources do:
                [ :source | reportStream tab.
                            reportStream nextPutAll: source.
                            reportStream tab.
                            reportStream nextPutAll: (self totalReceivedFrom: source).
                            reportStream cr].
            ↑reportStream contents
    incomeSources
            ↑incomes keys
    expenditureReasons
            ↑expenditures keys
```

A new category is added and the new methods typed in and accepted (Figure 17.38).

After adding the new methods, the instance of FinancialHistory can be asked for a report by evaluating an expression in the workspace (Figure 17.39). Instead of printing the report, a notifier appears on the screen (Figure 17.40).

Figure 17.38

Figure 17.39

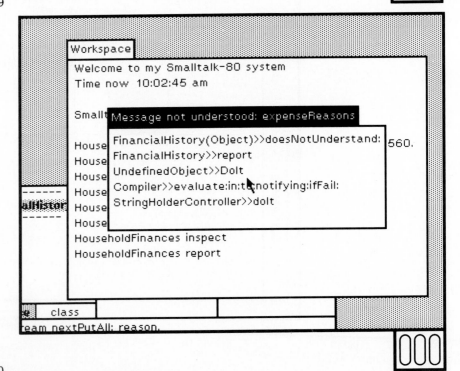

Figure 17.40

Notifiers

A notifier is a simple view of a process suspended after an error. The notifier's title indicates the nature of the error. Notifiers are created by sending an object the message error:. The argument of the message becomes the title of the notifier. The notifier shown in Figure 17.40 indicates that the message expenseReasons was sent to an object that did not understand it. The list visible in the notifier shows part of the state of the suspended process.

The cause of this error is evident from the title of the notifier. The message added to FinancialHistory was expenditureReasons not expenseReasons. The notifier and the erroneous process can be discarded by selecting the command close in the right mouse-button menu (Figure 17.41).

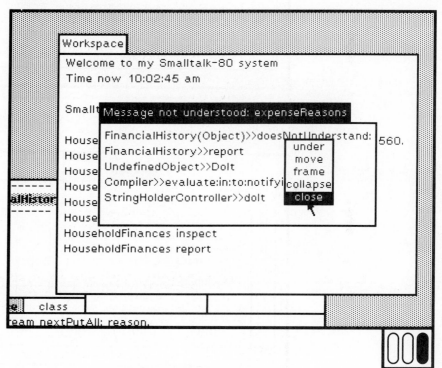

Figure 17.41

The misspelling in report can be corrected in the browser (Figures 17.42 and 17.43).

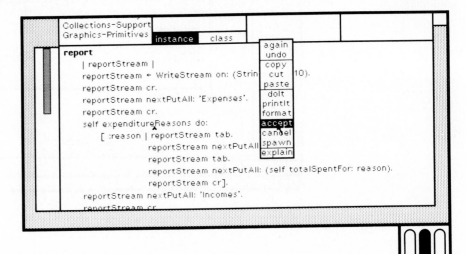

Figure 17.42

Figure 17.43

After fixing the misspelling in the browser, the original expression can be evaluated in the workspace again (Figures 17.44 and 17.45).

This creates another notifier. The cause of this error is not as obvious. The message do: was sent to an object that did not understand it. In order to learn more about the error, a more detailed view of the suspended process can be obtained by selecting the command debug in the middle-button menu.

Figure 17.44

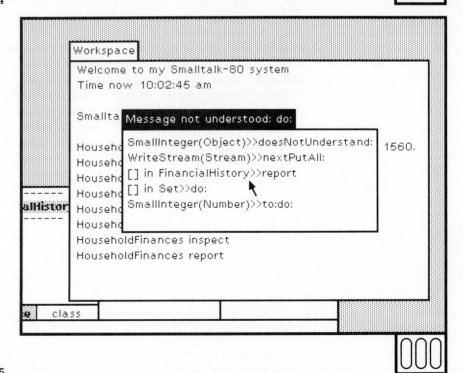

Figure 17.45

Debuggers

A debugger is a view of a suspended process that reveals more details than a notifier reveals. When debug is selected in a notifier's middle-button menu, a debugger is created viewing the same process the notifier viewed (Figure 17.46). After selecting debug, the user is prompted to supply a rectangular area in which to display the debugger. The rectangle is specified in the same way that the rectangular frame for a new inspector is specified (Figure 17.47).

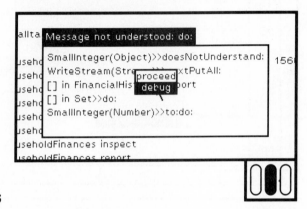

Figure 17.46

The debugger has six subviews. The top subview shows the same list that was visible through the notifier. This list gives a partial history of the process in which the error occurred. Each item corresponds to a message that was sent and whose response is not yet completed. The item contains the name of the receiver's class and the selector of the message, separated by "≫". The last item visible in the list, FinancialHistory ≫ report, indicates that an instance of FinancialHistory received the message report. This message was sent when the middle-button menu command printIt was selected while the expression HouseholdFinances report was the text selection. When one of the items in the debugger's upper list is selected, the method invoked by the corresponding message is displayed in the subview immediately below.

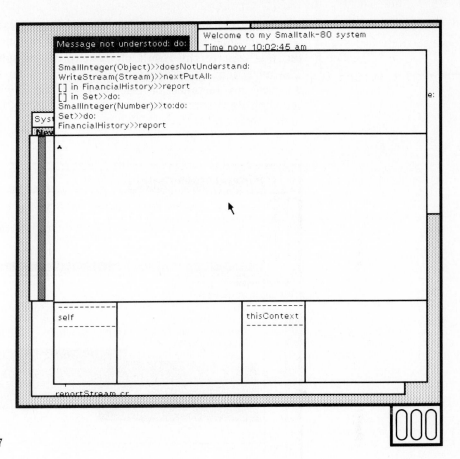

Figure 17.47

When a method is displayed, the last message sent before the process was suspended is complemented. Figure 17.48 shows that the message do: was sent to the result of the expression self expenditureReasons. The next item up on the list, Set >> do:, indicates that the receiver of do: was an instance of Set. The method invoked can be seen by selecting Set >> do: in the list.

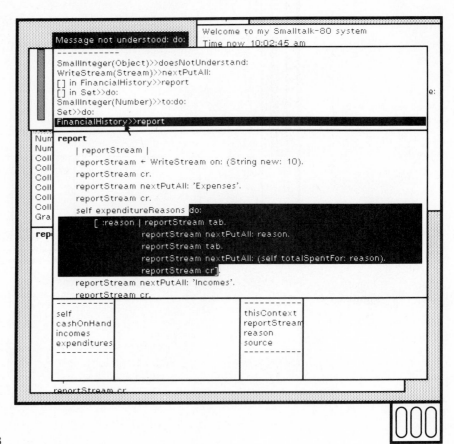

Figure 17.48

Figure 17.49 shows that this method sent a message to the object 1. The next item up on the list, SmallInteger(Number) >> to:do: shows that the receiver was an instance of SmallInteger. When the method invoked by a message was found in a superclass of the receiver's class, the name of that superclass is included in parentheses after the receiver's direct class. In the example, the method for to:do: was found in class Number.

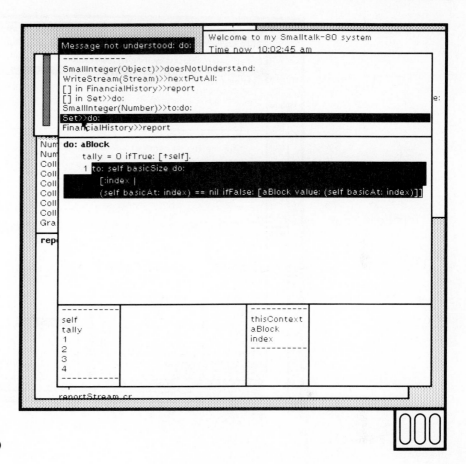

Figure 17.49

The top item on the list, SmallInteger(Object) >> doesNotUnderstand:, shows the last thing that happened before the process was suspended— an instance of SmallInteger received the message doesNotUnderstand:. This message was sent by the system when the do: message was not found in SmallInteger or in any of its superclasses. The doesNotUnderstand: message invoked a method that suspended the process and created the notifier viewing it. The second item from the top of the list, WriteStream(Stream) >> nextPutAll:, indicates that the misunderstood do: message was sent from the method for nextPutAll: in class Stream. Figure 17.50 shows the debugger with that item selected. The method displayed shows that do: was sent to the object named aCollection, which was provided as the argument of nextPutAll:.

The lower four subviews of a debugger are used to find the value of the variables used in the method. They function like two inspectors. The leftmost subview shows a list of the receiver (self) and its instance variable names. The third subview from the left shows the argument

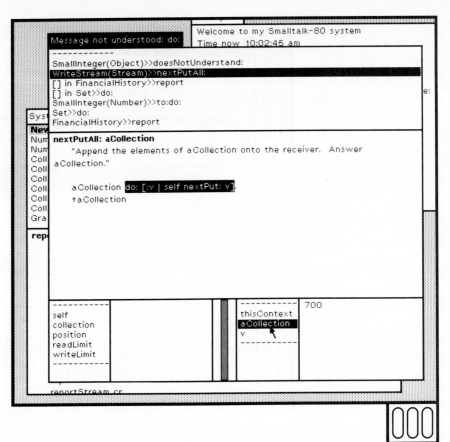

Figure 17.50

names and temporary variable names. When a name is selected in either one of these lists, the value of the associated variable is shown in the subview to its right. To display the receiver of the do: message, aCollection is selected in Figure 17.50.

The source of this error appears to be that the Stream was expecting a collection of elements as the argument of nextPutAll: and it got a number, 700, instead. Selecting the next item down from the top list shows where the argument came from. The argument was the result of evaluating the expression (self totalSpentFor: reason). In Figure 17.51, selections have been made in the bottom subviews to display the values of the instance variable, expenditures, and the argument, reason.

When text is selected and evaluated in the method displayed in the browser, the variable names are interpreted in that context. So the argument to nextPutAll: can be found by re-executing the expression (self totalSpentFor: reason) and printing the result (Figure 17.52).

Figure 17.51

Figure 17.52

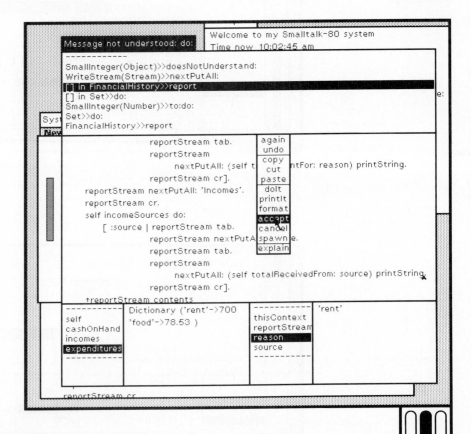

```
reportStream cr.
reportStream nextPutAll: 'Expenses'.
reportStream cr.
self expenditureReasons do:
    [ :reason | reportStream tab.
            reportStream nextPutAll: reason.
            reportStream tab.
            reportStream nextPutAll: (self totalSpentFor: reason 700).
            reportStream cr].
reportStream nextPutAll: 'Incomes'.
reportStream cr.
```

```
-----------          Dictionary ('rent'->700          -----------     'rent'
self                  'food'->78.53 )                 thisContext
cashOnHand                                            reportStream
incomes                                               reason
expenditures                                          source
-----------                                           -----------
```

Figure 17.53

```
                                    Welcome to my Smalltalk-80 system
Message not understood: do:        Time now 10:02:45 am
-----------
SmallInteger(Object)>>doesNotUnderstand:
WriteStream(Stream)>>nextPutAll:
[] in FinancialHistory>>report
[] in Set>>do:
SmallInteger(Number)>>to:do:
Set>>do:
FinancialHistory>>report
```

```
            reportStream tab.                  again
            reportStream                       undo
                nextPutAll: (self t            copy     ntFor: reason) printString.
                                                cut
            reportStream cr].                   paste
    reportStream nextPutAll: 'Incomes'.         doIt
    reportStream cr.                            printIt
    self incomeSources do:                      format
        [ :source | reportStream tab.           accept
            reportStream nextPutA                cancel   e.
            reportStream tab.                    spawn
            reportStream                         explain
                nextPutAll: (self totalReceivedFrom: source) printString.
            reportStream cr].
        treportStream contents
```

```
-----------          Dictionary ('rent'->700          -----------     'rent'
self                  'food'->78.53 )                 thisContext
cashOnHand                                            reportStream
incomes                                               reason
expenditures                                          source
-----------                                           -----------
```

```
reportStream cr.
```

Figure 17.54

The result is 700, as expected (Figure 17.53).

The report method had intended that the character representation of 700 be appended to reportStream, but it appended the number itself instead. This bug is fixed by sending the number the message printString. The correction can be made in the debugger (Figure 17.54). Now the expression can be evaluated again. The report is now successfully printed in the workspace (Figure 17.55).

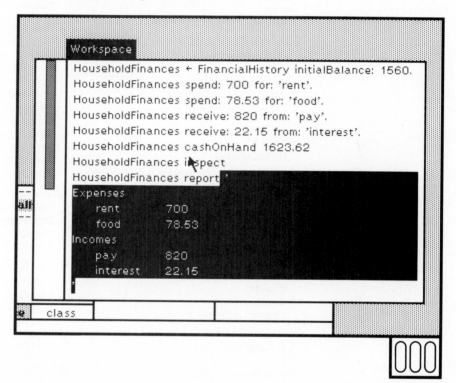

Figure 17.55

This completes the overview of the Smalltalk-80 programming interface. The ability to support this type of interaction with the user motivates the nature of many of the graphics classes discussed in subsequent chapters.

Implementation Classes

Protocols for each of the classes that implement the programming interface are not provided in this book. They are listed here, alphabetized within categories that describe the general or specific support they give to implementing the views described in this chapter.

Interface Framework and Support
Controller
ControlManager
Explainer
MouseMenuController
NoController
StandardSystemController
StandardSystemView
View
WindowingTransformation

Lists and List Selections
ListController
ListView
LockedListController
SelectionInListController
SelectionInListView
TextList

Scrolling
ScrollController

Confirmers and Prompteis
BinaryChoice
BinaryChoiceController
CRFillinTheBlankController
FillinTheBlank
FillinTheBlankController
FillinTheBlankView

Browsers
Browser
BrowserView
MethodListBrowser

Menus and Other Selectable Items
ActionMenu

BinaryChoiceView
Button
IndicatorOnSwitchController
LockedSwitchController
OneOnSwitch
PopUpMenu
Switch
SwitchController
SwitchView

Text and Code Support
AlwaysAcceptCodeController
CodeController
CodeView
OnlyWhenSelectedCodeController
OnlyWhenSelectedCodeView
ParagraphEditor
StringHolder
StringHolderController
StringHolderView
TextController
TextView

Inspectors
ContextInspector
DictionaryInspector
Inspector
InspectorView

Error Reporting—Notifiers and Debuggers
Debugger
NotifierController
NotifierView
ProcessHandle
SyntaxError

Not described in this book are the system files, transcripts, project, and change management support views.

File Access
FileList
FileModel

Transcript
TextCollector
TextCollectorController
TextCollectorView

Projects
Project
ProjectController
ProjectView

Change Management
ChangeController

ChangeList
ChangeListController
ChangeListView
Change
ChangeScanner
ChangeSet
ClassChange
ClassCommentChange
ClassDefinitionChange
ClassOtherChange
ClassRelatedChange
MethodChange
MethodDefinitionChange
MethodOtherChange
OtherChange

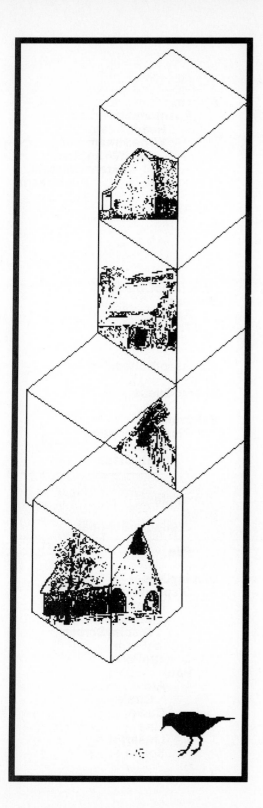

18

The Graphics Kernel

Object

Magnitude
    Character
    Date
    Time

    Number
      Float
      Fraction
      Integer
        LargeNegativeInteger
        LargePositiveInteger
        SmallInteger

    LookupKey
      Association

Link

    Process

Collection

    SequenceableCollection
      LinkedList

      Semaphore

    ArrayedCollection
      Array
      WordArray
        DisplayBitmap
      RunArray
      String
        Symbol
      Text
      ByteArray

    Interval
    OrderedCollection
      SortedCollection
  Bag
  MappedCollection
  Set
    Dictionary
      IdentityDictionary

Stream
    PositionableStream
      ReadStream
      WriteStream
        ReadWriteStream
        ExternalStream
          FileStream

    Random

UndefinedObject
Boolean
    False
    True

ProcessorScheduler
Delay
SharedQueue

Behavior
    ClassDescription
      Class
      MetaClass

Point
Rectangle
BitBlt
    CharacterScanner

Pen

DisplayObject
    DisplayMedium
      Form
        Cursor
        DisplayScreen
    InfiniteForm
    OpaqueForm
    Path
      Arc
        Circle
      Curve
      Line
      LinearFit
      Spline

Graphical Representation

Figure 18.1 shows a view of the display screen for a Smalltalk-80 system. It illustrates the wide range of graphical idiom available to the system. Rectangular areas of arbitrary size are filled with white, black, and halftone patterns. Text, in various typefaces, is placed on the screen from stored images of the individual characters. Halftone shades are "brushed" by the user to create freehand paintings. Moreover, although not shown on the printed page, images on the display can be moved or sequenced in time to provide animation.

The example interaction with the system given in the previous chapter illustrated some of the ways in which objects can be observed and manipulated graphically. Meaningful presentation of objects in the system demands maximum control over the display medium. One approach that provides the necessary flexibility is to allow the brightness of every discernible point in the displayed image to be independently controlled. An implementation of this approach is a contiguous block of storage in which the setting of each *bit* is mapped into the illumination of a corresponding picture element, or *pixel*, when displaying the image. The block of storage is referred to as a *bitmap*. This type of display is called a *bitmapped display*. The simplest form of bitmap allows only two brightness levels, white and black, corresponding to the stored bit values 0 or 1 respectively. The Smalltalk-80 graphics system is built around this model of a display medium.

Graphical Storage

Images are represented by instances of class Form. A Form has height and width, and a bitmap, which indicates the white and black regions of the particular image being represented. Consider, for example, the man-shape in Figure 18.2. The height of the Form is 40, its width is 14, and its appearance is described by the pattern of ones and zeros (shown as light and dark squares) in its bitmap. The height and width of the Form serve to impose the appropriate two-dimensional ordering on the otherwise unstructured data in the bitmap. We shall return to the representation of Forms in more detail later in this chapter.

New Forms are created by combining several Forms. The freehand drawing in the center of Figure 18.1 is an example of a large Form that was created by combining and repeating several Forms that serve as "paint brushes" in a Smalltalk-80 application system. The text in Figure 18.1 is a structured combination of Forms representing characters.

A Form can be presented to the display hardware as a buffer in memory of the actual data or of the image to be shown on a display

Figure 18.1

Figure 18.2

screen. Since the interface to the hardware is through a Form, there is no difference between combining images internally and displaying them on the screen. Animation can be displayed smoothly by using one Form as the display Form while the next image to be displayed is prepared in a second Form. As each image is completed, the two Forms exchange roles, causing the new image to be displayed and making the Form with the old image available for building yet another image in the sequence.

The Forms used as buffers for data to be shown on the display screen are instances of class DisplayScreen, a subclass of Form. Contiguous storage of bits is provided by instances of class WordArray. DisplayScreen's bitmap is an instance of DisplayBitmap, a subclass of WordArray. DisplayScreen and DisplayBitmap provide protocol specific to the actual hardware and to the fact that the Form represents the whole display screen rather than potential parts of it.

Graphical Manipulation

A basic operation on Forms, referred to as *BitBlt*, supports a wide range of graphical presentation. All text and graphic objects in the system are created and modified using this single graphical operation. The name

"BitBlt" derives from the generalization of data transfer to arbitrary bit locations, or pixels. One of the first computers on which a Smalltalk system was implemented had an instruction called BLT for *block transfer* of 16-bit words, and so "bit block transfer" became known as BitBlt.

Operations are represented by messages to objects. So BitBlt could have been implemented with a message to class Form. However, because BitBlts are fairly complicated operations to specify, they are represented by objects. These objects are instances of the class named BitBlt. The basic operation is performed by sending an appropriately initialized instance of BitBlt the message copyBits. The BitBlt operation is intentionally a very general operation, although most applications of it are graphically simple, such as "move this rectangle of pixels from here to there."

Figure 18.3 illustrates the process of copying a character of text into a region on the display. This operation will serve to illustrate most of the characteristics of BitBlt that are introduced in the remainder of this section.

Source and Destination Forms

The BitBlt copy operation involves two Forms, a source and a destination. The source in the example in Figure 18.3 is a *font* containing a set of character glyphs depicted in some uniform style and scale, and packed together horizontally. The destination in the example is assumed to be a Form that is used as the display buffer. Pixels are copied out of the source and stored into the destination. The width and height of the transfer correspond to the character size. The source x and y coordinates give the character's location in the font, and the destination coordinates specify the position on the display where its copy will appear.

Clipping Rectangle

BitBlt includes in its specification a rectangular area which limits the region of the destination that can be affected by its operation, independent of the other destination parameters. We call this area the *clipping rectangle*. Often it is desirable to display a partial *window* onto larger scenes, and the clipping rectangle ensures that all picture elements fall inside the bounds of the window. By its inclusion in the BitBlt primitive, the clipping function can be done efficiently and in one place, rather than being replicated in all application programs.

Figure 18.4 illustrates the result of imposing a clipping rectangle on the example of Figure 18.3. Pixels that would have been placed outside the clipping rectangle (the left edge of the "N" and half of the word "the") have not been transferred. Had there been other characters that fell above or below this rectangle, they would have been similarly clipped.

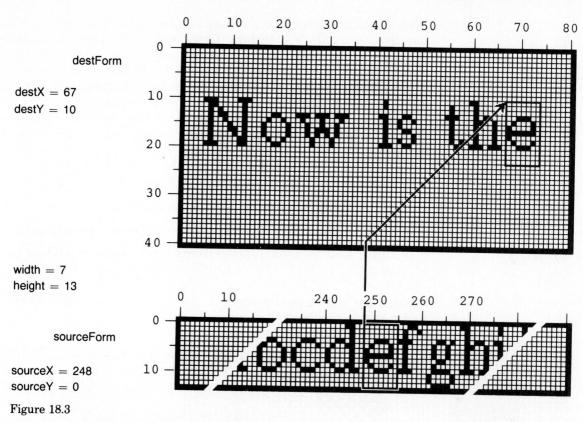

destForm

destX = 67
destY = 10

width = 7
height = 13

sourceForm

sourceX = 248
sourceY = 0

Figure 18.3

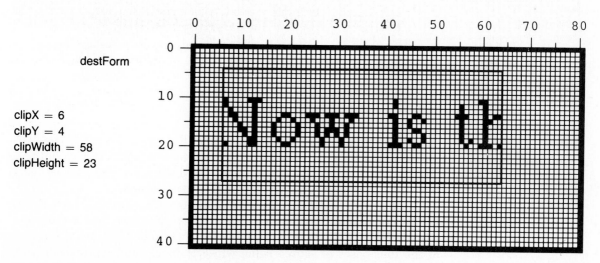

destForm

clipX = 6
clipY = 4
clipWidth = 58
clipHeight = 23

Figure 18.4

Halftone Form

Often it is desirable to fill areas with a regular pattern that provides the effect of gray tone or texture. To this end, BitBlt provides for reference to a third Form containing the desired pattern. This Form is referred to as a halftone or *mask*. It is restricted to have height and width of 16. When halftoning is specified, this pattern is effectively repeated every 16 units horizontally and vertically over the entire destination.

There are four "modes" of supplying pixels from the source and halftone controlled by supplying nil for the source form or the halftone form:

0. no source, no halftone (supplies solid black)

1. halftone only (supplies halftone pattern)

2. source only (supplies source pixels)

3. source AND halftone (supplies source bits masked by halftone pattern)

Figure 18.5 illustrates the effect of these four modes with the same source and destination and a regular gray halftone.

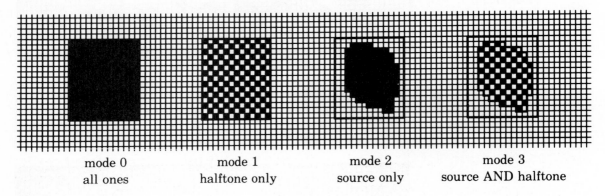

| mode 0 | mode 1 | mode 2 | mode 3 |
| all ones | halftone only | source only | source AND halftone |

Figure 18.5

Combination Rule

The examples above have all determined the new contents of the destination based only on the source and halftone, storing directly into the destination. The previous contents of the destination can also be taken into account in determining the result of the copying.

There are 16 possible rules for combining each source element **S** with the corresponding destination element **D** to produce the new destination element **D'**. Each rule must specify a white or black result for each of the four cases of source being white or black, and destination being white or black.

Figure 18.6 shows a box with four cells corresponding to the four cases encountered when combining source **S** and destination **D**. For instance, the cell numbered 2 corresponds to the case where the source was black and the destination was white. By appropriately filling the four cells with white or black, the box can be made to depict any combination rule. The numbers in the four cells map the rule as depicted graphically to the integer value which selects that rule. For example, to specify that the result should be black wherever the source or destination (or both) was black, we would blacken the cells numbered 4, 2, and 1. The associated integer for specifying that rule is the sum of the blackened cell numbers, or $4 + 2 + 1 = 7$.

Figure 18.6

Figure 18.7 illustrates four common combination rules graphically. In addition, each is described by a combination diagram, its integer rule number, and the actual logical function being applied. The full set of 16 combination rules appears later in the chapter as part of the detailed simulation of BitBlt.

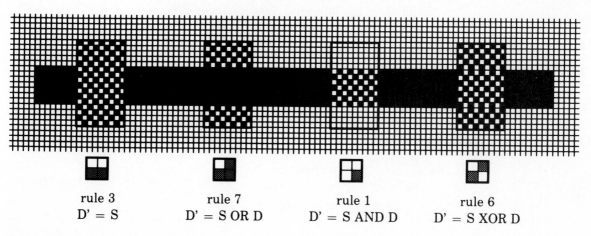

rule 3   rule 7   rule 1   rule 6
D' = S   D' = S OR D   D' = S AND D   D' = S XOR D

Figure 18.7

Classes Form and WordArray

Figure 18.8 shows further information about the Form shown in Figure 18.2. The width and height are stored as Integers. The actual pixels are stored in a separate object which is an instance of class WordArray. WordArrays have almost no protocol, since their sole purpose is to provide storage for Forms. They also have no intrinsic width and height, apart from that laid on by their owning Form, although the figure retains this structure for clarity. It can be seen that space has been provided in the WordArray for a width of 16; this is a manifestation of the hardware organization of storage and processing into 16-bit *words*. WordArrays are allocated with an integral number of words for each row of pixels. This row size is referred to as the *raster* size. The integral word constraint on raster size facilitates movement from one row to the next within the operation of BitBlt, and during the scanning of the display screen by the hardware. While this division of memory into words is significant at the primitive level, it is encapsulated in such a way that none of the higher-level graphical components in the system need consider the issue of word size.

Two classes, Rectangle and Point, are used extensively in working with stored images. A Point contains x and y coordinate values and is used to refer to a pixel location in a Form; a Rectangle contains two Points—the top left corner and the bottom right corner—and is used to define a rectangular area of a Form.

Class Form includes protocol for managing a rectangular pattern of black and white dots. The bitmap of a Form can be (re)set by copying bits from a rectangular area of the display screen (fromDisplay:), and the extent and offset of the Form can be set (extent:, extent:offset:). Two messages provide access to the individual bits (valueAt: and valueAt:put:). Constants for modes and masks are known to class Form and can be obtained by the following class messages of Form.

Form instance protocol

initialize-release

    fromDisplay: aRectangle   Copy the bits from the display screen within the boundaries defined by the argument, aRectangle, into the receiver's bitmap.

accessing

    extent: aPoint   Set the width and height of the receiver to be the coordinates of the argument, aPoint.

    extent: extentPoint offset: offsetPoint

        Set the width and height of the receiver to be the coordinates of the argument, extentPoint, and the offset to be offsetPoint.

Figure 18.8

pattern
    valueAt: aPoint   Answer the bit, 0 or 1, at location aPoint within the receiver's bitmap.

    valueAt: aPoint put: bitCode   Set the bit at location aPoint within the receiver's bitmap to be bitCode, either 0 or 1.

Form class protocol

instance creation
    fromDisplay: aRectangle   Answer a new Form whose bits are copied from the display screen within the boundaries defined by the argument, aRectangle, into the receiver's bitmap.

mode constants
    erase   Answer the Integer denoting mode erase.
    over   Answer the Integer denoting mode over.
    reverse   Answer the Integer denoting mode reverse.
    under   Answer the Integer denoting mode under.

mask constants
 black   Answer the Form denoting a black mask.
 darkGray   Answer the Form denoting a dark gray mask.
 gray   Answer the Form denoting a gray mask.
 lightGray   Answer the Form denoting a light gray mask.
 veryLightGray   Answer the Form denoting a very light gray mask.
 white   Answer the Form denoting a white mask.

Spatial Reference

Since the images represented by Forms are inherently two-dimensional, image manipulation is simplified by providing objects representing two-dimensional locations and areas. Instances of class Point represent locations and instances of class Rectangle represent areas.

Class Point

A Point represents an x–y pair of numbers usually designating a pixel in a Form. Points refer to pixel locations relative to the top left corner of a Form (or other point of reference). By convention, x increases to the right and y down, consistent with the layout of text on a page and the direction of display scanning. This is in contrast to the "right-handed" coordinate system in which y increases in the upward direction.

A Point is typically created using the binary message @ to a Number. For example, the result of evaluating the expression

 200 @ 150

is a Point with x and y coordinates 200 and 150. In addition, the class protocol of Point supports the instance creation message x: xInteger y: yInteger.

 Point x: 200 y: 150

represents the same location as 200@150. The instance protocol for Point supports accessing messages and messages for comparing two Points.

Point instance protocol

accessing

x	Answer the x coordinate.
x: aNumber	Set the x coordinate to be the argument, aNumber.
y	Answer the y coordinate.
y: aNumber	Set the y coordinate to be the argument, aNumber.

comparing

< aPoint	Answer whether the receiver is above and to the left of the argument, aPoint.
< = aPoint	Answer whether the receiver is neither below nor to the right of the argument, aPoint.
> aPoint	Answer whether the receiver is below and to the right of the argument, aPoint.
> = aPoint	Answer whether the receiver is neither above nor to the left of the argument, aPoint.
max: aPoint	Answer the lower right corner of the rectangle uniquely defined by the receiver and the argument, aPoint.
min: aPoint	Answer the upper left corner of the rectangle uniquely defined by the receiver and the argument, aPoint.

With respect to the coordinates labeled in Figure 18.9, example expressions are

expression	result
(45@230) < (175@270)	true
(45@230) < (175@200)	false
(45@230) > (175@200)	false
(175@270) > (45@230)	true
(45@230) max: (175@200)	175@230
(45@230) min: (175@200)	45@200

Arithmetic can be carried out between two Points or between a Point and a Number (a scaling factor). Each of the arithmetic messages takes either a Point or a Number (a scalar) as an argument, and returns a new Point as the result. Truncation and round off messages, similar to those for Numbers, are also provided in the instance protocol of Point.

Point instance protocol

arithmetic

* scale	Answer a new Point that is the product of the receiver and the argument, scale.

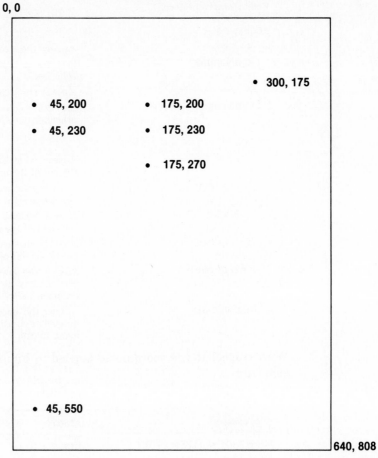

Figure 18.9

+ delta	Answer a new Point that is the sum of the receiver and the argument, delta.
− delta	Answer a new Point that is the difference of the receiver and the argument, delta.
/ scale	Answer a new Point that is the quotient of the receiver and the argument, scale.
// scale	Answer a new Point that is the quotient (defined by division with truncation toward negative infinity) of the receiver and the argument, scale.
abs	Answer a new Point whose x and y are the absolute values of the receiver's x and y.

truncation and round off

rounded	Answer a new Point that is the receiver's x and y rounded.
truncateTo: grid	Answer a new Point that is the receiver's x and y truncated to the argument, grid.

Thus

expression	result
(45@230) + (175@300)	220@530
(45@230) + 175	220@405
(45@230) − (175@300)	−130@−70
(160@240) / 50	(16/5)@(24/5)
(160@240) // 50	3@4
(160@240) // (50@50)	3@4
((45@230) − (175@300)) abs	130@70
(120.5 @ 220.7) rounded	121@221
(160 @ 240) truncateTo: 50	150@200

Various other operations can be performed on Points including computing the distance between two Points, computing the dot product of two Points, transposing a point, and determining Points within some gridded range.

Point instance protocol

point functions

    dist: aPoint — Answer the distance between the argument, aPoint, and the receiver.

    dotProduct: aPoint — Answer a Number that is the dot product of the receiver and the argument, aPoint.

    grid: aPoint — Answer a Point to the nearest rounded grid modules specified by the argument, aPoint.

    normal — Answer a Point representing the unit vector rotated 90 deg clockwise.

    transpose — Answer a Point whose x is the receiver's y and whose y is the receiver's x.

    truncatedGrid: aPoint — Answer a Point to the nearest truncated grid modules specified by the argument, aPoint.

Examples are

expression	result
(45@230) dist: 175@270	136.015
(160@240) dotProduct: 50@50	20000
(160@240) grid: 50@50	150@250
(160@240) normal	−0.83105 @ 0.5547
(160@240) truncatedGrid: 50@50	150@200
(175@300) transpose	300@175

Points and Rectangles are used together as support for graphical manipulation. A Rectangle contains two Points—origin, which specifies the top left corner, and corner, which indicates the bottom right corner of the region described. Class Rectangle provides protocol for access to all the coordinates involved, and other operations such as intersection with other rectangles. Messages to a Point provide an infix way to create a Rectangle with the Point as the origin.

Point instance protocol
_____

converting
    corner: aPoint   Answer a Rectangle whose origin is the receiver and whose corner is the argument, aPoint.

    extent: aPoint   Answer a Rectangle whose origin is the receiver and whose extent is the argument, aPoint.

Thus (45@200) corner: (175@270) represents the rectangular area shown earlier in the image of display coordinates.

Class Rectangle

Instances of Rectangle represent rectangular areas of pixels. Arithmetic operations take points as arguments and carry out scaling and translating operations to create new Rectangles. Rectangle functions create new Rectangles by determining intersections of Rectangles with Rectangles.

In addition to the messages to Point by which Rectangles can be created, class protocol for Rectangle supports three messages for creating instances. These messages specify either the boundaries of the rectangular area, the origin and corner coordinates, or the origin and width and height of the area.

Rectangle class protocol
_____

instance creation
    left: leftNumber right: rightNumber top: topNumber bottom: bottomNumber
                                     Answer a Rectangle whose left, right, top, and bottom coordinates are determined by the arguments.

    origin: originPoint corner: cornerPoint
                                       Answer a Rectangle whose top left and bottom right corners are determined by the arguments, originPoint and cornerPoint.

    origin: originPoint extent: extentPoint
                                       Answer a Rectangle whose top left corner is originPoint and width by height is extentPoint.

The accessing protocol for Rectangle is quite extensive. It supports detailed ways of referencing eight significant locations on the boundary of the Rectangle. These points are shown in Figure 18.10.

Messages for accessing these positions have selectors with names like those shown in the diagram.

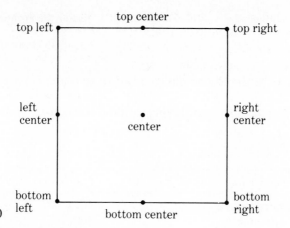

Figure 18.10

Rectangle instance protocol

---

accessing

topLeft	Answer the Point at the top left corner of the receiver.
topCenter	Answer the Point at the center of the receiver's top horizontal line.
topRight	Answer the Point at the top right corner of the receiver.
rightCenter	Answer the Point at the center of the receiver's right vertical line.
bottomRight	Answer the Point at the bottom right corner of the receiver.
bottomCenter	Answer the Point at the center of the receiver's bottom horizontal line.
bottomLeft	Answer the Point at the bottom left corner of the receiver.
leftCenter	Answer the Point at the center of the receiver's left vertical line.
center	Answer the Point at the center of the receiver.
area	Answer the receiver's area, the product of width and height.
width	Answer the receiver's width.
height	Answer the receiver's height.
extent	Answer the Point receiver's width @ receiver's height.
top	Answer the position of the receiver's top horizontal line.
right	Answer the position of the receiver's right vertical line.
bottom	Answer the position of the receiver's bottom horizontal line.
left	Answer the position of the receiver's left vertical line.

origin	Answer the Point at the top left corner of the receiver.
corner	Answer the Point at the bottom right corner of the receiver.

Suppose the Rectangle referred to as frame is created by the expression

frame ← Rectangle origin: 100@100 extent: 150@150

then

expression	result
frame topLeft	100@100
frame top	100
frame rightCenter	250@175
frame bottom	250
frame center	175@175
frame extent	150@150
frame area	22500

Each of the Rectangle's locations can be modified by an accessing message whose keyword is one of the positions named in Figure 18.10. In addition, the width and height can be set with the messages width: and height:, respectively. Two messages are listed below that are commonly used in the implementation of the system programming interface in order to reset the variables of a Rectangle.

Rectangle instance protocol

accessing
    origin: originPoint corner: cornerPoint
        Set the points at the top left corner and the bottom right corner of the receiver.
    origin: originPoint extent: extentPoint
        Set the point at the top left corner of the receiver to be originPoint and set the width and height of the receiver to be extentPoint.

Rectangle functions create new Rectangles and compute relationships between two Rectangles.

Rectangle instance protocol

rectangle functions
    amountToTranslateWithin: aRectangle
        Answer a Point, delta, such that the receiver, when moved by delta, will force the receiver to lie within the argument, aRectangle.

areasOutside: aRectangle	Answer a collection of Rectangles comprising the parts of the receiver which do not lie within the argument, aRectangle.
expandBy: delta	Answer a Rectangle that is outset from the receiver by delta, where delta is a Rectangle, Point, or scalar.
insetBy: delta	Answer a Rectangle that is inset from the receiver by delta, where delta is a Rectangle, Point, or scalar.
insetOriginBy: originDeltaPoint cornerBy: cornerDeltaPoint	
	Answer a Rectangle that is inset from the receiver by originDeltaPoint at the origin and cornerDeltaPoint at the corner.
intersect: aRectangle	Answer a Rectangle that is the area in which the receiver overlaps with the argument, aRectangle.
merge: aRectangle	Answer the smallest Rectangle that contains both the receiver and the argument, aRectangle.

Figure 18.11 shows three Rectangles, A, B, and C, created as follows.

A ← 50@50 corner: 200@200.
B ← 120@120 corner: 260@240.
C ← 100@300 corner: 300@400

Figure 18.11

Then expressions using these three Rectangles are listed below. Notice that Rectangles print in the form originPoint corner: cornerPoint.

expression	result
A amountToTranslateWithin: C	50@250
A areasOutside: B	OrderedCollection ((50@50 corner: 200 @120) (50@120 corner: 120@200))
C expandBy: 10	90@290 corner: 310@410
C insetBy: 10@20	110@320 corner: 290@380
A intersect: B	120@120 corner: 200@200
B merge: C	100@120 corner: 300@400

The testing protocol for Rectangles includes messages to determine whether a Point or other Rectangle is contained within the boundaries of a Rectangle, or whether two Rectangles intersect.

Rectangle instance protocol

testing

contains: aRectangle	Answer whether the receiver contains all Points contained by the argument, aRectangle.
containsPoint: aPoint	Answer whether the argument, aPoint, is within the receiver.
intersects: aRectangle	Answer whether the receiver contains any Point contained by the argument, aRectangle.

Continuing the above example

expression	result
A contains: B	false
C containsPoint: 200@320	true
A intersects: B	true

Like the messages for a Point, the coordinates of a Rectangle can be rounded to the nearest integer. A Rectangle can be moved by some amount, translated to a particular location, and the coordinates can be scaled or translated by some amount. Rectangles also respond to scaling and translating messages; they are part of the protocol for any object that can display itself on a display medium.

Rectangle instance protocol

---

truncation and round off

    rounded   Answer a Rectangle whose origin and corner coordinates are rounded to the nearest integer.

transforming

    moveBy: aPoint   Change the corner positions of the receiver so that its area translates by the amount defined by the argument, aPoint.

    moveTo: aPoint   Change the corners of the receiver so that its top left position is the argument, aPoint.

    scaleBy: scale   Answer a Rectangle scaled by the argument, scale, where scale is either a Point or a scalar.

    translateBy: factor   Answer a Rectangle translated by the argument, factor, where factor is either a Point or a scalar.

For example

expression	*result*
A moveBy: 50@50	100@100 corner: 250@250
A moveTo: 200@300	200@300 corner: 350@450
A scaleBy: 2	400@600 corner: 700@900
A translateBy: −100	100@200 corner: 250@350

Class BitBlt

The most basic interface to BitBlt is through a class of the same name. Each instance of BitBlt contains the variables necessary to specify a BitBlt operation. A specific application of BitBlt is governed by a list of parameters, which includes:

destForm   (destination form) a Form into which pixels will be stored

sourceForm   a Form from which pixels will be copied

halftoneForm   a Form containing a spatial halftone pattern

combinationRule	an Integer specifying the rule for combining corresponding pixels of the sourceForm and destForm
destX, destY, width, height	(destination area x, y, width, and height) Integers which specify the rectangular subregion to be filled in the destination
clipX, clipY, clipWidth, clipHeight	(clipping rectangular area x, y, width, and height) Integers which specify a rectangular area which restricts the affected region of the destination
sourceX, sourceY	Integers which specify the location (top left corner) of the subregion to be copied from the source

The BitBlt class protocol consists of one message for creating instances; this message contains a keyword and argument for each BitBlt variable. The BitBlt instance protocol includes messages for initializing the variables and a message, copyBits, which causes the primitive operation to take place. It also contains a message, drawFrom: startPoint to: stopPoint, for drawing a line defined by two Points.

BitBlt class protocol

---

instance creation
    destForm: destination
        sourceForm: source
        halftoneForm: halftone
        combinationRule: rule
        destOrigin: destOrigin
        sourceOrigin: sourceOrigin
        extent: extent
        clipRect: clipRect   Answer a BitBlt with values set according to each of the arguments, where rule is an Integer; destination, source, and halftone are Forms; destOrigin, sourceOrigin, and extent are Points; and clipRect is a Rectangle.

BitBlt instance protocol

---

accessing
    sourceForm: aForm   Set the receiver's source form to be the argument, aForm.

    destForm: aForm   Set the receiver's destination form to be the argument, aForm.

    mask: aForm   Set the receiver's halftone mask form to be the argument, aForm.

    combinationRule: anInteger   Set the receiver's combination rule to be the argument, anInteger, which must be an integer between 0 and 15.

    clipHeight: anInteger   Set the receiver's clipping area height to be the argument, anInteger.

    clipWidth: anInteger   Set the receiver's clipping area width to be the argument, anInteger.

clipRect	Answer the receiver's clipping rectangle.
clipRect: aRectangle	Set the receiver's clipping rectangle to be the argument, aRectangle.
clipX: anInteger	Set the receiver's clipping rectangle top left x coordinate to be the argument, anInteger.
clipY: anInteger	Set the receiver's clipping rectangle top left y coordinate to be the argument, anInteger.
sourceRect: aRectangle	Set the receiver's source form rectangular area to be the argument, aRectangle.
sourceOrigin: aPoint	Set the receiver's source form top left coordinates to be the argument, aPoint.
sourceX: anInteger	Set the receiver's source form top left x coordinate to be the argument, anInteger.
sourceY: anInteger	Set the receiver's source form top left y coordinate to be the argument, anInteger.
destRect: aRectangle	Set the receiver's destination form rectangular area to be the argument, aRectangle.
destOrigin: aPoint	Set the receiver's destination form top left coordinates to be the argument, aPoint.
destX: anInteger	Set the receiver's destination form top left x coordinate to be the argument, anInteger.
destY: anInteger	Set the receiver's destination form top left y coordinate to be the argument, anInteger.
height: anInteger	Set the receiver's destination form height to be the argument, anInteger.
width: anInteger	Set the receiver's destination form width to be the argument, anInteger.
copying	
copyBits	Perform the movement of bits from the source form to the destination form. Report an error if any variables are not of the right type (Integer or Form), or if the combination rule is not between 0 and 15 inclusive. Try to reset the variables and try again.

The state held in an instance of BitBlt allows multiple operations in a related context to be performed without the need to repeat all the initialization. For example, when displaying a scene in a display window, the destination form and clipping rectangle will not change from one operation to the next. Thus the instance protocol for modifying individual variables can be used to gain efficiency.

Line Drawing

Much of the graphics in the Smalltalk-80 system consists of lines and text. These entities are synthesized by repeated invocation of BitBlt.

The BitBlt protocol includes the messages drawFrom: startPoint to: stopPoint to draw a line whose end points are the arguments, startPoint and stopPoint.

BitBlt instance protocol
_____

line drawing
    drawFrom: startPoint to: stopPoint

> Draw a line whose end points are the arguments, startPoint and stopPoint. The line is formed by displaying copies of the current source form according to the receiver's halftone mask and combination rule.

By using BitBlt, one algorithm can draw lines of varying widths, different halftones, and any combination rule. To draw a line, an instance of BitBlt is initialized with the appropriate destination Form and clipping rectangle, and with a source that can be any Form to be applied as a pen or "brush" shape along the line. The message drawFrom:to: with Points as the two arguments is then sent to the instance. Figure 18.12 shows a number of different pen shapes and the lines they form when the BitBlt combination rule is 6 or 7.

The message drawFrom: startPoint to: stopPoint stores the destX and destY values. Starting from these stored values, the line-drawing loop, drawLoopX: xDelta Y: yDelta, shown next, accepts x and y delta values and calculates x and y step values to determine points along the line, and then calls copyBits in order to display the appropriate image at each point. The method used is the Bresenham plotting algorithm (*IBM Systems Journal*, Volume 4, Number 1, 1965). It chooses a principal direction and maintains a variable, p. When p's sign changes, it is time to move in the minor direction as well. This method is a natural unit to be implemented as a primitive method, since the computation is trivial and the setup in copyBits is almost all constant from one invocation to the next.

The method for drawLoopX: xDelta Y: yDelta in class BitBlt is

drawLoopX: xDelta Y: yDelta
```
| dx dy px py p |
dx ← xDelta sign.
dy ← yDelta sign.
px ← yDelta abs.
py ← xDelta abs.
self copyBits. "first point"
```

Figure 18.12

```
py > px
    ifTrue: "more horizontal"
        [p ← py // 2.
          1 to: py do:
             [ :i | destx ← destx + dx.
                 (p ← p − px) < 0
                      ifTrue: [desty ← desty + dy. p ← p + py].
                 self copyBits]]
    ifFalse: "more vertical"
        [p← px//2.
          1 to: px do:
             [ :i | desty ← desty + dy.
                 (p ← p − py) < 0
                      ifTrue: [destx ← destx + dx. p ← p + px].
                 self copyBits]]
```

Text Display

One of the advantages derived from BitBlt is the ability to store fonts compactly and to display them using various combination rules. The compact storage arises from the possibility of packing characters horizontally one next to another (as shown earlier in Figure 18.3), since BitBlt can extract the relevant bits if supplied with a table of left x coordinates of all the characters. This is called a *strike* format from the typographical term meaning a contiguous display of all the characters in a font.

The scanning and display of text are performed in the Smalltalk-80 system by a subclass of BitBlt referred to as CharacterScanner. This subclass inherits all the normal state, with destForm indicating the Form in which text is to be displayed and sourceForm indicating a Form containing all the character glyphs side by side (as in Figure 18.3). In addition CharacterScanner defines further state including:

text	a String of Characters to be displayed
textPos	an Integer giving the current position in text
xTable	an Array of Integers giving the left x location of each character in sourceForm
stopX	an Integer that sets a right boundary past which the inner loop should stop scanning
exceptions	an Array of Symbols that, if non-nil, indicate messages for handling the corresponding characters specially
printing	a Boolean indicating whether characters are to be printed

Once an instance has been initialized with a given font and text location, the scanWord: loop below will scan or print text until some horizontal position (stopX) is passed, until a special character (determined from exceptions) is found, or until the end of this range of text (endRun) is reached. Each of these conditions is denoted by a symbolic code referred to as stopXCode, exceptions (an Array of Symbols) and endRunCode.

```
scanword: endRun
    | charIndex |
    [textPos < endRun] whileTrue:
        ["pick character" charIndex ← text at: textPos.
         "check exceptions"
         (exceptions at: charIndex) > 0
            ifTrue: [↑exceptions at: charIndex].
         "left x of character in font" sourceX ← xTable at: charIndex.
         "up to left of next char"
         width ← (xTable at: charIndex+ 1) − sourceX.
         "print the character" printing ifTrue: [self copyBits].
```

```
    "advance by width of character" destX ← destX + width.
    destX > stopX ifTrue: [↑stopXCode]. "passed right boundary"
    "advance to next character"
    textPos ← textPos + 1].
textPos ← textPos − 1.
↑endRunCode
```

The check on exceptions handles many possibilities in one operation. The space character may have to be handled exceptionally in the case of text that is padded to achieve a flush right margin. Tabs usually require a computation or table lookup to determine their width. Carriage return is also identified in the check for exceptions. Character codes beyond the range given in the font are detected similarly, and are usually handled by showing an exceptional character, such as a little lightning bolt, so that they can be seen and corrected.

The printing flag can be set false to allow the same code to measure a line (break at a word boundary) or to find to which character the cursor points. While this provision may seem over-general, two benefits (besides compactness) are derived from that generality. First, if one makes a change to the basic scanning algorithm, the parallel functions of measuring, printing, and cursor tracking are synchronized by definition. Second, if a primitive implementation is provided for the loop, it exerts a threefold leverage on the system performance.

The scanword: loop is designed to be amenable to such primitive implementation; that is, the interpreter may intercept it and execute primitive code instead of the Smalltalk-80 code shown. In this way, much of the setup overhead for copyBits can be avoided at each character and an entire word or more can be displayed directly. Conversely, the Smalltalk text and graphics system requires implementation of only the one primitive operation (BitBlt) to provide full functionality.

Simulation of BitBlt

We provide here a simulation of an implementation of copyBits in a subclass of BitBlt referred to as BitBltSimulation. The methods in this simulation are intentionally written in the style of machine code in order to serve as a guide to implementors. No attempt is made to hide the choice of 16-bit word size. Although the copyBits method is presented as a Smalltalk-80 method in BitBltSimulation, it is actually implemented in machine-code as a primitive method in class BitBlt; the simulation does the same thing, albeit slower.

class name	BitBltSimulation
superclass	BitBlt
instance variable names	sourceBits sourceRaster
	destBits destRaster
	halftoneBits
	skew skewMask
	mask1 mask2
	preload nWords
	hDir vDir
	sourceIndex sourceDelta
	destIndex destDelta
	sx sy dx dy w h
class variable names	AllOnes RightMasks
class methods	

initialize
"Initialize a table of bit masks"
RightMasks ←
    #(0 16r1 16r3 16r7 16rF
        16r1F 16r3F 16r7F 16rFF
        16r1FF 16r3FF 16r7FF 16rFFF
        16r1FFF 16r3FFF 16r7FFF 16rFFFF).
AllOnes ← 16rFFFF

instance methods
operations

copyBits
"sets w and h"
self clipRange.
(w <=0 or: [h <=0]) ifTrue: [↑self]. "null range"
self computeMasks.
self checkOverlap.
self calculateOffsets.
self copyLoop

private

clipRange
"clip and adjust source origin and extent appropriately"
"first in x"
destX > = clipX
    ifTrue: [sx ← sourceX. dx ← destX. w ← width]
    ifFalse: [sx ← sourceX + (clipX − destX).
            w ← width − (clipX − destX).
            dx ← clipX].
(dx + w) > (clipX + clipWidth)
    ifTrue: [w ← w − ((dx + w) − (clipX + clipWidth))].

```
"then in y"
destY > = clipY
    ifTrue: [sy ← sourceY. dy ← destY. h ← height]
    ifFalse: [sy ← sourceY + clipY − destY.
              h ← height − clipY + destY.
              dy ← clipY].
(dy + h) > (clipY + clipHeight)
    ifTrue: [h ← h − ((dy + h) − (clipY + clipHeight))].
sx < 0
    ifTrue: [dx ← dx − sx. w ← w + sx. sx ← 0].
sx + w > sourceForm width
    ifTrue: [w ← w − (sx + w − sourceForm width)].
sy < 0
    ifTrue: [dy ← dy − sy. h ← h + sy. sy ← 0].
sy + h > sourceForm height
    ifTrue: [h ← h − (sy + h − sourceForm height)]
```

Clipping first checks whether the destination x lies to the left of the clipping rectangle and, if so, adjusts both destination x and width. As mentioned previously, the data to be copied into this adjusted rectangle comes from a shifted region of the source, so that the source x must also be adjusted. Next, the rightmost destination x is compared to the clipping rectangle and the width is decreased again if necessary. This whole process is then repeated for y and height. Then the height and width are clipped to the size of the source form. The adjusted parameters are stored in variables sx, sy, dx, dy, w, and h. If either width or height is reduced to zero, the entire call to BitBlt can return immediately.

computeMasks

```
| startBits endBits |
"calculate skew and edge masks"
destBits ← destForm bits.
destRaster ← destForm width −1 // 16 + 1.
sourceForm notNil
    ifTrue: [sourceBits ← sourceForm bits.
             sourceRaster← sourceForm width − 1//16 + 1].
halftoneForm notNil
    ifTrue: [halftoneBits ← halftoneForm bits].
skew ← (sx − dx) bitAnd: 15.
"how many bits source gets skewed to right"
startBits ← 16 − (dx bitAnd: 15).
"how many bits in first word"
mask1 ← RightMasks at: startBits + 1.
endBits ← 15 − ((dx + w−1) bitAnd: 15).
"how many bits in last word"
mask2 ← (RightMasks at: endBits + 1) bitInvert.
```

```
skewMask ←
    (skew=0
        ifTrue: [0]
        ifFalse: [RightMasks at: 16 − skew + 1]).
    "determine number of words stored per line; merge masks if necessary"
    w < startBits
        ifTrue: [mask1 ← mask1 bitAnd: mask2.
                 mask2 ← 0.
                 nWords ← 1]
        ifFalse: [nWords ← (w − startBits − 1) // 16 + 2].
```

In preparation for the actual transfer of data, several parameters are computed. First is skew, the horizontal offset of data from source to destination. This represents the number of bits by which the data will have to be rotated after being loaded from the source in order to line up with the final position in the destination. In the example of Figure 18.3, skew would be 5 because the glyph for the character "e" must be shifted left by 5 bits prior to being stored into the destination. From skew, skewMask is saved for use in rotating (this is unnecessary for machines with a rotate word instruction). Then mask1 and mask2 are computed for selecting the bits of the first and last partial words of each scan line in the destination. These masks would be 16r1FFF and 16rFFC0 respectively in the example of Figure 18.3 since startBits=13 and endBits=6. In cases such as this where only one word of each destination line is affected, the masks are merged to select the range within that word, here 16r1FC0.

checkOverlap

```
| t |
"check for possible overlap of source and destination"
hDir ← vDir ← 1. "defaults for no overlap"
(sourceForm == destForm and: [dy > = sy])
    ifTrue:
        [dy > sy "have to start at bottom"
        ifTrue: [vDir ← −1. sy ← sy + h − 1. dy ← dy + h − 1]
        ifFalse: [dx > sx "y's are equal, but x's are backward "
                ifTrue: [hDir ← −1.
                        sx ← sx + w − 1.
                        "start at right"
                        dx ← dx + w − 1.
                        "and fix up masks"
                        skewMask ← skewMask bitInvert.
                        t ← mask1.
                        mask1 ← mask2.
                        mask2 ← t]]]
```

A check must be made for overlapping source and destination. When source and destination lie in the same bitmap, there is the possibility of the copy operation destroying the data as it is moved. Thus when the data is being moved downward, the copy must start at the bottom and proceed upward. Similarly when there is no vertical movement, if the horizontal movement is to the right, the copy must start at the right and work back to the left. In all other cases the copy can proceed from top to bottom and left to right.

calculateOffsets

```
"check if need to preload buffer
(i.e., two words of source needed for first word of destination)"
preload ← (sourceForm notNil) and:
                    [skew ~= 0 and: [skew <= (sx bitAnd: 15)]].
hDir < 0 ifTrue: [preload ← preload == false].
"calculate starting offsets"
sourceIndex ← sy * sourceRaster + (sx // 16).
destIndex ← dy * destRaster + (dx // 16).
"calculate increments from end of 1 line to start of next"
sourceDelta ←
    (sourceRaster * vDir) −
        (nWords + (preload ifTrue: [1] ifFalse: [0]) * hDir).
destDelta ← (destRaster * vDir) − (nWords * hDir)
```

In cases where two words of source are needed to store the first word into the destination, a flag preload is set indicating the need to preload a 32-bit shifter prior to the inner loop of the copy (this is an optimization; one could simply always load an extra word initially). The offsets needed for the inner loop are the starting offset in words from the source and destination bases; deltas are also computed for jumping from the end of the data in one scanline to the start of data in the next.

inner loop

copyLoop

```
| prevWord thisWord skewWord mergeMask
  halftoneWord mergeWord word |
1 to: h do: "here is the vertical loop:"
  [ :i |
    (halftoneForm notNil)
      ifTrue:
          [halftoneWord ← halftoneBits at: (1 + (dy bitAnd: 15)).
           dy ← dy + vDir]
        ifFalse: [halftoneWord ← AllOnes].
      skewWord ← halftoneWord.
```

```
                                preload
                                  ifTrue: [prevWord ← sourceBits at: sourceIndex + 1.
                                        "load the 32-bit shifter"
                                        sourceIndex ← sourceIndex + hDir]
                                  ifFalse: [prevWord ← 0].
                                mergeMask ← mask1.
                                1 to to: nWords do: "here is the inner horizontal loop"
                                [ :word |
                                  sourceForm notNil "if source is used"
                                    ifTrue:
                                        [prevWord ← prevWord bitAnd: skewMask.
                                        thisWord ← sourceBits at: sourceIndex + 1.
                                                                "pick up next word"
                                        skewWord ←
                                            prevWord bitOr: (thisWord bitAnd: skewMask bitInvert).
                                        prevWord ← thisWord.
                                        skewWord ← (skewWord bitShift: skew) bitOr:
                                                        (skewWord bitShift: skew − 16)].
                                                                " 16-bit rotate"
                                  mergeWord ← self merge: (skewWord bitAnd: halftoneWord)
                                                        with: (destBits at: destIndex + 1).
                                destBits
                                    at: destIndex + 1
                                    put: ((mergeMask bitAnd: mergeWord)
                                                bitOr: (mergeMask bitInvert
                                                        bitAnd: (destBits at: destIndex + 1))).
                                  sourceIndex ← sourceIndex + hDir.
                                  destIndex ← destIndex + hDir.
                                  word = (nWords − 1)
                                    ifTrue: [mergeMask ← mask2]
                                    ifFalse: [mergeMask ← AllOnes]].
                                sourceIndex ← sourceIndex + sourceDelta.
                                destIndex ← destIndex + destDelta]
```

The outer, or vertical, loop includes the overhead for each line, selecting the appropriate line of halftone gray, preloading the shifter if necessary, and stepping source and destination pointers to the next scanline after the inner loop. It should be noted here that the reason for indexing the halftone pattern by the destination y is to eliminate "seams" which would occur if the halftones in all operations were not coordinated this way.

The inner, or horizontal, loop picks up a new word of source, rotates it with the previous, and merges the result with a word of the destination. The store into the destination must be masked for the first and last partial words on each scanline, but in the middle, no masking is really necessary.

merge: sourceWord with: destinationWord
```
"These are the 16 combination rules:"
combinationRule=0
    ifTrue: [↑0].
combinationRule=1
    ifTrue: [↑sourceWord bitAnd: destinationWord].
combinationRule=2
    ifTrue: [↑sourceWord bitAnd: destinationWord bitInvert].
combinationRule=3
    ifTrue: [↑sourceWord].
combinationRule=4
    ifTrue: [↑sourceWord bitInvert bitAnd: destinationWord].
combinationRule=5
    ifTrue: [↑destinationWord].
combinationRule=6
    ifTrue:[↑sourceWord bitXor: destinationWord].
combinationRule=7
    ifTrue: [↑sourceWord bitOr: destinationWord].
combinationRule=8
    ifTrue: [↑sourceWord bitInvert bitAnd: destinationWord bitInvert].
combinationRule=9
    ifTrue: [↑sourceWord bitInvert bitXor: destinationWord].
combinationRule=10
    ifTrue: [↑destinationWord bitInvert].
combinationRule=11
    ifTrue: [↑sourceWord bitOr: destinationWord bitInvert].
combinationRule=12
    ifTrue: [↑sourceWord bitInvert].
combinationRule=13
    ifTrue: [↑sourceWord bitInvert bitOr: destinationWord].
combinationRule=14
    ifTrue: [↑sourceWord bitInvert bitOr: destinationWord bitInvert].
combinationRule=15
    ifTrue: [↑AllOnes]
```

Efficiency Considerations

Our experience has demonstrated the value of BitBlt's generality. This one primitive is so central to the programming interface that any improvement in its performance has considerable effect on the interactive quality of the system as a whole. In normal use of the Smalltalk-80 system, most invocations of BitBlt are either in the extreme microscopic or macroscopic range.

In the macroscopic range, the width of transfer spans many words. The inner loop across a horizontal scan line gets executed many times, and the operations requested tend to be simple moves or constant stores. Examples of these are:

clearing a line of text to white

clearing an entire window to white

scrolling a block of text up or down

Most processors provide a fast means for block moves and stores, and these can be made to serve the applications above. Suppose we structure the horizontal loop of BitBlt as

1. move left partial word,

2. move many whole words (or none),

3. move right partial word (or none).

Special cases can be provided for 2 if the operation is a simple store or a simple copy with no skew (horizontal bit offset) from source to destination. In this way, most macroscopic applications of BitBlt can be made fast, even on processors of modest power.

The microscopic range of BitBlt is characterized by a zero count for the inner loop. The work on each scanline involves at most two partial words, and both overall setup and vertical loop overhead can be considerably reduced for these cases. Because characters tend to be less than a word wide and lines tend to be less than a word thick, nearly all text and line drawing falls into this category. A convenient way to provide such efficiency is to write a special case of BitBlt which assumes the microscopic parameters, but goes to the general BitBlt whenever these are not met. Because of the statistics (many small operations and a few very large ones), it does not hurt to pay the penalty of a false assumption on infrequent calls. One can play the same trick with clipping by assuming no clipping will occur and running the general code only when this assumption fails.

19

Pens

Class Pen

Geometric Designs
Spirals
Dragon Curve
Hilbert Curve

Commander Pen

Object

Magnitude
    Character
    Date
    Time

    Number
        Float
        Fraction
        Integer
            LargeNegativeInteger
            LargePositiveInteger
            SmallInteger

    LookupKey
        Association

Link

    Process

Collection

    SequenceableCollection
    LinkedList

        Semaphore

    ArrayedCollection
    Array

        WordArray
            DisplayBitmap

        RunArray
        String
            Symbol
        Text
        ByteArray

    Interval
    OrderedCollection
        SortedCollection
    Bag
    MappedCollection
    Set
    Dictionary
        IdentityDictionary

Stream
    PositionableStream
        ReadStream
        WriteStream
            ReadWriteStream
                ExternalStream
                    FileStream

    Random

UndefinedObject
Boolean
    False
    True

ProcessorScheduler
Delay
SharedQueue

Behavior
    ClassDescription
        Class
        MetaClass

Point
Rectangle
BitBlt
    CharacterScanner

Pen

DisplayObject
    DisplayMedium
        Form
            Cursor
            DisplayScreen
        InfiniteForm
        OpaqueForm
        Path
            Arc
                Circle
            Curve
            Line
            LinearFit
            Spline

As explained in the previous chapter, Forms represent images. Lines can be created by copying a Form to several locations in another Form at incremental distances between two designated points. Higher-level access to line drawing is provided by instances of class Pen.

Pen is a subclass of BitBlt. As such, it is a holder for source and destination Forms. The source Form can be colored black or white or different tones of gray, and copied into the destination Form with different combination rules, different halftone masks, and with respect to different clipping rectangles. The source Form is the Pen's writing tool or nib. The destination Form is the Pen's writing surface; it is usually the Form representing the display screen.

In addition to the implementations inherited from BitBlt, a Pen has a Point that indicates a position on the display screen and a Number that indicates a direction in which the Pen moves. A Pen understands messages that cause it to change its position or direction. When its position changes, the Pen can leave a copy of its Form at its former position. By moving the Pen to different screen positions and copying its Form to one or more of these positions, graphic designs are created.

Several programming systems provide this kind of access to line drawing. In these systems, the line drawer is typically called a "turtle" after the one first provided in the MIT/BBN Logo language (Seymour Papert, *MindStorms: Children, Computers and Powerful Ideas*, Basic Books, 1980; Harold Abelson and Andrea diSessa, *Turtle Geometry: The Computer as a Medium for Exploring Mathematics*, MIT Press, 1981). The protocol for Pens supports messages that are like the turtle commands provided in Logo. These consist of commands for telling the turtle to go some distance, turn some amount, to place a pen in a down position, and to place a pen in an up position. When the pen is down and it moves, a trace of the turtle's path is created. The corresponding Pen messages are go: distance, turn: amount, down, and up.

Multiple Pens can be created and their movement on the screen coordinated so that the process of creating a graphical design can itself be graphically pleasing. The next section contains the protocol that is provided in class Pen. Subsequent sections give examples of designs that can be created by sending messages to Pens.

Class Pen

Instances of class Pen are created by sending Pen the message new. A Pen created this way can draw anywhere on the display screen; its initial position is the center of the screen, facing in a direction towards the top of the screen. The Pen is set to draw (i.e., it is down) with a source Form or nib that is a 1 by 1 black dot.

There are two ways to change the source Form of a Pen. One way is to send the Pen the message defaultNib: widthInteger. The other way is to reset the source Form by sending the Pen the messages it inherits from its superclass, BitBlt. For example, the message sourceForm: changes the source form, or the message mask: changes the halftone form (the mask) used in displaying the source form. (Note that the default mask for displaying is black.)

Pen instance protocol

---

initialize-release

defaultNib: shape	A "nib" is the tip of a pen. This is an easy way to set up a default pen. The Form for the receiver is a rectangular shape with height and width equal to (1) the argument, shape, if shape is an Integer; or (2) the coordinates of shape if shape is a Point.

Thus

    bic ← Pen new defaultNib: 2

creates a Pen with a black Form that is 2 bits wide by 2 bits high.

The accessing protocol for a Pen provides access to the Pen's current direction, location, and drawing region. The drawing region is referred to as the Pen's *frame*.

Pen instance protocol

---

accessing

direction	Answer the receiver's current direction. 270 is towards the top of the screen.
location	Answer the receiver's current location.
frame	Answer the Rectangle in which the receiver can draw.
frame: aRectangle	Set the Rectangle in which the receiver can draw to be the argument, aRectangle.

Continuing to use the example, bic, and assuming that the display screen is 600 bits wide and 800 bits high, we have

expression	*result*
bic direction	270
bic location	300@400
bic frame: (50@50 extent: 200@200)	
bic location	300@400

Notice that when the Pen direction is towards the top of the display screen, the angle is 270 degrees. Notice also that the Pen is currently outside its drawing region and would have to be placed within the Rectangle, 50@50 corner: 250@250, before any of its marks could be seen.

The "turtle" drawing commands alter the Pen's drawing state, orient its drawing direction, and reposition it.

Pen instance protocol

---

moving

down	Set the state of the receiver to "down" so that it leaves marks when it moves.
up	Set the state of the receiver to "up" so that it does not leave marks when it moves.
turn: degrees	Change the direction that the receiver faces by an amount equal to the argument, degrees.
north	Set the receiver's direction to facing toward the top of the display screen.
go: distance	Move the receiver in its current direction a number of bits equal to the argument, distance. If the receiver status is "down," a line will be drawn using the receiver's Form as the shape of the drawing brush.
goto: aPoint	Move the receiver to position aPoint. If the receiver status is "down", a line will be drawn from the current position to the new one using the receiver's Form as the shape of the drawing brush. The receiver's direction does not change.
place: aPoint	Set the receiver at position aPoint. No lines are drawn.
home	Place the receiver at the center of the region in which it can draw.

Thus we can place bic in the center of its frame by evaluating the expression

    bic home

If we then ask

    bic location

the response would be 150@150.

Suppose that we drew a line with a Pen and then decided that we wanted to erase it. If the line had been drawn with a black Form, then we can erase it by drawing over it with a white Form of at least the same size. Thus

    bic go: 100

draws the black line. Then

    bic white

sets the drawing mask to be all white (the message white is inherited from the protocol of BitBlt), and then

    bic go: −100

draws over the original line, erasing it.

An exercise that is common in the Logo examples is to create various polygon shapes, such as a square.

    4 timesRepeat: [bic go: 100. bic turn: 90]

The following expression creates any polygon shape by computing the angle of turning as a function of the number of sides. If nSides is the number of sides of the desired polygon, then

    nSides timesRepeat: [bic go: 100. bic turn: 360 // nSides]

will draw the polygon. We can create a class Polygon whose instances refer to the number of sides and length of each side. In addition, each Polygon has its own Pen for drawing. In the definition that follows, we specify that a Polygon can be told to draw on the display screen; the method is the one described earlier.

class name	Polygon
superclass	Object
instance variable names	drawingPen
	nSides
	length

class methods

instance creation

new
    ↑super new default

instance methods

drawing

draw
    drawingPen black.
    nSides timesRepeat: [drawingPen go: length; turn: 360 // nSides]

accessing

length: n
    length ← n
sides: n
    nSides ← n

private

default
    drawingPen ← Pen new.
    self length: 100.
    self sides: 4

Then a Polygon can be created and a sequence of polygons drawn by evaluating the expressions

poly ← Polygon new.
3 to: 10 do: [:sides | poly sides: sides. poly draw]

The result is shown in Figure 19.1.

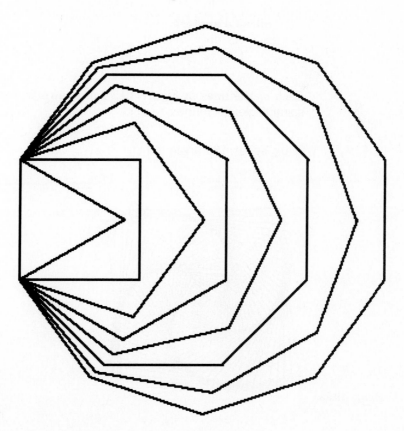

Figure 19.1

Geometric Designs

The Logo books mentioned earlier provide extensive examples of how to use this kind of access to line drawing in order to create images on a computer display screen. We provide several examples of methods that can be added to a Pen so that any Pen can draw a geometric design such as those shown in Figures 19.2 - 19.5. (Note: These methods are in the system as part of the description of Pen so that users can play with creating geometric designs.)

Spirals

The first design is called a *spiral*. A spiral is created by having the Pen draw incrementally longer lines; after each line is drawn, the Pen turns some amount. The lines drawn begin at length 1 and increase by 1 each time until reaching a length equal to the first argument of the message spiral:angle:. The second argument of the message is the amount the Pen turns after drawing each line.

```
spiral: n angle: a
    1 to: n do:
        [ :i | self go: i. self turn: a]
```

Each of the lines in Figure 19.2 was drawn by sending bic the message spiral:angle:, as follows.

    bic spiral: 150 angle: 89

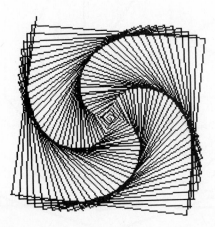

Figure 19.2a

bic spiral: 150 angle: 91

Figure 19.2b

bic spiral: 150 angle: 121

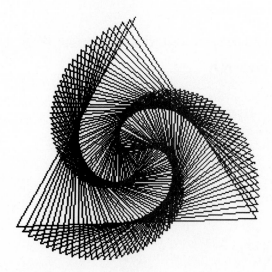

Figure 19.2c

bic home.
bic spiral: 150 angle: 89.
bic home.
bic spiral: 150 angle: 91

Figure 19.2d

Dragon Curve

Figure 19.3 is an image of a "dragon curve" of order 8 which was drawn in the middle of the screen by evaluating the expression

bic ← Pen new defaultNib: 4.
bic dragon: 9

The method associated with the message dragon: in class Pen is

```
dragon: n
    n = 0
        ifTrue: [self go: 10]
        ifFalse:
            [n > 0
                ifTrue:
                    [self dragon: n − 1.
                    self turn: 90.
                    self dragon: 1 − n]
                ifFalse:
                    [self dragon: −1 − n.
                    self turn: −90.
                    self dragon: 1 + n]]
```

Figure 19.3

Dragon curves were discussed by Martin Gardner in his mathematical games column in *Scientific American* (March 1967, p. 124, and April 1967, p. 119). Another discussion of dragon curves appears in Donald Knuth and Chandler Davis, "Number Representations and Dragon Curves," *Journal of Recreation Mathematics*, Vol. 3, 1970, pp. 66-81 and 133-149.

Hilbert Curve

Figure 19.4 is a space-filling curve attributed to the mathematician David Hilbert. A space-filling curve has an index; as the index increases to infinity, the curve tends to cover the points in a plane. The example is the result of evaluating the expression

    Pen new hilbert: 5 side: 8

The index for the example is 5; at each point, a line 8 pixels long is drawn. The corresponding method for the message hilbert:side is

```
hilbert: n side: s
    | a m |
    n = 0 ifTrue: [↑self turn: 180].
    n > 0 ifTrue: [a ← 90.
                  m ← n − 1]
        ifFalse: [a ← −90.
                  m ← n + 1].
```

Figure 19.4

```
self turn: a.
self hilbert: 0 — m side: s.
self turn: a.
self go: s.
self hilbert: m side: s.
self turn: 0 — a.
self go: s.
self turn: 0 — a.
self hilbert: m side: s.
self go: s.
self turn: a.
self hilbert: 0 — m side: s.
self turn: a
```

A Hilbert curve, where the source form is a different shape, creates a nice effect. Suppose the Form is three dots in a row and suppose that this Form is a system cursor referred to as dots that is a row of three dots. The image in Figure 19.5 was created by evaluating the expressions

```
bic ← Pen new sourceForm: Cursor dots.
bic combinationRule: Form under.
bic hilbert: 4 side: 16
```

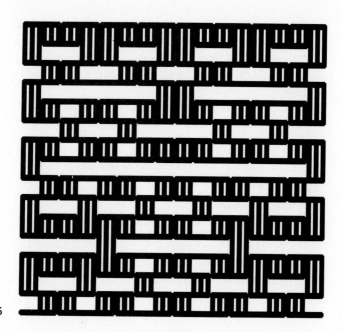

Figure 19.5

Expressions Cursor dots and Form under access a Form and a combination rule, respectively, that are constants in the system and that are known to the named classes. Other such constants are listed in a section of the next chapter. The messages sourceForm: and combinationRule: are inherited by Pens from their superclass BitBlt.

Commander Pen

The next example is shown in Figure 19.6. Although we can not show the process by which the design was created, it is a nice example for the reader to try. The basic idea is to create an object that controls several Pens and coordinates their drawing a design. We call the class of this kind of object, Commander. A Commander is an array of Pens. Pens controlled by a Commander can be given directions by having the Commander enumerate each Pen and evaluate a block containing Pen commands. So if a Commander's Pens should each go: 100, for example, then the Commander can be sent the message

    do: [:eachPen | eachPen go: 100]

A Commander also responds to messages to arrange its Pens so that interesting designs based on symmetries can be created. The two messages given in the description of Commander shown next are fanOut and lineUpFrom: startPoint to: endPoint. The first message arranges the Pens so that their angles are evenly distributed around 360 degrees. A Commander's Pens can be positioned evenly along a line using the message lineUpFrom:to:, where the arguments define the end points of the line.

A description for Commander follows. The message new: is redefined so that Pens are stored in each element of the Array.

class name	Commander
superclass	Array
class methods	

instance creation

new: numberOfPens
```
| newCommander |
newCommander ← super new: numberOfPens.
1 to: numberOfPens do:
        [ :index | newCommander at: index put: Pen new].
↑newCommander
```

instance methods

distributing

fanOut
```
1 to: self size do:
    [ :index |
    (self at: index) turn: (index − 1) * (360 / self size)]
```
lineUpFrom: startPoint to: endPoint
```
1 to: self size do:
    [ :index |
    (self at: index)
        place: startPoint + (stopPoint−startPoint*(index−1) / (self size−1))]
```

The methods are useful examples of sending messages to instances of class Point. The image in Figure 19.6 was drawn by evaluating the expressions

```
bic ← Commander new: 4.
bic fanOut.
bic do: [ :eachPen | eachPen up. eachPen go: 100. eachPen down].
bic do: [ :eachPen | eachPen spiral: 200 angle: 121]
```

The message do: to a Commander is inherited from its Collection superclass.

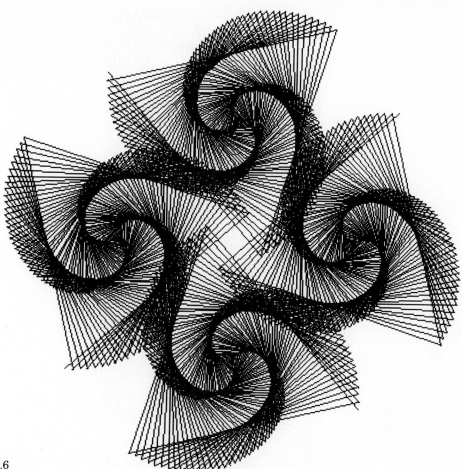

Figure 19.6

Another example of the use of a Commander is given in Figure 19.7. This image was created by using the message lineUpFrom:to:. It is a simple sequence of spirals arranged along a line at an angle, created by evaluating the expressions

```
bic ← Commander new: 6.
bic lineUpFrom: (300@150) to: (300@500).
bic do: [ :eachPen | eachPen spiral: 200 angle: 121]
```

☐ *Additional Protocol for Commander* Pen   An expanded description of Commander adds to Commander each message of the protocol of class Pen whose behavior changes position or orientation. This additional protocol supports the ability to send messages that are part of Pen's

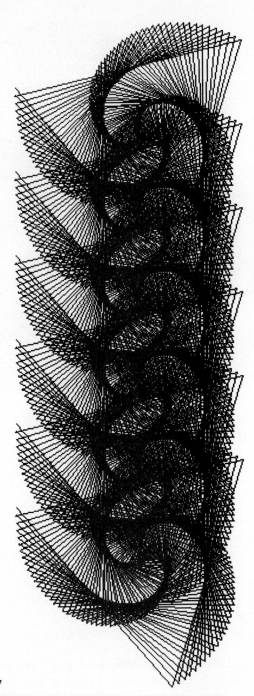

Figure 19.7

protocol to the Commander. Each such message is implemented as broadcasting the message to the elements of the collection. In this way, messages to Commander take the same form as messages to any Pen, rather than that of a do: message. With the class defined in this way, drawing sequences to a Commander appear more like drawing sequences to a Pen. Moreover, all the Pens commanded by a Commander draw in parallel; for example, all the spirals of Figures 19.6 or 19.7 would grow at once.

```
down
    self do: [ :each | each down]
up
    self do: [ :each | each up]
turn: degrees
    self do: [ :each | each turn: degrees]
north
    self do: [ :each | each north]
go: distance
    self do: [ :each | each go: distance]
goto: aPoint
    self do: [ :each | each goto: aPoint]
place: aPoint
    self do: [ :each | each place: aPoint]
home
    self do: [ :each | each home]
spiral: n angle: a
    1 to: n do:
        [ :i | self go: i. self turn: a]
```

With this additional protocol, Figure 19.6 can be drawn by evaluating the expressions

```
bic ← Commander new: 4.
bic fanOut.
bic up.
bic go: 100.
bic down.
bic spiral: 200 angle: 121
```

and Figure 19.7 by the expressions

```
bic ← Commander new: 6.
bic lineUpFrom: (300@150) to: (300@500).
bic spiral: 200 angle: 121
```

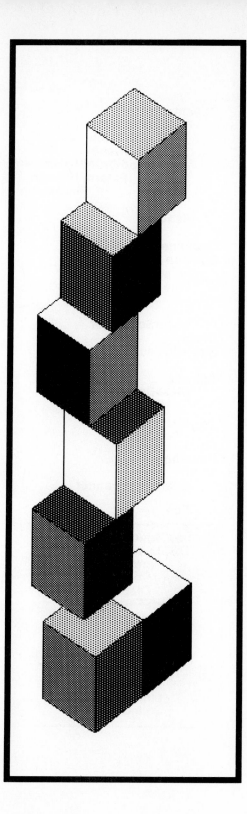

20

Display Objects

```
Object

    Magnitude                               Stream
        Character                               PositionableStream
        Date                                        ReadStream
        Time                                        WriteStream
                                                        ReadWriteStream
        Number                                          ExternalStream
            Float                                           FileStream
            Fraction
            Integer                             Random
                LargeNegativeInteger
                LargePositiveInteger        UndefinedObject
                SmallInteger                Boolean
                                                False
                                                True
        LookupKey
            Association
                                            ProcessorScheduler
    Link                                    Delay
                                            SharedQueue
        Process
                                            Behavior
    Collection                                  ClassDescription
                                                    Class
        SequenceableCollection                      MetaClass
            LinkedList
                                            Point
                                            Rectangle
                Semaphore                   BitBlt
                                                CharacterScanner
            ArrayedCollection
            Array                               Pen

                WordArray
                    DisplayBitmap        DisplayObject
                                             DisplayMedium
                RunArray                         Form
                String                               Cursor
                    Symbol                               DisplayScreen
                Text                         InfiniteForm
                ByteArray                    OpaqueForm
                                             Path
            Interval                             Arc
            OrderedCollection                        Circle
                SortedCollection             Curve
        Bag                                      Line
        MappedCollection                         LinearFit
        Set                                      Spline
            Dictionary
                IdentityDictionary
```

Graphics in the Smalltalk-80 system begin with the specification of BitBlt. Supported by Points, Rectangles, Forms, Pens, and Text, a wide variety of imagery can be created. The images in Figure 20.1 illustrate some of the graphical entities made possible by extending the use of these five kinds of objects.

The more artistic images in Figures 20.2 and 20.3 were created using the additional display objects available in the Smalltalk-80 system. The methods used in creating these images are described later. This chapter describes the available kinds of display objects and the various ways to manipulate them.

Class DisplayObject

A Form is a kind of display object. There are others in the system. The way in which these objects are implemented is as a hierarchy of classes whose superclass is named DisplayObject. Form is a subclass in this hierarchy.

A display object represents an image that has a width, a height, an assumed origin at 0@0, and an offset from this origin relative to which the image is to be displayed. All display objects are similar in their ability to copy their image into another image, to be scaled, and to be translated. They differ in how their image is created.

There are three primary subclasses of DisplayObject. They are DisplayMedium, DisplayText, and Path.

- DisplayMedium represents images that can be "colored" (that is, filled with a gray tone) and bordered (that is, their rectangular outline is colored).

- DisplayText represents textual images.

- Path represents images composed as collections of images.

A Form is a subclass of DisplayMedium; it adds the bitmap representation of the image. All DisplayObjects provide source information for images; Forms provide both the source and the destination information.

Class DisplayObject supports accessing messages for manipulating the various aspects of the image.

DisplayObject instance protocol

accessing	
width	Answer the width of the receiver's bounding box, a rectangle that represents the boundaries of the receiver's image.
height	Answer the height of the receiver's bounding box.
extent	Answer a Point representing the width and height of the receiver's bounding box.

TONES

ICONS

FONT

ABCDEFGHIJKLMNOPQRST
abcdefghijklmnopqrstuvwxyz
1234567890

SYMBOL

POINTS

TEXT

The modern age has brought to
Ikebana the concepts of individual
expression and abstract design
divorced from established rules.

LINE

Figure 20.1

DOCUMENT

IMAGE

BRUSHES

IDIOM

Figure 20.2

Figure 20.3

offset	Answer a Point representing the amount by which the receiver should be offset when it is displayed or its position is tested.
offset: aPoint	Set the receiver's offset.
rounded	Set the receiver's offset to the nearest integral amount.

DisplayObject also provides three kinds of messages that support *transforming* an image, *displaying* the image, and computing the *display box*, that is, a rectangular area that represents the boundaries of the area for displaying the image.

DisplayObject instance protocol

transforming

scaleBy: aPoint	Scale the receiver's offset by aPoint.
translateBy: aPoint	Translate the receiver's offset by aPoint.
align: alignmentPoint with: relativePoint	
	Translate the receiver's offset such that alignmentPoint aligns with relativePoint.

display box access

boundingBox	Answer the rectangular area that represents the boundaries of the receiver's space of information.

displaying

displayOn: aDisplayMedium at: aDisplayPoint clippingBox: clipRectangle rule: ruleInteger mask: aForm	
	Display the receiver at location aDisplayPoint with rule, ruleInteger, and halftone mask, aForm. Information to be displayed must be confined to the area that intersects with clipRectangle.

There are actually several displaying messages not shown above. Alternative displaying messages progressively omit a keyword (starting from the last one) and provide default masks, rules, clipping rectangles, and positions, when needed. Basically the display screen itself is the default clipping rectangle, 0@0 is the default display position, and the object that represents the system display screen, Display, (a global variable) is the default display medium.

The message displayAt: aDisplayPoint provides a generally useful message when the only parameter not defaulted is the location at which the image is to be placed. The message display assumes that the display location is 0@0.

DisplayObject instance protocol

displayAt: aDisplayPoint	Display the receiver at location aDisplayPoint with rule "over" or "storing"; halftone mask, a black Form; clipping rectangle the whose display screen; onto the display screen (Display).
display	Display the receiver at location 0@0.

These last two displaying messages are provided for textual objects such as String and Text as well, so that the programmer can place characters on the screen by evaluating an expression such as

'This is text to be displayed' displayAt: 100@100

Suppose locomotive is the Form that looks like

then it can be displayed on the screen with top left corner at location 50@150 by evaluating the expression

locomotive displayAt: 50@150

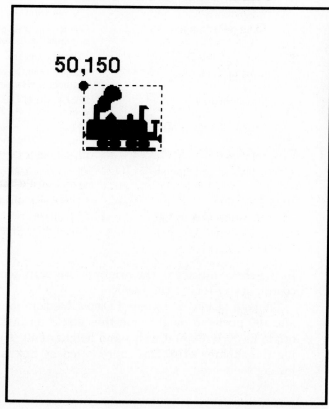

Class DisplayMedium

DisplayMedium is a subclass of DisplayObject that represents an object onto which images can be copied. In addition to those messages inherited from its superclass, DisplayMedium provides protocol for coloring the interior of images and placing borders around the display boxes of images. The "colors" are Forms that are already available in the system. These are black (the bitmap is all ones), white (all zeros), and various gray tones, either gray, veryLightGray, lightGray, or darkGray (mixtures of ones and zeros). Images of these colors are given below. All or portions of the DisplayMedium's area can be changed to one of these colors using the following messages.

DisplayMedium instance protocol

coloring

black	Change all of the receiver's area to black.
black: aRectangle	Change the area of the receiver defined by the argument, aRectangle, to black.
white	Change all of the receiver's area to white.
white: aRectangle	Change the area of the receiver defined by the argument, aRectangle, to white.
gray	Change all of the receiver's area to gray.
gray: aRectangle	Change the area of the receiver defined by the argument, aRectangle, to gray.
veryLightGray	Change all of the receiver's area to very light gray.
veryLightGray: aRectangle	Change the area of the receiver defined by the argument, aRectangle, to very light gray.
lightGray	Change all of the receiver's area to light gray.
lightGray: aRectangle	Change the area of the receiver defined by the argument, aRectangle, to light gray.
darkGray	Change all of the receiver's area to dark gray.
darkGray: aRectangle	Change the area of the receiver defined by the argument, aRectangle, to dark gray.

In the above messages, the origin of the argument, aRectangle, is in the coordinate system of the receiver.

Suppose picture is a kind of DisplayMedium that is 100 pixels in width and 100 pixels in height, and that box is an instance of Rectangle with origin at 30 @ 30 and width and height of 40. Then the protocol for filling the subarea of picture represented by box is illustrated by the following sequence.

expression	*result*
picture black: box	
picture white: box	
picture gray: box	
picture lightGray: box	
picture veryLightGray: box	

picture darkGray: box

Part of an image can be filled with a pattern by sending a DisplayMedium a message to fill a particular sub-area with a halftone pattern. The other coloring messages use these filling messages in their implementation.

DisplayMedium instance protocol

fill: aRectangle mask: aHalftoneForm

Change the area of the receiver defined by the argument, aRectangle, to white, by filling it with the 16 x 16-bit pattern, aHalftoneForm. The combination rule for copying the mask to the receiver is 3 (Form over).

fill: aRectangle rule: anInteger mask: aHalftoneForm

Change the area of the receiver defined by the argument, aRectangle, to white, by filling it with the 16 x 16 bit pattern, aHalftoneForm. The combination rule for copying the mask to the receiver is anInteger.

As an example, the result of evaluating the expressions

    box ← 16@16 extent: 64@64.
    picture fill: box mask: locomotive

where locomotive is a 16x16-bit Form, is

The result of evaluating the sequence of two expressions

    picture lightGray: box.
    picture fill: box rule: Form under mask: locomotive

is

Note that in the above, the rule Form under refers to an Integer combination rule. Messages to Form to access combination rules and halftone masks were defined in Chapter 18.

Reversing an image means changing all the bits in the area that are white to black and those that are black to white. Either all or part of an image can be reversed.

DisplayMedium instance Protocol

reverse: aRectangle mask: aHalftoneForm	Change the area in the receiver defined by the argument, aRectangle, so that, in only those bits in which the mask, aHalftoneForm, is black, white bits in the receiver become black and black become white.
reverse: aRectangle	Change the area in the receiver defined by the argument, aRectangle, so that white is black and black is white. The default mask is Form black.
reverse	Change all of the receiver's area so that white is black and black is white.

The result of

picture reverse: box

on the last image is

Bordering means coloring the outline of a rectangle. Bordering is done using a source Form and mask. Three messages provide methods for bordering an image.

DisplayMedium instance protocol

bordering

border: aRectangle widthRectangle: insets mask: aHalftoneForm

Color an outline around the area within the receiver defined by the argument, aRectangle. The color is determined by the mask, aHalftoneForm. The width of the outline is determined by the Rectangle, insets, such that, origin x is the width of the left side, origin y is the width of the top side, corner x is the width of the right side, and corner y is the width of the bottom side.

border: aRectangle width: borderWidth mask: aHalftoneForm

Color an outline around the area within the receiver defined by the argument, aRectangle. The color is determined by the mask, aHalftoneForm. The width of all the sides is borderWidth.

border: aRectangle width: borderWidth

Color an outline around the area within the receiver defined by the argument, aRectangle. The color is Form black. The width of all the sides is borderWidth.

Examples are

expression	*result*

picture
  border: box
  width: 8	

picture
  border: box
  width: 8
  mask: Form gray	

picture
  border: box
  widthRectangle:
      (4@16 corner: 4@16)
  mask: Form darkGray

picture
  border: box
  width: 16
  mask: locomotive

The next sequence of images shows how bordering can be done by manipulating the size of the rectangle used to designate which area within picture should be changed.

expression	*result*
frame ← 48@48 extent: 16@16. picture white. picture reverse: frame	

frame ← frame expandBy: 16.
picture
  fill: frame
  rule: Form reverse
  mask: Form black.

```
frame ← frame expandBy: 16.
picture
    border: frame
    width: 16
    mask: locomotive
```

```
picture
    border: frame
    width: 1
```

Forms

Class Form is the only subclass of DisplayMedium in the standard Smalltalk-80 system. It was introduced in Chapter 18 in which we defined messages that provide access to constants representing masks and combination rules (modes). As an illustration of the use of Forms in creating complex images, the following sequence of expressions creates the image shown at the beginning of this chapter as Figure 20.2.

Suppose we have two Forms available, each 120 bits wide and 180 bits high. We name them face25 and face75. These images were created using a scanner to digitize photographs of a gentleman when he was in his 20's and on the occasion of his 75th birthday.

The scanned images were scaled to the desired size and then combined with halftone masks in the following way. Two Arrays, each size 8, contain references to the halftone masks (masks) and the Forms (forms) used in creating each part of the final image.

```
masks ← Array new: 8.
masks at: 1 put: Form black.
masks at: 2 put: Form darkGray.
masks at: 3 put: Form gray.
masks at: 4 put: Form lightGray.
masks at: 5 put: Form veryLightGray.
masks at: 6 put: Form lightGray.
masks at: 7 put: Form gray.
masks at: 8 put: Form black.
forms ← Array new: 8.
forms at: 1 put: face25.
forms at: 2 put: face25.
forms at: 3 put: face25.
forms at: 4 put: face25.
forms at: 5 put: face75.
forms at: 6 put: face75.
forms at: 7 put: face75.
forms at: 8 put: face75
```

The variable i is the initial index into the first halftone and first Form used in forming the first sub-image of each row. Each time a complete row is displayed, i is incremented by 1. Each row consists of 5 elements. The variable index is used to index 5 halftones and five Forms; index is set to i at the outset of each row. Thus the first row is made up by combining elements 1, 2, 3, 4, and 5 of masks and forms; the second row is made up by combining elements 2, 3, 4, 5, and 6 of masks and forms; and so on. The y coordinate of each row changes by 180 pixels each time; the x coordinate of each column changes by 120 pixels.

```
i ← 1.
0 to: 540 by: 180 do:
    [ :y |  index ← i.
        0 to: 480 by: 120 do:
            [ :x |  (forms at: index)
                displayOn: Display
                at: x@y
                clippingBox: Display boundingBox
                rule: Form over
                mask: (masks at: index).
             index ← index + 1].
        i ← i + 1]
```

Other Forms

Two other kinds of forms exist in the system, InfiniteForm and OpaqueForm. These two classes are subclasses of DisplayObject, rather than of DisplayMedium. They therefore do not share Form's inherited ability to be colored and bordered. InfiniteForm represents a Form obtained by replicating a pattern Form indefinitely in all directions. Typically the overlapping views displayed in the Smalltalk-80 programming interface (as shown in Chapter 17) are placed over a light gray background; this background is defined by an InfiniteForm whose replicated pattern is Form gray. OpaqueForms represent a shape as well as a figure Form. The shape indicates what part of the background should be occluded in displaying the image, so that patterns other than black in the figure will still appear opaque. Instances of OpaqueForm support creating animations. Neither InfiniteForm nor OpaqueForm adds new protocol.

Cursors

Form has two subclasses of interest, class Cursor and class DisplayScreen. The Smalltalk-80 system makes extensive use of Forms to indicate both the current location of the hardware pointing device and the current status of the system. A Form used in this way is referred to as a *cursor* since its primary purpose is to move over the screen in order to locate screen coordinates.

Instances of class Cursor are Forms that are 16 pixels wide and 16 pixels high. Class Cursor adds three new messages to the displaying protocol that it inherits from DisplayObject.

Cursor instance protocol	
displaying	
show	Make the receiver be the current cursor shape.
showGridded: gridPoint	Make the receiver be the current cursor shape, forcing the location of cursor to the point nearest the location, gridPoint.
showWhile: aBlock	While evaluating the argument, aBlock, make the receiver be the cursor shape.

Several different cursors are supplied with the standard Smalltalk-80 system. They are shown in Figure 20.4 both small and enlarged in order to illustrate their bitmaps. The name of each cursor, given below its image, is the same as the message to class Cursor which accesses that particular Cursor. For example, the following expression shows a cursor that looks like eyeglasses on the screen while the system computes the factorial of 50. It then reverts to showing the original cursor shape.

normal   execute

up   down

origin   corner

read   write

crossHair   move

Figure 20.4   marker   wait

Cursor read showWhile: [50 factorial]

Changing the cursor shape is a very effective way of communicating with the user. Attention is always on the cursor, and changing its shape does not alter the appearance of the display.

The Display Screen

DisplayScreen is another subclass of Form. There is usually only one instance of DisplayScreen in the system. It is referred to as Display, a global variable used to handle general user requests to deal with the whole display screen. In addition to the messages it inherits from its superclasses, DisplayObject, DisplayMedium, and Form, DisplayScreen provides class protocol for resetting the width, height, and displayed image of the screen.

The one case when multiple instances of DisplayScreen may exist is when (double-buffered) full screen animation is being done by alternating which instance of DisplayScreen supplies bits to the display hardware. Typically, full screen animation is not used, rather, animation is done within a smaller rectangular area. A hidden buffer of bits is used to form the next image. Each new image is displayed by copying the bits to the rectangular area using the copyBits: message of a BitBlt.

DisplayText

The second subclass of DisplayObject is class DisplayText. An instance of Text provides a font index (1 through 10) and an emphasis (italic, bold, underline) for each character of an instance of String. DisplayText consists of a Text and a TextStyle. A TextStyle associates each font index with an actual font (set of glyphs). In addition to representing this mapping to the set of fonts, a DisplayText supports the ability to display the characters on the screen. It does not support the protocol needed to create a user interface for editing either the characters or the choice of fonts and emphasis; this protocol must be supplied by subclasses of DisplayText.

Paths

A third subclass of DisplayObject is class Path. A Path is an OrderedCollection of Points and a Form that should be displayed at each Point. Complex images can be created by copying the Form along the trajectory represented by the Points.

Class Path is the basic superclass of the graphic display objects that represent trajectories. Instances of Path refer to an OrderedCollection and to a Form. The elements of the collection are Points. They can be added to the Path (add:); all Points that are described by some criterion can be removed from the Path (removeAllSuchThat:); and the Points can be enumerated, collected, and selected (do:, collect, and select:).

Path instance protocol

accessing	
form	Answer the Form referred to by the receiver.
form: aForm	Set the Form referred to by the receiver to be aForm.
at: index	Answer the Point that is the indexth element of the receiver's collection.
at: index put: aPoint	Set the argument, aPoint, to be the indexth element of the receiver's collection.
size	Answer the number of Points in the receiver's collection.
testing	
isEmpty	Answer whether the receiver contains any Points.
adding	
add: aPoint	Add the argument, aPoint, as the last element of the receiver's collection of Points.
removing	
removeAllSuchThat: aBlock	Evaluate the argument, aBlock, for each Point in the receiver. Remove those Points for which aBlock evaluates to true.
enumerating	
do: aBlock	Evaluate the argument, aBlock, for each Point in the receiver.
collect: aBlock	Evaluate the argument, aBlock, for each Point in the receiver. Collect the resulting values into an OrderedCollection and answer the new collection.
select: aBlock	Evaluate the argument, aBlock, for each Point in the receiver. Collect into an Ordered-Collection those Points for which aBlock evaluates to true. Answer the new collection.

As an example, we create a "star" Path, and display a dot-shaped Form, referred to by the name dot, at each point on that Path.

```
aPath ← Path new form: dot.
aPath add: 150 @ 285.
aPath add: 400 @ 285.
aPath add: 185 @ 430.
aPath add: 280 @ 200.
aPath add: 375 @ 430.
```

```
aPath add: 150 @ 285.
aPath display
```

The resulting image is shown as the first path in Figure 20.5.

Figure 20.5

There are three paths in Figure 20.5.

- an instance of Path, created as indicated above

- an instance of LinearFit, using the same collection of Points

- an instance of Spline, using the same collection of Points

A LinearFit is displayed by connecting the Points in the collection, in order.

```
aPath ← LinearFit new form: dot.
aPath add: 150 @ 285.
aPath add: 400 @ 285.
aPath add: 185 @ 430.
aPath add: 280 @ 200.
aPath add: 375 @ 430.
aPath add: 150 @ 285.
aPath display
```

The Spline is obtained by fitting a cubic spline curve through the Points, again, in order. The order in which the Points are added to the Path significantly affects the outcome.

```
aPath ← Spline new form: dot.
aPath add: 150 @ 285.
aPath add: 400 @ 285.
aPath add: 185 @ 430.
aPath add: 280 @ 200.
aPath add: 375 @ 430.
aPath add: 150 @ 285.
aPath computeCurve.
aPath display
```

LinearFit and Spline are defined as subclasses of Path. In order to support the protocol of DisplayObject, each of these subclasses implements the message displayOn:at:clippingBox:rule:mask:.

Straight lines can be defined in terms of Paths. A Line is a Path specified by two points. An Arc is defined as a quarter of a circle. Instances of class Arc are specified to be one of the four possible quarters; they know their center Point and the radius of the circle. A Circle, then, is a kind of Arc that represents all four quarters. Again, in order to support the protocol of DisplayObject, each of these three classes (Line, Arc, and Circle) implements the messages displayOn:at:clippingBox:rule:mask:.

Class Curve is a subclass of Path. It represents a hyperbola that is tangent to lines determined by Points p1, p2 and p2, p3, and that passes through Points p1 and p3. The displaying message for Curve is defined as shown in the method below.

displayOn: aDisplayMedium
  at: aPoint
  clippingBox: aRectangle
  rule: anInteger
  mask: aForm
| pa pb k s p1 p2 p3 line |
line ← Line new.
line form: self form.
self size < 3 ifTrue: [self error: 'Curves are defined by three points'].
p1 ← self at: 1.
p2 ← self at: 2.
p3 ← self at: 3.
s ← Path new.
s add: p1.
pa ← p2 − p1.
pb ← p3 − p2.
k ← 5 max: pa x abs + pa y abs + pb x abs + pb y abs // 20.
"k is a guess as to how many line segments to use to approximate the curve."
1 to: k do:
  [:i | s add:
            pa∗i//k + p1∗(k−i) + (pb∗(i−1)//k + p2∗(i−1))//(k−1)].
s add: p3.
1 to: s size do:
  [:i |
    line at: 1 put: (s at: i).
    line at: 2 put: (s at: i + 1).
    line displayOn: aDisplayMedium
      at: aPoint
      clippingBox: aRectangle
      rule: anInteger
      mask: aForm]

The algorithm was devised by Ted Kaehler. Basically the idea is to divide the line segments p1, p2 and p2, p3 into 10 sections. Numbering the sections as shown in the diagram, draw a line connecting point 1 on p1, p2 to point 1 on p2, p3; draw a line connecting point 2 on p1, p2 to point 2 on p2, p3; and so on. The hyperbola is the path formed from p1 to p3 by interpolating along the line segments formed on the outer shell.

Several curves are shown in Figure 20.6. The curves are the black lines; the gray lines indicate the lines connecting the points that were used to define the curves.

Two Curves were used to create the image shown in Figure 20.3. The Form was one of the images of the gentleman used in Figure 20.2.

Image Manipulation with Forms

We have shown in Chapter 18 how BitBlt can copy shapes and how repeated invocation can synthesize more complex images such as text and lines. BitBlt is also useful in the manipulation of existing images. For example, text can be made to look bold by ORing over itself, shifted right by one pixel. Just as complex images can be built from simple ones, complex processing can be achieved by repeated application of simple operations. In addition to its obvious manisfestation in the DisplayObject protocol, the power of BitBlt is made available for manipulating images through such messages as copy:from:in:rule:.

We present here four examples of such structural manipulation: magnification, rotation, area filling, and the Game of Life.

Magnification

A simple way to magnify a stored Form would be to copy it to a larger Form, making a big dot for every little dot in the original. For a height h and width w, this would take h*w operations. The algorithm presented here (as two messages to class Form) uses only a few more than h + w operations.

```
magnify: aRectangle by: scale
    | wideForm bigForm spacing |
    spacing ← 0 @ 0.
```

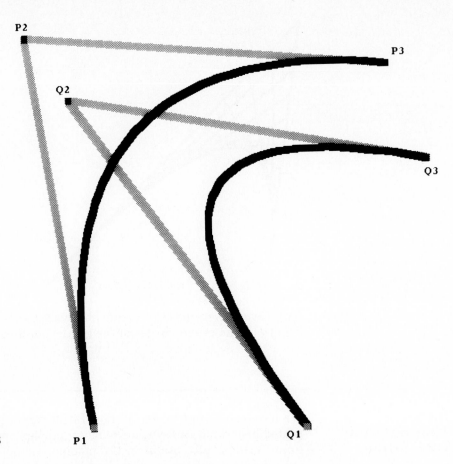

Figure 20.6

```
wideForm ←
    Form new
        extent: aRectangle width * scale x @ aRectangle height.
wideForm
    spread: aRectangle
    from: self
    by: scale x
    spacing: spacing x
    direction: 1 @ 0.
bigForm ← Form new extent: aRectangle extent * scale.
bigForm
    spread: wideForm boundingBox
    from: wideForm
    by: scale y
    spacing: spacing y
    direction: 0 @ 1.
↑bigForm
```

```
spread: rectangle
    from: aForm
    by: scale
    spacing: spacing
    direction: dir
| slice sourcePt |
slice ← 0@0 corner: dir transpose * self extent + dir.
sourcePt ← rectangle origin.
1 to: (rectangle extent dotProduct: dir) do:
    [ :i |
        "slice up original area"
        self copy: slice
            from: sourcePt
            in: aForm
            rule: 3.
        sourcePt ← sourcePt + dir.
        slice moveBy: dir * scale].
1 to: scale - spacing − 1 do:
    [ :i |
        "smear out the slices, leave white space"
        self copy: (dir corner: self extent)
            from: 0 @ 0
            in: self
            rule: 7]
```

The magnification proceeds in two steps. First, it slices up the image into vertical strips in wideForm separated by a space equal to the magnification factor. These are then smeared, using the ORing function, over the intervening area to achieve the horizontal magnification. The process is then repeated from wideForm into bigForm, with horizontal slices separated and smeared in the vertical direction, achieving the desired magnification. Figure 20.7 illustrates the progress of the above algorithm in producing the magnified "7".

Figure 20.7

Rotation

Another useful operation on images is rotation by a multiple of 90 degrees. Rotation is often thought to be a fundamentally different operation from translation, and this point of view would dismiss the possibility of using BitBlt to rotate an image. However, the first transformation shown in Figure 20.8 is definitely a step toward rotating the image shown; all that remains is to rotate the insides of the four cells that have been permuted. The remainder of the figure shows each of these cells being further subdivided, its cells being similarly permuted, and so on. Eventually each cell being considered contains only a single pixel. At this point, no further subdivision is required, and the image has been faithfully rotated.

Each transformation shown in Figure 20.8 would appear to require successively greater amounts of computation, with the last one requiring several times more than h*w operations. The tricky aspect of the algorithm below is to permute the subparts of every subdivided cell at once, thus performing the entire rotation in a constant times $\log_2(h)$ operations. The parallel permutation of many cells is accomplished with the aid of two auxiliary Forms. The first, mask, carries a mask that selects the upper left quadrant of every cell; the second, temp, is used for temporary storage. A series of operations exchanges the right and left halves of every cell, and then another series exchanges the diagonal quadrants, achieving the desired permutation.

```
rotate
    | mask temp quad all |
    all ← self boundingBox.
    mask ← Form extent: self extent.
    temp ← Form extent: self extent.
    mask white. "set up the first mask"
    mask black: (0@0 extent: mask extent // 2).
    quad ← self width // 2.
    [quad > = 1] whileTrue:
        ["First exchange left and right halves"
        temp copy: all from: 0@0 in: mask rule: 3.
        temp copy: all from: 0@quad negated in: mask rule: 7.
        temp copy: all from: 0@0 in: self rule: 1.
        self copy: all from: 0@0 in: temp rule: 6.
        temp copy: all from: quad@0 in: self rule: 6.
        self copy: all from: quad@0 in: self rule: 7.
        self copy: all from: quad negated@0 in: temp rule: 6.
        "then flip the diagonals"
        temp copy: all from: 0@0 in: self rule: 3.
        temp copy: all from: quad@quad in: self rule: 6.
        temp copy: all from: 0@0 in: mask rule: 1.
```

Figure 20.8

```
self copy: all from: 0@0 in: temp rule: 6.
self copy: all from: quad negated@quad negated in: temp rule: 6.
"Now refine the mask"
mask copy: all from: (quad//2)@(quad//2) in: mask rule: 1.
mask copy: all from: 0@quad negated in: mask rule: 7.
mask copy: all from: quad negated@0 in: mask rule: 7.
quad ← quad // 2]
```

Figure 20.9 traces the state of temp and self after each successive operation.

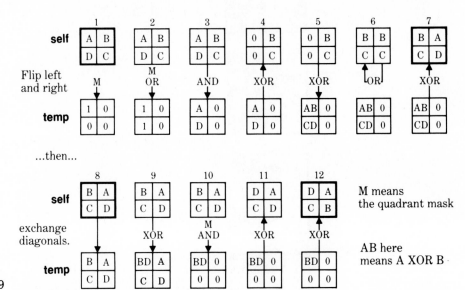

Figure 20.9

In the Figure 20.9, the offsets of each operation are not shown, though they are given in the program listing. After twelve operations, the desired permutation has been achieved. At this point the mask evolves to a finer grain, and the process is repeated for more smaller cells. Figure 20.10 shows the evolution of the mask from the first to the second stage of refinement.

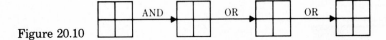

Figure 20.10

The algorithm presented here for rotation is applicable only to square forms whose size is a power of two. The extension of this technique to arbitrary rectangles is more involved. A somewhat simpler exercise is to apply the above technique to horizontal and vertical reflections about the center of a rectangle.

Area Filling

A useful operation on Forms is to be able to fill the interior of an outlined region with a halftone mask. The method given here takes as one argument a Point that marks a location in the interior of the region. A mark is placed at this location as a *seed*, and then the seed is smeared (in all four directions) into a larger blob until it extends to the region boundary. At each stage of the smearing process, the original Form is copied over the blob using the "erase" rule. This has the effect of trimming any growth which would have crossed the region borders. In addition, after every ten smear cycles, the resulting smear is compared with its previous version. When there is no change, the smear has filled the region and halftoning is applied throughout.

```
shapeFill: aMask interiorPoint: interiorPoint
    | dirs smearForm previousSmear all cycle noChange |
    all ← self boundingBox.
    smearForm ← Form extent: self extent.
    "Place a seed in the interior"
    smearForm valueAt: interiorPoint put: 1.
    previousSmear ← smearForm deepCopy.
    dirs ← Array with: 1@0 with: −1@0 with: 0@1 with: 0@−1.
    cycle ← 0.
    ["check for no change every 10 smears"
    (cycle ← cycle + 1)\\10 = 0 and:
        [previousSmear copy: all
                    from: 0@0
                    in: smearForm
                    rule: Form reverse.
        noChange ← previousSmear isAllWhite.
        previousSmear copy: all from: 0@0 in: smearForm rule: Form over.
        noChange]]
            whileFalse:
                [dirs do:
                    [ :dir |
                        "smear in each of the four directions"
                        smearForm copy: all
                                    from: dir
                                    in: smearForm
                                    rule: Form under.
                        "After each smear, trim around the region border"
                        smearForm copy: all from: 0@0 in: self rule: Form erase]].
    "Now paint the filled region in me with aMask"
    smearForm displayOn: self
                at: 0@0
                clippingBox: self boundingBox
                rule: Form under
                mask: aMask
```

Figure 20.11 shows a Form with a flower-shaped region to be filled. Successive smears appear below, along with the final result.

Figure 20.11

The Game of Life

Conway's Game of Life is a simple rule for successive populations of a bitmap. The rule involves the neighbor count for each cell—how many of the eight adjacent cells are occupied. Each cell will be occupied in the next generation if it has exactly three neighbors, or if it was occupied and has exactly two neighbors. This is explained as follows: three neighboring organisms can give birth in an empty cell, and an existing organism will die of exposure with less than two neighbors or from overpopulation with more than three neighbors. Since BitBlt cannot add, it would seem to be of no use in this application. However BitBlt's combination rules, available in the Form operations, do include the rules for partial sum (XOR) and carry (AND). With some ingenuity and a fair amount of extra storage, the next generation of any size of bitmap can be computed using a *constant* number of BitBlt operations.

```
nextLifeGeneration
    | nbr1 nbr2 nbr4 carry2 carry4 all delta |
    nbr1 ← Form extent: self extent.
    nbr2 ← Form extent: self extent.
    nbr4 ← Form extent: self extent.
    carry2 ← Form extent: self extent.
    carry4 ← Form extent: self extent.
    all ← self boundingBox.
    1 to: 8 do:
        [ :i |
        "delta is the offset of the eight neighboring cells"
        delta ← ((#(−1 0 1 1 1 0 −1 −1) at: i)
                    @ (#(−1 −1 −1 0 1 1 1 0) at: i)).
        carry2 copy: all from: 0@0 in: nbr1 rule: 3.
        carry2 copy: all from: delta in: self rule: 1. "AND for carry into 2"
```

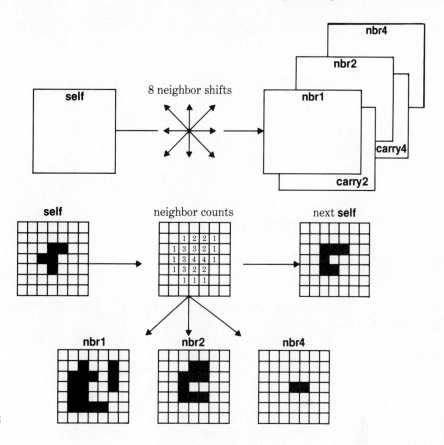

Figure 20.12

```
nbr1 copy: all from: delta in: self rule: 6. "XOR for sum 1"
carry4 copy: all from: 0@0 in: nbr2 rule: 3.
carry4 copy: all from: 0@0 in: carry2 rule: 1. "AND for carry into 4"
nbr2 copy: all from: 0@0 in: carry2 rule: 6. "XOR for sum 2"
nbr4 copy: all from: 0@0 in: carry4 rule: 6].
"XOR for sum 4 (ignore carry into 8)"
self copy: all from: 0@0 in: nbr2 rule: 1.
nbr1 copy: all from: 0@0 in: nbr2 rule: 1.
self copy: all from: 0@0 in: nbr1 rule: 7.
self copy: all from: 0@0 in: nbr4 rule: 4
"compute next generation"
```

As shown in Figure 20.12, the number of neighbors is represented using three image planes for the 1's bit, 2's bit and 4's bit of the count in binary. The 8's bit can be ignored, since there are no survivors in that case, which is equivalent to zero (the result of ignoring the 8's bit). This Smalltalk-80 method is somewhat wasteful, as it performs the full carry propagation for each new neighbor, even though nothing will propagate into the 4-plane until at least the fourth neighbor.

PART THREE

Part Three is an example of modeling discrete, event-driven simulations in the Smalltalk-80 system. A simulation is a representation of a system of objects in a real or fantasy world. The purpose of creating a computer simulation is to provide a framework in which to understand the simulation situation. In order to create the Smalltalk-80 simulations, we first describe a hierarchy of classes that represent probability distributions. Various kinds of probability distributions are used to determine arrival times of objects, such as customers, into a simulation; they are also used to randomly select response or service times for workers in a simulation. The example class SimulationObject represents any kind of object that enters into a simulation in order to carry out one or more tasks; class Simulation represents the simulation itself and provides the control structures for admitting and assigning tasks to new SimulationObjects.

The objects that participate in event-driven simulations operate more or less independently of one another. So it is necessary to consider the problem of coordinating and synchronizing their activities. The Smalltalk-80 system classes, Process, Semaphore, and SharedQueue, provide synchronization facilities for otherwise independent simulation events. The framework of classes defined in this part support the creation of simulations that use consumable, nonconsumable, and/or renewable resources. They also provide a number of ways in which a programmer can gather statistics about a running simulation.

Previous parts of the book described the Smalltalk-80 system from the programmer's view. The first chapter of this section provides a flavor of the system from the implementor's point of view.

21

The Implementation

The Compiler
Compiled Methods
The Bytecodes

The Interpreter
Contexts
Block Contexts
Messages
Primitive Methods

The Object Memory

The Hardware and Additional System Classes

Two major components of the Smalltalk-80 system can be distinguished: the *virtual image* and the *virtual machine*.

1. The *virtual image* consists of all of the objects in the system.

2. The *virtual machine* consists of the hardware devices and machine language (or microcode) routines that give dynamics to the objects in the virtual image.

The system implementer's task is to create a virtual machine. A virtual image can then be loaded into the virtual machine and the Smalltalk-80 system becomes the interactive entity described in earlier chapters.

The overview of the Smalltalk-80 implementation given in this chapter is organized in a top-down fashion, starting with the source methods written by programmers. These methods are translated by a *compiler* into sequences of eight-bit instructions called *bytecodes*. The compiler and bytecodes are the subject of this chapter's first section. The bytecodes produced by the compiler are instructions for an *interpreter*, which is described in the second section. Below the interpreter in the implementation is an *object memory* that stores the objects that make up the virtual image. The object memory is described in the third section of this chapter. At the bottom of any implementation is the *hardware*.

The Compiler

Source methods written by programmers are represented in the Smalltalk-80 system as instances of String. The Strings contain sequences of characters that conform to the syntax introduced in the first part of this book. For example, the following source method might describe how instances of class Rectangle respond to the unary message center. The center message is used to find the Point equidistant from a Rectangle's four sides.

center
    ↑origin + corner / 2

Source methods are translated by the system's *compiler* into sequences of instructions for a stack-oriented interpreter. The instructions are eight-bit numbers called *bytecodes*. For example, the bytecodes corresponding to the source method shown above are,

0, 1, 176, 119, 185, 124

Since a bytecode's value gives us little indication of its meaning to the interpreter, this chapter will accompany lists of bytecodes with comments about their functions. Any part of a bytecode's comment that depends on the context of the method in which it appears will be parenthesized. The unparenthesized part of the comment describes its general function. For example, the bytecode 0 always instructs the interpreter to push the value of the receiver's first instance variable on its stack. The fact that the variable is named origin depends on the fact that this method is used by Rectangles, so origin is parenthesized. The commented form of the bytecodes for Rectangle center is shown below.

Rectangle center

0	push the value of the receiver's first instance variable (origin) onto the stack
1	push the value of the receiver's second instance variable (corner) onto the stack
176	send a binary message with the selector +
119	push the SmallInteger 2 onto the stack
185	send a binary message with the selector /
124	return the object on top of the stack as the value of the message (center)

The stack mentioned in some of the bytecodes is used for several purposes. In this method, it is used to hold the receiver, arguments, and results of the two messages that are sent. The stack is also used as the source of the result to be returned from the center method. The stack is maintained by the interpreter and will be described in greater detail in the next section. A description of all the types of bytecodes will appear at the end of this section.

A programmer does not interact directly with the compiler. When a new source method is added to a class (Rectangle in this example), the class asks the compiler for an instance of CompiledMethod containing the bytecode translation of the source method. The class provides the compiler with some necessary information not given in the source method, including the names of the receiver's instance variables and the dictionaries containing accessible shared variables (global, class, and pool variables). The compiler translates the source text into a CompiledMethod and the class stores the method in its message dictionary. For example, the CompiledMethod shown above is stored in Rectangle's message dictionary associated with the selector center.

Another example of the bytecodes compiled from a source method illustrates the use of a store bytecode. The message extent: to a Rectangle changes the receiver's width and height to be equal to the x and y coordinates of the argument (a Point). The receiver's upper left corner (origin) is kept the same and the lower right corner (corner) is moved.

extent: newExtent
 corner ← origin + newExtent

Rectangle extent:

0	push the value of the receiver's first instance variable (origin) onto the stack
16	push the argument (newExtent) onto the stack
176	send a binary message with the selector +
97	pop the top object off of the stack and store it in the receiver's second instance variable (corner)
120	return the receiver as the value of the message (extent:)

The forms of source methods and compiled bytecodes are different in several respects. The variable names in a source method are converted into instructions to push objects on the stack, the selectors are converted into instructions to send messages, and the uparrow is converted into an instruction to return a result. The order of the corresponding components is also different in a source method and compiled bytecodes. Despite these differences in form, the source method and compiled bytecodes describe the same actions.

Compiled Methods

The compiler creates an instance of CompiledMethod to hold the bytecode translation of a source method. In addition to the bytecodes themselves, a CompiledMethod contains a set of objects called its *literal frame.* The literal frame contains any objects that could not be referred to directly by bytecodes. All of the objects in Rectangle center and Rectangle extent: were referred to directly by bytecodes, so the CompiledMethods for these methods do not need literal frames. As an example of a CompiledMethod with a literal frame, consider the method for Rectangle intersects:. The intersects: message inquires whether one Rectangle (the receiver) overlaps another Rectangle (the argument).

intersects: aRectangle
 ↑(origin max: aRectangle origin) < (corner min: aRectangle corner)

The four message selectors, max:, origin, min:, and corner are not in the set that can be directly referenced by bytecodes. These selectors are included in the CompiledMethod's literal frame and the send bytecodes refer to the selectors by their position in the literal frame. A CompiledMethod's literal frame will be shown after its bytecodes.

Rectangle intersects:

0	push the value of the receiver's first instance variable (origin) onto the stack
16	push the argument (aRectangle)

209	send a unary message with the selector in the second literal frame location (origin)
224	send a single argument message with the selector in the first literal frame location (max:)
1	push the value of the receiver's second instance variable (corner) onto the stack
16	push the argument (aRectangle) onto the stack
211	send a unary message with the selector in the fourth literal frame location (corner)
226	send a single argument message with the selector in the third literal frame location (min:)
178	send a binary message with the selector <
124	return the object on top of the stack as the value of the message (intersects:)

literal frame
#max:
#origin
#min:
#corner

The categories of objects that can be referred to directly by bytecodes are:

- the receiver and arguments of the invoking message

- the values of the receiver's instance variables

- the values of any temporary variables required by the method

- seven special constants (true, false, nil, −1, 0, 1, and 2)

- 32 special message selectors

The 32 special message selectors are listed below.

+	−	<	>
< =	> =	=	~=
*	/	\	@
bitShift:	\\	bitAnd:	bitOr:
(at:)	(at:put:)	(size)	(next)
(nextPut:)	(atEnd)	==	class
blockCopy:	value	value:	(do:)
(new)	(new:)	(x)	(y)

The selectors in parentheses may be replaced with other selectors by modifying the compiler and recompiling all methods in the system. The other selectors are built into the virtual machine.

Any objects referred to in a CompiledMethod's bytecodes that do not fall into one of the categories above must appear in its literal frame. The objects ordinarily contained in a literal frame are

- shared variables (global, class, and pool)

- most literal constants (numbers, characters, strings, arrays, and symbols)

- most message selectors (those that are not special)

Objects of these three types may be intermixed in the literal frame. If an object in the literal frame is referenced twice in the same method, it need only appear in the literal frame once. The two bytecodes that refer to the object will refer to the same location in the literal frame.

Two types of object that were referred to above, temporary variables and shared variables, have not been used in the example methods. The following example method for Rectangle merge: uses both types. The merge: message is used to find a Rectangle that includes the areas in both the receiver and the argument.

merge: aRectangle
```
| minPoint maxPoint |
minPoint ← origin min: aRectangle origin.
maxPoint ← corner max: aRectangle corner.
↑Rectangle origin: minPoint
         corner: maxPoint
```

When a CompiledMethod uses temporary variables (maxPoint and minPoint in this example), the number required is specified in the first line of its printed form. When a CompiledMethod uses a shared variable (Rectangle in this example) an instance of Association is included in its literal frame. All CompiledMethods that refer to a particular shared variable's name include the same Association in their literal frames.

Rectangle merge: requires 2 temporary variables

0	push the value of the receiver's first instance variable (origin) onto the stack
16	push the contents of the first temporary frame location (the argument aRectangle) onto the stack
209	send a unary message with the selector in the second literal frame location (origin)
224	send the single argument message with the selector in the first literal frame location (min:)
105	pop the top object off of the stack and store in the second temporary frame location (minPoint)
1	push the value of the receiver's second instance variable (corner) onto the stack
16	push the contents of the first temporary frame location (the argument aRectangle) onto the stack

211   send a unary message with the selector in the fourth literal frame location (corner)

226   send a single argument message with the selector in the third literal frame location (max:)

106   pop the top object off of the stack and store it in the third temporary frame location (maxPoint)

69   push the value of the shared variable in the sixth literal frame location (Rectangle) onto the stack

17   push the contents of the second temporary frame location (minPoint) onto the stack

18   push the contents of the third temporary frame location (maxPoint) onto the stack

244   send the two argument message with the selector in the fifth literal frame location (origin:corner:)

124   return the object on top of the stack as the value of the message (merge:)

literal frame
    #min:
    #origin
    #max:
    #corner
    #origin:corner:
    Association: #Rectangle ➤Rectangle

☐ *Temporary Variables*   Temporary variables are created for a particular execution of a CompiledMethod and cease to exist when the execution is complete. The CompiledMethod indicates to the interpreter how many temporary variables will be required. The arguments of the invoking message and the values of the temporary variables are stored together in the *temporary frame*. The arguments are stored first and the temporary variable values immediately after. They are accessed by the same type of bytecode (whose comments refer to a temporary frame location). Since merge: takes a single argument, its two temporary variables use the second and third locations in the temporary frame. The compiler enforces the fact that the values of the argument names cannot be changed by never issuing a store bytecode referring to the part of the temporary frame inhabited by the arguments.

☐ *Shared Variables*   Shared variables are found in dictionaries.

- *global variables* in a dictionary whose names can appear in any method

- *class variables* in a dictionary whose names can only appear in the methods of a single class and its subclasses

- *pool variables* in a dictionary whose names can appear in the methods of several classes

Shared variables are the individual associations that make up these dictionaries. The system represents associations in general, and shared variables in particular, with instances of Association. When the compiler encounters the name of a shared variable in a source method, the Association with the same name is included in the CompiledMethod's literal frame. The bytecodes that access shared variables indicate the location of an Association in the literal frame. The actual value of the variable is stored in an instance variable of the Association. In the CompiledMethod for Rectangle merge: shown above, class Rectangle is referenced by including the Association from the global dictionary whose name is the symbol #Rectangle and whose value is the class Rectangle.

The Bytecodes

The interpreter understands 256 bytecode instructions that fall into five categories: pushes, stores, sends, returns, and jumps. This section gives a general description of each type of bytecode without going into detail about which bytecode represents which instruction. Since more than 256 instructions for the interpreter are needed, some of the bytecodes take extensions. An extension is one or two bytes following the bytecode, that further specify the instruction. An extension is not an instruction on its own, it is only a part of an instruction.

□ *Push Bytecodes* A push bytecode indicates the source of an object to be added to the top of the interpreter's stack. The sources include

- the receiver of the message that invoked the CompiledMethod
- the instance variables of the receiver
- the temporary frame (the arguments of the message and the temporary variables)
- the literal frame of the CompiledMethod
- the top of the stack (i.e., this bytecode duplicates the top of the stack)

Examples of most of the types of push bytecode have been included in the examples. The bytecode that duplicates the top of the stack is used to implement cascaded messages.

Two different types of push bytecode use the literal frame as their source. One is used to push literal constants and the other to push the value of shared variables. Literal constants are stored directly in the literal frame, but the values of shared variables are stored in an Association that is pointed to by the literal frame. The following example method uses one shared variable and one literal constant.

incrementIndex
↑Index ← Index + 4

ExampleClass incrementIndex

64   push the value of the shared variable in the first literal frame location (Index) onto the stack

33   push the constant in the second literal frame location (4) onto the stack

176   send a binary message with the selector +

129,192 store the object on top of the stack in the shared variable in the first literal frame location (Index)

124   return the object on top of the stack as the value of the message (incrementIndex)

literal frame

Association: #Index ➤ 260
     4

☐ *Store Bytecodes*   The bytecodes compiled from an assignment expression end with a store bytecode. The bytecodes before the store bytecode compute the new value of a variable and leave it on top of the stack. A store bytecode indicates the variable whose value should be changed. The variables that can be changed are

- the instance variables of the receiver
- temporary variables
- shared variables

Some of the store bytecodes remove the object to be stored from the stack, and others leave the object on top of the stack, after storing it.

☐ *Send Bytecodes*   A send bytecode specifies the selector of a message to be sent and how many arguments it should have. The receiver and arguments of the message are taken off the interpreter's stack, the receiver from below the arguments. By the time the bytecode following the send is executed, the message's result will have replaced its receiver and arguments on the top of the stack. The details of sending messages and returning results is the subject of the next sections of this chapter. A set of 32 send bytecodes refer directly to the special selectors listed earlier. The other send bytecodes refer to their selectors in the literal frame.

☐ *Return Bytecodes*   When a return bytecode is encountered, the CompiledMethod in which it was found has been completely executed. Therefore a value is returned for the message that invoked that CompiledMethod. The value is usually found on top of the stack. Four special return bytecodes return the message receiver (self), true, false, and nil.

☐ *Jump Bytecodes*   Ordinarily, the interpreter executes the bytecodes sequentially in the order they appear in a CompiledMethod. The jump bytecodes indicate that the next bytecode to execute is not the one following the jump. There are two varieties of jump, *unconditional* and *conditional*. The unconditional jumps transfer control whenever they are encountered. The conditional jumps will only transfer control if the top of the stack is a specified value. Some of the conditional jumps transfer if the top object on the stack is true and others if it is false. The jump bytecodes are used to implement efficient control structures.

The control structures that are so optimized by the compiler are the conditional selection messages to Booleans (ifTrue:, ifFalse:, and ifTrue:ifFalse:), some of the logical operation messages to Booleans (and: and or:), and the conditional repetition messages to blocks (whileTrue: and whileFalse:). The jump bytecodes indicate the next bytecode to be executed relative to the position of the jump. In other words, they tell the interpreter how many bytecodes to skip. The following method for Rectangle includesPoint: uses a conditional jump.

includesPoint: aPoint
   origin < = aPoint
     ifTrue: [↑aPoint < corner]
     ifFalse: [↑false]

Rectangle includesPoint:

0	push the value of the receiver's first instance variable (origin) onto the stack
16	push the contents of the first temporary frame location (the argument aPoint) onto the stack
180	send a binary message with the selector < =
155	jump ahead 4 bytecodes if the object on top of the stack is false
16	push the contents of the first temporary frame location (the argument aPoint) onto the stack
1	push the value of the receiver's second instance variable (corner) onto the stack
178	send a binary message with the selector <
124	return the object on top of the stack as the value of the message (includesPoint:)
122	return false as the value of the message (includesPoint:)

The Interpreter

The Smalltalk-80 interpreter executes the bytecode instructions found in CompiledMethods. The interpreter uses five pieces of information and repeatedly performs a three-step cycle.

The State of the Interpreter

1. The CompiledMethod whose bytecodes are being executed.

2. The location of the next bytecode to be executed in that CompiledMethod. This is the interpreter's *instruction pointer*.

3. The receiver and arguments of the message that invoked the CompiledMethod.

4. Any temporary variables needed by the CompiledMethod.

5. A stack.

The execution of most bytecodes involves the interpreter's stack. Push bytecodes tell where to find objects to add to the stack. Store bytecodes tell where to put objects found on the stack. Send bytecodes remove the receiver and arguments of messages from the stack. When the result of a message is computed, it is pushed onto the stack.

The Cycle of the Interpreter

1. Fetch the bytecode from the CompiledMethod indicated by the instruction pointer.

2. Increment the instruction pointer.

3. Perform the function specified by the bytecode.

As an example of the interpreter's function, we will trace its execution of the CompiledMethod for Rectangle center. The state of the interpreter will be displayed after each of its cycles. The instruction pointer will be indicated by an arrow pointing at the next bytecode in the CompiledMethod to be executed.

> ▶ 0   push the value of the receiver's first instance variable (origin) onto the stack

The receiver, arguments, temporary variables, and objects on the stack will be shown as normally printed (their responses to printString). For example, if a message is sent to a Rectangle, the receiver will be shown as

Receiver   100@100 corner: 200@200

At the start of execution, the stack is empty and the instruction pointer indicates the first bytecode in the CompiledMethod. This CompiledMethod does not require temporaries and the invoking message did not have arguments, so these two categories are also empty.

Method for Rectangle center

▶ 0	push the value of the receiver's first instance variable (origin) onto the stack
1	push the value of the receiver's second instance variable (corner) onto the stack
176	send a binary message with the selector +
119	push the SmallInteger 2 onto the stack
185	send a binary message with the selector /
124	return the object on top of the stack as the value of the message (center)

Receiver   100@100 corner: 200@200

Arguments

Temporary Variables

Stack

Following one cycle of the interpreter, the instruction pointer has been advanced and the value of the receiver's first instance variable has been copied onto the stack.

Method for Rectangle center

0	push the value of the receiver's first instance variable (origin) onto the stack
▶ 1	push the value of the receiver's second instance variable (corner) onto the stack
176	send a binary message with the selector +
119	push the SmallInteger 2 onto the stack
185	send a binary message with the selector /
124	return the object on top of the stack as the value of the message (center)

Receiver   100@100 corner: 200@200

Arguments

Temporary Variables

Stack   100@100

The interpreter's second cycle has an effect similar to the first. The top of the stack is shown toward the bottom of the page. This corresponds to the commonly used convention that memory locations are shown with addresses increasing toward the bottom of the page.

Method for Rectangle center

0	push the value of the receiver's first instance variable (origin) onto the stack
1	push the value of the receiver's second instance variable (corner) onto the stack
◆ **176**	send a binary message with the selector +
119	push the SmallInteger 2 onto the stack
185	send a binary message with the selector /
124	return the object on top of the stack as the value of the message (center)

Receiver   100@100 corner: 200@200

Arguments

Temporary Variables

Stack   100@100
             200@200

The interpreter's third cycle encounters a send bytecode. It removes two objects from the stack and uses them as the receiver and argument of a message with selector + . The procedure for sending the message will not be described in detail here. For the moment, it is only necessary to know that eventually the result of the + message will be pushed onto the stack. Sending messages will be described in later sections.

Method for Rectangle center

0	push the value of the receiver's first instance variable (origin) onto the stack
1	push the value of the receiver's second instance variable (corner) onto the stack
176	send a binary message with the selector +
◆ **119**	push the SmallInteger 2 onto the stack
185	send a binary message with the selector /
124	return the object on top of the stack as the value of the message (center)

Receiver   100@100 corner: 200@200

Arguments

Temporary Variables

Stack   300@300

The interpreter's next cycle pushes the constant 2 onto the stack.

Method for Rectangle center

0	push the value of the receiver's first instance variable (origin) onto the stack
1	push the value of the receiver's second instance variable (corner) onto the stack
176	send a binary message with the selector +
119	push the SmallInteger 2 onto the stack
▸ **185**	send a binary message with the selector /
124	return the object on top of the stack as the value of the message (center)

Receiver	100@100 corner: 200@200
Arguments	
Temporary Variables	
Stack	300@300
	2

The interpreter's next cycle sends another message whose result replaces its receiver and arguments on the stack.

Method for Rectangle center

0	push the value of the receiver's first instance variable (origin) onto the stack
1	push the value of the receiver's second instance variable (corner) onto the stack
176	send a binary message with the selector +
119	push the SmallInteger 2 onto the stack
185	send a binary message with the selector /
▸ **124**	return the object on top of the stack as the value of the message (center)

Receiver	100@100 corner: 200@200
Arguments	
Temporary Variables	
Stack	150@150

The final bytecode returns a result to the center message. The result is found on the stack (150@150). It is clear by this point that a return bytecode must involve pushing the result onto another stack. The details of returning a value to a message will be described after the description of sending a message.

Contexts

Push, store, and jump bytecodes require only small changes to the state of the interpreter. Objects may be moved to or from the stack, and the instruction pointer is always changed; but most of the state remains the same. Send and return bytecodes may require much larger changes to the interpreter's state. When a message is sent, all five parts of the interpreter's state may have to be changed in order to execute a different CompiledMethod in response to this new message. The interpreter's old state must be remembered because the bytecodes after the send must be executed after the value of the message is returned.

The interpreter saves its state in objects called *contexts*. There will be many contexts in the system at any one time. The context that represents the current state of the interpreter is called the *active context*. When a send bytecode in the active context's CompiledMethod requires a new CompiledMethod to be executed, the active context becomes *suspended* and a new context is created and made active. The suspended context retains the state associated with the original CompiledMethod until that context becomes active again. A context must remember the context that it suspended so that the suspended context can be resumed when a result is returned. The suspended context is called the new context's *sender*. A pseudo-variable named thisContext can be used in expressions to refer to the active contexts.

The form used to show the interpreter's state in the last section will be used to show contexts as well. The active context will be indicated by the word Active in its top delimiter. Suspended contexts will say Suspended. For example, consider a context representing the execution of the CompiledMethod for Rectangle rightCenter with a receiver of 100@ 100 corner: 200@200. The source method for Rectangle rightCenter is

rightCenter
    ↑ self right @ self center y

The interpreter's state following execution of the first bytecode is shown below. The sender is some other context in the system.

Active

Method for Rectangle rightCenter

112	push the receiver (self) onto the stack
▶ **208**	send a unary message with the selector in the first literal (right)
112	push the receiver (self) onto the stack
209	send the unary message with the selector in the second literal (center)
207	send the unary message with the selector y
187	send the binary message with the selector @
124	return the object on top of the stack as the value of the message (rightCenter)

literal frame
    #right
    #center

Receiver	100@100 corner: 200@200
Arguments	
Temporary Variables	
Stack	100@100 corner: 200@200
Sender	⇩

After the next bytecode is executed, that context will be suspended. The object pushed by the first bytecode has been removed to be used as the receiver of a new context, which becomes active. The new active context is shown above the suspended context.

_____ **Active** _____

Method for Rectangle right

▶ 1	push the value of the receiver's second instance variable (corner) onto the stack
206	send a unary message with the selector x
124	return the object on top of the stack as the value of the message (right)

Receiver   100@100 corner: 200@200

Arguments

Temporary Variables

Stack

Sender ⬇

_____ **Suspended** _____

Method for Rectangle rightCenter

112	push the receiver (self) onto the stack
208	send a unary message with the selector in the first literal (right)
▶ 112	push the receiver (self) onto the stack
209	send the unary message with the selector in the second literal (center)
207	send the unary message with the selector y
187	send the binary message with the selector @
124	return the object on top of the stack as the value of the message (rightCenter)

literal frame
   #right
   #center

Receiver   100@100 corner: 200@200

Arguments

Temporary Variables

Stack

Sender ⬇

The next cycle of the interpreter advances the new context instead of the previous one.

───────────────────────────── **Active** ─────────────────────────────

Method for Rectangle right

1	push the value of the receiver's second instance variable (corner) onto the stack
▶ **206**	send a unary message with the selector x
124	return the object on top of the stack as the value of the message (right)

Receiver   100@100 corner: 200@200

Arguments

Temporary Variables

Stack   200@200

Sender ⇩

───────────────────────────── **Suspended** ─────────────────────────────

Method for Rectangle rightCenter

112	push the receiver (self) onto the stack
208	send a unary message with the selector in the first literal (right)
▶ **112**	push the receiver (self) onto the stack
209	send the unary message with the selector in the second literal (center)
207	send the unary message with the selector y
187	send the binary message with the selector @
124	return the object on top of the stack as the value of the message (rightCenter)

literal frame
   #right
   #center

Receiver   100@100 corner: 200@200

Arguments

Temporary Variables

Stack

Sender ⇩

In the next cycle, another message is sent, perhaps creating another context. Instead of following the response of this new message (x), we will skip to the point that this context returns a value (to right). When the result of x has been returned, the new context looks like this:

_____ **Active** _____

Method for Rectangle right

1	push the value of the receiver's second instance variable (corner) onto the stack
206	send a unary message with the selector x
▸ 124	return the object on top of the stack as the value of the message (right)

Receiver 100@100 corner: 200@200

Arguments

Temporary Variables

Stack 200

Sender ⇩

_____ **Suspended** _____

Method for Rectangle rightCenter

112	push the receiver (self) onto the stack
208	send a unary message with the selector in the first literal (right)
▸ 112	push the receiver (self) onto the stack
209	send the unary message with the selector in the second literal (center)
207	send the unary message with the selector y
187	send the binary message with the selector @
124	return the object on top of the stack as the value of the message (rightCenter)

literal frame
  #right
  #center

Receiver 100@100 corner: 200@200

Arguments

Temporary Variables

Stack

Sender ⇩

The next bytecode returns the value on the top of the active context's stack (200) as the value of the message that created the context (right). The active context's sender becomes the active context again and the returned value is pushed on its stack.

_____ **Active** _____

Method for Rectangle rightCenter

112	push the receiver (self) onto the stack
208	send a unary message with the selector in the first literal (right)
▶ 112	push the receiver (self) onto the stack
209	send the unary message with the selector in the second literal (center)
207	send the unary message with the selector y
187	send the binary message with the selector @
124	return the object on top of the stack as the value of the message (rightCenter)

literal frame
#right
#center

Receiver   100@100 corner: 200@200

Arguments

Temporary Variables

Stack   200

Sender ⇩

Block Contexts

The contexts illustrated in the last section are represented in the system by instances of MethodContext. A MethodContext represents the execution of a CompiledMethod in response to a message. There is another type of context in the system, which is represented by instances of BlockContext. A BlockContext represents a block in a source method that is not part of an optimized control structure. The compilation of the optimized control structures was described in the earlier section on jump bytecodes. The bytecodes compiled from a nonoptimized control structure are illustrated by the following hypothetical method in Collection. This method returns a collection of the classes of the receiver's elements.

classes
↑self collect: [:element | element class]

Collection classes requires 1 temporary variable

112	push the receiver (self) onto the stack
137	push the active context (thisContext) onto the stack
118	push the SmallInteger 1 onto the stack
200	send a single argument message with the selector blockCopy:
164,4	jump around the next 4 bytes
104	pop the top object off of the stack and store in the first temporary frame location (element)

16   push the contents of the first temporary frame location (element) onto the stack

199   send a unary message with the selector class

125   return the object on top of the stack as the value of the block

224   send a single argument message with the selector in the first literal frame location (collect:)

124   return the object on top of the stack as the value of the message (classes)

literal frame
    #collect:

A new BlockContext is created by the blockCopy: message to the active context. The bytecode that pushes the active context was not described along with the rest of the push bytecodes since the function of contexts had not been described at that point. The argument to blockCopy: (1 in this example) indicates the number of block arguments the block requires. The BlockContext shares much of the state of the active context that creates it. The receiver, arguments, temporary variables, CompiledMethod, and sender are all the same. The BlockContext has its own instruction pointer and stack. Upon returning from the blockCopy: message, the newly created BlockContext is on the stack of the active context and the next instruction jumps around the bytecodes that describe the actions of the block. The active context gave the BlockContext an initial instruction pointer pointing to the bytecode after this jump. The compiler always uses an extended (two-byte) jump after a blockCopy: so that the BlockContext's initial instruction pointer is always two more than the active context's instruction pointer when it receives the blockCopy: message.

The method for Collection classes creates a BlockContext, but does not execute its bytecodes. When the collection receives the collect: message, it will repeatedly send value: messages to the BlockContext with the elements of the collection as arguments. A BlockContext responds to value: by becoming the active context, which causes its bytecodes to be executed by the interpreter. Before the BlockContext becomes active, the argument to value: is pushed onto the BlockContext's stack. The first bytecode executed by the BlockContext stores this value in a temporary variable used for the block argument.

A BlockContext can return a value in two ways. After the bytecodes in the block have been executed, the final value on the stack is returned as the value of the message value or value:. The block can also return a value to the message that invoked the CompiledMethod that created the BlockContext. This is done with the regular return bytecodes. The hypothetical method for Collection containsInstanceOf: uses both types of return from a BlockContext.

containsInstanceOf: aClass
    self do: [:element | (element isKindOf: aClass) ifTrue: [↑true]].
    ↑false

Collection containsInstanceOf: requires 1 temporary variable

112	push the receiver (self) onto the stack
137	push the active context (thisContext) onto the stack
118	push the SmallInteger 1 onto the stack
200	send a single argument message with the selector blockCopy:
164,8	jump around the next 8 bytes
105	pop the top object off of the stack and store in the second temporary frame location (element)
17	push the contents of the second temporary frame location (element) onto the stack
16	push the contents of the first temporary frame location (aClass) onto the stack
224	send a single argument message with the selector in the first literal frame location (isKindOf:)
152	pop the top object off of the stack and jump around 1 byte if it is false
121	return true as the value of the message (containsInstanceOf:)
115	push nil onto the stack
125	return the object on top of the stack as the value of the block
203	send the single argument message with the selector do:
135	pop the top object off the stack
122	return false as the value of the message (containsInstanceOf:)

literal frame

#isKindOf:

Messages

When a send bytecode is encountered, the interpreter finds the CompiledMethod indicated by the message as follows.

1. *Find the message receiver.* The receiver is below the arguments on the stack. The number of arguments is indicated in the send bytecode.

2. *Access a message dictionary.* The original message dictionary is found in the receiver's class.

3. *Look up the message selector in the message dictionary.* The selector is indicated in the send bytecode.

4. *If the selector is found,* the associated CompiledMethod describes the response to the message.

5. *If the selector is not found,* a new message dictionary must be searched (returning to step 3). The new message dictionary will be found in the superclass of the last class whose message dictionary was searched. This cycle may be repeated several times, traveling up the superclass chain.

If the selector is not found in the receiver's class nor in any of its superclasses, an error is reported, and execution of the bytecodes following the send is suspended.

☐ *Superclass Sends*   A variation of the send bytecodes called *super-sends* uses a slightly different algorithm to find the CompiledMethod associated with a message. Everything is the same except for the second step, which specifies the original message dictionary to search. When a super-send is encountered, the following second step is substituted.

> **2.** *Access a message dictionary.* The original message dictionary is found in the superclass of the class in which the currently executing CompiledMethod was found.

Super-send bytecodes are used when super is used as the receiver of a message in a source method. The bytecode used to push the receiver will be the same as if self had been used, but a super-send bytecode will be used to describe the selector.

As an example of the use of a super-send, imagine a subclass of Rectangle called ShadedRectangle that adds an instance variable named shade. A Rectangle might respond to the message shade: by producing a new ShadedRectangle. ShadedRectangle provides a new method for the message intersect:, returning a ShadedRectangle instead of a Rectangle. This method must use super to access its own ability to actually compute the intersection.

intersect: aRectangle
> ↑ (super intersect: aRectangle)
>   shade: shade

ShadedRectangle intersect:

112	push the receiver (self) onto the stack
16	push the contents of the first temporary frame location (the argument aRectangle) onto the stack
133,33	send to super a single argument message with the selector in the second literal frame location (intersect:)
2	push the value of the receiver's third instance variable (shade) onto the stack
224	send a single argument message with the selector in the first literal frame location (shade:)
124	return the object on top of the stack as the value of the message (intersect:)

literal frame
> #shade:
> #intersect:
> Association: #ShadedRectangle ➔ ShadedRectangle

It is important to note that the initial class searched in response to a super-send will be the superclass of the receiver's class only if the CompiledMethod containing the super-send was originally found the receiver's class. If the CompiledMethod was originally found in a superclass of the receiver's class, the search will start in *that* class's superclass. Since the interpreter's state does not include the class in which it found each CompiledMethod, that information is included in the CompiledMethod itself. Every CompiledMethod that includes a super-send bytecode refers to the class in whose message dictionary it is found. The last entry of the literal frame of those CompiledMethods contains an association referring to the class.

Primitive Methods

The interpreter's actions after finding a CompiledMethod depend on whether or not the CompiledMethod indicates that a *primitive method* may be able to respond to the message. If no primitive method is indicated, a new MethodContext is created and made active as described in previous sections. If a primitive method is indicated in the CompiledMethod, the interpreter may be able to respond to the message without actually executing the bytecodes. For example, one of the primitive methods is associated with the + message to instances of SmallInteger.

+ addend
　< primitive: 1 >
　↑ super + addend

SmallInteger + associated with primitive #1

112	push the receiver (self) onto the stack
16	push the contents of the first temporary frame location (the argument addend) onto the stack
133,32	send to super a single argument message with the selector in the first literal frame location (+)
124	return the object on top of the stack as the value of the message (+)

literal frame
　# +
　#SmallInteger → SmallInteger

Even if a primitive method is indicated for a CompiledMethod, the interpreter may not be able to respond successfully. For example, the argument of the + message might not be another instance of SmallInteger or the sum might not be representable by a SmallInteger. If the interpreter cannot execute the primitive for some reason, the primitive is said to *fail*. When a primitive fails, the bytecodes in the CompiledMethod are executed as if the primitive method had not been indicated. The method for SmallInteger + indicates that the + method in the superclass (Integer) will be used if the primitive fails.

There are about a hundred primitive methods in the system that perform four types of operation.

1. Arithmetic

2. Storage management

3. Control

4. Input-output

The Object Memory

The object memory provides the interpreter with an interface to the objects that make up the Smalltalk-80 virtual image. Each object is associated with a unique identifier called its *object pointer*. The object memory and interpreter communicate about objects with object pointers. The size of object pointers determines the maximum number of objects a Smalltalk-80 system can contain. This number is not fixed by anything about the language, but the implementation described in this book uses 16-bit object pointers, allowing 65536 objects to be referenced. Implementation of the Smalltalk-80 system with larger object references will require changing certain parts of the virtual machine specification. It is not within the scope of this book to detail the relevant changes.

The object memory associates each object pointer with a set of other object pointers. Every object pointer is associated with the object pointer of a class. If an object has instance variables, its object pointer is also associated with the object pointers of their values. The individual instance variables are referred to by zero-relative integer indices. The value of an instance variable can be changed, but the class associated with an object cannot be changed. The object memory provides the following five fundamental functions to the interpreter.

1. *Access* the value of an object's *instance variable*. The object pointer of the instance and the index of the instance variable must be supplied. The object pointer of the instance variable's value is returned.

2. *Change* the value of an object's *instance variable*. The object pointer of the instance and the index of the instance variable must be supplied. The object pointer of the new value must also be supplied.

3. *Access* an object's *class*. The object pointer of the instance must be supplied. The object pointer of the instance's class is returned.

4. *Create* a new *object*. The object pointer of the new object's class and the number of instance variables it should have must be supplied. The object pointer of the new instance is returned.

5. Find the *number of instance variables* an object has. The object's pointer must be supplied. The number of instance variables is returned.

There is no explicit function of the object memory to remove an object no longer being used because these objects are reclaimed automatically. An object is reclaimed when there are no object pointers to it from other objects. This reclamation can be accomplished either by reference counting or garbage collection.

There are two additional features of the object memory that provide efficient representation of numerical information. The first of these sets aside certain object pointers for instances of class SmallInteger. The second allows objects to contain integer values instead of object pointers.

☐ *Representation of Small Integers* The instances of class SmallInteger represent the integers −16384 through 16383. Each of these instances is assigned a unique object pointer. These object pointers all have a 1 in the low-order bit position and the two's complement representation of their value in the high-order 15 bits. An instance of SmallInteger needs no instance storage since both its class and its value can be determined from its object pointer. Two additional functions are provided by the object memory to convert back and forth between SmallInteger object pointers and numerical values.

6. Find the numerical value represented by a SmallInteger. The object pointer of the SmallInteger must be supplied. The two's complement value is returned.

7. Find the SmallInteger representing a numerical value. The two's complement value must be supplied. A SmallInteger object pointer is returned.

This representation for SmallIntegers implies that there can be 32768 instances of the other classes in the system. It also implies that equality (=) and equivalence (==) will be the same for instances of SmallInteger. Integers outside the range −16384 through 16383 are represented by instances of class LargePositiveInteger or LargeNegativeInteger. There may be several instances representing the same value, so equality and equivalence are different.

☐ *Collections of Integer Values* Another special representation is included for objects representing collections of integers. Instead of storing the object pointers of the SmallIntegers representing the contents of the collection, the actual numerical values are stored. The values in these special collections are constrained to be positive. There are two varieties of collection, one limiting its values to be less than 256 and the other limiting its values to be less than 65536. The object memory provides functions analogous to the first five listed in this section, but for objects whose contents are numerical values instead of object pointers.

The distinction between objects that contain object pointers and those that contain integer values is never visible to the Smalltalk-80 programmer. When one of these special numerical collections is accessed by sending it a message, the object pointer of an object representing the value is returned. The nature of these special collections is only evident in that they may refuse to store objects that do not represent integers within the proper range.

The Hardware and Additional System Classes

The Smalltalk-80 implementation has been described as a virtual machine to avoid unnecessary hardware dependencies. Some hardware requirements, input-output devices and clocks, are imposed by the primitives that the virtual image depends on.

1. A bitmap display. It is convenient if the bitmap being displayed can be located in the object memory.

2. A pointing device with three associated buttons. It is most convenient if these are physically located on the device.

3. A keyboard, either decoded ASCII or undecoded ALTO.

4. A disk. The virtual image skeleton disk system must be tailored to the actual disk used.

5. A millisecond timer.

6. A real time clock with one second resolution.

Three system classes, whose implementation details are not provided in this book, create the desired interface between user input devices. They are InputSensor, InputState, and KeyboardEvent. Sensor, an instance of class InputSensor, acts as the primary intermediary among applications that wish to set and test input devices and the primitives that actually access the hardware.

Other system classes not included for discussion in this book support compilation. They are class Complier, Decompiler, DecompilerConstructor, LiteralDictionary, Scanner, Parser, ParseStack, and ParseNode and the several subclasses of ParseNode. No detailed protocol is given for CompiledMethod, InstructionStream, ContextPart (whose subclasses are BlockContext and MethodContext), InstructionPointer, Message, MethodDescription, MethodDictionary, SystemDictionary (whose single instance Smalltalk provides users with a system query interface), and MetaclassForMultipleInheritance. This last class is used to support multiple inheritance, as described in the paper by Dan Ingalls and Alan Borning: "Multiple Inheritance in Smalltalk-80" in *Proceedings of the National Conference on Artificial Intelligence,* Pittsburgh, PA, August, 1982.

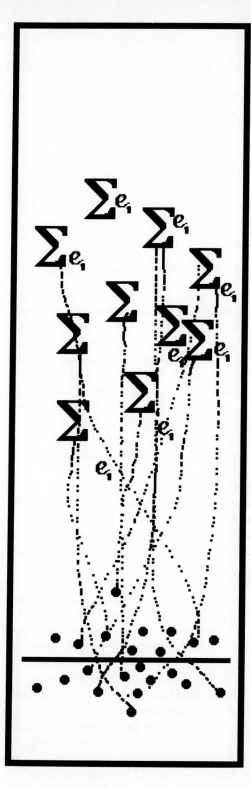

22

Probability Distributions

Probability Distribution Framework

Applications, such as simulations, often wish to obtain values associated with the outcomes of chance experiments. In such experiments, a number of possible questions might be asked, such as:

- What is the probability of a certain event occurring?
- What is the probability of one of several events occurring?
- What is the probability that, in the next N trials, at least one successful event will occur?
- How many successful events will occur in the next N trials?
- How many trials until the next successful event occurs?

Definitions

In the terminology of simulations, a *trial* is a tick of the simulated clock (where a clock tick might represent seconds, minutes, hours, days, months, or years, depending on the unit of time appropriate to the situation). An *event* or *success* is a job arrival such as a car arriving to a car wash, a customer arriving in a bank, or a broken machine arriving in the repair shop.

In the realm of statistics, the probability that an event will occur is typically obtained from a large number of observations of actual trials. For example, a long series of observations of a repair shop would be needed in order to determine the probability of a broken machine arriving in the shop during a fixed time interval. In general, several events might occur during that time interval. The set of possible events is called a *sample space*. A *probability function* on a sample space is defined as an association of a number between 0 and 1 with each event in the sample space. The probability or chance that at least one of the events in the sample space will occur is defined as 1; if p is the probability that event E will occur, then the probability that E will not occur is defined as $1 - p$.

Sample spaces are classified into two types: *discrete* and *continuous*. A sample space is discrete if it contains a finite number of possible events or an infinite number of events that have a one-to-one relationship with the positive integers. For example, the six possible outcomes of a throw of a die constitute a discrete sample space. A sample space is continuous if it contains an ordered, infinite number of events, for example, any number between 1.0 and 4.0. Probability functions on each of these types of sample spaces are appropriately named *discrete probability functions* and *continuous probability functions*.

A *random variable* is a real-valued function defined over the events in a sample space. The adjectives "discrete" and "continuous" apply to random variables according to the characteristic of their range. The probability function of a random variable is called a *probability distri-*

bution; the values in the range of the function are the probabilities of occurrence of the possible values of the random variable. The *density* is a function that assigns probabilities to allowed ranges of the random variable. Any function can be a *density* function (discrete or continuous) if it has only positive values and its integral is 1.

Another useful function that plays an important role in simulations is called the *cumulative distribution function*. It gives the probability that the value of the random variable is within a designated range. For example, the cumulative distribution function answers the question: what is the probability that, in the throw of a die, the side is 4 or less?

The *mean* is defined as the average value that the random variable takes on. The *variance* is a measure of the spread of the distribution. It is defined as the average of the square of the deviations from the mean.

---

*Introductory
Examples*

Two examples of sample spaces are given here before entering into a detailed description of the Smalltalk-80 classes. Suppose the sample space is the possible outcomes of a toss of a die. The sample space consists of

    event 1: 1 is thrown
    event 2: 2 is thrown
    event 3: 3 is thrown
    event 4: 4 is thrown
    event 5: 5 is thrown
    event 6: 6 is thrown

Then, for this discrete probability distribution, the probability function for any event is

    f(event) = 1/6

If X is a random variable over the sample space, then the probability distribution of X is g(X) such that

    g(X=1) = f(event1) = 1/6, ... , g(X=6) = f(event6) = 1/6.

The density of X is 1/6 for any value of X.
    The cumulative distribution function of X is

    $c(a, b) = \Sigma_a^b g(X)$

For example,

    c(2,4) = g(X=2) + g(X=3) + g(X=4) = 1/6 + 1/6 + 1/6 = 1/2

As an example of a continuous probability distribution, let the sample space be the time of day where the start of the day is time = 12:00 a.m.

and the end of the day is time = 11:59:59.99... p.m. The sample space is the interval between these two times.

The probability function is

$$f(event) = probability\ (event_i \le time < event_j)$$

where $event_i < event_j$. The density of X is

$$g(X = any\ specified\ time) = 0$$

Suppose this is a 24-hour clock. Then the probability that, upon looking at a clock, the time is between 1:00 p.m. and 3:00 p.m., is defined by the cumulative distribution function

$$c(1{:}00,\ 3{:}00) = \int_{1{:}00}^{3{:}00} g(X)$$

g(X) is uniform over 24 hours. So

$$c(1{:}00,\ 3{:}00) = c(1{:}00,\ 2{:}00) + c(2{:}00,\ 3{:}00) = 1/24 + 1/24 = 1/12.$$

Class ProbabilityDistribution

The superclass for probability distributions provides protocol for obtaining one or more random samplings from the distribution, and for computing the density and cumulative distribution functions. It has a class variable U which is an instance of class Random. Class Random provides a simple way in which to obtain a value with uniform probability distribution over the interval [0,1].

Like class Random, ProbabilityDistribution is a Stream that accesses elements generated algorithmically. Whenever a random sampling is required, the message next is sent to the distribution. ProbabilityDistribution implements next by returning the result of the message inverseDistribution: var, where the argument var is a random number between 0 and 1. Subclasses of ProbabilityDistribution must implement inverseDistribution: in order to map [0,1] onto their sample space, or else they must override the definition of next. The message next: is inherited from the superclass Stream.

class name	ProbabilityDistribution
superclass	Stream
class variable names	U
class methods	

class initialization

initialize
   "Uniformly distributed random numbers in the range [0,1]."
   U ← Random new

instance creation

new
   ↑self basicNew

instance methods

random sampling

next

"This is a general random number generation method for any probability law; use the (0, 1) uniformly distributed random variable U as the value of the law's distribution function. Obtain the next random value and then solve for the inverse. The inverse solution is defined by the subclass."
↑self inverseDistribution: U next

testing

atEnd

↑ false

probability functions

density: x

"This is the density function."
self subclassResponsibility

distribution: aCollection

"This is the cumulative distribution function. The argument is a range of contiguous values of the random variable. The distribution is mathematically the area under the probability curve within the specified interval."
self subclassResponsibility

private

inverseDistribution: x

self subclassResponsibility

computeSample: m outOf: n

"Compute the number of ways one can draw a sample without replacement of size m from a set of size n."
m > n ifTrue: [↑0.0].
↑n factorial / (n−m) factorial

In order to initialize the class variable U, evaluate the expression

ProbabilityDistribution initialize

Computing the number of ways one can draw a sample without replacement of size m from a set of size n will prove a useful method shared by the subclass implementations that follow.

Class
DiscreteProbability

The two types of probability distributions, discrete and continuous, are specified as subclasses of class ProbabilityDistribution; each provides an implementation of the cumulative distribution function which depends on the density function. These implementations assume that the density function will be provided in subclasses.

class name	DiscreteProbability
superclass	ProbabilityDistribution
instance methods	

probability functions

distribution: aCollection

"Answer the sum of the discrete values of the density function for each element in the collection."
| t |
t ← 0.0.
aCollection do: [:i | t ← t + (self density: i)].
↑t

Class
ContinuousProbability

class name	ContinuousProbability
superclass	ProbabilityDistribution
instance methods	

probability functions

distribution: aCollection

"This is a slow and dirty trapezoidal integration to determine the area under the probability function curve y=density(x) for x in the specified collection. The method assumes that the collection contains numerically-ordered elements."
| t aStream x1 x2 y1 y2 |
t ← 0.0.
aStream ← ReadStream on: aCollection.
x2 ← aStream next.
y2 ← self density: x2.
[x1 ← x2. x2 ← aStream next]
    whileTrue:
        [y1 ← y2.
        y2 ← self density: x2.
        t ← t + ((x2−x1)∗(y2+y1))].
↑t∗0.5

In order to implement the various kinds of probability distributions as subclasses of class DiscreteProbability or ContinuousProbability, both the density function and the inverse distribution function (or a different response to next) must be implemented.

Discrete Probability Distributions

As an example of a discrete probability distribution, take the heights of a class of 20 students and arrange a table indicating the frequency of students having the same heights (the representation of height is given in inches). The table might be

measured height	number of students
60″	3
62″	2
64″	4
66″	3
68″	5
70″	3

Given this information, we might ask the question: what is the probability of randomly selecting a student who is 5′4″ tall? This question is answered by computing the density function of the discrete probability associated with the observed information. In particular, we can define the density function in terms of the following table.

height	density
60″	3/20
62″	2/20
64″	4/20
66″	3/20
68″	5/20
70″	3/20

Suppose we define a subclass of DiscreteProbability which we name SampleSpace, and provide the above table as the value of an instance variable of SampleSpace. The response to the message density: x is the value associated with x in the table (in the example, the value of x is one of the possible heights); the value of the density of x, where x is not in the table, is 0. The probability of sampling each element of the collection is equally likely, so the density function is the reciprocal of the size of the collection. Since there may be several occurrences of a data element, the probability must be the appropriate sum of the probability for each occurrence. The implementation of the cumulative distribution function is inherited from the superclass.

class name	SampleSpace
superclass	DiscreteProbability
instance variable names	data
class methods	

instance creation

data: aCollection
    ↑self new setData: aCollection

instance methods

probability functions

density: x
    "x must be in the sample space; the probability must sum over all occurrences of x in the sample space"
    (data includes: x)
        ifTrue: [↑(data occurrencesOf: x) / data size]
        ifFalse: [↑0]

private

inverseDistribution: x
    ↑data at: (x∗data size) truncated + 1
setData: aCollection
    data ← aCollection

Suppose heights is an instance of SampleSpace. The data is an array of 20 elements, the height of each student in the example.

heights ← SampleSpace data:
        #(60 60 60 62 62 64 64 64 64 66 66 66 68 68 68 68
          68 70 70 70)

Then we can ask heights the question, what is the probability of randomly selecting a student with height 64, or what is the probability of randomly selecting a student whose height is between 60″ and 64″? The answer to the first question is the density function, that is, the response to the message density: 64. The answer to the second is the cumulative distribution function; that is, the answer is the response to the message distribution: (60 to: 64 by: 2).

SampleSpace, in many ways, resembles a discrete uniform distribution. In general, a discrete uniform distribution is defined over a finite range of values. For example, we might specify a uniform distribution defined for six values: 1, 2, 3, 4, 5, 6, representing the sides of a die. The density function, as the constant 1/6, indicates that the die is "fair," i.e., the probability that each of the sides will be selected is the same.

We define four kinds of discrete probability distributions that are useful in simulation studies. They are Bernoulli, Binomial, Geometric, and Poisson. A Bernoulli distribution answers the question, will a success occur in the next trial? A binomial distribution represents N repeated, independent Bernoulli distributions, where N is greater than or equal to one. It answers the question, how many successes are there in N trials? Taking a slightly different point of view, the geometric distribution answers the question, how many repeated, independent Bernoulli trials are needed before the first success is obtained? A Poisson distribution is used to answer the question, how many events occur in a particular time interval? In particular, the Poisson determines the probability that K events will occur in a particular time interval, where K is greater than or equal to 0.

The Bernoulli Distribution

A Bernoulli distribution is used in the case of a sample space of two possibilities, each with a given probability of occurrence. Examples of sample spaces consisting of two possibilities are

- The throw of a die, in which I ask, did I get die side 4? The probability of success if the die is fair is 1/6; the probability of failure is 5/6.

- The toss of a coin, in which I ask, did I get heads? The probability of success if the coin is fair is 1/2; the probability of failure is 1/2.

- The draw of a playing card, in which I ask, is the playing card the queen of hearts? The probability of success if the card deck is standard is 1/52; the probability of failure is 51/52.

According to the specification of class Bernoulli, we create a Bernoulli distribution using expressions of the form

Bernoulli parameter: 0.17

In this example, we have created a Bernoulli distribution with a probability of success equal to 0.17. The probability of success is also referred to as the mean of the Bernoulli distribution.

The parameter, prob, of a Bernoulli distribution is the probability that one of the two possible outcomes will occur. This outcome is typically referred to as the successful one. The parameter prob is a number between 0.0 and 1.0. The density function maps the two possible outcomes, 1 or 0, onto the parameter prob or its inverse. The cumulative distribution, inherited from the superclass, can only return values prob or 1.

class name	Bernoulli
superclass	DiscreteProbability
instance variable names	prob

class methods

instance creation

parameter: aNumber
(aNumber between: 0.0 and: 1.0)
    ifTrue: [↑self new setParameter: aNumber]
    ifFalse: [self error: ' The probability must be between 0.0 and 1.0 ']

instance methods

accessing

mean
↑prob
variance
↑prob * (1.0 − prob)

probability functions

density: x
" let 1 denote success"
x = 1 ifTrue: [↑prob].
" let 0 denote failure"
x = 0 ifTrue: [↑1.0−prob].
self error: ' outcomes of a Bernoulli can only be 1 or 0 '

private

inverseDistribution: x
" Depending on the random variable x, the random sample is 1 or 0,
denoting success or failure of the Bernoulli trial."
x < = prob
    ifTrue: [↑1]
    ifFalse: [↑0]
setParameter: aNumber
prob ← aNumber

Suppose, at some stage of playing a card game, we wish to determine whether or not the first draw of a card is an ace. Then a possible (randomly determined) answer is obtained by sampling from a Bernoulli distribution with mean of 4/52.

(Bernoulli parameter: 4/52) next

Let's trace how the response to the message next is carried out.

The method associated with the unary selector next is found in the method dictionary of class ProbabilityDistribution. The method returns the value of the expression self inverseDistribution: U next. That is, a uniformly distributed number between 0 and 1 is obtained (U next) in order to be the argument of inverseDistribution:. The method associated with the selector inverseDistribution: is found in the method dictionary of class Bernoulli. This is the inverse distribution function, a mapping from a value prob of the cumulative distribution function onto a value, x, such that prob is the probability that the random variable is less than or equal to x. In a Bernoulli distribution, x can only be one of two values; these are denoted by the integers 1 and 0.

The Binomial Distribution

In simulations, we use a Bernoulli distribution to tell us whether or not an event occurs, for example, does a car arrive in the next second or will a machine break down today? The binomial distribution answers how many successes occurred in N trials. The density function of a Bernoulli distribution tells us the probability of occurrence of one of two events. In contrast, the density function of a binomial answers the question, what is the probability that x successes will occur in the next N trials?

The binomial distribution represents N repeated, independent Bernoulli trials. It is the same as Bernoulli for $N = 1$. In the description of class Binomial, a subclass of class Bernoulli, the additional instance variable, N, represents the number of trials. That is, given an instance of Binomial, the response to the message next answers the question, how many successes are there in N trials?

The probability function for the binomial is

$$\frac{N!}{x!(N-x)!}\, p^x (1-p)^{N-x}$$

where x is the number of successes and p is the probability of success on each trial. The notation "!" represents the mathematical factorial operation. The first terms can be reduced to computing the number of ways to obtain x successes out of N trials, divided by the number of ways to obtain x successes out of x trials. Thus the implementation given below makes use of the method computeSample: a outOf: b provided in the superclass ProbabilityDistribution.

class name	Binomial
superclass	Bernoulli
instance variable names	N
class methods	

instance creation

events: n mean: m
    n truncated < = 0 ifTrue: [self error: 'number of events must be > 0'].
    ↑self new: events: n mean: m

instance methods

random sampling

next
| t |
"A surefire but slow method is to sample a Bernoulli N times. Since the
Bernoulli returns 0 or 1, the sum will be between 0 and N."
t ← 0.
N timesRepeat: [t ← t + super next].
↑t

probability functions

density: x
(x between: 0 and: N)
ifTrue: [↑((self computeSample: x outOf: N)
/ (self computeSample: x outOf: x))
* (prob raisedTo: x) * ⟨(1.0−prob) raisedTo: N−x)]
ifFalse: [↑0.0]

private

events: n mean: m
N ← n truncated.
self setParameter: m/N
"setParameter: is implemented in my superclass"

Let's use flipping coins as our example. In five trials of a coin flip,
where the probability of heads is 0.5, the Bernoulli distribution with parameter 0.5 represents one trial, i.e., one coin flip.

sampleA ← Bernoulli parameter: 0.5

The result of

sampleA next

is either 1 or 0, answering the question, did I get heads?
Suppose instead we create

sampleB ← Binomial events: 5 mean: 2.5

The result of

sampleB next

is a number between 0 and 5, answering the question, how many heads did I get in 5 trials?

The message

    sampleB density: 3

is a number between 0 and 1, answering the question, what is the probability of getting heads 3 times in 5 trials?

The Geometric Distribution

Suppose we wish to answer the question, how many repeated, independent Bernoulli trials are needed before the first success is obtained? This new perspective on a Bernoulli distribution is the geometric distribution. As in the Bernoulli and binomial cases, the probability of a success is between 0.0 and 1.0; the mean of the geometric is the reciprocal of the success probability. Thus if we create a geometric distribution as

    Geometric mean: 5

then the mean is 5 and the probability of a success is 1/5. The mean must be greater than or equal to 1.

A geometric distribution is more suitable for an event-driven simulation design than a Bernoulli or binomial. Instead of asking how many cars arrive in the next 20 seconds (a binomial question), the geometric distribution asks, how many seconds before the next car arrives. In event-driven simulations, the (simulated) clock jumps to the time of the next event. Using a geometric distribution, we can determine when the next event will occur, set the clock accordingly, and then carry out the event, potentially "saving" a great deal of real time.

The probability distribution function is

$$p(1-p)^{x-1}$$

where x is the number of trials required and p is the probability of success on a single trial.

class name	Geometric
superclass	Bernoulli
class methods	

instance creation

mean: m
    ↑self parameter: 1/m
    "Note that the message parameter: is implemented in the superclass"

instance methods

accessing

mean
> ↑ 1.0 / prob

variance
> ↑ (1.0−prob) / prob squared

probability functions

density: x
> x > 0 ifTrue: [↑prob ∗ ((1.0−prob) raisedTo: x−1)]
>   ifFalse: [↑0.0]

private

inverseDistribution: x
> "Method is from Knuth, Vol. 2, pp.116−117"
> ↑(x ln / (1.0−prob) ln) ceiling

Suppose, on the average, two cars arrive at a ferry landing every minute. We can express this statistical information as

> sample ← Geometric mean: 60/2

The density function can be used to answer the question, what is the probability that it will take N trials before the next success? For example, what is the probability that it will take 30 seconds before the next car arrives?

> sample density: 30

The cumulative distribution function can be used to answer the question, did the next car arrive in 30 to 40 seconds?

> sample distribution: (30 to: 40)

---

*The Poisson
Distribution*

Suppose the question we wish to ask is, how many events occur in a unit time (or space interval)? The binomial distribution considers the occurrence of two independent events, such as drawing a king of hearts or a king of spades from a full deck of cards. There are random events, however, that occur at random points in time or space. These events do not occur as the outcomes of trials. In these circumstances, it does not make sense to consider the probability of an event happening or not happening. One does not ask how many cars did not arrive at a ferry or how many airplanes did not land at the airport; the appropriate questions are how many cars did arrive at the ferry and how many airplanes did land at the airport, in the next unit of time?

In simulations, the Poisson distribution is useful for sampling potential demands by customers for service, say, of cashiers, salesmen, technicians, or Xerox copiers. Experience has shown that the rate at which the service is provided often approximates a Poisson probability law.

The Poisson law describes the probability that exactly x events occur in a unit time interval, when the mean rate of occurrence per unit time is the variable mu. For a time interval of dt, the probability is mu*dt; mu must be greater than 0.0.

The probability function is

$$\frac{a^x e^{-a}}{x!}$$

where a is the mean rate (or mu), e the base of natural logarithms, x is the number of occurrences, and ! the factorial notation.

class name	Poisson
superclass	DiscreteProbability
instance variable names	mu
class methods	

instance creation

mean: p
> "p is the average number of events happening per unit interval."
> p > 0.0
>> ifTrue: [↑self new setMean: p]
>> ifFalse: [self error: 'mean must be greater than 0.0']

instance methods

accessing

mean
> ↑mu
variance
> ↑mu

random sampling

next
> "how many events occur in the next unit interval?"
> | p n q |
> p ← mu negated exp.
> n ← 0.
> q ← 1.0.
> [q ← q * U next.
> q >= p]
>> whileTrue: [n ← n+ 1].
> ↑n

probability functions

density: x
"the probability that in a unit interval, x events will occur"
x > = 0
    ifTrue: [↑((mu raisedTo: x) * (mu negated exp)) / x factorial]
    ifFalse: [↑0.0]

private

setMean: p
mu ← p

The response to the message next answers the question, how many events occur in the next unit of time or space? The density function of x determines the probability that, in a unit interval (of time or space), x events will occur. The cumulative distribution function of x determines the probability that, in a unit interval, x events or fewer will occur.

Continuous Probability Distributions

A continuous random variable can assume any value in an interval or collection of intervals. In the continuous case, questions similar to those asked in the discrete case are asked and the continuous probability distributions show strong correspondence to the discrete ones. An example of a question one asks of a continuous probability distribution is, what is the probability of obtaining a temperature at some moment of time. Temperature is a physical property which is measured on a continuous scale.

We define four kinds of continuous probability distributions; they are uniform, exponential, gamma, and normal distributions. The uniform distribution answers the question, given a set of equally likely events, which one occurs? Given that the underlying events are Poisson distributed, the exponential distribution is used to answer the question, how long before the first (next) event occurs? The gamma distribution is related in that it answers the question, how long before the Nth event occurs? The normal or Gaussian distribution is useful for approximating limiting forms of other distributions. It plays a significant role in statistics because it is simple to use; symmetrical about the mean; completely determined by two parameters, the mean and the variance; and reflects the distribution of everyday events.

The Uniform Distribution

We have already examined the uniform distribution from the perspective of selecting discrete elements from a finite sample space. The question we asked was, given a set of equally likely descriptions, which one to pick? In the continuous case, the sample space is a continuum, such as time or the interval between 0 and 1. The class Uniform provided here extends the capabilities of class Random by generating a random variable within any interval as a response to the message next.

class name	Uniform
superclass	ContinuousProbability
instance variable names	startNumber
	stopNumber

class methods

instance creation

from: begin to: end
begin > end
ifTrue: [self error: ' illegal interval ']
ifFalse: [↑self new setStart: begin toEnd: end]

instance methods

accessing

mean
↑(startNumber + stopNumber)/2
variance
↑(stopNumber − startNumber) squared / 12

probability functions

density: x
(x between: startNumber and: stopNumber)
ifTrue: [↑1.0 / (stopNumber − startNumber)]
ifFalse: [↑0]

private

inverseDistribution: x
"x is a random number between 0 and 1"
↑startNumber + (x * (stopNumber − startNumber))
setStart: begin toEnd: end
startNumber ← begin.
stopNumber ← end

The Exponential Distribution

Given that the underlying events are Poisson distributed, the exponential distribution determines how long before the next event occurs. This is more suitable for a simulation design than is Poisson in the same sense that the geometric distribution was more suitable than the binomial, because we can jump the simulated clock setting to the next occurrence of an event, rather than stepping sequentially through each time unit.

As an example of sampling with an exponential, we might ask, when will the next car arrive? The density function of x is the probability that the next event will occur in the time interval x, for example, what is the probability of the next car arriving in the next 10 minutes?

Exponential is typically used in situations in which the sample deteriorates with time. For example, an exponential is used to determine the probability that a light bulb or a piece of electronic equipment will fail prior to some time x. Exponential is useful in these cases because the longer the piece of equipment is used, the less likely it is to keep running.

As in the case of a Poisson, the parameter of the exponential distribution, mu, is in terms of events per unit time, although the domain of this distribution is time (not events).

The probability function for the exponential distribution is

$$\frac{e^{-\frac{x}{a}}}{a}$$

where a is the mean rate (mu = 1/a) between occurrences.

class name	Exponential
superclass	ContinuousProbability
instance variable names	mu
class methods	

instance creation

mean: p
> "Since the exponential parameter mu is the same as Poisson mu, if we are given the mean of the exponential, we take reciprocal to get the probability parameter"
> ↑self parameter: 1.0/p

parameter: p
> p > 0.0
>   ifTrue: [↑self new setParameter: p]
>   ifFalse: [self error:
>   ' The probability parameter must be greater than 0.0 ']

instance methods

accessing

mean
> ↑1.0/mu

variance
> ↑1.0/(mu ∗ mu)

probability functions

density: x
  x > 0.0
    ifTrue: [↑mu * (mu*x) negated exp]
    ifFalse: [↑0.0]
distribution: anInterval
  anInterval last < = 0.0
    ifTrue: [↑0.0]
    ifFalse: [↑ 1.0 − (mu * anInterval last) negated exp −
                (anInterval first > 0.0
                  ifTrue: [self distribution:
                            (0.0 to: anInterval first)]
                  ifFalse: [0.0])]

private

inverseDistribution: x
  "implementation according to Knuth, Vol. 2, p. 114"
  ↑x ln negated / mu
setParameter: p
  mu ← p

---

*The Gamma
Distribution*

A distribution related to the exponential is gamma, which answers the question, how long before the Nth event occurs? For example, we use a gamma distribution to sample how long before the Nth car arrives at the ferry landing. Each instance of class Gamma represents an Nth event and the probability of occurrence of that Nth event (inherited from the superclass Exponential). The variable N specified in class Gamma must be a positive integer.

The probability function is

$$\frac{x^{k-1} e^{-\frac{x}{a}}}{a^k (k-1)!}$$

where k is greater than zero and the probability parameter mu is 1/a. The second term of the denominator, (k-1)!, is the gamma function when it is known that k is greater than 0. The implementation given below does not make this assumption.

class name	Gamma
superclass	Exponential
instance variable names	N

class methods

instance creation

events: k mean: p

| events |

events ← k truncated.

events > 0

ifTrue: [↑ (self parameter: events/p) setEvents: events]

ifFalse: [self error: 'the number of events must be greater than 0']

instance methods

accessing

mean

↑super mean * N

variance

↑super variance * N

probability functions

density: x

| t |

x > 0.0

ifTrue: [t ← mu * x.

↑(mu raisedTo: N) / (self gamma: N)

* (x raisedTo: N−1)

* t negated exp]

ifFalse: [↑0.0]

private

gamma: n

| t |

t ← n − 1.0.

↑self computeSample: t outOf: t

setEvents: events

N ← events

*The Normal
Distribution*

The normal distribution, also called the Gaussian, is useful for summarizing or approximating other distributions. Using the normal distribution, we can ask questions such as how long before a success occurs (similar to the discrete binomial distribution) or how many events occur in a certain time interval (similar to the Poisson). Indeed, the normal can be used to approximate a binomial when the number of events is very large or a Poisson when the mean is large. However, the approximation is only accurate in the regions near the mean; the errors in approximation increase towards the tail.

A normal distribution is used when there is a central dominating value (the mean), and the probability of obtaining a value decreases with a deviation from the mean. If we plot a curve with the possible values on the x-axis and the probabilities on the y-axis, the curve will look like a bell shape. This bell shape is due to the requirements that the probabilities are symmetric about the mean, the possible values from the sample space are infinite, and yet the probabilities of all of these infinite values must sum to 1. The normal distribution is useful when determining the probability of a measurement, for example, when measuring the size of ball bearings. The measurements will result in values that cluster about a central mean value, off by a small amount.

The parameters of a normal distribution are the mean (mu) and a standard deviation (sigma). The standard deviation must be greater than 0. The probability function is

$$\frac{e^{\frac{1}{2}\left(\frac{x-a}{b}\right)^2}}{b\sqrt{2\pi}}$$

where a is the parameter mu and b is the standard deviation sigma.

class name	Normal
superclass	ContinuousProbability
instance variable names	mu
	sigma

class methods

instance creation

mean: a deviation: b
    b > 0.0
        ifTrue: [↑self new setMean: a standardDeviation: b]
        ifFalse: [self error: 'standard deviation must be greater than 0.0']

instance methods

accessing

mean
    ↑mu
variance
    ↑sigma squared

random sampling

next
    "Polar method for normal deviates, Knuth vol. 2, pp. 104, 113"
    | v1 v2 s rand u |
    rand ← Uniform from: −1.0 to: 1.0.
    [v1 ← rand next.
    v2 ← rand next.
    s ← v1 squared + v2 squared.
    s > = 1] whileTrue.
    u ← (−2.0 * s ln / s) sqrt.
    ↑mu + (sigma * v1 * u)

probability functions

density: x
```
| twoPi t |
twoPi ← 2 * 3.1415926536.
t ← x − mu / sigma.
↑(−0.5 * t squared) exp / (sigma * twoPi sqrt)
```

private

setMean: m standardDeviation: s
```
mu ← m.
sigma ← s
```

In subsequent chapters, we define and provide examples of using class descriptions that support discrete, event-driven simulation. The probability distributions defined in the current chapter will be used throughout the example simulations.

23

Event-Driven Simulations

A simulation is a representation of a system of objects in a real or fantasy world. The purpose of creating a computer simulation is to provide a framework in which to understand the simulated situation, for example, to understand the behavior of a waiting line, the workload of clerks, or the timeliness of service to customers. Certain kinds of simulations are referred to as "counter simulations." They represent situations for which there are places or counters in which clerks work. Customers arrive at a place in order to get service from a clerk. If a clerk is not available, the customer enters a waiting line. The first customer in the line is serviced by the next available clerk. Often a given simulation has several kinds of places and several customers, each with an agenda of places to visit. There are many examples of such situations: banks, car washes, barber shops, hospitals, cafeterias, airports, post offices, amusement parks, and factories. A computer simulation makes it possible to collect statistics about these situations, and to test out new ideas about their organization.

The objects that participate in a counter simulation operate more or less independently of one another. So, it is necessary to consider the problem of coordinating or synchronizing the activities of the various simulated objects. They typically coordinate their actions through the mechanism of message passing. Some objects, however, must synchronize their actions at certain critical moments; some objects can not proceed to carry out their desired actions without access to specific resources that may be unavailable at a given moment. The Smalltalk-80 system classes, Process, Semaphore, and SharedQueue, provide synchronization facilities for otherwise independent activities. To support a general description of counter simulations, mechanisms are needed for coordinating

- the use of fixed-size resources,

- the use of fluctuating resources, and

- the appearance of simultaneity in the actions of two objects.

Fixed resources can either be *consumable* or *nonconsumable*. For example, jelly beans are consumable, fixed resources of a candy store; books are non-consumable resources of a library. Fluctuating resources are typically referred to as *renewable* or producer/consumer synchronized. A store can model its supply of jelly beans as a fluctuating resource because the supply can be renewed. One can also imagine a resource that is both renewable and nonconsumable. Such a resource might be modeled in a simulation of car rentals: cars are renewable resources since new ones are manufactured and added to the available supply of cars to rent; the cars are also nonconsumable because a rented car is returned to the dealer for use by other customers. Actually, most nonconsumable resources are consumable, for example, library books eventually become too tattered for continued circulation; the rental cars eventually get junked. "Nonconsumable" means, minimally, that they are not consumed during the period of interest in the simulation.

When the actions of two objects in a simulation must be synchronized to give the appearance of carrying out a task together, the two objects are said to be in a server/client relationship. For example, a doctor needs the cooperation of the patient in order to carry out an examination. The server is a *coordinated* resource; it is a simulation object whose tasks can only be carried out when one or more clients request the resource.

An important aspect of simulations is that they model situations that change over time; customers enter and leave a bank; cars enter, get washed, get dried, and leave a car wash; airplanes land, unload passengers, load passengers, and take off from airports. It is often the case that these activities are time-related; at certain times or with certain intervals of time, events occur. Therefore, actions have to be synchronized with some notion of time. Often this notion of time is itself simulated.

There are a number of ways in which to represent the actions of simulated objects with respect to real or simulated time. In one approach, the clock runs in its usual manner. At each tick of the clock, all objects are given the opportunity to take any desired action. The clock acts as a synchronization device for the simulation, providing the opportunity to give the appearance of parallelism since the clock waits until all actions appropriate at the given time are completed. Often, no actions will take place at a given tick of the clock.

Alternatively, the clock can be moved forward according to the time at which the next action will take place. In this case, the system is driven by the next discrete action or event scheduled to occur. The implementation of a simulation using this approach depends on maintaining a queue of events, ordered with respect to simulated time. Each time an event is completed, the next one is taken from the queue and the clock is moved to the designated time.

The simulations presented in this chapter are based on this *event-driven* approach. They include simulations in which a collection of independent objects exist, each with a set of tasks to do (services or resources to obtain), and each needing to coordinate its activity's times with other objects in the simulated situation.

This chapter describes a framework in which such simulations can be developed. The class SimulationObject describes a general kind of object that might appear in a simulation, that is, one with a set of tasks to do. The message protocol of the class provides a framework in which the tasks are carried out. An instance of class Simulation maintains the simulated clock and the queue of events. The specification of the arrival of new objects into the system (objects such as customers) and the specification of resources (such as the clerks) are coordinated in this class.

The next chapter, Chapter 24, deals with ways to collect the data generated in running a simulation. Statistics gathering can be handled by providing a general mechanism in subclasses of class Simulation and/or class SimulationObject. Alternatively, each example simulation can provide its own mechanism for collecting information about its behavior.

Chapter 25 describes example simulations that make use of two kinds of synchronizations, shared use of fixed resources and shared use of fluctuating resources; Chapter 26 introduces additional support for coordination between two simulation objects—those wanting service and those providing service.

A Framework for Simulations

This section contains a description of the classes that provide the basic protocol for classes SimulationObject and Simulation. These classes are presented twice. First, a description of the protocol is given with an explanation of how to create a default example; second, an implementation of these classes is given.

Simulation Objects

Consider simulating a car wash. Major components of a car wash are washing places, drying places, paying places, washers, dryers, cashiers, and vehicles of different sorts such as trucks and cars. We can classify these components according to behavior. Major classifications are: places, where workers are located and work is performed; workers, such as washers, dryers, and cashiers; and the vehicles that are the customers of the places. These classifications might be translated into three classes of Smalltalk objects: Place, Worker, and Customer. But each of these classes of objects is similar in that each describes objects that have tasks to do—a Customer requests service, a Worker gives service, and a Place provides resources. In particular, a Place provides a waiting queue for the times when there are more customers than its workers can handle. These similarities are modeled in the superclass SimulationObject, which describes objects that appear in a simulated situation; a SimulationObject is any object that can be given a sequence of tasks to do. Each object defines a main sequence of activity that is initiated when the object enters the simulation. For example, the activities of a car in a car wash are to request a washer, wait while being washed, request a dryer, wait while being dried, pay for the service, and leave.

Class SimulationObject specifies a general control sequence by which the object enters, carries out its tasks, and leaves the simulation. This sequence consists of sending the object the messages startUp, tasks, and finishUp. Initialization of descriptive variables is specified as the response to message initialize. These messages are invoked by the method associated with startUp. Response to the messages tasks and initialize are implemented by subclasses of SimulationObject.

SimulationObject instance protocol

initialization	
initialize	Initialize instance variables, if any.
simulation control	
startUp	Initialize instance variables. Inform the simulation that the receiver is entering it, and then initiate the receiver's tasks.
tasks	Define the sequence of activities that the receiver must carry out.
finishUp	The receiver's tasks are completed. Inform the simulation.

There are several messages that any SimulationObject can use in order to describe its tasks. One is holdFor: aTimeDelay, where the argument aTimeDelay is some amount of simulated time for which the object delays further action. The idea of this delay is to create a period of time in which the object is presumably carrying out some activity.

We call the category of these messages, the modeler's task language to indicate that these are the messages sent to a SimulationObject as part of the implementation of the message tasks.

A simulation can contain simple or *static* resources, like "jelly beans," that can be acquired by a simulation object. Or a simulation can consist of *coordinated* resources, that is, simulation objects whose tasks must be synchronized with the tasks of other simulation objects. The task language includes messages for accessing each kind of resource, either to get or to give the resource.

There are 4 kinds of messages for static resources. There are 2 messages for getting an amount of the resource named resourceName. They are

    acquire: amount ofResource: resourceName
    acquire: amount ofResource: resourceName withPriority: priorityInteger

There is one for giving an amount of the resource named resourceName,

    produce: amount ofResource: resourceName

and one for giving up an acquired static resource,

    release: aStaticResource

There are also 3 kinds of messages for coordinated resources. The message for getting the resource named resourceName (here, the resource is a SimulationObject that models a kind of customer, and the asker is a server such as a clerk) is

>   acquireResource: resourceName

To produce the resource named resourceName (the asker is a customer), the message is

>   produceResource: resourceName

and to give up an acquired resource (which is a SimulationObject whose task events can now be resumed), the message is

>   resume: anEvent

When a SimulationObject makes a static resource request, it can do so by stating the level of importance of the request. The number 0 represents the last important request, successively higher numbers represent successively higher levels of importance. The message acquire:ofResource: assumes a priority level of 0; acquire:ofResource:with Priority: specifies particular levels in its third argument.

Two queries check whether a static resource is in the simulation and how much of the resource is available. These are resourceAvailable: resourceName, which answers whether or not the simulation has a resource referred to by the String, resourceName; and inquireFor: amount ofResource: resourceName, which answers whether there is at least amount of the resource remaining.

When a SimulationObject is synchronizing its tasks with that of another SimulationObject, it might be useful to know whether such an object is available. Two additional inquiry messages support finding out whether a provider or requester of a coordinated task is available—numberOfProvidersOfResource: resourceName and numberOf-RequestersOfResource: resourceName.

In addition, a message to a SimulationObject can request that the Simulation it is in stop running. This is the message stopSimulation.

SimulationObject instance protocol
_____

task language
   holdFor: aTimeDelay   Delay carrying out the receiver's next task until aTimeDelay amount of simulated time has passed.

acquire: amount ofResource: resourceName

> Ask the simulation to provide a simple resource that is referred to by the String, resourceName. If one exists, ask it to give the receiver amount of resources. If one does not exist, notify the simulation user (programmer) that an error has occurred.

acquire: amount ofResource: resourceName withPriority: priorityNumber

> Ask the simulation to provide a simple resource that is referred to by the String, resourceName. If one exists, ask it to give the receiver amount of resources, taking into account that the priority for acquiring the resource is to be set as priorityNumber. If one does not exist, notify the simulation user (programmer) that an error has occurred.

produce: amount ofResource: resourceName

> Ask the simulation to provide a simple resource that is referred to by the String, resourceName. If one exists, add to it amount more of its resources. If one does not exist, create it.

release: aStaticResource

> The receiver has been using the resource referred to by the argument, aStaticResource. It is no longer needed and can be recycled.

inquireFor: amount ofResource: resourceName

> Answer whether or not the simulation has at least a quantity, amount, of a resource referred to by the String, resourceName.

resourceAvailable: resourceName

> Answer whether or not the simulation has a resource referred to by the String, resourceName.

acquireResource: resourceName

> Ask the simulation to provide a resource simulation object that is referred to by the String, resourceName. If one exists, ask it to give the receiver its services. If one does not exist, notify the simulation user (programmer) that an error has occurred.

produceResource: resourceName

> Have the receiver act as a resource that is referred to by the String, resourceName. Wait for another SimulationObject that provides service to (acquires) this resource.

resume: anEvent

> The receiver has been giving service to the resource referred to by the argument, anEvent. The service is completed so that the resource, a SimulationObject, can continue its tasks.

numberOfProvidersOfResource: resourceName

> Answer the number of SimulationObjects waiting to coordinate its tasks by acting as the resource referred to by the String, resourceName.

numberOfRequestersOfResource: resourceName

> Answer the number of SimulationObjects waiting to coordinate its tasks by acquiring the resource referred to by the String, resourceName.

stopSimulation	Tell the simulation in which the receiver is running to stop. All scheduled events are removed and nothing more can happen in the simulation.

The examples we present in subsequent chapters illustrate each message in the modeler's task language.

Simulations

The purpose of class Simulation is to manage the topology of simulation objects and to schedule actions to occur according to simulated time. Instances of class Simulation maintain a reference to a collection of SimulationObjects, to the current simulated time, and to a queue of events waiting to be invoked.

The unit of time appropriate to the simulation is saved in an instance variable and represented as a floating-point number. The unit might be milliseconds, minutes, days, etc. A simulation advances time by checking the queue to determine when the next event is scheduled to take place, and by setting its instance variable to the time associated with that next event. If the queue of events is empty, then the simulation terminates.

Simulation objects enter a simulation in response to one of several scheduling messages such as

scheduleArrivalOf: aSimulationObjectClass
     accordingTo: aProbabilityDistribution or
scheduleArrivalOf: aSimulationObject at: aTimeInteger.

These messages are sent to the simulation either at the time that the simulation is first initialized, in response to the message defineArrivalSchedule, or as part of the sequence of tasks that a SimulationObject carries out. The second argument of the first message, aProbabilityDistribution, is an instance of a probability distribution such as those defined in Chapter 21. In this chapter, we assume the availability of the definitions given in Chapter 21. The probability distribution defines the interval at which an instance of the first argument, aSimulationObjectClass, is to be created and sent the message startUp.

In addition, Simulation supports messages having to do with scheduling a particular sequence of actions. These are schedule: actionBlock at: timeInteger and schedule: actionBlock after: amountOfTime.

In order to define the resources in the simulation, the modeler can send the simulation one or more of two possible messages. Either

self produce: amount of: resourceName

where the second argument, resourceName, is a String that names a simple quantifiable resource available in the simulation; the first argument is the (additional) quantity of this resource to be made available.

Or

    self coordinate: resourceName

The argument, resourceName, is a String that names a resource that is to be provided by some objects in the simulation and requested by other objects. For example, the resource is car washing, the provider is a washer object and the requestor is a car object.

Simulation instance protocol

---

initialization

    initialize   Initialize the receiver's instance variables.

modeler's initialization language

    defineArrivalSchedule   Schedule simulation objects to enter the simulation at specified time intervals, typically based on probability distribution functions. This method is implemented by subclasses. It involves a sequence of messages to the receiver (i.e., to self) that are of the form
                                        schedule:at:, scheduleArrivalOf:at:,
                                        scheduleArrivalOf:accordingTo:, or
                                        scheduleArrivalOf:accordingTo:startingAt:.
                                    See the next category of messages for descriptions of these.

    defineResources   Specify the resources that are initially entered into the simulation. These typically act as resources to be acquired. This method is implemented by subclasses and involves a sequence of messages to the receiver (i.e., to self) of the form produce: amount of: resourceName.

modeler's task language

    produce: amount of: resourceName
                                    An additional quantity of amount of a resource referred to by the String, resourceName, is to be part of the receiver. If the resource does not as yet exist in the receiver, add it; if it already exists, increase its available quantity.

    coordinate: resourceName   Use of a resource referred to by the String, resourceName, is to be coordinated by the receiver.

    schedule: actionBlock after: timeDelayInteger
                                    Set up a program, actionBlock, that will be evaluated after a simulated amount of time, timeDelayInteger, passes.

    schedule: actionBlock at: timeInteger
                                    Schedule the sequence of actions (actionBlock) to occur at a particular simulated time, timeInteger.

    scheduleArrivalOf: aSimulationObject at: timeInteger
                                    Schedule the simulation object, aSimulationObject, to enter the simulation at a specified time, timeInteger.

scheduleArrivalOf: aSimulationObjectClass
accordingTo: aProbabilityDistribution

> Schedule simulation objects that are instances of aSimulationObjectClass to enter the simulation at specified time intervals, based on the probability distribution aProbabilityDistribution. The first such instance should be scheduled to enter now. See Chapter 21 for definitions of possible probability distributions.

scheduleArrivalOf: aSimulationObjectClass
accordingTo: aProbabilityDistribution
startingAt: timeInteger

> Schedule simulation objects that are instances of aSimulationObjectClass to enter the simulation at specified time intervals, based on the probability distribution aProbabilityDistribution. The first such instance should be scheduled to enter at time timeInteger.

Notice that in the above scheduling messages, scheduleArrivalOf:at: takes a SimulationObject instance as its first argument, while scheduleArrivalOf:accordingTo: takes a SimulationObject class. These messages are used differently; the first one can be used by the SimulationObject itself to reschedule itself, while the second is used to initiate the arrival of SimulationObjects into the system.

The protocol for Simulation includes several accessing messages. One, the message includesResourceFor: resourceName, can be sent by a SimulationObject in order to determine whether or not a resource having a given name exists in the simulation.

Simulation instance protocol
___

accessing
    includesResourceFor: resourceName

> Answer if the receiver has a resource that is referred to by the String, resourceName. If such a resource does not exist, then report an error.

    provideResourceFor: resourceName

> Answer a resource that is referred to by the String, resourceName.

    time

> Answer the receiver's current time.

The simulation control framework is like that of class SimulationObject. Initialization is handled by creating the Simulation and sending it the message startUp. Simulation objects and the scheduling of new objects create events that are placed in the event queue. Once initialized, the Simulation is made to run by sending it the message proceed until there are no longer any events in the queue.

In the course of running the simulation, objects will enter and exit. As part of the protocol for scheduling a simulation object, the object informs its simulation that it is entering or exiting. The corresponding messages are enter: anObject and exit: anObject. In response to these messages, statistics might be collected about simulation objects upon their entrance and their exit to the simulation. Or a subclass might choose to deny an object entrance to the simulation; or a subclass might choose to reschedule an object rather than let it leave the simulation.

Simulation instance protocol

---

simulation control
    startUp | Specify the initial simulation objects and the arrival schedule of new objects.

    proceed | This is a single event execution. The first event in the queue, if any, is removed, time is updated to the time of the event, and the event is initiated.

    finishUp | Release references to any remaining simulation objects.

    enter: anObject | The argument, anObject, is informing the receiver that it is entering.

    exit: anObject | The argument, anObject, is informing the receiver that it is exiting.

Of the above messages, the default responses in class Simulation are mostly to do nothing. In particular, the response to messages enter: and exit: are to do nothing. Messages defineArrivalSchedule and defineResources also do nothing. As a result, the message startUp accomplishes nothing. These messages provide the framework that subclasses are to use—a subclass is created that overrides these messages in order to add simulation-specific behavior.

A "Default" Example: NothingAtAll

Unlike many of the system class examples of earlier chapters, the superclasses Simulation and SimulationObject typically do not implement their basic messages as

    self subclassResponsibility

By not doing so, instances of either of these classes can be successfully created. These instances can then be used as part of a basic or a "default" simulation that serves as a skeletal example. As we have seen, such simulation objects are scheduled to do nothing and consist of no events. Development of more substantive simulations can proceed by gradual refinement of these defaults. With a running, default example, the designer/programmer can incrementally modify and test the simulation, replacing the uninteresting instances of the superclasses with instances of appropriate subclasses. The example simulation NothingAtAll illustrates the idea of a "default" simulation.

Suppose we literally do nothing other than to declare the class NothingAtAll as a subclass of Simulation. A NothingAtAll has no initial resources since it does nothing in response to the message defineResources. And it has no simulation objects arriving at various intervals, because it does nothing in response to the message defineArrivalSchedule. Now we execute the following statement.

NothingAtAll new startUp proceed

The result is that an instance of NothingAtAll is created and sent the message startUp. It is a simulation with no resources and no objects scheduled, so the queue of events is empty. In response to the message proceed, the simulation determines that the queue is empty and does nothing.

As a modification of the description of NothingAtAll, we specify a response to the message defineArrivalSchedule. In it, the objects scheduled for arrival are instances of class DoNothing. DoNothing is created simply as a subclass of SimulationObject. A DoNothing has no tasks to carry out, so as soon as it enters the simulation, it leaves.

class name	DoNothing
superclass	SimulationObject
instance methods	

no new methods

class name	NothingAtAll
superclass	Simulation
instance methods	

initialization

defineArrivalSchedule
    self scheduleArrivalOf: DoNothing
      accordingTo: (Uniform from: 1 to: 5)

This version of NothingAtAll might represent a series of visitors entering an empty room, looking around without taking time to do so, and leaving. The probability distribution, Uniform, in the example in this chapter is assumed to be the one specified in Chapter 21. According to the above specification, new instances of class DoNothing should arrive in the simulation every 1 to 5 units of simulated time starting at time 0. The following expressions, when evaluated, create the simulation, send it the message startUp, and then iteratively send it the message proceed.

aSimulation ← NothingAtAll new startUp.
20 timesRepeat: [aSimulation proceed].

The message startUp invokes the message defineArrivalSchedule which schedules instances of DoNothing. Each time the message proceed is sent to the simulation, a DoNothing enters or exits. Evaluation might result in the following sequence of events. The time of each event is shown on the left and a description of the event is shown on the right.

0.0	a DoNothing enters
0.0	a DoNothing exits
3.21	a DoNothing enters
3.21	a DoNothing exits
7.76	a DoNothing enters
7.76	a DoNothing exits

and so on.

We can now make the simulation more interesting by scheduling the arrival of more kinds of simulation objects, ones that have tasks to do. We define Visitor to be a SimulationObject whose task is to enter the empty room and look around, taking between 4 and 10 simulated units to do so, that is, a random amount determined by evaluating the expression (Uniform from: 4 to: 10) next.

class name	Visitor
superclass	SimulationObject
instance methods	

simulation control

tasks
    self holdFor: (Uniform from: 4.0 to: 10.0) next

NothingAtAll is now defined as

class name	NothingAtAll
superclass	Simulation
instance methods	

initialization

defineArrivalSchedule
    self scheduleArrivalOf: DoNothing
        accordingTo: (Uniform from: 1 to: 5).
    self scheduleArrivalOf: Visitor
        accordingTo: (Uniform from: 4 to: 8)
        startingAt: 3

Two kinds of objects enter the simulation, one that takes no time to look around (a DoNothing) and one that visits a short while (a Visitor). Execution of

aSimulation ← NothingAtAll new startUp.
20 timesRepeat: [aSimulation proceed].

might result in the following sequence of events.

0.0	a DoNothing enters
0.0	a DoNothing exits
3.0	a Visitor enters
3.21	a DoNothing enters
3.21	a DoNothing exits
7.76	a DoNothing enters
7.76	a DoNothing exits
8.23	a (the first) Visitor exits after 5.23 seconds

and so on.

Implementation of the Simulation Classes

In order to trace the way in which the sequence of events occurs in the examples provided so far, it is necessary to show an implementation of the two classes. The implementations illustrate the control of multiple independent processes in the Smalltalk-80 system that were described in Chapter 15.

Class SimulationObject

Every SimulationObject created in the system needs access to the Simulation in which it is functioning. Such access is necessary, for example, in order to send messages that inform the simulation that an object is entering or exiting. In order to support such access, Simulation responds to the message active. The tasks for any subclass of SimulationObject send messages to Simulation active in order to ask the simulation for information, to get resources, or to produce resources.

class name	SimulationObject
superclass	Object

instance creation

new
    ↑super new initialize

The simulation control framework, sometimes referred to as the "life cycle" of the object, involves the sequence startUp—tasks—finishUp. When the SimulationObject first arrives at the simulation, it is sent the message startUp.

instance methods

initialization

initialize

"Do nothing. Subclasses will initialize instance variables."
↑ self

simulation control

startUp

Simulation active enter: self.
"First tell the simulation that the receiver is beginning to do my tasks."
self tasks.
self finishUp.

tasks

"Do nothing. Subclasses will schedule activities."
↑ self

finishUp

"Tell the simulation that the receiver is done with its tasks."
Simulation active exit: self.

The category **task language** consists of messages the modeler can use in specifying the SimulationObject's sequence of actions. The object might hold for an increment of simulated time (holdFor:). The object might try to acquire access to another simulation object that is playing the role of a resource (acquire:ofResource:). Or the object might determine whether a resource is available (resourceAvailable:).

task language

holdFor: aTimeDelay

Simulation active delayFor: aTimeDelay

acquire: amount ofResource: resourceName

"Get the resource and then tell it to acquire amount of it. Answers an instance of StaticResource"
↑(Simulation active provideResourceFor: resourceName)
acquire: amount
withPriority: 0

acquire: amount
ofResource: resourceName
withPriority: priority

↑(Simulation active provideResourceFor: resourceName)
acquire: amount
withPriority: priority

produce: amount ofResource: resourceName

Simulation active produce: amount of: resourceName

release: aWaitingSimulationObject
↑aWaitingSimulationObject

inquireFor: amount ofResource: resourceName
↑(Simulation active provideResourceFor: resourceName)
amountAvailable > = amount

resourceAvailable: resourceName
"Does the active simulation have a resource with this attribute available?"
↑Simulation active includesResourceFor: resourceName

acquireResource: resourceName
↑(Simulation active provideResourceFor: resourceName)
acquire

produceResource: resourceName
↑(Simulation active provideResourceFor: resourceName)
producedBy: self

resume: anEvent
↑anEvent resume

numberOfProvidersOfResource: resourceName
| resource |
resource ← Simulation active provideResourceFor: resourceName.
resource serversWaiting
ifTrue: [↑resource queueLength]
ifFalse: [↑0]

numberOfRequestersOfResource: resourceName
| resource |
resource ← Simulation active provideResourceFor: resourceName.
resource customersWaiting
ifTrue: [↑resource queueLength]
ifFalse: [↑0]

stopSimulation
Simulation active finishUp

A Simulation stores a Set of resources. In the case of static resources, instances of class ResourceProvider are stored; in the case of resources that consist of tasks coordinated among two or more simulation objects, instances of ResourceCoordinator are stored.

When a SimulationObject requests a static resource (acquire:ofResource:) and that request succeeds, then the SimulationObject is given an instance of class Resource. A Resource refers to the resource that created it and the quantity of the resource it represents. Given the methods shown for class SimulationObject, we can see that a resource responds to the message amountAvailable to return the currently available quantity of the resource that the SimulationObject might acquire. This message is sent in the method associated with inquireFor:ofResource:.

In the methods associated with SimulationObject messages acquire:of-Resource: and acquire:ofResource:withPriority:, a ResourceProvider is obtained and sent the message acquire: amount withPriority: priorityNumber. The result of this message is an instance of class StaticResource. However, if the amount is not available, the process in which the request was made will be suspended until the necessary resources become available. A StaticResource is sent the message release in order to recycle the acquired resource.

When a SimulationObject requests a coordinated resource (acquireResource:) and that request succeeds, then the object co-opts another simulation object acting as the resource (the object in need of service) until some tasks (services) are completed. If such a resource is not available, the process in which the request was made will be suspended until the necessary resources become available. Instances of class ResourceCoordinator understand messages acquire in order to make the request to coordinate service tasks and producedBy: aSimulationObject in order to specify that the argument is to be co-opted by another object in order to synchronize activities. As indicated by the implementation of SimulationObject, a ResourceCoordinator can answer queries such as customersWaiting or serversWaiting to determine if resources (customers) or service givers (servers) are waiting to coordinate their activities, and queueLength to say how many are waiting.

Explanations of the implementations of classes ResourceProvider and ResourceCoordinator are provided in Chapters 25 and 26.

Class DelayedEvent

The implementation of a scheduling mechanism for class Simulation makes extensive use of the Smalltalk-80 processor scheduler classes presented in the chapter on multiple processes (Chapter 15). There are several problems that have to be solved in the design of class Simulation. First, how do we store an event that must be delayed for some increment of simulated time? Second, how do we make certain that all processes initiated at a particular time are completed before changing the clock? And third, in terms of the solutions to the first two problems, how do we implement the request to repeatedly schedule a sequence of actions, in particular, instantiation and initiation of a particular kind of SimulationObject?

In order to solve the first problem, the Simulation maintains a queue of all the scheduled events. This queue is a SortedCollection whose elements are the events, sorted with respect to the simulated time in which they must be invoked. Each event on the queue is placed there within a package that is an instance of class DelayedEvent. At the time the package is created, the event is the system's active process. As such, it can be stored with its needed running context by creating a Semaphore. When the event is put on the queue, the DelayedEvent is sent the message pause which sends its Semaphore the message wait; when the event is taken off the queue, it is continued by sending it the message resume. The method associated with resume sends the DelayedEvent's Semaphore the message signal.

The protocol for instances of class DelayedEvent consists of five messages.

DelayedEvent instance protocol
_____

accessing

    condition   Answer a condition under which the event should be sequenced.

    condition: anObject   Set the argument, anObject, to be the condition under which the event should be sequenced.

scheduling

    pause   Suspend the current active process, that is, the current event that is running.

    resume   Resume the suspended process.

comparing

    < = aDelayedEvent   Answer whether the receiver should be sequenced before the argument, aDelayedEvent.

A DelayedEvent is created by sending the class the message new or onCondition: anObject. The implementation of class DelayedEvent is given next.

class name	DelayedEvent
superclass	Object
instance variable names	resumptionSemaphore resumptionCondition
class methods	

instance creation

    new
        ↑super new initialize
    onCondition: anObject
        ↑super new setCondition: anObject

instance methods

accessing

    condition
        ↑resumptionCondition
    condition: anObject
        resumptionCondition ← anObject

comparing

    < = aDelayedEvent
        resumptionCondition isNil
            ifTrue: [↑true]
            ifFalse: [↑resumptionCondition < = aDelayedEvent condition]

scheduling

pause
> Simulation active stop process.
> resumptionSemaphore wait

resume
> Simulation active start process.
> resumptionSemaphore signal.
> ↑resumptionCondition

private

initialize
> resumptionSemaphore ← Semaphore new

setCondition: anObject
> self initialize.
> resumptionCondition ← anObject

According to the above specification, any object used as a resumption condition must respond to the message < =.

Class Simulation

Instances of class Simulation own four instance variables: a Set of objects that act as resources of the simulation (resources), a Number representing the current time (currentTime), a SortedCollection representing a queue of delayed events (eventQueue), and an Integer denoting the number of processes active at the current time (processCount). A class variable maintains reference to the currently active Simulation, allowing multiple instances to exist but only one in control at a time.

Initialization of a Simulation sets the instance variables to initial values. When the instance is sent the scheduling message startUp, it sends itself the message activate which informs interested other classes which Simulation is now the active one.

class name	Simulation
superclass	Object
instance variable names	resources currentTime
	eventQueue processCount
class variable names	RunningSimulation
class methods	

instance creation

new
> ↑super new initialize

accessing

active

> ↑ RunningSimulation

instance methods

initialization

initialize
resources ← Set new.
currentTime ← 0.0.
processCount ← 0.
eventQueue ← SortedCollection new

activate
"This instance is now the active simulation."
Running Simulation ← self.

Initialization messages are also needed by the subclasses. The messages provided for the modeler to use in specifying arrival schedules and resource objects provides an interface to the process scheduling messages.

defineArrivalSchedule
"A subclass specifies the schedule by which simulation objects dynamically enter into the simulation."
↑self
defineResources
"A subclass specifies the simulation objects that are initially entered into the simulation."
↑self

task language

produce: amount of: resourceName
(self includesResourceFor: resourceName)
  ifTrue: [(self provideResourceFor: resourceName) produce: amount]
  ifFalse: [resources add:
       (ResourceProvider named: resourceName with: amount)]
coordinate: resourceName
(self includesResourceFor: resourceName)
  ifFalse: [resources add:
       (ResourceCoordinator named: resourceName)]
schedule: actionBlock after: timeDelayInteger
self schedule: actionBlock at: currentTime + timeDelayInteger
schedule: aBlock at: timeInteger
"This is the mechanism for scheduling a single action"
self newProcessFor:
  [self delayUntil: timeInteger.
  aBlock value]
scheduleArrivalOf: aSimulationObject at: timeInteger
self schedule: [aSimulationObject startUp] at: timeInteger

scheduleArrivalOf: aSimulationObjectClass
accordingTo: aProbabilityDistribution
    "This means start now"
    self scheduleArrivalOf: aSimulationObjectClass
        accordingTo: aProbabilityDistribution
        startingAt: currentTime

scheduleArrivalOf: aSimulationObjectClass
accordingTo: aProbabilityDistribution
startingAt: timeInteger
    "Note that aSimulationObjectClass is the class SimulationObject or
    one of its subclasses. The real work is done in the private message
    schedule:startingAt:andThenEvery:"
    self schedule: [aSimulationObjectClass new startUp]
        startingAt: timeInteger
        andThenEvery: aProbabilityDistribution

[Note, to define produce:of: and coordinate: first define classes ResourceProvider (page 512) and ResourceCoordinator (page 543), respectively.]

The scheduling messages of the task language implement a reference-counting solution to keeping track of initiated processes. This is the technique used to solve the second problem cited earlier, that is, how to make certain that all processes initiated for a particular time are carried out by the single Smalltalk-80 processor scheduler before a different process gets the opportunity to change the clock. Using reference counting, we guarantee that simulated time does not change unless the reference count is zero.

The key methods are the ones associated with schedule: aBlock at: timeInteger and schedule: aBlock startingAt: timeInteger andThenEvery: aProbabilityDistribution. This second message is a private one called by the method associated with scheduleArrivalOf: aSimulationObjectClass accordingTo: aProbabilityDistribution startingAt: timeInteger. It provides a general mechanism for scheduling repeated actions and therefore represents a solution to the third design problem mentioned earlier, how we implement the request to repeatedly schedule a sequence of actions.

The basic idea for the schedule: aBlock at: timeInteger is to create a process in which to delay the evaluation of the sequence of actions (aBlock) until the simulation reaches the appropriate simulated time (timeInteger). The delay is performed by the message delayUntil: delayedTime. The associated method creates a DelayedEvent to be added to the simulation's event queue. The process associated with this DelayedEvent is then suspended (by sending it the message pause). When this instance of DelayedEvent is the first in the queue, it will be removed and the time will be bumped to the stored (delayed) time. Then this instance of DelayedEvent will be sent the message resume which will cause the evaluation of the block; the action of this block is to schedule some simulation activity.

A process that was active is suspended when the DelayedEvent is signaled to wait. Therefore, the count of the number of processes must be decremented (stopProcess). When the DelayedEvent resumes, the process continues evaluation with the last expression in the method delayedUntil:; therefore the count of the number of processes must be incremented (startProcess).

scheduling

delayUntil: aTime
    | delayEvent |
    delayEvent ← DelayedEvent onCondition: aTime.
    eventQueue add: delayEvent.
    delayEvent pause.

delayFor: timeDelay
    self delayUntil: currentTime + timeDelay

startProcess
    processCount ← processCount + 1

stopProcess
    processCount ← processCount − 1

Reference counting of processes is also handled in the method associated with class Simulation's scheduling message newProcessFor: aBlock. It is implemented as follows.

newProcessFor: aBlock
    self startProcess.
    [aBlock value.
     self stopProcess] fork

The first expression increments the count of processes. The second expression is a block that is forked. When the Smalltalk processor scheduler evaluates this block, the simulation sequence of actions, aBlock, is evaluated. The completion of evaluating aBlock signals the need to decrement the count of processes. In this way, a single sequence of actions is scheduled in the event queue of the Simulation and delayed until the correct simulated time. In summary, the reference count of processes increments whenever a new sequence of actions is initiated, decrements whenever a sequence completes, decrements whenever a DelayedEvent pauses, and increments whenever the DelayedEvent resumes.

The method for the private message schedule: aBlock startingAt: timeInteger andThenEvery: aProbabilityDistribution forks a process that repeatedly schedules actions. The algorithm consists of iterations of two messages,

self delayUntil: timeInteger.
self newProcessFor: aBlock

Repetition of the two messages delayUntil: and newProcessFor: depends on a probability distribution function. The number of repetitions equals the number of times the distribution can be sampled. The number that is sampled represents the next time that the sequence of actions (aBlock) should be invoked. Elements of the distribution are enumerated by sending the distribution the message do:.

private

schedule: aBlock
      startingAt: timeInteger
      andThenEvery: aProbabilityDistribution
    self newProcessFor:
      [" This is the first time to do the action."
      self delayUntil: timeInteger.
      "Do the action."
      self newProcessFor: aBlock copy.
      aProbabilityDistribution
        do: [:nextTimeDelay |
            "For each sample from the distribution,
            delay the amount sampled,"
            self delayFor: nextTimeDelay.
            "then do the action"
            self newProcessFor: aBlock copy]]

Simulation itself has a control framework similar to that of SimulationObject. The response to startUp is to make the simulation the currently active one and then to define the simulation objects and arrival schedule. The inner loop of scheduled activity is given as the response to the message proceed. Whenever the Simulation receives the message proceed, it checks the reference count of processes (by sending the message readyToContinue). If the reference count is not zero, then there are still processes active for the current simulated time. So, the system-wide processor, Processor, is asked to yield control and let these processes proceed. If the reference count is zero, then the event queue is checked. If it is not empty, the next event is removed from the event queue, time is changed, and the delayed process is resumed.

simulation control

startUp
    self activate.
    self defineResources.
    self defineArrivalSchedule

proceed
>| eventProcess |
>[self readyToContinue] whileFalse: [Processor yield].
>eventQueue isEmpty
>>ifTrue: [↑self finishUp]
>>ifFalse: [eventProcess ← eventQueue removeFirst.
>>>currentTime ← eventProcess condition.
>>>eventProcess resume]

finishUp
>"Empty out the event queue"
>eventQueue ← SortedCollection new.
>↑ nil

enter: anObject
>↑self

exit: anObject
>↑self

atEnd
>"Push the simulation to the point of readiness to continue and then
>answer whether it is ready to continue,"
>[self readyToContinue]
>whileFalse: [processor—yield].
>↑ eventQueue is empty.

private

readyToContinue
>↑processCount = 0

In addition to these various modeler's languages and simulation control
messages, several accessing messages are provided in the protocol of
Simulation.

accessing

includesResourceFor: resourceName
>| test |
>test ← resources
>>detect: [:each | each name = resourceName]
>>ifNone: [nil].
>↑test notNil

provideResourceFor: resourceName
>↑resources detect: [:each | each name = resourceName]

time
>↑currentTime

The implementations of Simulation and SimulationObject illustrate the
use of messages fork to a BlockContext, yield to a ProcessorScheduler,
and signal and wait to a Semaphore.

We can now trace the execution of the first example of the simulation, NothingAtAll, in which DoNothings only were scheduled. After sending the message

NothingAtAll new

the instance variables of the new simulation consist of

```
resources = Set ()
currentTime = 0.0
processCount = 0
eventQueue = SortedCollection ()
```

We then send this simulation the message startUp, which invokes the message scheduleArrivalOf: DoNothing accordingTo: (Uniform from: 1 to: 5). This is identical to sending the simulation the message

```
schedule: [DoNothing new startUp]
startingAt: 0.0
andThenEvery: (Uniform from: 1 to: 5)
```

The response is to call on newProcessFor:.

Step 1. newProcessFor: increments the processCount (self startProcess) and then creates a new Process that evaluates the following block, which will be referred to as block A.

```
[self delayUntil: timeInteger.
 self newProcessFor: block copy.
 aProbabilityDistribution do:
        [ :nextTimeDelay |
          self delayFor: nextTimeDelay.
          self newProcessFor: block copy]
```

where the variable block is

```
[DoNothing new startUp]
```

which will be referred to as block B.

Step 2. When the process returns to the second expression of the method newProcessFor:, execution continues by evaluating block A. Its first expression decrements the process count and suspends an activity until time is 0.0 (i.e., create a DelayedEvent for the active simulation scheduler to tell the DoNothing to startUp at time 0.0; put it on the event queue).

```
resources = Set ()
currentTime = 0.0
processCount = 0
eventQueue = SortedCollection (a DelayedEvent 0.0)
```

Now we send the simulation the message proceed. The process count is 0 so readyToContinue returns true; the event queue is not empty so the first DelayedEvent is removed, time is set to 0.0, and the delayed process is resumed (this was the scheduler block A). The next action increments the process count and evaluates block B. This lets a DoNothing enter and do its task, which is nothing, so it leaves immediately. The new processFor: message decrements the process count to 0, gets a number from the probability distribution, delays for this number of time units, and schedules a new process for some time later. The sequence continues indefinitely, as long as the message proceed is re-sent to the simulation.

Other tasks will enter the event queue depending on the method associated with the message tasks in a subclass of SimulationObject. Thus if Visitor is scheduled in NothingAtAll, then the expresson self holdFor: someTime will enter an event on the queue, intermingled with events that schedule new arrivals of Visitors and DoNothings.

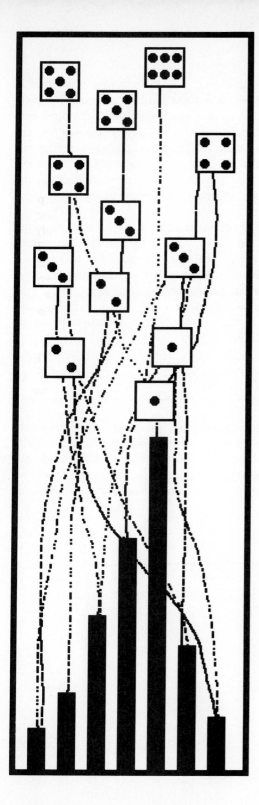

24

Statistics Gathering in Event-Driven Simulations

Duration Statistics

Throughput Histograms

Tallying Events

Event Monitoring

A framework for specifying event-driven simulations was presented in the previous chapter. This framework did not include methods for gathering statistics about a simulation as it is running. Statistics might consist of the amount of time each simulation object spends in the simulation (and, therefore, how well the model supports carrying out the kinds of tasks specified by the objects); information about the length of the queues such as the maximum, minimum and average lengths and amount of time spent in each queue; and information about the utilization of the simulation's resources.

There are a number of ways to add statistics gathering to class Simulation or class SimulationObject. In this chapter, we provide four examples of statistics gathering: duration statistics, throughput histograms, event tallying, and event monitoring. Each of these examples involves creating a subclass of Simulation or SimulationObject in order to provide a dictionary in which data can be stored or a file into which data can be written, and, in that subclass, modifying the appropriate methods in order to store the appropriate data.

Duration Statistics

For the first example of statistics gathering, we create a general subclass of Simulation that simply stores the time an object enters and exits the simulation. The times are kept in a special record whose fields are the time at which the object entered the simulation (entranceTime) and the length of time the object spent in the simulation (duration). Records are described as follows.

class name	SimulationObjectRecord
superclass	Object
instance variable names	entranceTime
	duration

instance methods

accessing

entrance: currentTime
    entranceTime ← currentTime
exit: currentTime
    duration ← currentTime − entranceTime
entrance
    ↑entranceTime
exit
    ↑entranceTime + duration
duration
    ↑duration

printing

printOn: aStream
>   entranceTime printOn: aStream.
>   aStream tab.
>   duration printOn: aStream

An example subclass of Simulation which uses SimulationObjectRecords for gathering statistics is StatisticsWithSimulation. It is defined as follows.

class name	StatisticsWithSimulation
superclass	Simulation
instance variable names	statistics
instance methods	

initialization

initialize
>   super initialize.
>   statistics ← Dictionary new

simulation scheduling

enter: anObject
>   statistics at: anObject
>   put: (SimulationObjectRecord new entrance: currentTime)

exit: anObject
>   (statistics at: anObject) exit: currentTime

statistics

printStatisticsOn: aStream
> | stat |
>   aStream cr.
>   aStream nextPutAll: 'Object'.
>   aStream tab.
>   aStream nextPutAll: 'Entrance Time'.
>   aStream tab.
>   aStream nextPutAll: 'Duration'.
>   aStream cr.
>   "Sort with respect to the time the object entered the simulation. Because the keys as well as the values are needed, it is necessary to first obtain the set of associations and then sort them."
>   stat ← SortedCollection
>   sortBlock: [:i :j | i value entrance <= j value entrance].
>   statistics associationsDo: [:each | stat add: each].

```
stat do:
    [ :anAssociation |
    aStream cr.
    anAssociation key printOn: aStream.
    aStream tab.
    anAssociation value printOn: aStream
    "The value is a SimulationObjectRecord which prints the entrance
    time and duration"]
```

Suppose we created NothingAtAll as a subclass of StatisticsWithSimulation. In this example, NothingAtAll schedules two simulation objects: one that does nothing (a DoNothing), arriving according to a uniform distribution from 3 to 5 units of time starting at 0; and one that looks around for 5 units of simulated time (a Visitor), arriving according to a uniform distribution from 5 to 10 units of time starting at 1. Whenever one of these objects enters the simulation, an entry is put in the statistics dictionary. The key is the object itself; the equals (=) test is the default (==), so each object is a unique key. The value is an instance of SimulationObjectRecord with entrance data initialized. When the object exits, the record associated with it is retrieved and a message is sent to it in order to set the exit data.

class name	DoNothing
superclass	SimulationObject
instance methods	

no new methods

class name	Visitor
superclass	SimulationObject
instance methods	

simulation control

tasks
```
self holdFor: 5
```

class name	NothingAtAll
superclass	StatisticsWithSimulation
instance methods	

initialization

defineArrivalSchedule
```
self scheduleArrivalOf: DoNothing
    accordingTo: (Uniform from: 3 to: 5).
self scheduleArrivalOf: Visitor
    accordingTo: (Uniform from: 5 to: 10)
    startingAt: 1
```

Whenever we halt the simulation, we can send the message printStatisticsOn: aFile (where aFile is a kind of FileStream). The result might look like:

Object	Entrance Time	Duration
a DoNothing	0.0	0.0
a Visitor	1.0	5.0
a DoNothing	4.58728	0.0
a Visitor	6.71938	5.0
a DoNothing	9.3493	0.0
a DoNothing	13.9047	0.0
a Visitor	16.7068	5.0
a DoNothing	17.1963	0.0
a DoNothing	21.7292	0.0
a Visitor	23.2563	5.0
a DoNothing	25.6805	0.0
a DoNothing	29.3202	0.0
a Visitor	32.1147	5.0
a DoNothing	32.686	0.0
a DoNothing	36.698	0.0
a DoNothing	41.1135	0.0
a Visitor	41.1614	5.0
a DoNothing	44.3258	0.0
a Visitor	48.4145	5.0
a DoNothing	48.492	0.0
a DoNothing	51.7833	0.0
a Visitor	53.5166	5.0
a DoNothing	56.4262	0.0
a DoNothing	60.5357	0.0
a Visitor	63.4532	5.0
a DoNothing	64.8572	0.0
a DoNothing	68.7634	0.0
a Visitor	68.921	5.0
a DoNothing	72.4788	0.0
a DoNothing	75.8567	0.0

Throughput Histograms

A common statistic gathered in simulations is the throughput of objects, that is, how many objects pass through the simulation in some amount of time; this is proportional to how much time each object spends in the simulation. Gathering such statistics involves keeping track of the number of objects that spend time within predetermined intervals of time. Reporting the results involves displaying the number of objects, the minimum time, maximum time, and the number of objects whose times fall within each specified interval. Such statistics are especially useful in simulations involving resources in order to determine whether or not there are sufficient resources to handle requests— if objects have to wait a long time to get a resource, then they must spend more time in the simulation.

In order to support the gathering of throughput statistics, we provide class Histogram. Histograms maintain a tally of values within prespecified ranges. For example, we might tally the number of times various values fall between 1 and 5, 5 and 10, 10 and 20, 20 and 25, 25 and 30, 30 and 35, 35 and 40, and 40 and 45. That is, we divide the interval 5 to 45 into bins of size 5 and keep a running count of the number of times a value is stored into each bin.

Class Histogram is created by specifying the lower bound, the upper bound, and the bin size. To obtain a Histogram for the above example, evaluate

Histogram from: 5 to: 45 by: 5

Besides data on the bins, a Histogram keeps track of minimum, maximum, and total values entered. An entry might not fit within the bounds of the interval; an additional variable is used to store all such entries (extraEntries). The bins are stored as elements of an array; the array size equals the number of bins (that is, upper bound - lower bound // bin size). The message store: aValue is used to put values in the Histogram. The index of the array element to be incremented is 1 + (aValue - lower bound // bins size). Most of the methods shown support printing the collected information.

class name	Histogram
superclass	Object
instance variable names	tallyArray
	lowerBound upperBound
	step
	minValue maxValue
	totalValues
	extraEntries
class methods	

class initialization

from: lowerNum to: upperNum by: step
   ↑self new newLower: lowerNum upper: upperNum by: step

instance methods

accessing

contains: aValue

↑lowerBound < = aValue and: [aValue < upperBound]

store: aValue

```
| index |
minValue isNil
    ifTrue: [minValue ← maxValue ← aValue]
    ifFalse: [minValue ← minValue min: aValue.
              maxValue ← maxValue max: aValue].
totalValues ← totalValues + aValue.
(self contains: aValue)
    ifTrue: [index ← (aValue - lowerBound // step) + 1.
            tallyArray at: index put: (tallyArray at: index) + 1]
    ifFalse: [extraEntries ← extraEntries + 1]
```

printing

printStatisticsOn: aStream

```
| totalObjs pos |
self firstHeader: aStream.
aStream cr; tab.
totalObjs ← extraEntries.
"count the number of entries the throughput records know"
tallyArray do: [ :each | totalObjs ← totalObjs + each].
totalObjs printOn: aStream.
aStream tab.
minValue printOn: aStream.
aStream tab.
maxValue printOn: aStream.
aStream tab.
(totalValues / totalObjs) asFloat printOn: aStream.
aStream cr.
self secondHeader: aStream.
aStream cr.
pos ← lowerBound.
tallyArray do:
    [ :entry |
      pos printOn: aStream.
      aStream nextPut: $—.
      (pos ← pos + step) printOn: aStream.
      aStream tab.
      entry printOn: aStream.
      aStream tab.
      (entry / totalObjs) asFloat printOn: aStream.
```

Statistics Gathering in Event-Driven Simulations

```
        aStream tab.
        aStream nextPut: $| .
        "print the X's"
        entry rounded timesRepeat: [aStream nextPut: $X].
        aStream cr]
```

firstHeader: aStream

```
    aStream cr; tab.
    aStream nextPutAll: 'Number of'.
    aStream tab.
    aStream nextPutAll: 'Minimum'.
    aStream tab.
    aStream nextPutAll: 'Maximum'.
    aStream tab.
    aStream nextPutAll: 'Average'.
    aStream cr; tab.
    aStream nextPutAll: 'Objects'.
    aStream tab.
    aStream nextPutAll: 'Value'.
    aStream tab.
    aStream nextPutAll: 'Value'.
    aStream tab.
    aStream nextPutAll: 'Value'
```

secondHeader: aStream

```
    aStream cr; tab.
    aStream nextPutAll: 'Number of'.
    aStream cr.
    aStream nextPutAll: 'Entry'.
    aStream tab.
    aStream nextPutAll: 'Objects'.
    aStream tab.
    aStream nextPutAll: 'Frequency'.
```

private

newLower: lowerNum upper: upperNum by: stepAmount

```
    tallyArray ← Array new: (upperNum − lowerNum // stepAmount).
    tallyArray atAllPut: 0.
    lowerBound ← lowerNum.
    upperBound ← upperNum.
    step ← stepAmount.
    minValue ← maxValue ← nil.
    totalValues ← 0.
    extraEntries ← 0
```

A simulation of visitors to a museum serves as an example of the use of a Histogram. Museum is like NothingAtAll in that Visitors arrive and look around. The Visitors take a varying amount of time to look around, depending on their interest in the museum artifacts. We assume that this time is normally distributed with a mean of 20 and a standard deviation of 5. Visitors come to the museum throughout the day, one every 5 to 10 units of simulated time.

class name	Museum
superclass	Simulation
instance variable names	statistics
instance methods	

initialization

initialize
```
super initialize.
statistics ← Histogram from: 5 to: 45 by: 5
```
defineArrivalSchedule
```
self scheduleArrivalOf: Visitor
    accordingTo: (Uniform from: 5 to: 10)
```

scheduling

exit: aSimulationObject
```
super exit: aSimulationObject.
statistics store: currentTime - aSimulationObject entryTime
```
printStatisticsOn: aStream
```
statistics printStatisticsOn: aStream
```

In order for class Museum to update the statistics, Visitors must keep track of when they entered the museum and be able to respond to an inquiry as to their time of entry.

class name	Visitor
superclass	SimulationObject
instance variable names	entryTime
instance methods	

initialization

initialize
```
super initialize.
entryTime ← Simulation active time
```

accessing

entryTime
```
↑entryTime
```

simulation control

tasks
```
self holdFor: (Normal mean: 20 deviation: 5) next
```

To create and run the simulation, we evaluate

    aSimulation ← Museum new startUp.
    [aSimulation time < 50] whileTrue: [aSimulation proceed]

When the Museum was created, a Histogram for statistics was created. Each time a Visitor left the Museum, data was stored in the Histogram. The data consists of the duration of the visit.

After running the simulation until time 50, we ask the Museum for a report.

    aSimulation printStatisticsOn: (FileStream fileNamed: 'museum.report')

The method associated with printStatisticsOn: sends the same message, printStatisticsOn:, to the Histogram, which prints the following information on the file museum.report.

Number of Objects	Minimum Value	Maximum Value	Average Value
64	10.0202	31.2791	20.152

Entry	Number of Objects	Frequency	
5-10	0	0	|
10-15	14	0.21875	| XXXXXXXXXXXXX
15-20	16	0.25	| XXXXXXXXXXXXXXX
20-25	20	0.3125	| XXXXXXXXXXXXXXXXXXX
25-30	13	0.203125	| XXXXXXXXXXXX
30-35	1	0.015625	| X
35-40	0	0	|
40-45	0	0	|

Tallying Events

As another example of tallying the events in a simulation, we present a commonly-used example of a simulation of Traffic. In this simulation, we tally the number of cars that enter an intersection, distinguishing those that drive straight through the intersection from those that turn left and those that turn right. By observation, we note that twice as many cars go straight as turn right or left, but twice as many turn left as right. A new car arrives at the intersection according to a uniform distribution every 0.5 to 2 units of time (self scheduleArrivalOf: Car accordingTo: (Uniform from: 0.5 to: 2)). We will run the simulation until simulated time exceeds 100.

class name	Traffic
superclass	Simulation
instance variable names	statistics
instance methods	

initialization

initialize
```
super initialize.
statistics ← Dictionary new: 3.
statistics at: #straight put: 0.
statistics at: #right put: 0.
statistics at: #left put: 0
```
defineArrivalSchedule
```
self scheduleArrivalOf: Car accordingTo: (Uniform from: 0.5 to: 2).
self schedule: [self finishUp] at: 100
```

statistics

update: key
```
statistics at: key put: (statistics at: key) + 1
```
printStatisticsOn: aStream
```
aStream cr.
aStream nextPutAll: 'Car Direction       Tally'.
statistics associationsDo:
    [ :assoc |
     aStream cr.
     assoc key printOn: aStream.
     aStream tab.
     assoc value printOn: aStream]
```

Note that in the method associated with defineArrivalSchedule, the action self finishUp is scheduled to occur at simulated time 100. This event will terminate the simulation as desired.

class name	Car
superclass	SimulationObject
instance methods	

simulation control

tasks
```
"Sample, without replacement, the direction through the intersection that
the car will travel."
| sample |
sample ← SampleSpace data:
                #(left left right straight straight straight
                    straight straight straight).
Simulation active update: sample next
```

SampleSpace was a class we introduced in Chapter 21. Cars are scheduled to enter the simulation with the sole task of picking a direction to tell the simulation. After running the simulation, we ask the Traffic simulation to report the tallies by sending it the printStatisticsOn: message. A possible outcome of evaluating

aSimulation ← Traffic new startUp.
[aSimulation proceed notNil] whileTrue.
aSimulation printStatisticsOn: (FileStream fileNamed: 'traffic.data')

is the following information written on the file traffic.data.

Car Direction	Tally
straight	57
right	8
left	15

Event Monitoring

Another possible technique for gathering data from a simulation is to note the occurrence of each (major) event, including the entering and exiting of simulation objects. This is accomplished by creating a subclass of SimulationObject that we call EventMonitor. In this example, a class variable refers to a file onto which notations about their events can be stored. Each message that represents an event to be monitored must be overridden in the subclass to include the instructions for storing information on the file. The method in the superclass is still executed by distributing the message to the pseudo-variable super.

Basically, the notations consist of the time and identification of the receiver (a kind of SimulationObject), and an annotation such as "enters" or "requests" or "releases."

class name	EventMonitor
superclass	SimulationObject
class variable names	DataFile
class methods	

class initialization

file: aFile
    DataFile ← aFile

instance methods

scheduling

startUp

    self timeStamp.
    DataFile nextPutAll: ' enters '.
    super startUp

finishUp

    super finishUp.
    self timeStamp.
    DataFile nextPutAll: ' exits '

task language

holdFor: aTimeDelay

    self timeStamp.
    DataFile nextPutAll: ' holds for '.
    aTimeDelay printOn: DataFile.
    super holdFor: aTimeDelay

acquire: amount ofResource: resourceName

    | waiting |
    "Store fact that resource is being requested."
    self timeStamp.
    DataFile nextPutAll: ' requests '.
    amount printOn: DataFile.
    DataFile nextPutAll: ' of ', resourceName.
    "Now try to get the resource."
    waiting ← super acquire: amount
                    ofResource: resourceName.
    "Returns here when resource is obtained; store the fact."
    self timeStamp.
    DataFile nextPutAll: ' obtained '.
    amount printOn: DataFile.
    DataFile nextPutAll: ' of ', resourceName.
    ↑ waiting

acquire: amount
ofResource: resourceName
withPriority: priorityNumber

    | waiting |
    "Store fact that resource is being requested"
    self timeStamp.
    DataFile nextPutAll: ' requests '.
    amount printOn: DataFile.
    DataFile nextPutAll: ' at priority '.
    priorityNumber printOn: DataFile.
    DataFile nextPutAll: ' of ', resourceName.

```
"Now try to get the resource."
waiting ←
    super acquire: amount
            ofResource: resourceName
            withPriority: priorityNumber.
"Returns here when resource is obtained; store the fact."
self timeStamp.
DataFile nextPutAll: 'obtained '.
amount printOn: DataFile.
DataFile nextPutAll: 'of ', resourceName.
↑ waiting
```

produce: amount ofResource: resourceName

```
self timeStamp.
DataFile nextPutAll: 'produces '.
amount printOn: DataFile.
DataFile nextPutAll: 'of ', resourceName.
super produce: amount ofResource: resourceName
```

release: waiting

```
self timeStamp.
DataFile nextPutAll: 'releases '.
waiting amount printOn: DataFile.
DataFile nextPutAll: 'of', waiting
super release: waiting
```

acquireResource: resourceName

```
| anEvent |
"Store fact that resource is being requested"
self timeStamp.
DataFile nextPutAll: 'wants to serve for '.
DataFile nextPutAll: resourceName.
"Now try to get the resource."
anEvent ← super acquireResource: resourceName.
"Returns here when resource is obtained; store the fact."
self timeStamp.
DataFile nextPutAll: 'can serve '.
anEvent resource printOn: DataFile.
↑anEvent
```

produceResource: resourceName

```
self timeStamp.
DataFile nextPutAll: 'wants to get service as '.
DataFile nextPutAll: resourceName.
super produceResource: resourceName
```

resume: anEvent

```
self timeStamp.
DataFile nextPutAll: 'resumes '.
```

anEvent resource printOn: DataFile.
super resume: anEvent

private

timeStamp
DataFile cr.
Simulation active time printOn: DataFile.
DataFile tab.
self printOn: DataFile.

We can monitor the events of the NothingAtAll simulation consisting of arrivals of Visitors and default simulations (DoNothings). Except for creating Visitor and DoNothing as subclassses of EventMonitor rather than of SimulationObject, the class definitions are the same.

class name	DoNothing
superclass	EventMonitor
instance methods	

no new methods

class name	Visitor
superclass	EventMonitor
instance methods	

simulation control

tasks
self holdFor: (Uniform from: 4.0 to: 10.0) next

NothingAtAll is redefined with a new arrival schedule.

class name	NothingAtAll
superclass	Simulation
instance methods	

initialization

defineArrivalSchedule
self scheduleArrivalOf: DoNothing
accordingTo: (Uniform from: 1 to: 5).
self scheduleArrivalOf: Visitor
accordingTo: (Uniform from: 4 to: 8)
startingAt: 3

After executing

Statistics Gathering in Event-Driven Simulations

Visitor file: (FileStream fileNamed: 'NothingAtAll.events').
                                   "This informs DoNothing too"
aSimulation ← NothingAtAll new startUp.
[aSimulation time < 25] whileTrue: [aSimulation proceed]

the file 'NothingAtAll.events' contains the following information

0.0	a DoNothing enters
0.0	a DoNothing exits
3.0	a Visitor enters
3.0	a Visitor holds for 7.5885
4.32703	a DoNothing enters
4.32703	a DoNothing exits
7.74896	a Visitor enters
7.74896	a Visitor holds for 4.14163
8.20233	a DoNothing enters
8.20233	a DoNothing exits
10.5885	a Visitor exits
11.8906	a Visitor exits
12.5153	a DoNothing enters
12.5153	a DoNothing exits
14.2642	a Visitor enters
14.2642	a Visitor holds for 4.51334
16.6951	a DoNothing enters
16.6951	a DoNothing exits
18.7776	a Visitor exits
19.8544	a Visitor enters
19.8544	a Visitor holds for 5.10907
20.5342	a DoNothing enters
20.5342	a DoNothing exits
23.464	a DoNothing enters
23.464	a DoNothing exits
24.9635	a Visitor exits

Distinctively labeling each arriving SimulationObject might improve the ability to follow the sequence of events. The goal is to have a trace for an execution of the NothingAtAll simulation look like the following.

0.0	DoNothing 1 enters
0.0	DoNothing 1 exits
3.0	Visitor 1 enters
3.0	Visitor 1 holds for 7.5885
4.32703	DoNothing 2 enters
4.32703	DoNothing 2 exits
7.74896	Visitor 2 enters

7.74896	Visitor 2 holds for 4.14163
8.20233	DoNothing 3 enters
8.20233	DoNothing 3 exits
10.5885	Visitor 1 exits
11.8906	Visitor 2 exits
12.5153	DoNothing 4 enters
12.5153	DoNothing 4 exits
14.2642	Visitor 3 enters
14.2642	Visitor 3 holds for 4.51334
16.6951	DoNothing 5 enters
16.6951	DoNothing 5 exits
18.7776	Visitor 3 exits
19.8544	Visitor 4 enters
19.8544	Visitor 4 holds for 5.10907
20.5342	DoNothing 6 enters
20.5342	DoNothing 6 exits
23.464	DoNothing 7 enters
23.464	DoNothing 7 exits
24.9635	Visitor 4 exits

Each subclass of EventMonitor must create its own sequence of labels. EventMonitor sets up a label framework in which the subclass can implement a way of distinguishing its instances. EventMonitor itself provides a model that the subclasses can duplicate; in this way, a default simulation using instances of EventMonitor can be used to produce the trace shown above. In addition to the scheduling, task language and private messages shown in the earlier implementation of EventMonitor, the class description has the following messages.

class name	EventMonitor
superclass	SimulationObject
instance variable names	label
class variable names	DataFile
	Counter

class methods

class initialization

  file: aFile
    DataFile ← aFile.
    Counter ← 0

instance methods

initialization

  initialize
    super initialize.
    self setLabel

accessing

setLabel
> Counter ← Counter + 1.
> label ← Counter printString

label
> ↑label

printing

printOn: aStream
> self class name printOn: aStream.
> aStream space.
> aStream nextPutAll: self label

Visitor, as a subclass of **EventMonitor**, has to have an independent class variable to act as the counter of its instances. The class description of Visitor is now

class name	Visitor
superclass	EventMonitor
class variable names	MyCounter
class methods	

class initialization

file: aFile
> super file: aFile.
> MyCounter ← 0

instance methods

accessing

setLabel
> MyCounter ← MyCounter + 1.
> label ← MyCounter printString

simulation control

tasks
> self holdFor: (Uniform from: 4.0 to: 10.0) next

MyCounter is set to 0 when the instance is told initialize; the method is found in class EventMonitor. Printing retrieves the label that Visitor redefines with respect to MyCounter. We let DoNothing use the class variable, Counter, of its superclass. Then the desired trace will be produced using these definitions.

25

The Use of Resources in Event-Driven Simulations

Implementing Classes ResourceProvider **and** WaitingSimulationObject

Consumable Resources

Nonconsumable Resources
Example of a File System

Renewable Resources
Example of a Ferry Service

In the previous chapters, we introduced a framework in which to specify event-driven simulations and to gather statistics about such simulations. Without resources to contend for and use, the only real task that an object can perform in a simulation is to hold (wait) for some specified amount of simulated time. Two kinds of resources are illustrated in this chapter: fixed resources and fluctuating resources. These kinds of resources were introduced in Chapter 23; the example in that chapter of classes Simulation and SimulationObject defined a support for resources coordination that will be further described in this chapter.

A fixed resource can be *consumable*. The simulation with a consumable resource begins with a given quantity of some resource, say, jelly beans. As the simulation proceeds, objects acquire the resource, ultimately using up all that were originally available. New objects needing the resource either terminate without successfully completing their tasks, or are indefinitely delayed waiting for a resource that will never be provided. Alternatively, a fixed resource can be *nonconsumable*. The simulation begins with a given quantity of some nonconsumable resource, say, glass jars. As the simulation proceeds, objects acquire the resource. When an object no longer needs the resource, it is recycled. Objects needing the resource either obtain it immediately or are delayed until a recycled one becomes available.

A fluctuating resource models producer/consumer relationships. A simulation can begin with a given quantity of some resource, say cars. As the simulation proceeds, objects acquire the resource; when they no longer need the resource, they recycle it (such as in the used car market). New resources can be added (produced), increasing the supply of the resource. Objects needing the resource either obtain it immediately or must wait until a recycled one or a new one becomes available. A fluctuating resource for which additional quantities can be produced is called a *renewable* resource. The example of the car is an example of a resource that is both renewable and nonconsumable.

Implementing ResourceProvider and WaitingSimulation-Object

The modeler's language for specifying resources in a Simulation includes expressions of the form

    self produce: amount of: resourceName

The response to this message is either to create an instance of class Resource with amount as its available quantity of resources, or to retrieve an existing Resource and increment its resources by amount. Instances of ResourceProvider are created by sending ResourceProvider the message named: aString or named: aString with: amount.

When a SimulationObject requests a resource (acquire: amount ofResource: resourceName), the currently active simulation (Simulation active) is asked to provide the corresponding resource (provideResourceFor:). Presumably the resource exists in the simulation as a result of the initialization of the Simulation; the Simulation refers to a Set of instances of ResourceProvider and can enumerate this Set in order to find one whose name is resourceName.

Once the SimulationObject has access to a ResourceProvider it can

ask how many resources it has available,
ask its name,
ask to acquire some amount (and with a particular access priority),
ask to produce some amount.

When a SimulationObject asks to acquire some resources, this request is added to a queue of such requests, ordered with respect to priority and, within identical priority levels, on a first-come first-served basis. Each time a request is made or more resources are produced, the ResourceProvider checks to see if one or more of its pending requests can be satisfied.

Each request is stored as a kind of DelayedEvent, an instance of class WaitingSimulationObject. Whenever a request is made, the request is stored on the waiting queue, pending, and then an attempt is made to provide the resource.

Class ResourceProvider is a subclass of class Resource. Class ResourceCoordinator, to be presented in the next chapter, is also a subclass of Resource. Resource represents the resource in terms of its name and the queue of requests that must be satisfied.

class name	Resource
superclass	Object
instance variable names	pending
	resourceName

class methods

instance creation

named: resourceName
↑ self new setName: resourceName

instance methods

accessing

acquire
↑ self

addRequest: aWaitingSimulationObject
> pending add: aWaitingSimulationObject.
> self provideResources.
> aWaitingSimulationObject pause.

name
> ↑ resourceName

private

provideResources
> ↑ self

setName: aString
> resourceName ← aString.
> pending ← SortedCollection new

Class ResourceProvider represents resources as simple quantifiable items that have no tasks to do and are, therefore, not created as actual SimulationObjects. Rather, a numerical count is kept of the number of the items. When a SimulationObject successfully acquires this kind of resource, the SimulationObject is given access to an instance of WaitingSimulationObject. The response in ResourceProvider to acquire:withPriority: removes a WaitingSimulationObject from the queue of pending requests, decrements the amount currently available, and returns the obtained WaitingSimulationObject.

class name	ResourceProvider
superclass	Resource
instance variable names	amountAvailable
class methods	

instance creation

named: aResourceName with: amount
> ↑ self new setName: aResourceName with: amount

named: aResourceName
> ↑ self new setName: aResourceName with: 0

instance methods

accessing

amountAvailable
    ↑ amountAvailable

task language

acquire: amountNeeded withPriority: priorityNumber
    | waiting |
    waiting ← WaitingSimulationObject
                  for: amountNeeded
                  of: self
                  withPriority: priorityNumber.
    self addRequest: waiting.
    ↑ waiting

produce: amount
    amountAvailable − amountAvailable + amount
    self provideResources

private

provideResources
    | waiting |
    [pending isEmpty not
        and: [pending first amount < = amountAvailable]]
        whileTrue:
            [waiting ← pending removeFirst.
            amountAvailable ← amountAvailable - waiting amount.
            waiting resume]

setName: aResourceName with: amount
    super setName: aResourceName.
    amountAvailable ← amount

A WaitingSimulationObject represents a delayed event, either a request to give some amount of resource (to be a server), or a request to get some amount of a resource (to be a customer).

class name	WaitingSimulationObject
superclass	DelayedEvent
instance variable names	amount
	resource
class methods	
instance creation	

for: amount of: aResource withPriority: aNumber

↑ (self onCondition: aNumber) setAmount: amount resource: aResource

for: amount withPriority: aNumber

↑ (self onCondition: aNumber) setAmount: amount resource: nil

instance methods

accessing

amount

↑ amount

name

↑ resource name

resource

↑ resource

resource: aResource

resource ← aResource

rask language

consume: aNumber

amount ← (amount − aNumber) max: 0

release

resource produce: amount.
amount ← 0

release: anAmount

resource produce: anAmount.
amount ← amount − anAmount

private

setAmount: aNumber
    resource: aResource

amount ← aNumber.
resource ← aResource.

When a Simulationobject acquires a resource, it is presumably consuming that resource until that resource is returned to the simulation. The amount of resource held in the WaitingSimulationObject is returned to the simulation by sending the WaitingSimulationObject the message release. Typically, however, the SimulationObject sends itself the message release: aWaitingSimulationObject so that a uniform style of sending messages to self is maintained in the method associated with the object's tasks. This uniformity simplifies the design of a method for tracing or monitoring the events of a simulation. Because all task messages are sent as messages to self and therefore to a SimulationObject, it is possible to create a subclass of SimulationObject (EventMonitor was the example we presented in Chapter 24) in which all task messages are intercepted in order to store a notation that the task is being done.

Using SimulationObject task message acquire:ofResource: and release:, the resource can be treated as a nonconsumable resource. A mixture is possible. The SimulationObject can acquire some amount of a resource, say 10, consume 5, and return 5. The message consume: is used to remove resources from the simulation. Thus the example would be accomplished by sending a WaitingSimulationObject acquired with 10 resources, the message consume: 5, and then the message release (or sending release: aStaticResource to self).

Consumable Resources

A simple jelly bean example illustrates the idea of a consumable resource. Recall the simulation example, NothingAtAll, introduced in Chapter 23. Suppose that whenever a Visitor enters the simulation and looks around, it has a task to acquire 2 jelly beans, take 2 units of time eating the beans, and leave. The simulation is initialized with one resource consisting of 15 jelly beans. The definition of this version of NothingAtAll is

class name	NothingAtAll
superclass	Simulation
instance methods	

initialization

defineResources
    self produce: 15 of: ' jelly beans '
defineArrivalSchedule
    self scheduleArrivalOf: Visitor accordingTo: (Uniform from: 1 to: 3)

The Visitor's tasks are expressed in two messages to self found in its method for tasks.

tasks
    self acquire: 2 ofResource: ' jelly beans ' .
    self holdFor: 2

An example execution of this simulation, in which only exits and entries are monitored, is

0.0	Visitor 1 enters
2.0	Visitor 1 exits
2.03671	Visitor 2 enters

4.03671	Visitor 2 exits	
4.34579	Visitor 3 enters	
5.92712	Visitor 4 enters	
6.34579	Visitor 3 exits	
7.92712	Visitor 4 exits	
8.46271	Visitor 5 enters	
10.4627	Visitor 5 exits	
10.5804	Visitor 6 enters	
12.5804	Visitor 6 exits	
12.7189	Visitor 7 enters	
14.7189	Visitor 7 exits	last visitor to get jelly beans
15.0638	Visitor 8 enters	endless waiting from now on
17.6466	Visitor 9 enters	
19.8276	Visitor 10 enters	

After the seventh Visitor enters, there are no more jelly beans, so all the subsequent Visitors are endlessly delayed waiting for resources that will never be made available. Alternatively, the Visitor could check to see if any jelly beans remain available (inquireFor:ofResource:). If none remain, the Visitor can leave rather than getting caught in the queue. This corresponds to the following method for tasks.

tasks
```
(self inquireFor: 2 ofResource: 'jelly beans')
    ifTrue: [self acquire: 2 ofResource: 'jelly beans'.
             self holdFor: 2]
```

One additional refinement might be to inform the simulation that all resources are used up and that it is time to "close the store." This is done by sending the Visitor the message stopSimulation. If we were to send this message the first time a Visitor enters who can not acquire enough jelly beans, then it is possible that a Visitor who has entered the store will get locked in. We have to make certain that a Visitor who acquires the last jelly beans, closes the store upon exit; in this way, a later Visitor will not lock this last successful one into the store. This corresponds to the following method for tasks.

tasks
```
| flag |
(self inquireFor: 2 ofResource: 'jelly beans')
    ifTrue: [self acquire: 2 ofResource: 'jelly beans'.
             flag ← self inquireFor: 2 ofResource: 'jelly beans'.
             "Are there still 2 left so that the next Visitor can be served?"
             self holdFor: 2.
             flag ifFalse: [self stopSimulation]]
```

Here is another example execution of the simulation NothingAtAll, in which only exits and entries are monitored.

0.0	Visitor 1 enters	
2.0	Visitor 1 exits	
2.26004	Visitor 2 enters	
4.26004	Visitor 2 exits	
4.83762	Visitor 3 enters	
6.34491	Visitor 4 enters	
6.83762	Visitor 3 exits	
8.34491	Visitor 4 exits	
8.51764	Visitor 5 enters	
9.9006	Visitor 6 enters	
10.5176	Visitor 5 exits	
11.9006	Visitor 6 exits	
12.6973	Visitor 7 enters	last successful requestor
14.0023	Visitor 8 enters	nothing available for this Visitor
14.0023	Visitor 8 exits	
14.6973	Visitor 7 exits	last successful requestor closes shop on exit

The EventMonitor class described in the previous chapter also monitors the use of resources. So, a trace of NothingAtAll would include the times at which jelly beans were requested and obtained.

0.0	Visitor 1 enters
0.0	Visitor 1 requests 2 of jelly beans
0.0	Visitor 1 obtained 2 of jelly beans
0.0	Visitor 1 holds for 2
1.40527	Visitor 2 enters
1.40527	Visitor 2 requests 2 of jelly beans
1.40527	Visitor 2 obtained 2 of jelly beans
1.40527	Visitor 2 holds for 2
2.0	Visitor 1 exits
2.56522	Visitor 3 enters
2.56522	Visitor 3 requests 2 of jelly beans
2.56522	Visitor 3 obtained 2 of jelly beans
2.56522	Visitor 3 holds for 2
3.40527	Visitor 2 exits
4.56522	Visitor 3 exits
5.3884	Visitor 4 enters
5.3884	Visitor 4 requests 2 of jelly beans
5.3884	Visitor 4 obtained 2 of jelly beans
5.3884	Visitor 4 holds for 2
6.69794	Visitor 5 enters
6.69794	Visitor 5 requests 2 of jelly beans
6.69794	Visitor 5 obtained 2 of jelly beans
6.69794	Visitor 5 holds for 2

7.3884	Visitor 4 exits
7.72174	Visitor 6 enters
7.72174	Visitor 6 requests 2 of jelly beans
7.72174	Visitor 6 obtained 2 of jelly beans
7.72174	Visitor 6 holds for 2
8.69794	Visitor 5 exits
9.72174	Visitor 6 exits
10.153	Visitor 7 enters
10.153	Visitor 7 requests 2 of jelly beans
10.153	Visitor 7 obtained 2 of jelly beans
10.153	Visitor 7 holds for 2
11.875	Visitor 8 enters
11.875	Visitor 8 exits
12.153	

At time 11.875, all but one jelly bean has been consumed. At time 12.153 Visitor number 7 stops the simulation.

Nonconsumable Resources

A car rental simulation serves to illustrate the use of a nonconsumable resource. The example simulation is a short-term car rental agency that opens up with 15 cars and 3 trucks available. Renters of cars arrive with a mean rate of one every 30 minutes, and those requiring trucks one every 120 minutes. The first car renter arrives when the shop opens, and the first truck renter arrives 10 minutes later. Classes CarRenter and TruckRenter represent these simulation objects.

RentalAgency is specified as a subclass of Simulation. It implements the two initialization messages, defineArrivalSchedule and defineResources.

class name	RentalAgency
superclass	Simulation
instance methods	

initialization

defineArrivalSchedule
    self scheduleArrivalOf: CarRenter
        accordingTo: (Exponential mean: 30).
    self scheduleArrivalOf: TruckRenter
        accordingTo: (Exponential mean: 120)
        startingAt: 10
defineResources
    self produce: 15 of: 'car'.
    self produce: 3 of: 'truck'

The tasks for CarRenter and TruckRenter are similar. First acquire a car or truck; if none are available, wait. Once the vehicle is obtained, use it. A CarRenter keeps the car between 4 and 8 hours (uniformly distributed); a TruckRenter keeps the truck between 1 and 4 hours (uniformly distributed). These usage times are indicated by having the renter hold for the appropriate amount of time before returning the vehicle (i.e., releasing the resource).

In order to monitor the two kinds of SimulationObject, and to have labels that separately identify each kind, the implementations of CarRenter and TruckRenter duplicate the labeling technique demonstrated earlier for class Visitor.

class name	CarRenter
superclass	EventMonitor
class variable names	CarCounter
	Hour

class methods

class initialization

file: file
        super file: file.
        CarCounter ← 0.
        Hour ← 60

instance methods

accessing

setLabel
        CarCounter ← CarCounter + 1.
        label ← CarCounter printString

simulation control

tasks
        | car |
        car ← self acquire: 1 ofResource: 'car'.
        self holdFor: (Uniform from: 4*Hour to: 8*Hour) next.
        self release: car

class name	TruckRenter
superclass	EventMonitor
class variable names	TruckCounter
	Hour

class methods

class initialization

file: file
        super file: file.
        TruckCounter ← 0
        Hour ← 60

instance methods

accessing

setLabel
> TruckCounter ← TruckCounter + 1.
> label ← TruckCounter printString

simulation control

tasks
> | truck |
> truck ← self acquire: 1 ofResource: ' truck '.
> self holdFor: (Uniform from: Hour to: 4∗Hour) next.
> self release: truck

The rental agency simulation is run by invoking

> aFile ← FileStream fileNamed: 'rental.events'.
> CarRenter file: aFile.
> TruckRenter file: aFile.
> anAgency ← RentalAgency new startUp.
> [anAgency time < 600] whileTrue: [anAgency proceed]

The trace on file rental.events after 10 hours (600 minutes) shows the following sequence of events.

0	CarRenter 1 enters
0	CarRenter 1 requests 1 of Car
0	CarRenter 1 obtained 1 of Car
0	CarRenter 1 holds for 460.426
10	TruckRenter 1 enters
10	TruckRenter 1 requests 1 of Truck
10	TruckRenter 1 obtained 1 of Truck
10	TruckRenter 1 holds for 87.2159
26.2079	CarRenter 2 enters
26.2079	CarRenter 2 requests 1 of Car
26.2079	CarRenter 2 obtained 1 of Car
26.2079	CarRenter 2 holds for 318.966
27.4147	CarRenter 3 enters
27.4147	CarRenter 3 requests 1 of Car
27.4147	CarRenter 3 obtained 1 of Car
27.4147	CarRenter 3 holds for 244.867
51.5614	CarRenter 4 enters
51.5614	CarRenter 4 requests 1 of Car
51.5614	CarRenter 4 obtained 1 of Car
51.5614	CarRenter 4 holds for 276.647
78.0957	CarRenter 5 enters

78.0957	CarRenter 5 requests 1 of Car
78.0957	CarRenter 5 obtained 1 of Car
78.0957	CarRenter 5 holds for 333.212
93.121	CarRenter 6 enters
93.121	CarRenter 6 requests 1 of Car
93.121	CarRenter 6 obtained 1 of Car
93.121	CarRenter 6 holds for 359.718
97.2159	TruckRenter 1 releases 1 of Truck
97.2159	TruckRenter 1 exits
99.0265	CarRenter 7 enters
99.0265	CarRenter 7 requests 1 of Car
99.0265	CarRenter 7 obtained 1 of Car
99.0265	CarRenter 7 holds for 417.572
106.649	CarRenter 8 enters
106.649	CarRenter 8 requests 1 of Car
106.649	CarRenter 8 obtained 1 of Car
106.649	CarRenter 8 holds for 294.43
107.175	CarRenter 9 enters
107.175	CarRenter 9 requests 1 of Car
107.175	CarRenter 9 obtained 1 of Car
107.175	CarRenter 9 holds for 314.198
121.138	CarRenter 10 enters
121.138	CarRenter 10 requests 1 of Car
121.138	CarRenter 10 obtained 1 of Car
121.138	CarRenter 10 holds for 467.032
127.018	TruckRenter 2 enters
127.018	TruckRenter 2 requests 1 of Truck
127.018	TruckRenter 2 obtained 1 of Truck
127.018	TruckRenter 2 holds for 74.5047
145.513	CarRenter 11 enters
145.513	CarRenter 11 requests 1 of Car
145.513	CarRenter 11 obtained 1 of Car
145.513	CarRenter 11 holds for 243.776
166.214	CarRenter 12 enters
166.214	CarRenter 12 requests 1 of Car
166.214	CarRenter 12 obtained 1 of Car
166.214	CarRenter 12 holds for 429.247
172.253	CarRenter 13 enters
172.253	CarRenter 13 requests 1 of Car
172.253	CarRenter 13 obtained 1 of Car
172.253	CarRenter 13 holds for 370.909
191.438	TruckRenter 3 enters
191.438	TruckRenter 3 requests 1 of Truck
191.438	TruckRenter 3 obtained 1 of Truck
191.438	TruckRenter 3 holds for 225.127

201.523	TruckRenter 2 releases 1 of Truck
201.523	TruckRenter 2 exits
220.102	CarRenter 14 enters
220.102	CarRenter 14 requests 1 of Car
220.102	CarRenter 14 obtained 1 of Car
220.102	CarRenter 14 holds for 334.684
252.055	CarRenter 15 enters
252.055	CarRenter 15 requests 1 of Car
252.055	CarRenter 15 obtained 1 of Car
252.055	CarRenter 15 holds for 408.358
269.964	CarRenter 16 enters
269.964	CarRenter 16 requests 1 of Car
272.282	CarRenter 3 releases 1 of Car
272.282	CarRenter 3 exits
272.282	CarRenter 16 obtained 1 of Car
272.282	CarRenter 16 holds for 281.349
292.375	CarRenter 17 enters
292.375	CarRenter 17 requests 1 of Car
328.208	CarRenter 4 releases 1 of Car
328.208	CarRenter 4 exits
328.208	CarRenter 17 obtained 1 of Car
328.208	CarRenter 17 holds for 270.062
345.174	CarRenter 2 releases 1 of Car
345.174	CarRenter 2 exits
350.53	CarRenter 18 enters
350.53	CarRenter 18 requests 1 of Car
350.53	CarRenter 18 obtained 1 of Car
350.53	CarRenter 18 holds for 297.154
354.126	CarRenter 19 enters
354.126	CarRenter 19 requests 1 of Car
358.269	TruckRenter 4 enters
358.269	TruckRenter 4 requests 1 of Truck
358.269	TruckRenter 4 obtained 1 of Truck
358.269	TruckRenter 4 holds for 173.648
367.88	TruckRenter 5 enters
367.88	TruckRenter 5 requests 1 of Truck
367.88	TruckRenter 5 obtained 1 of Truck
367.88	TruckRenter 5 holds for 175.972
389.289	CarRenter 11 releases 1 of Car
389.289	CarRenter 11 exits
389.289	CarRenter 19 obtained 1 of Car
389.289	CarRenter 19 holds for 379.017
401.079	CarRenter 8 releases 1 of Car
401.079	CarRenter 8 exits
402.224	CarRenter 20 enters

402.224	CarRenter 20 requests 1 of Car
402.224	CarRenter 20 obtained 1 of Car
402.224	CarRenter 20 holds for 341.188
410.431	TruckRenter 6 enters
410.431	TruckRenter 6 requests 1 of Truck
411.307	CarRenter 5 releases 1 of Car
411.307	CarRenter 5 exits
416.566	TruckRenter 3 releases 1 of Truck
416.566	TruckRenter 3 exits
416.566	TruckRenter 6 obtained 1 of Truck
416.566	TruckRenter 6 holds for 119.076
421.373	CarRenter 9 releases 1 of Car
421.373	CarRenter 9 exits
422.802	CarRenter 21 enters
422.802	CarRenter 21 requests 1 of Car
422.802	CarRenter 21 obtained 1 of Car
422.802	CarRenter 21 holds for 241.915
452.839	CarRenter 6 releases 1 of Car
452.839	CarRenter 6 exits
460.426	CarRenter 1 releases 1 of Car
460.426	CarRenter 1 exits
512.263	CarRenter 22 enters
512.263	CarRenter 22 requests 1 of Car
512.263	CarRenter 22 obtained 1 of Car
512.263	CarRenter 22 holds for 277.035
516.598	CarRenter 7 releases 1 of Car
516.598	CarRenter 7 exits
531.917	TruckRenter 4 releases 1 of Truck
531.917	TruckRenter 4 exits
535.642	TruckRenter 6 releases 1 of Truck
535.642	TruckRenter 6 exits
543.162	CarRenter 13 releases 1 of Car
543.162	CarRenter 13 exits
543.852	TruckRenter 5 releases 1 of Truck
543.852	TruckRenter 5 exits
553.631	CarRenter 16 releases 1 of Car
553.631	CarRenter 16 exits
554.786	CarRenter 14 releases 1 of Car
554.786	CarRenter 14 exits
574.617	CarRenter 23 enters
574.617	CarRenter 23 requests 1 of Car
574.617	CarRenter 23 obtained 1 of Car
574.617	CarRenter 23 holds for 436.783
588.171	CarRenter 10 releases 1 of Car
588.171	CarRenter 10 exits

591.51	CarRenter 24 enters
591.51	CarRenter 24 requests 1 of Car
591.51	CarRenter 24 obtained 1 of Car
591.51	CarRenter 24 holds for 430.067
595.461	CarRenter 12 releases 1 of Car
595.461	CarRenter 12 exits
598.27	CarRenter 17 releases 1 of Car
598.27	CarRenter 17 exits
599.876	CarRenter 25 enters
599.876	CarRenter 25 requests 1 of Car
599.876	CarRenter 25 obtained 1 of Car
599.876	CarRenter 25 holds for 472.042
642.188	TruckRenter 7 enters
642.188	TruckRenter 7 requests 1 of Truck
642.188	TruckRenter 7 obtained 1 of Truck
642.188	TruckRenter 7 holds for 190.586

A snapshot of the simulation shows that, at time 642.188, the following events are queued in anAgency and the following resources are available.

Resource (car) no pending requests; 6 available
Resource (truck) no pending requests; 2 available
Event Queue
    CarRenter for creation and start up
    TruckRenter for creation and start up
    9 CarRenters holding
    1 TruckRenter holding

Note that a nonconsumable resource differs from the description of a consumable resource only in the SimulationObject's sending the message release: in order to recycle acquired resources.

Example of a File System

The car rental is an open simulation in which objects (car renters and truck renters) arrive, do their tasks, and leave again. A closed simulation is one in which the same objects remain in the simulation for the duration of the simulation run. The next example is of a file system; it was adopted from a book by Graham Birtwistle that presents a Simula-based system named Demos [*A System for Discrete Event Modelling on Simula*, Graham M. Birtwistle, MacMillan, London, England, 1979]. The purpose of Demos is to support teaching about the kinds of event-driven simulations discussed in this chapter. The book is a thorough introduction to this class of simulations and to their implementation in Simula. There are many useful examples, each of which could be implemented in the context of the Smalltalk-80 simulation framework provided in this and in the previous chapter. We use variations of a Demos file system, a car ferry, and an information system example for illustration in this chapter so that, after seeing how we approach the Smalltalk-80 implementations, the interested reader can try out more of Birtwistle's examples.

In the example file system, "writer" processes update a file, and "reader" processes read it. Any number of readers may access the file at the same time, but writers must have sole access to the file. Moreover, writers have priority over readers. The individual sequencing of events is shown in the programs below. The example illustrates the use of priority queueing for resources as well as another approach to collecting statistics. In this case, the statistics gathered is a tally of the number of reads and the number of writes.

Suppose there are three system file readers and two file writers, and only three (nonconsumable) file resources. The initialization method specifies a statistics dictionary with two zero-valued entries, reads and writes. The simulation is to run for 25 simulated units of time; it schedules itself to receive the message finishUp at time 25.

Note in the implementation of defineArrivalSchedule that the FileSystemReaders and FileSystemWriters are given attributes so that they can be identified in the event traces.

class name	FileSystem
superclass	Simulation
instance variable names	statistics

instance methods

initialization

initialize
```
super initialize.
statistics ← Dictionary new: 2.
statistics at: #reads put: 0.
statistics at: #writes put: 0
```

defineArrivalSchedule
```
self scheduleArrivalOf: (FileSystemReader new label: 'first')
    at: 0.0.
self scheduleArrivalOf: (FileSystemWriter new label: 'first')
    at: 0.0.
self scheduleArrivalOf: (FileSystemReader new label: 'second')
    at: 0.0.
self scheduleArrivalOf: (FileSystemWriter new label: 'second')
    at: 1.0.
self scheduleArrivalOf: (FileSystemReader new label: 'third')
    at: 2.0.
self schedule: [self finishUp] at: 25
```

defineResources
```
self produce: 3 of: 'File'
```

statistics

statisticsAt: aKey changeBy: anInteger
> statistics at: aKey
>> put: (statistics at: aKey) + anInteger

printStatisticsOn: aStream
> statistics printOn: aStream

The FileSystemReader repeatedly carries out a sequence of five tasks: acquire one File resource, hold for an amount of time appropriate to reading the file, release the resource, update the tally of read statistics, and then hold for an amount of time appropriate to using the information read from the file. FileSystemWriters acquire three file resources, hold in order to write on the file, release the resources, and update the write statistics. The priority of a FileSystemReader is set to 1; the priority of a FileSystemWriter is 2. In this way, the nonconsumable ResourceProvider 'File' will give attention to FileSystemWriters before FileSystemReaders.

In order to obtain a trace of the events, the two simulation objects are created as subclasses of EventMonitor. Since each has a single label that will serve to identify it, only the response to printOn: aStream is reimplemented.

class name	FileSystemReader
superclass	EventMonitor
instance methods	

accessing

label: aString
> label ← aString

simulation control

tasks
> | file |
> "The repeated sequence of tasks is as follows"
> [true]
>> whileTrue:
>>> [file ← self acquire: 1 ofResource: 'File' withPriority: 1.
>>> self holdFor: 2.0.
>>> self release: file.
>>> Simulation active statisticsAt: #reads changeBy: 1.
>>> self holdFor: 5.0]

printing

printOn: aStream
> aStream nextPutAll: label.
> aStream space.
> self class name printOn: aStream

class name	FileSystemWriter
superclass	EventMonitor
instance methods	

accessing

label: aString
> label ← aString

simulation control

tasks
> | file |
> "The repeated sequence of tasks is as follows"
> [true]
>> whileTrue:
>>> ["Gather information"
>>> self holdFor: 5.0.
>>> file ← self acquire: 3 ofResource: 'File' withPriority: 2.
>>> self holdFor: 3.0.
>>> self release: file.
>>> Simulation active statisticsAt: #writes changeBy: 1]

printing

printOn: aStream
> aStream nextPutAll: label.
> aStream space.
> self class name printOn: aStream

The five simulation objects carry out their tasks, until the simulation stops itself at time 25. In specifying the tasks of a SimulationObject, the modeler has available all the control structures of the Smalltalk-80 language. A trace of the events shows how FileSystemReaders are held up because of the higher priority and larger resource needs of the FileSystemWriters. For example, the first and second FileSystemReaders are held up at time 7.0; the third at time 9.0; and all until time 11.0, the time at which no FileSystemWriter requires resources.

0.0	first FileSystemReader enters
0.0	first FileSystemReader requests 1 of File
0.0	first FileSystemReader obtained 1 of File
0.0	first FileSystemReader holds for 2.0
0.0	first FileSystemWriter enters
0.0	first FileSystemWriter holds for 5.0
0.0	second FileSystemReader enters
0.0	second FileSystemReader requests 1 of File
0.0	second FileSystemReader obtained 1 of File
0.0	second FileSystemReader holds for 2.0

1.0	second FileSystemWriter enters
1.0	second FileSystemWriter holds for 5.0
2.0	second FileSystemReader releases 1 of File
2.0	second FileSystemReader holds for 5.0
2.0	first FileSystemReader releases 1 of File
2.0	first FileSystemReader holds for 5.0
2.0	third FileSystemReader enters
2.0	third FileSystemReader requests 1 of File
2.0	third FileSystemReader obtained 1 of File
2.0	third FileSystemReader holds for 2.0
4.0	third FileSystemReader releases 1 of File
4.0	third FileSystemReader holds for 5.0
5.0	first FileSystemWriter requests 3 of File
5.0	first FileSystemWriter obtained 3 of File
5.0	first FileSystemWriter holds for 3.0
6.0	second FileSystemWriter requests 3 of File
7.0	first FileSystemReader requests 1 of File
7.0	second FileSystemReader requests 1 of File
8.0	first FileSystemWriter releases 3 of File
8.0	first FileSystemWriter holds for 5.0
8.0	second FileSystemWriter obtained 3 of File
8.0	second FileSystemWriter holds for 3.0
9.0	third FileSystemReader requests 1 of File
11.0	second FileSystemWriter releases 3 of File
11.0	second FileSystemWriter holds for 5.0
11.0	first FileSystemReader obtained 1 of File
11.0	first FileSystemReader holds for 2.0
11.0	second FileSystemReader obtained 1 of File
11.0	second FileSystemReader holds for 2.0
11.0	third FileSystemReader obtained 1 of File
11.0	third FileSystemReader holds for 2.0
13.0	third FileSystemReader releases 1 of File
13.0	third FileSystemReader holds for 5.0
13.0	second FileSystemReader releases 1 of File
13.0	second FileSystemReader holds for 5.0
13.0	first FileSystemReader releases 1 of File
13.0	first FileSystemReader holds for 5.0
13.0	first FileSystemWriter requests 3 of File
13.0	first FileSystemWriter obtained 3 of File
13.0	first FileSystemWriter holds for 3.0
16.0	first FileSystemWriter releases 3 of File
16.0	first FileSystemWriter holds for 5.0
16.0	second FileSystemWriter requests 3 of File
16.0	second FileSystemWriter obtained 3 of File
16.0	second FileSystemWriter holds for 3.0

18.0	first FileSystemReader requests 1 of File
18.0	second FileSystemReader requests 1 of File
18.0	third FileSystemReader requests 1 of File
19.0	second FileSystemWriter releases 3 of File
19.0	second FileSystemWriter holds for 5.0
19.0	first FileSystemReader obtained 1 of File
19.0	first FileSystemReader holds for 2.0
19.0	second FileSystemReader obtained 1 of File
19.0	second FileSystemReader holds for 2.0
19.0	third FileSystemReader obtained 1 of File
19.0	third FileSystemReader holds for 2.0
21.0	third FileSystemReader releases 1 of File
21.0	third FileSystemReader holds for 5.0
21.0	second FileSystemReader releases 1 of File
21.0	second FileSystemReader holds for 5.0
21.0	first FileSystemReader releases 1 of File
21.0	first FileSystemReader holds for 5.0
21.0	first FileSystemWriter requests 3 of File
21.0	first FileSystemWriter obtained 3 of File
21.0	first FileSystemWriter holds for 3.0
24.0	first FileSystemWriter releases 3 of File
24.0	first FileSystemWriter holds for 5.0
24.0	second FileSystemWriter requests 3 of File
24.0	second FileSystemWriter obtained 3 of File
24.0	second FileSystemWriter holds for 3.0

At this point, the current time is 25 and the statistics gathered is printed by sending the FileSystem the message printStatisticsOn: aStream where the Stream is, for example, a FileStream. The result is

| reads | 9 |
| writes | 5 |

Note that if the FileSystemReaders were not held up by lack of resources and lower priority, there would have been 12 reads during this timeframe.

Renewable Resources

In simulations involving producer/consumer synchronizations, simulation objects acting as producers make resources available to other objects acting as consumers. The simulation starts out with some fixed amount of resource, perhaps 0. Producer objects increase the available resources, consumer objects decrease them. This type of resource differs from a nonconsumable resource in that there is no limit to the amounts of resource that can be made available. Such resources are called *renewable* resources.

A simulation of a car dealership provides a simple example of a renewable resource. Suppose a customer comes in to buy a car every two to six days. The car dealer starts out with 12 cars on the lot; when these are sold, orders must wait until new cars are delivered. Ten to twelve new cars are shipped to the dealer every 90 days. We assume that all the cars are the same and that every customer is willing to wait so that no sales are lost if a car is not immediately available. The car dealer is interested in giving good service, but he is also unwilling to keep too large an inventory. By examining the average length of the queue of waiting customers, the dealer can modify his quarterly order of cars in order to minimize customer dissatisfaction and still maintain a small inventory of new cars.

Statistics on the amount of time that car buyers have to wait to get a car are kept by the simulation. The method used is the same as the method demonstrated in Chapter 24 for collecting information on Visitors to a Museum; a Histogram is maintained by the CarDealer. Each CarBuyer remembers its entry time; when it exits the simulation, the length of time the CarBuyer spent in the simulation is logged in the Histogram. This length of time is equivalent to the amount of time the CarBuyer had to wait to get a car because the CarBuyer's only task is to acquire a car.

class name	CarDealer
superclass	Simulation
instance variable names	statistics
instance methods	

initialization

initialize
    super initialize.
    statistics ← Histogram from: 1 to: 365 by: 7

defineArrivalSchedule
    self scheduleArrivalOf: CarBuyer
        accordingTo: (Uniform from: 2 to: 6)
        startingAt: 1.0.
    self scheduleArrivalOf: (CarDelivery new) at: 90.0
    "only one delivery is scheduled; the instance of CarDelivery will reschedule itself as the last of its tasks"

defineResources
    self produce: 12 of: 'Car'

accessing

exit: aSimulationObject
> super exit: aSimulationObject.
> " A CarDelivery could be exiting—ignore it"
> (aSimulationObject isKindOf: CarBuyer)
> > ifTrue: [statistics store: currentTime − aSimulationObject entryTime]

printing

printStatisticsOn: aStream
> statistics printStatisticsOn: aStream

All the CarBuyer wants to do is get a car; the CarBuyer only waits if a car is not immediately available.

class name	CarBuyer
superclass	SimulationObject
instance variable names	entryTime
instance methods	

accessing

entryTime
> ↑entryTime

initialization

initialize
> super initialize.
> entryTime ← Simulation active time

simulation control
tasks
> self acquire: 1 ofResource: 'Car'

The CarDelivery produces 10 to 12 new cars. After producing the new cars, the CarDelivery object schedules itself to return in 90 days. An alternative implementation would have the CarDelivery hold for 90 days and then repeat its task.

class name	CarDelivery
superclass	SimulationObject
instance methods	

simulation control

tasks
> "Get access to the Car resource and produce 10, 11, or 12 new cars"
> self produce: ((SampleSpace data: #(10 11 12)) next)
> > ofResource: 'Car'.
> "Schedule a new delivery in 90 days"
> Simulation active scheduleArrivalOf: self
> > at: Simulation active time + 90

The statistics give us the number of buyers, minimum, maximum, and average wait times for the buyers, and the number of buyers within each wait-time interval. No one waited longer than 204 days. 91 car buyers came to the dealer; 12 did not have to wait because the dealer had cars already. Of the 43 that waited and were served, they waited on the average of 78.5 days.

At time 360.0 the statistics indicates the following information.

Number of Objects	Minimum Value	Maximum Value	Average Value
55	0.0	197.168	78.5476

Entry	Number of Objects	Frequency	
1-8	2	0.0363636	| XX
8-15	3	0.0545454	| XXX
15-22	2	0.0363636	| XX
22-29	1	0.0181818	| X
29-36	2	0.0363636	| XX
36-43	1	0.0181818	| X
43-50	0	0.0	|
50-57	1	0.0181818	| X
57-64	2	0.0363636	| XX
64-71	1	0.0181818	| X
71-78	2	0.0363636	| XX
78-85	2	0.0363636	| XX
85-92	2	0.0363636	| XX
92-99	0	0.0	|
99-106	0	0.0	|
106-113	1	0.0181818	| X
113-120	3	0.0545454	| XXX
120-127	2	0.0363636	| XX
127-134	2	0.0363636	| XX
134-141	2	0.0363636	| XX
141-148	1	0.0181818	| X
148-155	0	0.0	|
155-162	1	0.0181818	| X
162-169	2	0.0363636	| XX
169-176	2	0.0363636	| XX
176-183	1	0.0181818	| X
183-190	2	0.0363636	| XX
190-197	2	0.0363636	| XX
197-204	1	0.0181818	| X
204-211	0	0.0	|

Pending Requests 36 buyers waiting for a car

From the above information, we can estimate that the number of cars delivered could safely be increased, even doubled, to meet the consumer demand.

Example of a Ferry Service

This next example is like one in the Birtwistle book. The example is of a ferry shuttling between an island and the mainland, carrying cars back and forth. The ferry starts service at 7:00 a.m. (420 minutes into the day) and stops at 10:45 p.m. (1365 minutes into the day) once it has reached one of its docking locations. The ferry has a capacity of only six cars.

The ferry's task is to load no more than six of the waiting cars and then to cross over the waterway. The crossing takes about eight minutes with a standard deviation of 0.5 minutes. The activity of crossing from one side to the other continues until the time is 1365 minutes. The FerrySimulation described next simulates one day's ferry service. Note in the definition of Ferry the use of the Smalltalk-80 whileFalse: control structure to repetitively send the Ferry from one side to another; also note the use of messages to split up the task description into parts load, holdFor: (cross over), unload, and changeSide.

class name	Ferry
superclass	SimulationObject
instance variable names	carsOnBoard
	currentSide

instance methods

initialization

initialize
```
    super initialize.
    carsOnBoard ← 0.
    currentSide ← 'Mainland'
```

simulation control

tasks
```
    "Initialize the count of loaded cars and then keep loading until at most 6
    are on board. Stop loading if no more cars are waiting at the dock."
    [Simulation active time > 1365.0] whileFalse:
        [carsOnBoard ← 0.
        self load.
        self holdFor: (Normal mean: 8 deviation: 0.5) next.
        self unload.
        self changeSide]
```
load
```
    "It takes 0.5 minutes to load each car. Only try to acquire a resource, a
    car from this side's dock, if it is there. The conditional for the repetition
    checks remaining resources and only continues if a car is waiting."
```

```
        [carsOnBoard < 6
            and: [self inquireFor: 1 of: currentSide]]
                whileTrue:
                    [self acquire: 1 ofResource: currentSide.
                    self holdFor: 0.5.
                    carsOnBoard ← carsOnBoard + 1]
```

changeSide
```
    currentSide ← currentSide = 'Mainland'
                        ifTrue: ['Island']
                        ifFalse: ['Mainland']
```

unload
```
    "It takes 0.5 minutes to unload each car."
    self holdFor: carsOnBoard*0.5.
```

We will need two SimulationObjects in order to simulate the cars arriving at the dock of the Mainland or at the Island, that is, to produce a car at these locations.

class name	IslandArrival
superclass	SimulationObject
instance methods	

simulation control

> **tasks**
> ```
>     self produce: 1 ofResource: 'Island'
> ```

class name	MainlandArrival
superclass	SimulationObject
instance methods	

simulation control

> **tasks**
> ```
>     self produce: 1 ofResource: 'Mainland'
> ```

The ferry simulation has two kinds of Resources, one for the mainland and one for the island, in which to queue the arriving cars. When these resources are first created, i.e., the day begins, there are three cars already waiting at the mainland dock and no cars waiting at the island dock. The arrival schedule says that cars arrive with a mean rate of 0.15 every minute.

class name	FerrySimulation
superclass	Simulation
instance methods	

initialization

> **defineArrivalSchedule**
> ```
>     self scheduleArrivalOf: MainlandArrival
> ```

        accordingTo: (Exponential parameter: 0.15)
        startingAt: 420.0.
    self scheduleArrivalOf: IslandArrival
        accordingTo: (Exponential parameter: 0.15)
        startingAt: 420.0.
    self scheduleArrivalOf: Ferry new at: 420.0

defineResources
    self produce: 3 of: 'Mainland'.
    self produce: 0 of: 'Island'

There is some data that the simulation should collect while it is accumulating. First, the Ferry should count the total number of trips it takes, the total cars it carries, and the number of trips it takes carrying no cars. This data is obtained by adding three instance variables (trips, totalCars, and emptyTrips) in the definition of class Ferry and modifying three methods.

class name	Ferry
superclass	SimulationObject
instance variable names	emptyTrips
	carsOnBoard
	currentSide
	trips
	totalCars
	emptyTrips

instance methods

initialization

initialize
    super initialize.
    carsOnBoard ← 0.
    currentSide ← 'Mainland'.
    trips ← 0.
    totalCars ← 0.
    emptyTrips ← 0

simulation control

load
    "Keep a running tally of the cars carried"
    [carsOnBoard < 6
        and: [self inquireFor: 1 ofResource: currentSide]]
            whileTrue:
                [self acquire: 1 ofResource: currentSide.
                self holdFor: 0.5.
                carsOnBoard ← carsOnBoard + 1.
                totalCars ← totalCars + 1]

tasks
```
"Check for an empty trip and keep a tally of trips"
[Simulation active time > 1365.0] whileFalse:
    [carsOnBoard ← 0.
    self load.
    carsOnBoard = 0 ifTrue: [emptyTrips ← emptyTrips + 1].
    self holdFor: (Normal mean: 8 deviation: 0.5) next.
    self unload.
    self changeSide.
    trips ← trips + 1]
```

In addition, we would like to know the maximum size of the number of
Mainland and Island arrivals, that is, the maximum queue waiting for
the Ferry. The FerrySimulation can determine this information by adding two instance variables, maxMainland and maxIsland; each time the
message produce: amount of: resourceName is sent to the simulation
and a resource amount is increased, the corresponding variable can be
reset to the maximum of its current value and that of the resource.

The trace we provide shows the beginning and the ending sequence
of events. The arrival of cars at the Island and the Mainland is listed
separately from the repetitive tasks of the Ferry.

420.000	IslandArrival 1
420.000	MainlandArrival 1
425.290	MainlandArrival 2
429.380	MainlandArrival 3
430.830	IslandArrival 2
431.302	IslandArrival 3
434.209	IslandArrival 4
438.267	IslandArrival 5
440.864	IslandArrival 6
441.193	MainlandArrival 4
448.044	IslandArrival 7
448.827	IslandArrival 8
453.811	IslandArrival 9
458.804	MainlandArrival 5
467.860	IslandArrival 10
470.800	IslandArrival 11
473.957	MainlandArrival 6
475.508	IslandArrival 12

This continues until ...

1300.87	IslandArrival 169
1301.11	MainlandArrival 124
1301.19	IslandArrival 170

1306.75	IslandArrival 171
1309.30	IslandArrival 172
1315.24	MainlandArrival 125
1319.65	MainlandArrival 126
1321.80	MainlandArrival 127
1322.39	MainlandArrival 128
1328.45	IslandArrival 173
1328.99	IslandArrival 174
1329.77	MainlandArrival 129
1331.63	IslandArrival 175
1335.43	MainlandArrival 130
1338.93	IslandArrival 176
1342.46	MainlandArrival 131
1348.11	IslandArrival 177
1358.63	MainlandArrival 132
1359.10	IslandArrival 178
1360.79	MainlandArrival 133

The Ferry starts at the Mainland where there were three cars waiting; no cars are at the Island. Immediately a car arrives at each place.

420.0   Ferry 1 enters
         load at Mainland: there are now 4 cars waiting at Mainland and 1 car waiting at Island
420.0   Ferry 1 obtained 1 of Mainland, holds for 0.5
420.5   Ferry 1 obtained 1 of Mainland, holds for 0.5
421.0   Ferry 1 obtained 1 of Mainland, holds for 0.5
421.5   Ferry 1 obtained 1 of Mainland, holds for 0.5
         cross over
422.0   Ferry 1 holds for 8.56369
         unload 4 cars at Island: there are now 2 cars waiting at Mainland and 1 car waiting at Island
430.564 Ferry 1 holds for 2.0
         load at Island: there are now 2 cars at Mainland and 3 cars at Island
432.564 Ferry 1 obtained 1 of Island, holds for 0.5
433.064 Ferry 1 obtained 1 of Island, holds for 0.5
433.564 Ferry 1 obtained 1 of Island, holds for 0.5
         cross over
434.064 Ferry 1 holds for 8.55344
         unload 3 cars at Mainland: there are now 3 cars waiting at Mainland and 3 cars waiting at Island
442.617 Ferry 1 holds for 1.5
         load at Mainland: there is now 3 cars waiting at Mainland and 0 cars waiting at Island

444.117   Ferry 1 obtained 1 of Mainland, holds for 0.5
444.617   Ferry 1 obtained 1 of Mainland, holds for 0.5
445.117   Ferry 1 obtained 1 of Mainland, holds for 0.5
          cross over
445.617   Ferry 1 holds for 8.98081
          unload 3 cars at Island: there are now 0 cars waiting
          at Mainland and 6 cars waiting at Island
454.598   Ferry 1 holds for 1.5
          load at Island: there are now 0 cars waiting at Main-
          land and 6 cars waiting at Island
456.098   Ferry 1 obtained 1 of Island, holds for 0.5
456.598   Ferry 1 obtained 1 of Island, holds for 0.5
457.098   Ferry 1 obtained 1 of Island, holds for 0.5
457.598   Ferry 1 obtained 1 of Island, holds for 0.5
458.098   Ferry 1 obtained 1 of Island, holds for 0.5
458.598   Ferry 1 obtained 1 of Island, holds for 0.5

          cross over
459.098   Ferry 1 holds for 7.96448
          unload 6 cars at Mainland: there is now 1 car waiting
          at Mainland and 0 cars waiting at Island
467.062   Ferry 1 holds for 3.0
          load at Mainland: there is now 1 car waiting at Main-
          land and 1 car waiting at Island
470.062   Ferry 1 obtained 1 of Mainland, holds for 0.5
          continues until
          load at Island
1299.52   Ferry 1 obtained 1 of Island, holds for 0.5
1300.02   Ferry 1 obtained 1 of Island, holds for 0.5
          cross over
1300.52   Ferry 1 holds for 7.23914
          unload 2 cars at Mainland
1307.76   Ferry 1 holds for 1.0
          load at Mainland: there is now 1 car waiting at Main-
          land and 3 cars waiting at Island
1308.76   Ferry 1 obtained 1 of Mainland, holds for 0.5
          cross over
1309.26   Ferry 1 holds for 7.78433
          load at Island: there are now 2 cars waiting at
          Mainland and 4 cars waiting at Island
1317.54   Ferry 1 obtained 1 of Island, holds for 0.5
1318.04   Ferry 1 obtained 1 of Island, holds for 0.5
1318.54   Ferry 1 obtained 1 of Island, holds for 0.5
1319.04   Ferry 1 obtained 1 of Island, holds for 0.5
          cross over

1319.54	Ferry 1 holds for 8.51123
	unload 4 cars at Mainland: there are now 3 cars waiting at Mainland and 0 cars waiting at Island
1328.05	Ferry 1 holds for 2.0
	load at Mainland: there are now 5 cars waiting at Mainland and 2 cars waiting at Island
1330.05	Ferry 1 obtained 1 of Mainland, holds for 0.5
1330.55	Ferry 1 obtained 1 of Mainland, holds for 0.5
1331.05	Ferry 1 obtained 1 of Mainland, holds for 0.5
1331.55	Ferry 1 obtained 1 of Mainland, holds for 0.5
1332.05	Ferry 1 obtained 1 of Mainland, holds for 0.5
	cross over
1332.55	Ferry 1 holds for 8.17247
	unload 5 cars at Island: there is now 1 car waiting at Mainland and 4 cars waiting at Island
1340.72	Ferry 1 holds for 2.5
	load at Island: there are now 2 cars waiting at Mainland and 4 cars waiting at Island
1343.22	Ferry 1 obtained 1 of Island, holds for 0.5
1343.72	Ferry 1 obtained 1 of Island, holds for 0.5
1344.22	Ferry 1 obtained 1 of Island, holds for 0.5
1344.72	Ferry 1 obtained 1 of Island, holds for 0.5
	cross over
1345.22	Ferry 1 holds for 7.75318
	unload at Mainland: there are 2 cars waiting at Mainland and 1 car waiting at Island
1352.98	Ferry 1 holds for 2.0
	load at Mainland: there are 2 cars waiting at Mainland and 1 car waiting at Island
1354.98	Ferry 1 obtained 1 of Mainland, holds for 0.5
1355.48	Ferry 1 obtained 1 of Mainland, holds for 0.5
	cross over
1355.98	Ferry 1 holds for 8.54321
	unload 2 cars at Island: there are 2 cars waiting at Mainland and 2 cars waiting at Island
1364.52	Ferry 1 holds for 1.0
	quitting time
1365.52	Ferry 1 exits

The data collected shows that the Ferry took 79 trips, carrying a total of 310 cars (an average of 3.9 cars per trip). None of the trips was done with an empty load. The Mainland waiting line had a maximum of 7 cars while the Island had a maximum of 18. At the time that the Ferry closed, two cars were left at each location.

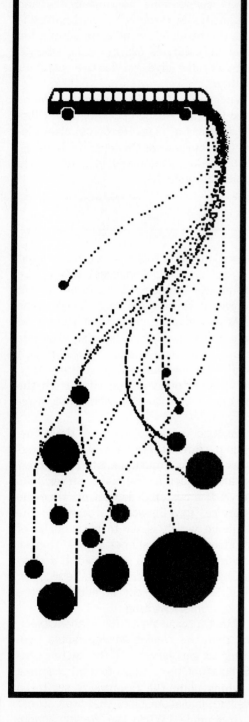

26

Coordinated Resources for Event-Driven Simulations

The three kinds of simulation objects, consumable, nonconsumable, and renewable, coordinate access to quantifiable resources. Coordination is also needed in order to synchronize the tasks of two or more simulation objects. For example, a car washer only carries out its tasks when a vehicle appears in the car wash; a bank teller gives service to a customer when the customer appears in the bank.

The mechanism for providing synchronization of tasks among two or more SimulationObjects is supported by class ResourceCoordinator. Class ResourceCoordinator is a concrete subclass of class Resource; class Resource was defined in Chapter 25. The purpose of this chapter is to describe the implementation of ResourceCoordinator and to give several examples using this synchronization technique.

The Implementation of Class Resource- Coordinator

A ResourceCoordinator represents a SimulationObject whose tasks must be synchronized with the tasks of another SimulationObject. One of the objects is considered the resource or the "customer"; the other object acquires this resource in order to give it service and can, therefore, be thought of as a "server" or clerk. At any given time, customers may be waiting for a server or servers may be waiting for customers, or no one may be waiting. Only one queue has to be maintained; a variable of a ResourceCoordinator keeps track of whether that queue contains customers, servers, or is empty. The variable pending, inherited from the superclass Resource, refers to the queue; the variable whoIsWaiting refers to the status of the queue.

Three inquiries can be made of a ResourceCoordinator, are there customers waiting? (customersWaiting), are there servers waiting? (serversWaiting), and how many are waiting? (queueLength). The message acquire comes from a SimulationObject acting as a server who wants to acquire a customer to serve. If a customer is waiting, then the SimulationObject can give it service (giveService); otherwise, the SimulationObject is added to the queue which is set to be a queue of servers waiting. The message producedBy: aCustomer comes from a SimulationObject acting as a customer who wants to be served. If a server is waiting, then the SimulationObject can get service (getServiceFor: aCustomerRequest); otherwise, the SimulationObject is added to the queue which is set to be a queue of customers waiting.

In all cases, the queue consists of instances of WaitingSimulationObject. If the queue consists of customers, then the WaitingSimulationObject refers to the SimulationObject waiting to get service. If the queue consists of servers, then the WaitingSimulationObject refers to a nil resource until a customer is acquired, at which point the resource is set to be the customer request (itself a WaitingSimulationObject that was stored when the customer request was first made). When the WaitingSimulationObject is resumed, the resource is returned to the requestor; in this way, a server gains access to a customer request. Once the synchronized tasks are completed, the server can resume the customer's activities by resuming the request.

class name	ResourceCoordinator
superclass	Resource
instance variable names	whoIsWaiting
instance methods	

accessing

customersWaiting
↑ whoIsWaiting == #customer

serversWaiting
↑ whoIsWaiting == #server

queueLength
↑ pending size

task language

acquire
|waiting|
self customersWaiting ifTrue: [↑ self giveService].
"get here if there is no customer waiting for the server."
waiting ← WaitingSimulationObject for: 1 withPriority: 0.
whoIsWaiting ← #server.
self addRequest: waiting.
↑ waiting resource

producedBy: aCustomer
|waiting|
waiting ← WaitingSimulationObject for: 1
                of: aCustomer
                withPriority: 0.
self serversWaiting ifTrue: [↑ self getServiceFor: waiting].
whoIsWaiting ← #customer.
self addRequest: waiting

private

getServiceFor: aCustomerRequest
| aServerRequest |
aServerRequest ← pending removeFirst.
pending isEmpty ifTrue: [whoIsWaiting ← #none].
aServerRequest resource: aCustomerRequest.
aServerRequest resume.
aCustomerRequest pause

giveService
  | aCustomerRequest |
  aCustomerRequest ← pending removeFirst.
  pending isEmpty ifTrue: [whoIsWaiting ← #none].
  ↑aCustomerRequest
setName: aString
  super setName: aString.
  whoIsWaiting ← #none

Notice that when a server gives service to a customer, the customer request is suspended (pause) in which case the simulation process reference count must be decremented until the service task is resumed.

Example: A Car Wash Simulation

The example of a CarWash simulation consists of cars that arrive and ask to be washed or washed and waxed. Washers are available to do the washing and waxing; when there are no cars to service, the Washers are idle. The definition of the simulation CarWash follows. There is one resource coordinator for the various car customers. Cars arrive for washing about one every 20 minutes; cars arrive for washing and waxing about one every 30 minutes. The Washer arrives when the CarWash first starts and stays as long as the simulation proceeds.

class name	CarWash
superclass	Simulation

instance methods

initialization

defineArrivalSchedule
  self scheduleArrivalOf: Wash
    accordingTo: (Exponential mean: 20).
  self scheduleArrivalOf: WashAndWax
    accordingTo: (Exponential mean: 30).
  self scheduleArrivalOf: Washer new at: 0.0
defineResources
  self coordinate: 'CarCustomer'

Each kind of car customer can report the service it requires. The Washer tasks depend on the kind of service each car customer wants. First a customer is obtained. Then it is given service (wash, wax, or both) and then the customer's own activities are continued.

class name	Washer
superclass	SimulationObject

instance methods

simulation control

tasks

```
| carRequest |
[true] whileTrue:
   [carRequest ← self acquireResource: 'CarCustomer'.
   (carRequest resource wants: 'wash')
      ifTrue: [self holdFor: (Uniform from: 12.0 to: 26.0) next].
   (carRequest resource wants: 'wax')
      ifTrue: [self holdFor: (Uniform from: 8.0 to: 12.0) next].
   self resume: carRequest]
```

The vehicles Wash and WashAndWax are defined next. Each contains an attribute which defines the kinds of service they require. The tasks of these vehicles are simply to ask for service and, after getting the service, to leave.

class name	Wash
superclass	SimulationObject
instance variable names	service
instance methods	

accessing

wants: aService

```
↑service includes: aService
```

initialization

initialize

```
super initialize.
service ← #('wash')
```

simulation control

tasks

```
self produceResource: 'CarCustomer'
```

class name	WashAndWax
superclass	Wash
instance methods	

initialization

initialize

```
super initialize.
service ← #('wash' 'wax')
```

WashAndWax is defined as a subclass of Wash since the only difference between the two is setting the service attributes. The following trace was produced by making the SimulationObject's subclasses of EventMonitor.

0	Wash 1 enters
0	Wash 1 wants to get service as CarCustomer

0	WashAndWax 1 enters
0	WashAndWax 1 wants to get service as CarCustomer
0	Washer 1 enters
0	Washer 1 wants to serve for CarCustomer
0	Washer 1 can serve Wash 1
0	Washer 1 holds for 14.2509
7.95236	WashAndWax 2 enters
7.95236	WashAndWax 2 wants to get service as CarCustomer
8.42388	Wash 2 enters
8.42388	Wash 2 wants to get service as CarCustomer
12.9404	Wash 3 enters
12.9404	Wash 3 wants to get service as CarCustomer
14.2509	Washer 1 resumes Wash 1
14.2509	Washer 1 wants to serve for CarCustomer
14.2509	Washer 1 can serve WashAndWax 1
14.2509	Washer 1 holds for 25.502 (wash part)
14.2509	Wash 1 exits
26.6023	WashAndWax 3 enters
26.6023	WashAndWax 3 wants to get service as CarCustomer
26.8851	Wash 4 enters
26.8851	Wash 4 wants to get service as CarCustomer
29.5632	Wash 5 enters
29.5632	Wash 5 wants to get service as CarCustomer
32.1979	Wash 6 enters
32.1979	Wash 6 wants to get service as CarCustomer
38.7616	Wash 7 enters
38.7616	Wash 7 wants to get service as CarCustomer
39.753	Washer 1 holds for 9.21527 (wax part)
43.5843	Wash 8 enters
43.5843	Wash 8 wants to get service as CarCustomer
48.9683	Washer 1 resumes WashAndWax 1
48.9683	Washer 1 wants to serve for CarCustomer
48.9683	Washer 1 can serve WashAndWax 2
48.9683	Washer 1 holds for 14.2757 (wash part)
48.9683	WashAndWax 1 exits
51.8478	WashAndWax 4 enters
51.8478	WashAndWax 4 wants to get service as CarCustomer
63.244	Washer 1 holds for 11.7717 (wax part)
68.9328	Wash 9 enters
68.9328	Wash 9 wants to get service as CarCustomer
70.6705	WashAndWax 5 enters
70.6705	WashAndWax 5 wants to get service as CarCustomer
75.0157	Washer 1 resumes WashAndWax 2
75.0157	Washer 1 wants to serve for CarCustomer
75.0157	Washer 1 can serve Wash 2
75.0157	Washer 1 holds for 18.6168

75.0157	WashAndWax 2 exits
78.0228	Wash 10 enters
78.0228	Wash 10 wants to get service as CarCustomer
78.2874	WashAndWax 6 enters
78.2874	WashAndWax 6 wants to get service as CarCustomer

At 78.2874, there are 12 customers waiting—8 are Wash and 4 are WashAndWax; 2 Wash and 2 WashAndWax have been served.

From this trace one can see that more Washers are needed to service the demand in this CarWash. It is also possible to collect specific data on the amount of time customers wait (using the duration statistics gathering technique and throughput histogram from the previous chapter) and the percentage of time a worker is busy or idle.

Example: A Ferry Service for a Special Truck

The last example in Chapter 25 was of a ferry service in which a ferry crosses between an island and the mainland carrying cars. The cars were modeled as static resources that a ferry could acquire. The ferry's task was to load as many as six cars, cross over the water, unload the cars it carried, and repeat the process. The example was like one provided in the book on Demos by Graham Birtwistle. In that book, Birtwistle describes the ferry service as coordinating the ferry service with the travels of a truck. A truck goes from the mainland to the island in order to make deliveries, returns to the mainland to get more supplies, and then goes to the island again, etc. The ferry only crosses from one side to the other if it is carrying the truck. This version of the ferry simulation requires a coordination of SimulationObjects representing the ferry and the truck; each has its own tasks to do, but the truck can not do its tasks without the assistance of the ferry and the ferry has no tasks to do in the absence of a truck to carry.

Ferry service starts at 7:00 a.m. (420.0 minutes into the day) and ends at 7:00 p.m. (1140 minutes into the day).

class name	FerrySimulation
superclass	Simulation
instance methods	

initialization

defineArrivalSchedule
>   self scheduleArrivalOf: Truck new at: 420.0.
>   self scheduleArrivalOf: Ferry new at: 420.0.

defineResources
>   self coordinate: ' TruckCrossing '

The Truck and the Ferry are defined in terms of producing and acquiring the resource 'TruckCrossing'.

class name	Ferry
superclass	SimulationObject
instance methods	

simulation control

tasks
```
| truckRequest |
Simulation active time > 1140.0] whileFalse:
      [truckRequest ← self acquireResource: 'TruckCrossing'.
      self load.
      self crossOver.
      self unload.
      self resume: truckRequest]
```
load
```
      self holdFor: 5.0
```
unload
```
      self holdFor: 3.0
```
crossOver
```
      self holdFor: (Normal mean: 8 deviation: 0.5) next
```

The Truck delivers supplies on the island and picks up supplies on the mainland.

class name	Truck
superclass	SimulationObject
instance methods	

simulation control

tasks
```
[true]
   whileTrue:
      [self produceResource: 'TruckCrossing'.
      self deliverSupplies.
      self produceResource: 'TruckCrossing'.
      self pickUpSupplies]
```
deliverSupplies
```
      self holdFor: (Uniform from: 15 to: 30) next
```
pickUpSupplies
```
      self holdFor: (Uniform from: 30 to: 45) next
```

There is no check in the definition of Truck or Ferry for a particular side, mainland or island, because we assume that both simulations objects start on the same side (the mainland) and their synchronization for crossing over guarantees that they stay on the same side. A trace of the events for running FerrySimulation is

Start at the mainland

420.0	Ferry enters
420.0	Ferry wants to serve for TruckCrossing
420.0	Truck enters
420.0	Truck wants to get service as TruckCrossing
420.0	Ferry can serve Truck
420.0	Ferry load truck
420.0	Ferry holds for 5.0
425.0	Ferry cross over
425.0	Ferry holds for 7.84272

unload the truck at the island side

432.843	Ferry unload truck
432.843	Ferry holds for 3.0
435.843	Ferry resumes Truck
435.843	Ferry wants to serve for TruckCrossing
435.843	Truck deliver supplies
435.843	Truck holds for 21.1949
457.038	Truck wants to get service as TruckCrossing
457.038	Ferry can serve Truck
457.038	Ferry load truck
457.038	Ferry holds for 5.0

cross over back to the mainland

462.038	Ferry cross over
462.038	Ferry holds for 8.28948
470.327	Ferry unload truck
470.327	Ferry holds for 3.0
473.327	Ferry resumes Truck
473.327	Ferry wants to serve for TruckCrossing
473.327	Truck pick up supplies
473.327	Truck holds for 40.0344
513.361	Truck wants to get service as TruckCrossing
513.361	Ferry can serve Truck
513.361	Ferry load truck
513.361	Ferry holds for 5.0

back to the island

518.361	Ferry cross over
518.361	Ferry holds for 8.05166
526.413	Ferry unload truck
526.413	Ferry holds for 3.0
529.413	Ferry resumes Truck
529.413	Ferry wants to serve for TruckCrossing
529.413	Truck delivers supplies
529.413	Truck holds for 27.1916
556.605	Truck wants to get service as TruckCrossing
556.605	Ferry can serve Truck
556.605	Ferry load truck

556.605	Ferry holds for 5.0
	back to mainland, etc.
561.605	Ferry cross over
561.605	Ferry holds for 7.53188
569.137	Ferry unload truck
569.137	Ferry holds for 3.0
572.136	Ferry resumes Truck
572.136	Ferry wants to serve for TruckCrossing
572.136	Truck pick up supplies
572.136	Truck holds for 36.8832

The ferry tasks do not guarantee that the resting place for the evening
is the mainland side. This can be done by monitoring which side the
ferry is on and then stopping only after returning to the mainland.
Only the definition of Ferry must change since the Truck side is synchronized with it.

class name	Ferry
superclass	SimulationObject
instance variable names	currentSide
instance methods	

simulation control

initialize
```
    super initialize.
    currentSide ← 'Mainland'
```
tasks
```
    | truckRequest finished |
    finished ← false
    [finished] whileFalse:
        [truckRequest ← self acquireResource: 'TruckCrossing'.
        self load.
        self crossOver.
        self unload.
        self resume: truckRequest.
        finished ←
            Simulation active time > 1140.0 and: [currentSide = 'Mainland']]
```
load
```
    self holdFor: 5.0
```
unload
```
    self holdFor: 3.0
```
crossOver
```
    self holdFor: (Normal mean: 8 deviation: 0.5) next.
    currentSide ←
        currentSide = 'Mainland'
            ifTrue: ['Island']
            ifFalse: ['Mainland']
```

Suppose now that cars can arrive at the ferry ramp in order to be carried across. The ferry can carry as many as 4 cars in addition to the truck, but the ferry will not cross over unless there is a truck to carry. Then the definition of the simulation changes by the addition of cars arriving at the mainland or the island; we introduce cars in the same way we did in Chapter 25—as static resources.

class name	FerrySimulation
superclass	Simulation
instance methods	

initialization

defineArrivalSchedule
    self scheduleArrivalOf: Truck new at: 420.0.
    self scheduleArrivalOf: Ferry new at: 420.0.
    self scheduleArrivalOf: MainlandArrival
        accordingTo: (Exponential parameter: 0.15)
        startingAt: 420.0.
    self scheduleArrivalOf: IslandArrival
        accordingTo: (Exponential parameter: 0.15)
        startingAt: 420.0
defineResources
    self coordinate: 'TruckCrossing'.
    self produce: 3 ofResource: 'Mainland'.
    self produce: 0 ofResource: 'Island'

The definitions for MainlandArrival and IslandArrival are the same as those given in Chapter 25.

class name	MainlandArrival
superclass	SimulationObject
instance methods	

simulation control

tasks
    self produce: 1 ofResource: 'Mainland'

class name	IslandArrival
superclass	SimulationObject
instance methods	

simulation control

tasks
    self produce: 1 ofResource: 'Island'

The Ferry now must take into consideration loading and unloading any cars waiting at the ramp of the current side.

class name	Ferry
superclass	SimulationObject
instance variable names	currentSide
	carsOnBoard

instance methods

simulation control

initialize
    super initialize.
    currentSide ← 'Mainland'.
    carsOnBoard ← 0

tasks
    | truckRequest finished |
    finished ← false.
    [finished] whileFalse:
        [truckRequest ← self acquireResource: 'TruckCrossing'.
        self load.
        self crossOver.
        self unload.
        self resume: truckRequest.
        finished ←
            Simulation active time > 1140.0 and: [currentSide = 'Mainland']]

load
    "load the truck first"
    self holdFor: 5.0
    "now load any cars that are waiting on the current side"
    [carsOnBoard < 4
        and: [self inquireFor: 1 ofResource: currentSide]]
                whileTrue:
                    [self acquire: 1 ofResource: currentSide.
                    self holdFor: 0.5.
                    carsOnBoard ← carsOnBoard + 1]

unload
    "unload the cars and the truck"
    self holdFor: (carsOnBoard * 0.5) + 3.0

crossOver
    self holdFor: (Normal mean: 8 deviation: 0.5) next.
    currentSide ←
        currentSide = 'Mainland'
            ifTrue: ['Island']
            ifFalse: ['Mainland']

Example: A Bank

A bank teller only carries out tasks when a customer appears at the teller's window and asks for service. Since the teller's services are dependent on the needs of the customer, the specification of the teller's tasks includes requests for information from the customer.

Suppose the bank assigns two bank tellers to work all day. The bank opens at 9:00 a.m. and closes at 3:00 p.m. Throughout the day, customers arrive every 10 minutes with a standard deviation of 5 minutes. At the noon lunch hour, the number of customers increases dramatically, averaging one every three minutes. Two additional bank tellers are added to handle the increased demand for service. When a regular bank teller is not serving a customer, the teller has desk work to do.

The arrival of customers and regular workers into the bank is scheduled in the response to the message defineArrivalSchedule to BankSimulation. The lunchtime increase is represented by a discrete probability distribution that is a sample space of twenty 3's, representing a total of the 60 minutes during which lunchtime customers appear. Mixed with the normal load of customers, this means that 20 or more customers appear in that busiest hour.

We define simulation objects BankTeller, LunchtimeTeller, BankCustomer, as well as the BankSimulation. Initialize BankSimulation by sending it the message initialize.

class name	BankSimulation
superclass	Simulation
class variable names	Hour
class methods	

class initialization

initialize
    Hour ← 60

instance methods

initialization

defineArrivalSchedule
    self scheduleArrivalOf: BankCustomer
        accordingTo: (Normal mean: 10 deviation: 5)
        startingAt: 9*Hour.
    self scheduleArrivalOf: (BankTeller name: 'first') at: 9*Hour.
    self scheduleArrivalOf: (BankTeller name: 'second') at: 9*Hour.
    self scheduleArrivalOf: BankCustomer
        accordingTo:
          (SampleSpaceWithoutReplacement
               data: ((1 to: 20) collect: [:i | 3]))
        startingAt: 12*Hour.
    self schedule: [self hireMoreTellers] at: 12*Hour.
    self schedule: [self finishUp] at: 15*Hour

defineResources
    self coordinate: 'TellerCustomer'

simulation control

hireMoreTellers
```
self schedule: [(LunchtimeTeller name: 'first') startUp] after: 0.0.
self schedule: [(LunchtimeTeller name: 'second') startUp] after: 0.0
```

The ResourceCoordinator is responsible for matching customers (takers of service) with bank tellers (givers of service). The bank customer's task is simple. After entering the bank, the customer gets the attention of a bank teller and asks for service. After obtaining service, the customer leaves. The amount of time the customer spends in the bank depends on how long the customer must wait for a teller and how long the teller takes giving service.

class name	BankCustomer
superclass	SimulationObject
instance methods	

simulation control

tasks
```
self produceResource: 'TellerCustomer'
```

The bank teller's tasks depend on the needs of the customer. To keep this example simple, we will assume that a BankTeller does about the same work for each customer, taking between 2 and 15 minutes. Another alternative would be to give each BankCustomer a list of desired services as was done in the car wash example; the BankTeller would enumerate over the set, taking times appropriate to each kind of service. Whenever a customer is not available, the teller does other tasks. These tasks are small and take a short amount of time; however, the teller can not be interrupted. When one of these background desk tasks is completed, the teller checks to see if a customer has arrived and is waiting for service.

class name	BankTeller
superclass	SimulationObject
instance methods	

simulation control

tasks
```
[true] whileTrue:
    [(self numberOfProvidersOfResource: 'TellerCustomer') > 0
        ifTrue: [self counterWork]
        ifFalse: [self deskWork]]
```

counterWork
```
| customerRequest |
customerRequest ← self acquireResource: 'TellerCustomer'.
self holdFor: (Uniform from: 2 to: 15) next.
self resume: customerRequest
```

deskWork
>   self holdFor: (Uniform from: 1 to: 5) next

A LunchtimeTeller has to schedule itself to leave the bank after an hour. This scheduling can be specified in the response to initialize. When it is time to leave, the LunchtimeTeller has to make certain that all its tasks are completed before leaving. Therefore, a signal (getDone) is set to true the first time the message finishUp is sent; this signal is checked each time the teller's counter work completes. The second time finishUp is sent, the signal is true and the teller can exit. The LunchtimeTeller, unlike the regular BankTeller, does not do any desk work when customers are not available.

class name	LunchtimeTeller
superclass	BankTeller
instance variable names	getDone
instance methods	

initialization

initialize
>   super initialize.
>   getDone ← false.
>   Simulation active schedule: [self finishUp] after: 60

simulation control

finishUp
>   getDone
>   ifTrue: [super finishUp]
>   ifFalse: [getDone ← true]

tasks
>   [getDone] whileFalse: [self counterWork].
>   self finishUp

A partial trace of the events follows.

540	BankCustomer 1 enters
540	BankCustomer 1 wants to get service as TellerCustomer
540	BankTeller first enters
540	BankTeller first wants to serve for TellerCustomer
540	BankTeller first can serve BankCustomer 1
540	BankTeller first holds for 9.33214
540	BankTeller second enters
540	BankTeller second does desk work
540	BankTeller second holds for 3.33594
543.336	BankTeller second does desk work

543.336	BankTeller second holds for 2.96246
546.298	BankTeller second does desk work
546.298	BankTeller second holds for 3.56238
549.332	BankTeller first resumes BankCustomer 1
549.332	BankTeller first does desk work
549.332	BankTeller first holds for 1.83978
549.332	BankCustomer 1 exits
549.819	BankCustomer 2 enters
549.819	BankCustomer 2 wants to get service as TellerCustomer
549.861	BankTeller second wants to serve for TellerCustomer
549.861	BankTeller second can serve BankCustomer 2
549.861	BankTeller second holds for 14.3192
551.172	BankTeller first does desk work
551.172	BankTeller first holds for 4.16901
555.341	BankTeller first does desk work
555.341	BankTeller first holds for 2.60681
557.948	BankTeller first does desk work
557.948	BankTeller first holds for 4.58929
559.063	BankCustomer 3 enters
559.063	BankCustomer 3 wants to get service as TellerCustomer
562.537	BankTeller first wants to serve for TellerCustomer
562.537	BankTeller first can serve BankCustomer 3
562.537	BankTeller first holds for 13.4452
564.18	BankTeller second resumes BankCustomer 2
564.18	BankTeller second does desk work
564.18	BankTeller second holds for 2.63007
564.18	BankCustomer 2 exits
565.721	BankCustomer 4 enters
565.721	BankCustomer 4 wants to get service as TellerCustomer
566.81	BankTeller second wants to serve for TellerCustomer
566.81	BankTeller second can serve BankCustomer 4
566.81	BankTeller second holds for 5.08139
571.891	BankTeller second resumes BankCustomer 4
571.891	BankTeller second does desk work
571.891	BankTeller second holds for 4.69818
571.891	BankCustomer 4 exits
575.982	BankTeller first resumes BankCustomer 3
575.982	BankTeller first does desk work
575.982	BankTeller first holds for 2.10718
575.982	BankCustomer 3 exits
576.59	BankTeller second does desk work
576.59	BankTeller second holds for 4.04327

... and so on until lunch hour when the extra help arrives;
at this point, 18 customers have entered; BankTeller first is
giving BankCustomer 18 service...

720	BankCustomer 19 enters
720	BankCustomer 19 wants to get service as TellerCustomer
720	LunchtimeTeller first enters
720	LunchtimeTeller first wants to serve for TellerCustomer
720	LunchtimeTeller first can serve BankCustomer 19
720	LunchtimeTeller first holds for 11.9505
720	LunchtimeTeller second enters
720	LunchtimeTeller second wants to serve for TellerCustomer
721.109	BankTeller second does desk work
721.109	BankTeller second holds for 2.09082
721.663	BankTeller first resumes BankCustomer 18
721.663	BankTeller first does desk work
721.663	BankTeller first holds for 3.43219
721.663	BankCustomer 18 exits
722.085	BankCustomer 20 enters
722.085	BankCustomer 20 wants to get service as TellerCustomer
722.085	LunchtimeTeller second can serve BankCustomer 20
722.085	LunchtimeTeller second holds for 9.51483
723	BankCustomer 21 enters
723	BankCustomer 21 wants to get service as TellerCustomer
723.2	BankTeller second wants to serve for TellerCustomer
723.2	BankTeller second can serve BankCustomer 21
723.2	BankTeller second holds for 9.66043
725.095	BankTeller first does desk work
725.095	BankTeller first holds for 4.97528
726	BankCustomer 22 enters
726	BankCustomer 22 wants to get service as TellerCustomer
729	BankCustomer 23 enters
729	BankCustomer 23 wants to get service as TellerCustomer
730.071	BankTeller first wants to serve for TellerCustomer
730.071	BankTeller first can serve BankCustomer 22
730.071	BankTeller first holds for 8.17746
731.6	LunchtimeTeller second resumes BankCustomer 20
731.6	LunchtimeTeller second wants to serve for TellerCustomer

731.6	LunchtimeTeller second can serve BankCustomer 23
731.6	LunchtimeTeller second holds for 6.27971
731.6	BankCustomer 20 exits
731.95	LunchtimeTeller first resumes BankCustomer 19
731.95	LunchtimeTeller first wants to serve for TellerCustomer
731.95	BankCustomer 19 exits
732	BankCustomer 24 enters
732	BankCustomer 24 wants to get service as TellerCustomer
732	LunchtimeTeller first can serve BankCustomer 24
732	LunchtimeTeller first holds for 9.52138

... BankCustomer 40 just left and lunch time is over; there are 3 other customers in the bank; as soon as they finish with their current customers, the LunchtimeTellers will leave...

780.0	BankCustomer 44 enters
780.0	BankCustomer 44 wants to get service as TellerCustomer
780.918	BankTeller first wants to serve for TellerCustomer
780.918	BankTeller first can serve BankCustomer 44
780.918	BankTeller first holds for 13.1566
781.968	BankCustomer 45 enters
781.968	BankCustomer 45 wants to get service as TellerCustomer
784.001	LunchtimeTeller second resumes BankCustomer 43
784.001	LunchtimeTeller second exits
784.001	BankCustomer 43 exits
787.879	LunchtimeTeller first resumes BankCustomer 42
787.879	LunchtimeTeller first exits
787.879	BankCustomer 42 exits
789.189	BankTeller second resumes BankCustomer 41
789.189	BankTeller second wants to serve for TellerCustomer
789.189	BankTeller second can serve BankCustomer 45
789.189	BankTeller second holds for 2.38364
789.189	BankCustomer 41 exits
791.572	BankTeller second resumes BankCustomer 45
791.572	BankTeller second does desk work
791.572	BankTeller second holds for 2.34467
791.572	BankCustomer 45 exits
793.917	BankTeller second does desk work
793.917	BankTeller second holds for 3.19897

and so on...

The data that would be collected here includes the busy/idle percentages of the tellers and the customers' average wait time.

Example: An Information System

Our last example is also in the Birtwistle book and, according to Birtwistle, is a popular example for simulation systems such as GPSS. The example is an information system simulation that describes remote terminals at which users can arrive and make retrieval requests. A customer with a query arrives at one or the other of the terminals and queues, if necessary, to use it. The system scanner rotates from terminal to terminal seeing if a request is waiting and, if so, provides service. Service means that the scanner copies the query to a buffer unit capable of holding three queries simultaneously; if no buffer position is available, the copying process must wait until one becomes available. Once copying to the buffer succeeds, the system processes the query and places the answer in the buffer to return to the terminal without need for the scanner again.

Using the data provided by Birtwistle, we will model a system with six terminals. Customers arrive at terminals with an exponential mean time of 5 minutes. The buffers are modeled as static resources; the terminals are also static resources; while the terminal services are objects whose tasks are coordinated with the tasks of the queries.

class name	InformationSystem
superclass	Simulation
instance methods	

initialization

defineArrivalSchedule
"Schedule many queries and only one scanner"
self scheduleArrivalOf: Query
accordingTo: (Exponential parameter: 5)
startingAt: 0.0.
self scheduleArrivalOf: SystemScanner new at: 0.0

defineResources
self produce: 3 of: 'Buffer'.
0 to: 5 do:
[:n |
self produce: 1 of 'Terminal', n printString.
self coordinate: 'TerminalService', n printString]

In the above method, we use string concatenation to form the attribute names of six terminals as static resources and six terminal services as coordinated services; the names are Terminal0,...,Terminal5 and TerminalService0,...,TerminalService5.

The ResourceCoordinators for terminal service for each of the six terminals are being handled differently here than in the bank and car wash simulation examples. At any time, the queues of customers or servers will contain only one or no elements. During the simulation, a Query will enter a queue to wait for terminal service. A SystemScanner moves from coordinator to coordinator, round-robin fashion, to act as the giver of service if a Query is waiting.

The customer, a Query, must first access a terminal resource to get a reply. On accessing one of the six terminals, the customer keys in a request and awaits the reply. It takes between 0.3 and 0.5 minutes (uniformly distributed) to enter a query. Then terminal service is requested. The query now waits for the SystemScanner; when the SystemScanner notices the waiting query, it gives it the needed service. This means that the SystemScanner obtains a buffer slot for the query and copies the request into the buffer. It takes 0.0117 minutes to transfer a query to the buffer. Now the reply can be transferred to the terminal and read, the buffer can be freed up, and the terminal released. It takes between 0.05 and 0.10 (uniformly distributed) to process a query, and 0.0397 minutes to transfer the reply back to the terminal. Customers take between 0.6 and 0.8 minutes (uniformly distributed) to read a reply.

class name	Query
superclass	SimulationObject
instance methods	

scheduling

tasks
```
| terminal terminalNum |
"pick a terminal"
terminalNum ← (SampleSpace data: #('0' '1' '2' '3' '4' '5')) next.
"get a terminal resource"
terminal ← self acquire: 1 ofResource: 'Terminal', terminalNum.
"got the terminal, now enter the query"
self holdFor: (Uniform from: 0.3 to: 0.5) next.
"act as a resource for a terminal service in order to process the query"
self produceResource: 'TerminalService', terminalNum.
"the query is now processed; now read the reply"
self holdFor: (Uniform from: 0.6 to: 0.8) next.
"and release the terminal"
self release: terminal
```

The scanner's job is to rotate from terminal to terminal seeing if a request is pending and, if so, to wait to transfer a query into a buffer and then move on. Scanner rotation takes 0.0027 minutes and the same amount of time to test a terminal.

```
class name                        SystemScanner
superclass                        SimulationObject
instance variable names           n
instance methods
initialization
    initialize
        super initialize.
        n ← 5
simulation control
    tasks
        | terminalServiceRequest buffer test |
        [true]
            whileTrue:
                [n ← (n + 1) \\ 6.
                self holdFor: 0.0027.
                test ←
                  self numberOfProvidersOfResource:
                                    'TerminalService', n printString.
                self holdFor: 0.0027.
                test = 0 ifFalse:
                  [terminalServiceRequest ←
                      self acquireResource: ('TerminalService', n printString).
                  buffer ← self acquire: 1 ofResource: 'Buffer'.
                  "copy the request"
                  self holdFor: 0.0117.
                  "process the query"
                  self holdFor: (Uniform from: 0.05 to: 0.10) next.
                  "return the reply to the terminal"
                  self holdFor: 0.0397.
                  "done, release the resources"
                  self release: buffer.
                  self resume: terminalServiceRequest]]
```

The SystemScanner is not idle when no Query is waiting; it continually moves from terminal to terminal checking for a Query. This movement stops when a Query is found in order to provide service. When the service is completed, the SystemScanner returns to circulating around, looking for another Query.

Not much happens at first. The first Query enters but it holds for 0.360428 units of time in order to enter its query at Terminal1; meanwhile the SystemScanner moves around the terminals. A second Query enters at 0.0472472 and requests Terminal3; a third enters at 0.130608 and requests Terminal4. At 0.360428, the first Query requests service at Terminal1 which is given a short time later at time 0.367198. Between this time and time 0.478235, the SystemScanner gives service by getting a Buffer, copying the query to the Buffer, processing it, transferring the reply, and then releasing the Buffer and resuming the Query. In the meantime, the second Query requested service, and a fourth Query entered at Terminal4. The SystemScanner then rotates to Terminal3 to give service to the second Query waiting there.

0.0	Query 1 enters
0.0	Query 1 requests 1 of Terminal1
0.0	Query 1 obtained 1 of Terminal1
0.0	Query 1 holds for 0.360428
0.0	SystemScanner enters
0.0	SystemScanner holds for 0.0027
0.0027	SystemScanner holds for 0.0027
0.0054	SystemScanner holds for 0.0027

...etc...

0.0432	SystemScanner holds for 0.0027
0.0459	SystemScanner holds for 0.0027
0.0472472	Query 2 enters
0.0472472	Query 2 requests 1 of Terminal3
0.0472472	Query 2 obtained 1 of Terminal3
0.0472472	Query 2 holds for 0.363611
0.0486	SystemScanner holds for 0.0027
0.0513	SystemScanner holds for 0.0027

...etc...

0.1269	SystemScanner holds for 0.0027
0.1296	SystemScanner holds for 0.0027
0.130608	Query 3 enters
0.130608	Query 3 requests 1 of Terminal4
0.130608	Query 3 obtained 1 of Terminal4
0.130608	Query 3 holds for 0.445785
0.1323	SystemScanner holds for 0.0027
0.135	SystemScanner holds for 0.0027

...etc...

0.356398	SystemScanner holds for 0.0027
0.359098	SystemScanner holds for 0.0027
0.360428	Query 1 wants to get service as TerminalService1
0.361798	SystemScanner holds for 0.0027

0.364498	SystemScanner holds for 0.0027
0.367198	SystemScanner wants to give service as TerminalService1
0.367198	SystemScanner can serve as TerminalService1
0.367198	SystemScanner requests 1 of Buffer
0.367198	SystemScanner obtained 1 of Buffer
0.367198	SystemScanner holds for 0.0117
0.378898	SystemScanner holds for 0.0596374
0.410858	Query 2 wants to get service as TerminalService3
0.41396	Query 4 enters
0.41396	Query 4 requests 1 of Terminal4
0.438535	SystemScanner holds for 0.0397
0.478235	SystemScanner releases 1 of Buffer
0.478235	SystemScanner resumes Query 1
0.478235	SystemScanner holds for 0.0027
0.478235	Query 1 got served as TerminalService1
0.478235	Query 1 holds for 0.740207
0.480935	SystemScanner holds for 0.0027
0.483635	SystemScanner holds for 0.0027
0.486335	SystemScanner holds for 0.0027
0.489035	SystemScanner wants to give service as TerminalService3
0.489035	SystemScanner can serve as TerminalService3
0.489035	SystemScanner requests 1 of Buffer
0.489035	SystemScanner obtained 1 of Buffer
0.489035	SystemScanner holds for 0.0117
0.500735	SystemScanner holds for 0.0515655
0.552301	SystemScanner holds for 0.0397
0.576394	Query 3 wants to get service as TerminalService4
0.592001	SystemScanner releases 1 of Buffer
0.592001	SystemScanner resumes Query 2
0.592001	SystemScanner holds for 0.0027
0.592001	Query 2 got served as TerminalService3
0.592001	Query 2 holds for 0.655313

...etc...

For more examples to try, see the Birtwistle book.

Subject Index

Abelson, Harold, 365
abstract classes
    in collections, 134
    defined, 66, 73
    example of, 66-67
    implementation description for, 67-72
    for metaclasses, 78
    purpose of, 66
    in streams, 198
    and subclass framework messages, 72-73
accept command, 303-304, 306
accessing
    of class hierarchy, 277-278
    of contents of method dictionary, 275-726
    of elements of collection, 153-155, 195
    of files, 208-210, 288
    of instances and variables, 276-277, 288
    mutually exclusive, 258-262
    of parts of object, 99-100
    of text, 231
active context, 431-436
active process, 254
active simulation, 478
addition
    of elements, 134-135, 214
    of numbers. *See* number(s)
Algol, 13, 34, 119, 165
alphabetical order, 114-116, 160

animation, 331, 333, 400
arc, 403
area filling, 392-393, 411-412
argument(s)
    block, 35-36, 37, 138, 253, 436-437
    in compiler, 419, 423-425
    defined, 25, 37
    expression syntax for, 25-27
    in interpreter, 427, 436-437, 439
argument name(s)
    defined, 49, 53
    in error reporting, 323-324
    in protocol description, 42
    vs. temporary variables, 51
arithmetic. *See* number(s)
arithmetic progressions, 163-165
array(s)
    accessing of, 126
    in block arguments, 36
    classes for, 145, 165-166, 231
    comparison of, 96
    defined, 37
    in dictionaries, 69
    expression syntax for, 21
    system classes for, 13
assignments, 22-23, 27, 37, 50
association, 148
audit trail, 286-287

System Index

#, 21, 168
$, 20
', 20
@, 182, 340
    See also Point
Arc, 403
Array, 46, 52, 72, 96, 98, 100, 133, 136, 139, 145, 154-157, 165, 172-174, 197, 202, 216, 219, 231, 253, 269, 276, 376, 397
    used on, 68-69, 71, 242, 259, 411, 498
ArrayedCollection, 145, 157, 165-166, 219, 231, 269, 278
Association, 148-150, 220, 225-226, 422
    used on, 224
    See also association (subject index)
at:, 46, 148, 153
    defined on, 99, 229, 232, 234
at:put:, 46-47, 148, 153, 308
    defined on, 99, 230, 232, 234
Bag, 133-135, 140-141, 145, 148, 152, 169, 181, 183, 185
    defined on, 147, 220-222
    used on, 184, 217
become:
    defined on, 246
    used on, 247
Behavior, 269-270, 272, 283, 288
    defined on, 273-282, 285

BitBlt, 334, 349, 355, 361-362, 365-366, 368, 375, 383, 400, 405
    defined on, 350-352
BlockContext, 253, 435-436, 488
    defined on, 254-255
    See also block (subject index)
Boolean, 15, 23, 34, 119, 215, 237, 239, 436
    defined on, 238
    See also true; false
ByteArray, 112, 145, 165-166, 231
Character, 107, 114, 133, 136, 139-140, 145, 165-166, 168, 201, 209
    defined on, 115-116
CharacterScanner, 354
Circle, 403
Class, 76, 78, 81, 84, 87-89, 269-271, 281, 283-284, 289-290
    defined on, 288-289
ClassDescription, 81, 269-270, 283-284, 288
    defined on, 285-286
collect:, 36, 38, 138
    defined on, 137, 215, 225, 227, 230, 233-234
Collection, 95, 145-148, 150-151, 153, 163, 165, 168, 174, 188, 201, 212, 227, 269, 282, 376
    defined on, 134, 136-137, 139-141, 213-219, 221
    used on, 284

Example Class Index

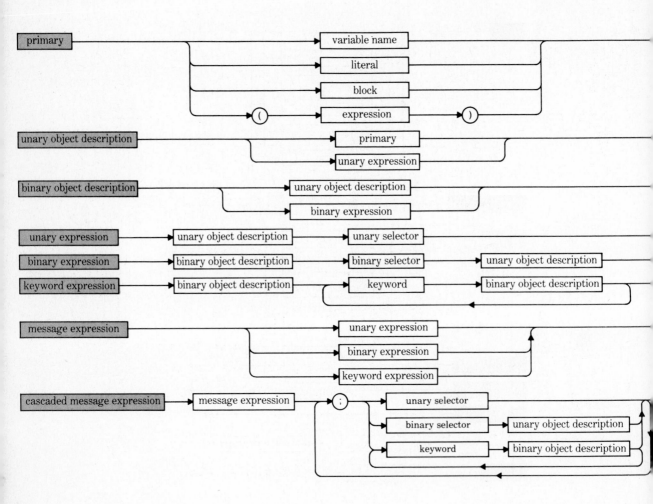